The Role of Intelligence in Countering Violent Extremism

Eugene de Silva
https://orcid.org/0009-0006-8631-7472
Virginia Research Institute, USA

Sinduja Umandi W. Jayaratne
Bandaranaike Centre for International Studies, Sri Lanka

IGI Global
Scientific Publishing
Publishing Tomorrow's Research Today

Vice President of Editorial	Melissa Wagner
Director of Acquisitions	Mikaela Felty
Director of Book Development	Jocelynn Hessler
Production Manager	Mike Brehm
Cover Design	Jose Rosado

Published in the United States of America by
IGI Global Scientific Publishing
701 East Chocolate Avenue
Hershey, PA, 17033, USA
Tel: 717-533-8845 | Fax: 717-533-7115
Website: https://www.igi-global.com E-mail: cust@igi-global.com

Library of Congress Cataloging-in-Publication Data

CIP Data Pending
ISBN13: 979-8-3693-3522-2
Isbn13Softcover: 979-8-3693-5213-7
EISBN13: 979-8-3693-3523-9

British Cataloguing in Publication Data
A Cataloguing in Publication record for this book is available from the British Library.

Eugene de Silva: To my parents, Angelo de Silva and Latha de Silva, for instilling in me wisdom and perseverance.

Sinduja Umandi W. Jayaratne: To my parents, Yamuna Jayasekera and Kumara Jayaratne, for their unwavering support.

Table of Contents

Detailed Table of Contents

mitigate the threat of rising violent extremism in the country. Finally. this research would recommend how to minimize the gaps in the existing CVE approaches in UK.

Hamas-led attack on Israel (October 7, 2023) was considered to be a spectacular military surprise similar to the "Yom Kippur War" (1973). There are parallel lines to the attack and the war, most of them in the field of intelligence, such as ignoring intelligence reports and failure to connect the dots, i.e., failing to interpret the large amounts of data accumulated in the intelligence division, and identified in the two events, that a war was about to break out. Israeli intelligence also failed in both wars by sticking to the wrong concepts. According to the first case study ("The 1973 War"), the Egyptian and the Syrian armies would not start a war because the Israeli military had remarkably won the "1967 War". According to the second case study (Hamas-led attack on Israel), "Hamas is deterred," and the conflict between Israel and the Hamas organization controlling in Gaza strip, could be contained by Israel. Though both conceptions were incorrect, they prevented political and military decision-makers and heads of the IDF from "reading" the intelligence reports, which explicitly described the most likely option of war and attack in both situations. In the research, a top-tier intelligence agency, the IDF intelligence, failed miserably to connect the dots twice, 50 years apart. In our research, the "Yom Kippur War" and the Hamas-led attack on Israel (October 7, 2023) are compared using a close tables and artificial intelligence.

After the Cold War ended in 1991, extremism surged, seeking expression through violence, while science advanced to embrace Artificial Intelligence (AI), creating intelligent machines. AI blends software and machines, with computers as a fundamental form and robots as advanced versions. In Pakistan, using robots in the field is both novel and costly. This study explores how science and intelligence can counter violent extremism at the induction, training, and action levels of terrorists and their organizations. Through structured, open-ended interviews with Punjab's counter-terrorism officials, the study found five key insights. First, a hide-and-seek dynamic exists between violent perpetrators and counter-efforts. Second, human intelligence remains vital, but AI's potential in thwarting terrorism is significant. Third, combining science and intelligence in AI offers an edge. Fourth, as extremism

Foreword

The 21st century confronts us with a sobering reality: security is no longer the domain of armed forces and intelligence agencies alone, but a shared responsibility across all sectors of society. The threats we face are not only more numerous but also more sophisticated, transnational, and multifaceted than those of previous generations. This book, edited by Prof. Eugene de Silva and Ms. Sinduja U. W. Jayaratne, is both timely and essential in addressing these realities.

What distinguishes this volume is its breadth of vision and depth of analysis. It does not confine itself to a single discipline or narrow definition of security but embraces a genuinely interdisciplinary approach. The contributors who are scholars, practitioners, and analysts from across continents bring with them a wealth of perspectives informed by experience in intelligence operations, cybersecurity, geopolitical strategy, and the ethical governance of technology.

One of the book's strengths is its deliberate juxtaposition of theory and practice. The opening chapter aptly compares the HUMINT and AI use in intelligence services followed by the scientific approach to intelligence analysis in assessing terror threats. The collective chapters do not simply represent an academic exercise; they provide a roadmap for enhancing the precision and reliability of intelligence in an age where the cost of error is measured in human lives.

The chapters on cyber terrorism and cyber warfare remind us that the digital revolution, while a source of unprecedented connectivity, has also created vulnerabilities on a scale unimaginable just decades ago. The authors do not merely catalogue threats; they critically examine preparedness, attribution, and the capacity of state and non-state actors to respond. This is vital reading for anyone involved in national security, law enforcement, or the governance of critical infrastructure.

Equally compelling is the exploration of historical intelligence failures and their lessons for today. The parallels drawn between the Yom Kippur War and the events of October 7, 2023, which are here framed as cautionary lessons about the risks of conceptual rigidity and the need to adapt. These lessons resonate beyond the Middle East, speaking to the universal challenges faced by intelligence services worldwide.

I am also struck by the book's engagement with the ethical dimensions of security. In a world increasingly reliant on artificial intelligence, the question is not whether to use AI in countering violent extremism, but how to do so without eroding the democratic values we seek to defend. The chapter on the ethical implications of AI offers a balanced, principled framework that should inform both national policy and international norms.

Perhaps most importantly, this book recognizes that security is as much about people as it is about technology or strategy. Whether in the community dynamics that determine the flow of intelligence in Iraq, the ideological landscapes of South Asia, or the policy responses to extremism in the UK, the debate between HUMINT and AI remains central. Without trust, legitimacy, and a deep understanding of context, even the most advanced tools will fail to deliver lasting security.

For policymakers, scholars, and practitioners, this volume offers both insight and guidance. It challenges us to think critically, to learn from the past, and to anticipate the future. Above all, it calls for cooperation across disciplines, sectors, and borders because only by working together can we hope to address the complex threats of our time.

I commend the editors and contributors for producing a collection of work of such relevance and quality. It deserves a place on the desk of every serious student and practitioner of security in the modern age.

Kriengsak Chareonwongsak
Harvard University, USA

Preface

In an age where the boundaries between peace and conflict, reality and cyberspace, human and artificial intelligence are increasingly blurred, the field of security studies demands fresh perspectives, innovative tools, and cross-disciplinary approaches. This volume brings together a diverse range of scholars and practitioners from across the globe, each addressing pressing questions that sit at the heart of our collective security.

The genesis of this book lies in a recognition: the threats we face today are neither singular nor confined by geography. Terrorism, violent extremism, and political instability manifest in varied forms from calculated acts of violence rooted in historical grievances to faceless cyberattacks traversing boundless digital networks. The challenge for intelligence and security professionals is not simply to respond, but to anticipate, understand, and, where possible, prevent such threats.

Our contributing authors examine these challenges through an impressive variety of lenses. We open with rigorous analytical models, such as the use of the Analytic Hierarchy Process (AHP) to assess terrorist intentions and capabilities. This methodology, with its focus on structured decision-making, offers an antidote to the dangers of intuition-driven intelligence, showing how even limited information can be transformed into actionable insights.

From there, the discourse expands to the cyber domain, where the evolution of terrorism is both accelerated and obscured by technology. Cyber terrorism and cyber warfare as explored by our contributors represent not just new battlefields, but entirely new paradigms for conflict. The omnipresence of digital connectivity renders no institution immune, from national security agencies to financial institutions and educational systems. The contributors highlight the critical need for robust preparedness, realistic attribution frameworks, and a candid acknowledgment of the vulnerabilities inherent in our connected world.

The book also turns to historical case studies with modern parallels, such as the comparative analysis of the Yom Kippur War (1973) and the October 7, 2023 Hamas-led attack on Israel. These events underscore a recurring intelligence failure:

the inability to connect the dots despite ample warning signals. Through such studies, the authors remind us that technology and data are only as useful as the conceptual frameworks guiding their interpretation.

Other chapters delve into the interplay between science, human intelligence (HUMINT), and artificial intelligence (AI) in countering violent extremism. Whether in the context of Pakistan's counter-terrorism operations, UK policy responses to radicalization, or the integration of AI into global intelligence networks, these contributions converge on a shared truth: the future of security depends on synergizing human insight with technological innovation while preserving ethical principles.

We also engage with geopolitical and regional perspectives. Analyses of extremism in South Asia, Islamic political thought, and the radicalization risks surrounding China's Belt and Road Initiative reveal how ideology, history, and economic strategy intersect with global security dynamics.

Finally, the volume closes with a critical examination of the ethical implications of AI in countering violent extremism. As algorithmic decision-making becomes more deeply embedded in security operations, questions of privacy, accountability, and governance take on existential importance.

CHAPTER OVERVIEW

Chapter 1: HUMINT vs AI in Intelligence and Security Services

Eugene de Silva explores the complementary yet distinct roles of Human Intelligence (HUMINT) and Artificial Intelligence (AI) in modern security operations. By analyzing historical precedents and technological developments, the chapter evaluates how both intelligence types can be effectively integrated for more responsive and nuanced decision-making.

Chapter 2: Prioritizing Threats: AHP-Based Assessment of Terrorist Intention and Capability

I. Made Wardhana introduces the Analytic Hierarchy Process (AHP) as a method to enhance objectivity in threat prioritization. By focusing on the twin pillars of terrorist intention and capability, the chapter provides a replicable, data-driven model that aids intelligence professionals in quantifying and ranking threats.

Chapter 3: Islamic Political Thought in Historical Perspective

Sinduja Jayaratne offers a historical analysis of Islamic political philosophy in South Asia and its reinterpretation by contemporary extremist ideologues. The chapter connects theological and political ideas across centuries to explain the ideological underpinnings of modern extremist movements.

Chapter 4: Extremism in the UK: Historical Roots and Policy Responses

Kavindu Peiris and Sinduja Jayaratne examine the UK's experiences with radicalization, mapping its historical and contemporary challenges. The chapter evaluates UK counter-extremism policies and offers recommendations to bridge existing gaps in preventing and responding to violent extremism.

Chapter 5: Failure to Connect the Dots: Yom Kippur and October 7

Galit Ben-Israel presents a comparative case study of two intelligence failures: the 1973 Yom Kippur War and the Hamas-led October 7, 2023, attack on Israel. The chapter emphasizes institutional rigidity, cognitive bias, and conceptual errors in intelligence analysis, drawing critical lessons for the future.

Chapter 6: Countering Violent Extremism with Science and Intelligence

Tehmina Aslam explores the intersection of science, AI, and counter-terrorism efforts in Pakistan. Through interviews with counter-terrorism officials, the study reveals both the promise and limitations of using AI-enhanced intelligence in real-world operations, especially in resource-constrained settings.

Chapter 7: Radicalization and the Belt and Road Initiative

Bhagya Senaratne and Asif Fuard analyze how China's Belt and Road Initiative (BRI) intersects with regional extremism in Afghanistan, Pakistan, and Xinjiang. The chapter dissects how geopolitical ambitions can be undermined by radical actors, stressing the need for integrated security frameworks.

Chapter 8: Cyber Security Threats, Cyber Terrorism, Cyber Warfare

Pankaj Bhambri and Alex Khang provide a panoramic view of the growing cyber threat landscape. Highlighting the spectrum of cyber-attacks from phishing to state-sponsored cyber warfare, this chapter underscores the need for advanced and adaptive cyber defense mechanisms.

Chapter 9: Attribution: Challenges in Cyber Terrorism and Preparedness

Aishwarya Majumdar, Pranjal Chaturvedi, and Bhupinder Singh delve into the complex issue of attribution in cyber terrorism. This chapter critically examines legal, technical, and diplomatic hurdles in identifying perpetrators and improving global cyber security readiness.

Chapter 10: Ethical Implications of AI in Countering Violent Extremism

Aamer Khan addresses the ethical tensions inherent in deploying AI for security and surveillance purposes. The chapter calls for the development of international legal and ethical norms that reconcile security needs with the preservation of civil liberties and human rights.

In curating this collection, our aim has been to assemble a body of work that is both academically rigorous and practically relevant. We have encouraged our contributors to draw upon empirical evidence, historical insight, and forward-looking analysis, in the belief that the fight against extremism and terrorism requires not only sharper tools but also deeper understanding.

It is our hope that this book serves as a resource for policymakers, intelligence professionals, scholars, and students alike; a compendium that informs, challenges, and inspires. The threats we face are complex, but so too are the capacities of the human mind and spirit when guided by collaboration, critical thinking, and an unwavering commitment to security and justice.

Eugene de Silva
Sinduja U. W. Jayaratne
August 15, 2025

Chapter 1
HUMINT vs. AI in Intelligence and Security Services

Eugene de Silva
https://orcid.org/0009-0006-8631-7472
Virginia Research Institute, USA

ABSTRACT

In the evolving domain of global intelligence and security services, the interplay between Human Intelligence (HUMINT) and Artificial Intelligence (AI) has become increasingly significant. HUMINT, which draws on human operatives and interpersonal communication, and AI, which leverages computational power for vast data analysis, each provide unique strengths and limitations in modern intelligence-gathering operations. This chapter examines the historical development, key contributions, strengths, and weaknesses of both HUMINT and AI. It analyzes the challenges and controversies surrounding their deployment in intelligence work, including issues of ethical governance, data privacy, and operational security. Drawing on global case studies from the United States, United Kingdom, Russia, France, the Middle East, and other regions, the chapter explores how an integrated HUMINT-AI framework can enhance security operations. It also provides solutions and recommendations for future research and policy directions aimed at optimizing intelligence services while safeguarding human rights and ethical standards.

INTRODUCTION

In today's rapidly evolving global security landscape, the methods by which intelligence is gathered, analyzed, and applied are undergoing significant transfor-

DOI: 10.4018/979-8-3693-3522-2.ch001

mation. Traditional Human Intelligence (HUMINT), which relies on human operatives, interpersonal communication, and contextual judgment, has long served as the cornerstone of intelligence operations. However, the rise of Artificial Intelligence (AI) has introduced a new era of computational capabilities, enabling unprecedented speed and scope in data processing, pattern recognition, and predictive modeling.

This chapter explores the dynamic and sometimes contentious relationship between HUMINT and AI within the domains of intelligence and security services. While both approaches offer unique strengths, they also present distinct limitations that challenge their integration into cohesive operational frameworks. HUMINT excels in understanding cultural nuance, deception detection, and motivation analysis in areas where machines still struggle. In contrast, AI systems can analyze vast data streams in real time, detect anomalies, and perform complex tasks with minimal human oversight.

The purpose of this chapter is not to pit HUMINT and AI against each other as mutually exclusive tools, but rather to evaluate how they can complement each other in modern intelligence work. Through a review of historical developments, global case studies, and ethical considerations, the chapter aims to provide a comprehensive understanding of how these two modes of intelligence can be synthesized. Furthermore, the discussion extends into policy implications, multidisciplinary applications, and the future of hybrid intelligence operations.

As intelligence agencies and security professionals navigate the complexities of the digital age, understanding the respective roles of human insight and artificial cognition becomes essential. The integration of HUMINT and AI, when done ethically and effectively, has the potential to revolutionize not only how we gather intelligence, but how we protect nations, prevent conflict, and respond to emerging threats.

BACKGROUND

Intelligence services have long depended on human operatives, often referred to as HUMINT (Human Intelligence) agents to gather, interpret, and disseminate critical information that supports national security, strategic policy formulation, and military operations. These operatives functioned in the shadows, cultivating relationships, infiltrating adversarial organizations, and transmitting sensitive intelligence under conditions of extreme risk. Their contributions have historically been indispensable in navigating international crises, combating espionage, and preventing acts of aggression. However, the landscape of intelligence has undergone a dramatic transformation in recent decades, propelled by the exponential growth of artificial intelligence (AI) technologies.

AI's integration into intelligence frameworks represents a paradigm shift. Intelligence agencies are no longer solely reliant on individual field agents or physical surveillance. Today, they leverage massive data sets, automated surveillance systems, and predictive algorithms to identify threats, track targets, and assess risk. AI can process terabytes of information in seconds, mine data from a wide array of sources including social media, financial records, and satellite imagery and offer real-time insights that would be virtually impossible to achieve through human analysis alone. As a result, AI has become a powerful force multiplier, enhancing the scope, speed, and precision of modern intelligence operations.

The historical development of HUMINT dates back thousands of years. Ancient military treatises, such as *The Art of War* by Sun Tzu (1910), emphasized the strategic value of espionage and the necessity of infiltrating enemy ranks. In the modern era, the two World Wars and the Cold War gave rise to sophisticated espionage networks. Institutions such as the Office of Strategic Services (OSS); a precursor to the CIA and the British Secret Intelligence Service (MI6) trained operatives in counterintelligence, covert operations, and psychological warfare. Figures like Richard Sorge, the Cambridge Five, and Aldrich Ames exemplified the operational impact that a single human agent could have on the global balance of power (Prados, 1996).

In parallel, AI's intellectual origins can be traced to the mid-20th century. Mathematician Alan Turing laid the theoretical foundation for machine-based intelligence, while John McCarthy, often called the "father of AI," formally coined the term in 1956 (Nilsson, 2009). Despite early optimism, AI remained largely confined to academic and theoretical research until the early 21st century. The 9/11 terrorist attacks served as a catalyst for its adoption by intelligence agencies, leading to significant investments in technologies such as biometric surveillance, pattern recognition, natural language processing (NLP), and data mining (Lowenthal, 2016). These systems were deployed to track terrorist networks, monitor cross-border activities, and predict future threats based on behavioral analysis.

The intersection of HUMINT and AI presents an unprecedented opportunity to create hybrid intelligence frameworks that combine the nuanced understanding of human behavior with the computational power of machine learning. HUMINT remains critical in situations where AI is limited in cases such as deciphering intent, gauging loyalty, or navigating cultural subtleties that algorithms cannot yet interpret effectively. In contrast, AI excels in identifying patterns across diverse and fragmented datasets, supporting decision-making processes with predictive modeling and real-time alerts.

However, this convergence also introduces complex ethical, operational, and technological challenges. From an ethical standpoint, the use of AI in intelligence raises questions about privacy, consent, and the potential for algorithmic bias. Misinterpretations by AI systems can lead to wrongful targeting or surveillance of innocent individuals. Operationally, there is a risk of overreliance on machine-generated data, sidelining the intuitive judgment and contextual understanding that human operatives provide. Moreover, ensuring interoperability between legacy HUMINT practices and AI-driven systems requires robust training, infrastructure upgrades, and organizational restructuring.

In addition, adversaries are also adopting AI, creating a new kind of arms race in intelligence capabilities. Nations and non-state actors are deploying AI for cyberattacks, disinformation campaigns, and social engineering. The dual-use nature of AI technology being accessible to both state and non-state entities further complicates the strategic environment. Thus, intelligence services must not only integrate AI responsibly but also develop counter-AI strategies to protect national interests.

Therefore, while AI dramatically enhances the scope and efficiency of modern intelligence operations, it does not render HUMINT obsolete. Rather, the future of intelligence lies in synergizing human insight with artificial processing power. Striking the right balance between the two will determine how effectively intelligence agencies can navigate an increasingly complex and digitized global landscape.

MAIN FOCUS OF THE CHAPTER

Human Intelligence (HUMINT) continues to be a core pillar of intelligence gathering, deeply entrenched in methods such as clandestine infiltration, agent recruitment, psychological manipulation, and deep cultural immersion. Unlike other forms of intelligence collection, HUMINT depends on interpersonal skills, psychological acuity, and the cultivation of trust or deception to elicit sensitive information from human sources. The methodology's adaptability and strategic depth were particularly notable during World War II, when the British Double-Cross System transformed captured German spies into double agents. These operatives helped orchestrate one of the most successful deception campaigns in military history such as the Operation Fortitude, which misled the Nazis about the true location of the D-Day landings (Hinsley & Simkins, 1990).

During the Cold War, HUMINT evolved into a sophisticated apparatus of global espionage. Western agencies such as the CIA and MI6 employed agents in adversarial territories to collect intelligence, while Eastern Bloc nations like the Soviet Union infiltrated Western governments. The infamous “Cambridge Five,” including Kim Philby, highlighted the dangers of counterintelligence failures, as Soviet moles within British intelligence compromised major operations (Prados, 1996). In parallel, HUMINT proved crucial in regional conflicts such as the French-Algerian

War, where the French security apparatus relied heavily on local informants and controversial psychological operations to suppress the National Liberation Front (FLN). The ethical dilemmas surrounding these operations, particularly those involving torture and coercion, underscore the persistent tension between tactical gain and moral restraint (Horne, 2006).

In the contemporary period, HUMINT continues to serve as an essential mechanism in conflict zones. For example, during Operation Iraqi Freedom, U.S. operatives developed tribal networks to track insurgents and identify al-Qaeda leadership. The CIA's engagement with Afghan mujahideen during the Soviet-Afghan War offered similarly valuable ground-level intelligence, with informants embedded within communities providing strategic updates and targeting data (Bamford, 2001; Coll, 2004). Moreover, the enduring need for cultural fluency and emotional intelligence ensures that HUMINT remains irreplaceable in environments where human motivation, sentiment, and trust play defining roles. Similarly, in Latin American conflicts such as Plan Colombia, HUMINT helped counter narcoterrorism through embedded intelligence agents and local partnerships, underscoring its versatility across regions (Crandall, 2002).

Artificial Intelligence (AI), by contrast, introduces a mechanized paradigm of intelligence collection that thrives on speed, scale, and precision. While early uses of AI were confined to signal intelligence (SIGINT) and electronic intelligence (ELINT), contemporary intelligence agencies have adopted AI for mass data analysis, facial recognition, biometric surveillance, and predictive modeling. Agencies like the NSA led the charge in automating surveillance systems. Their controversial PRISM program, revealed by Edward Snowden, showcased how AI could enable governments to mine massive datasets from corporations like Google and Facebook (Pasquale, 2015).

Internationally, AI applications have proliferated. China's *Skynet* surveillance system, for instance, integrates facial recognition and behavioral analytics to monitor over a billion citizens, raising serious concerns about authoritarian overreach and mass social control (Mozur, 2019; Creemers, 2022; Zuboff, 2019). Similarly, Israel's Unit 8200 has pioneered advanced applications of AI in cybersecurity and battlefield telemetry, utilizing real-time data to disrupt adversarial communications and predict insurgent movements (Singer & Friedman, 2014). France's ANSSI has also employed AI to protect critical infrastructure from cyberattacks, demonstrating how machine learning supports defensive postures in cyber warfare. In the UK, GCHQ has faced increasing scrutiny over its digital surveillance and data collection practices, reflecting broader debates about accountability in intelligence operations (Gentry, 2019).

The strategic strengths of AI lie in its capacity for pattern detection, anomaly recognition, and real-time response. During operations against ISIS in Iraq and

Syria, predictive analytics enabled precision airstrikes by identifying logistical routes, safe houses, and operational timelines (Roff, 2019). These capabilities have become central to modern counterterrorism and cyber defense. However, AI lacks interpretive nuance. It cannot gauge intent or loyalty, nor can it negotiate, manipulate, or build rapport—functions at which human operatives excel. More importantly, AI systems often rely on historical data, which may not accurately reflect fast-evolving geopolitical realities.

Despite these strengths, both HUMINT and AI present vulnerabilities. HUMINT is constrained by human limitations: susceptibility to error, manipulation, and betrayal. The damage caused by double agents like Aldrich Ames and Robert Hanssen illustrated how trust violations can devastate agency networks and compromise lives (Prados, 1996). Conversely, AI systems risk bias and error on a structural level. Algorithms trained on skewed datasets have produced discriminatory outcomes, as demonstrated by the COMPAS tool used in U.S. courts to predict recidivism, which disproportionately flagged Black defendants (O'Neil, 2016).

Moreover, the deployment of AI in predictive policing has sparked controversy in liberal democracies. Studies show that these systems can replicate and amplify existing inequalities, disproportionately targeting marginalized communities (Mehrabi et al., 2021). In authoritarian regimes, AI becomes a tool of oppression, as seen in the surveillance of Uyghur Muslims in China's Xinjiang region, where facial recognition and behavioral analytics are used to monitor movement, social interactions, and political loyalty (Human Rights Watch, 2019).

AI's limitations were also evident in its failure to predict or interpret the sociopolitical unrest that led to the Arab Spring. Despite massive surveillance capabilities, intelligence agencies were caught off-guard because AI could not assess emotional currents, social grievances, or the tipping points of public sentiment (Zegart, 2021). These failures highlight the indispensable value of HUMINT in capturing the "human terrain" of conflict. HUMINT operatives are uniquely capable of interpreting subtle signs of unrest, such as shifts in cultural norms, religious discourse, or underground political rhetoric—that escape algorithmic detection.

The integration of HUMINT and AI offers a promising but complex future. A hybridized intelligence model that leverages the strengths of both could revolutionize national security and strategic planning. For example, HUMINT-sourced insights can contextualize AI-generated alerts, enabling nuanced and responsive action plans. However, to achieve this synergy, institutions must address structural issues such as interdepartmental data sharing, ethical frameworks, and training for human-machine collaboration. Case studies such as NATO's Allied Command Transformation (ACT) experiments with AI-driven decision-support and threat-detection systems highlight the practical potential of this integration (Pomerleau, 2020).

Another emerging concern involves adversarial use of AI. State and non-state actors are increasingly developing offensive AI tools for cyber warfare, misinformation, and subversion. Russian disinformation campaigns during Western elections, often amplified by AI bots and content farms, illustrate how artificial intelligence can be weaponized to manipulate public opinion (Polyakova & Boyer, 2018). Consequently, HUMINT will be vital not only in verifying the authenticity of information but also in assessing the psychological impact of adversarial narratives on target populations.

Finally, the evolution of intelligence practices reflects an ongoing dialogue between tradition and innovation. HUMINT, grounded in human experience and emotional depth, remains irreplaceable in many aspects of intelligence work. AI, with its computational advantages, complements but cannot supplant the human dimension. Together, they form the dual engines of 21st-century intelligence, each indispensable, and each demanding vigilant oversight.

ISSUES, CONTROVERSIES, AND PROBLEMS: ETHICAL, LEGAL, AND OPERATIONAL CHALLENGES IN HUMINT AND AI INTEGRATION

The integration of Artificial Intelligence (AI) into intelligence operations has expanded the scope of surveillance, threat detection, and predictive modeling. However, this transformation is accompanied by pressing ethical, legal, and operational challenges. While Human Intelligence (HUMINT) traditionally faces issues of reliability, betrayal, and ethical conduct, AI introduces newer dimensions such as algorithmic bias, opaque decision-making, and threats to civil liberties. As intelligence frameworks become increasingly hybrid, composed of both human and machine components, understanding and addressing these issues becomes essential for ethical and effective national security operations.

Ethical and Legal Concerns

The use of AI for mass surveillance and predictive analytics has triggered global concerns over privacy violations and civil liberties. One of the most significant milestones in public awareness of state surveillance came with Edward Snowden's 2013 disclosures about the National Security Agency's (NSA) PRISM program. The leaked documents revealed that U.S. intelligence agencies had accessed vast amounts of private communications from tech companies without user consent (Greenwald, 2014; Pasquale, 2015). These revelations initiated a worldwide debate on the balance between national security and individual privacy. In the United Kingdom, Liberty Human Rights (2021) highlighted that the widespread use of facial recognition technology by police has expanded with minimal oversight, posing threats to privacy, freedom of assembly, and nondiscrimination. The report emphasized that algorithmic bias embedded in such systems disproportionately affects minority communities and undermines public trust in security institutions. These findings illustrate how the integration of AI into HUMINT operations can erode the principles of accountability and proportionality unless governed by clear, transparent frameworks.

Similarly, in China, the deployment of AI-powered surveillance systems has reached an unprecedented scale. The Chinese government's Skynet and Sharp Eyes projects use facial recognition and real-time tracking to monitor public behavior, particularly targeting ethnic minorities like the Uighur population in Xinjiang (Qiang, 2019). Reports have detailed how biometric data, movement patterns, and social media activity are monitored to assess individual loyalty to the Communist Party, raising severe human rights concerns (Mozur, 2019).

These developments challenge international norms surrounding human rights and the rule of law. While the International Covenant on Civil and Political Rights (ICCPR) guarantees protection against arbitrary interference in privacy (Article 17), the deployment of AI technologies in opaque and intrusive ways often circumvents such protections. Moreover, the lack of clear, global regulatory frameworks governing AI use in surveillance creates legal gray zones that are often exploited by states in the name of national security.

The ethical concerns surrounding AI are not confined to authoritarian regimes. Democratic states have also faced criticism for deploying surveillance tools without adequate oversight. In the United Kingdom, for instance, the use of Live Facial Recognition (LFR) by the Metropolitan Police has been contested in court due to concerns over disproportionate targeting of minority communities and lack of public consent (Liberty, 2020). In the United States, cities like San Francisco and Boston have passed ordinances banning or restricting facial recognition use by public agencies due to similar concerns.

Reliability and Bias in AI Systems

Another core issue is the reliability of AI systems, especially those deployed in high-stakes environments like law enforcement, intelligence, and national defense. AI algorithms are only as good as the data on which they are trained. If datasets are biased, incomplete, or unrepresentative, the outputs of AI systems will reflect those same flaws, often amplifying systemic inequalities.

The COMPAS (Correctional Offender Management Profiling for Alternative Sanctions) algorithm, used in U.S. courts to assess the likelihood of criminal recidivism, exemplifies this problem. A ProPublica investigation found that COMPAS disproportionately flagged Black defendants as high-risk compared to white defendants with similar criminal histories (Angwin et al., 2016; O'Neil, 2016). Such outcomes not only compromise justice but also erode public trust in institutions that rely on algorithmic decision-making.

Predictive policing tools have similarly come under scrutiny in the UK and U.S. These systems use historical crime data to predict future criminal activity and allocate policing resources accordingly. However, critics argue that these models reinforce existing biases by over-policing already marginalized communities (Mehrabi et al., 2021; Brayne, 2017). As such, AI-based systems may not reduce bias but rather encode and perpetuate it.

Operational Risks and Failures

While AI faces concerns regarding algorithmic transparency and reliability, Human Intelligence (HUMINT) is vulnerable to distinctly human limitations, most notably betrayal, cognitive bias, emotional stress, and manipulation. The historical record of intelligence failures is replete with examples of double agents and informants who compromised critical operations. The case of Aldrich Ames, a CIA counterintelligence officer who spied for the Soviet Union, is one of the most damaging breaches in U.S. intelligence history. Ames exposed the identities of numerous CIA assets, leading to their arrest or execution (Prados, 1996).

Similarly, Robert Hanssen, another U.S. intelligence official, sold classified information to Moscow for over two decades, underscoring how even highly vetted personnel can become internal threats. These examples illustrate how the subjective nature of HUMINT, including personal motivations, ideological leanings, and emotional vulnerabilities, can result in catastrophic operational outcomes.

AI, while not subject to emotional failings, carries its own set of operational risks. Chief among them is the inability of AI to interpret complex human behaviors, particularly those driven by cultural nuance, sarcasm, or deception. This was evident in the intelligence community's failure to predict the 2011 Arab Spring. Despite the existence of massive AI-powered surveillance networks monitoring communication flows across North Africa and the Middle East, the spontaneous nature of the uprisings and the emotional undercurrents of collective dissent were missed by analytical models that prioritized quantifiable indicators over human sentiment (Zegart, 2021).

Technical vulnerabilities also make AI a target for cyberattacks and data manipulation. Adversarial machine learning, a technique in which bad actors feed false or misleading data into AI systems, can distort algorithmic predictions and decision-making. This represents a serious threat in intelligence settings, where false positives or negatives can have life-or-death consequences.

SOLUTIONS AND RECOMMENDATIONS

Addressing these multifaceted risks requires a combination of policy reform, technical innovation, and operational restructuring. Several key strategies can enhance the ethical and effective deployment of AI in intelligence, while also reinforcing the strengths of HUMINT.

1. Integration of HUMINT and AI

The most promising approach lies in the integration of AI with HUMINT rather than the replacement of one by the other. A hybrid model leverages the contextual, cultural, and emotional acuity of human operatives alongside the speed, scale, and precision of machine processing. The U.S. Department of Defense's Project Maven is a model example. It uses AI to analyze drone footage and flag potential threats but leaves the final determination to human analysts (Singer & Friedman, 2014). Such collaborative frameworks help minimize both human and machine error.

2. Ethical AI Development

To curb the misuse of AI, especially in surveillance, governments and multilateral organizations must develop binding ethical frameworks. The European Union's proposed Artificial Intelligence Act, for instance, categorizes AI systems by risk and imposes strict obligations on high-risk applications, including those used in law enforcement and border control (European Commission, 2021). Transparency, auditability, and accountability must become foundational design principles for any AI system used in intelligence.

3. Training and Capacity Building

Modern intelligence personnel must be proficient in both traditional fieldcraft and contemporary technologies. This requires a significant investment in interdisciplinary training that spans behavioral psychology, cyber operations, data science, and machine learning. Agencies should also foster partnerships with academic institutions and private-sector innovators to stay current with AI advancements.

4. Cross-Border Collaboration

Given the global nature of cyber threats and terrorism, intelligence services must work across national boundaries to develop shared protocols, interoperable systems, and joint task forces. NATO's Cooperative Cyber Defence Centre of Excellence

(CCDCOE) represents a model for multinational cooperation in intelligence sharing and cyber defense (Fidler et al., 2013). The European Union's Intelligence and Situation Centre (EU INTCEN) provides a parallel example within the EU framework.

5. Future Research Priorities

Further research should investigate how AI can augment HUMINT processes. This includes the use of sentiment analysis to gauge the emotional state and reliability of informants in real-time, as well as natural language processing (NLP) tools to analyze communication patterns. Quantum computing also represents a major frontier. As quantum machines evolve, they may soon render current encryption techniques obsolete, transforming the field of signals intelligence (Russell & Norvig, 2016).

FUTURE RESEARCH DIRECTIONS

The evolution of intelligence in the 21st century demands not only technological adoption but also systematic inquiry into future capabilities. Emerging technologies like artificial intelligence (AI), quantum computing, and cross-border surveillance architecture are redefining the parameters of modern intelligence work. As intelligence services shift toward hybrid models that blend Human Intelligence (HUMINT) with machine-driven systems, focused research is essential to optimize, regulate, and ethically harness these innovations.

AI-Powered HUMINT Support

One of the most compelling avenues for future research lies in the augmentation of HUMINT through AI. While AI excels at processing large datasets and identifying anomalies, it cannot replicate the intuitive, cultural, and emotional depth of human field agents. Future studies should explore how AI can act as a support mechanism rather than a replacement.

For instance, AI-driven sentiment analysis tools can evaluate the tone, emotional state, and linguistic patterns of informants in real-time. By processing voice inflections, facial micro-expressions, and textual cues, these systems can help analysts detect deception or stress. Natural Language Processing (NLP) algorithms can be used to monitor shifts in communication tone over time, allowing intelligence operatives to assess trustworthiness or emerging ideological shifts in their human sources.

Moreover, AI tools could enhance informant management. AI-enabled dashboards may prioritize agent reports based on their assessed reliability, geographic value, or alignment with ongoing intelligence missions. These systems would require significant oversight but could revolutionize how intelligence operatives' triage and validate vast volumes of human-sourced data.

Research is also needed on using machine learning to support operational logistics in HUMINT missions, predicting optimal meeting locations, timing for contact, or even risk-level assessments for human assets based on known environmental and political variables. These applications could greatly enhance field safety while preserving agent anonymity.

Simulation and Predictive Modeling of HUMINT-AI Interactions

Future research should also explore simulation environments where interactions between human agents and AI systems can be modeled, tested, and optimized. Such simulations can help identify scenarios where AI can enhance HUMINT operations (e.g., source validation, location tracking) and where reliance on AI may be risky due to adversarial manipulation or contextual blind spots.

While most discussions of AI in intelligence focus on surveillance and data analytics, research by Chandrasekera et al. (2024) highlights another crucial dimension — the role of AI in enhancing human creativity and decision-making. Their study demonstrates that AI systems can augment human intuition by supporting early-stage design thinking and complex problem-solving. Applied to the intelligence context, such human–AI collaboration suggests that analytical and operational planning could similarly benefit from AI's capacity to model scenarios, visualize data relationships, and inspire novel strategic approaches without replacing human judgment.

Quantum Computing and Intelligence

Quantum computing is poised to disrupt every aspect of digital information security. Its potential to break traditional encryption schemes through quantum algorithms such as Shor's Algorithm presents both a threat and an opportunity for intelligence services. Future research must prioritize two key tracks: quantum-safe encryption and offensive quantum capabilities.

In the defensive sphere, the development and implementation of post-quantum cryptographic algorithms is essential. Intelligence agencies must anticipate the eventuality that current standards such as RSA and ECC will become obsolete. Collaboration with institutions such as NIST (National Institute of Standards and Technology), which is leading post-quantum standardization efforts, will be key to remaining secure in a quantum-enabled world.

On the offensive front, quantum computing could offer intelligence agencies unprecedented capabilities in codebreaking, simulations, and optimization problems. For example, quantum computers could analyze adversarial communication networks in near real-time, simulate behavioral outcomes in counterintelligence scenarios, or optimize surveillance routes and satellite tasking with a precision unmatched by classical computing (Russell & Norvig, 2016).

However, such power also poses ethical risks. Asymmetric access to quantum computing may lead to power imbalances and the erosion of privacy on a global scale. Future research must explore governance models and treaties to mitigate the destabilizing effects of quantum supremacy in intelligence domains.

Cross-Border Collaboration

Given the transnational nature of cyber threats, terrorism, and disinformation campaigns, intelligence can no longer function effectively within isolated national silos. Cross-border collaboration, both multilateral and bilateral, must become a cornerstone of future intelligence research.

Projects such as NATO's Cooperative Cyber Defence Centre of Excellence (CCDCOE) have already demonstrated the effectiveness of multinational cooperation in cyberspace. However, further research is needed into how such models can be extended to the integration of AI-supported HUMINT. How can trust be fostered between partner agencies when sharing sensitive algorithmic tools? What protocols are required to ensure interoperability without compromising operational secrecy or national security interests?

The European Union's Intelligence and Situation Centre (EU INTCEN) also offers a model for regional integration. However, limitations in real-time data sharing, standardization of AI ethics, and legal harmonization remain persistent barriers. Future research should address these gaps by proposing policy frameworks, secure infrastructure models, and joint AI oversight mechanisms that respect national sovereignty while maximizing collaborative potential.

Cross-border research initiatives should also examine how global crises such as pandemics, migration flows, and climate instability impact the coordination of intelligence. AI-supported HUMINT in disaster zones, refugee monitoring, and pandemic response could become essential to national resilience. Building intelligence frameworks that can respond to these challenges in real-time requires both technical innovation and geopolitical coordination.

In is imperative that the future of intelligence lies not only in the adoption of emerging technologies but in the rigorous, interdisciplinary research that guides their ethical and strategic use. From augmenting human capabilities with AI, securing communications in a post-quantum world, to redefining the geopolitical map of intelligence sharing, future research directions must be comprehensive, collaborative, and foresighted.

Ethics and Accountability in Intelligence AI

As AI becomes more embedded in intelligence operations, there is an urgent need for research into ethical governance frameworks. This includes establishing protocols for transparency, human oversight, accountability, and bias mitigation. Comparative studies between national security agencies may yield insights into best practices and ethical pitfalls.

Cross-Disciplinary Applications and Impacts

Interdisciplinary research is essential to understand how AI and HUMINT strategies can be co-applied in areas beyond military intelligence, such as cybersecurity, counterterrorism, public health crisis management, and economic surveillance. Each of these domains presents unique challenges that require customized integration of human and machine reasoning.

Training and Education for Hybrid Intelligence Analysts

There is a pressing need to develop educational curricula and professional training programs for the next generation of intelligence analysts. These programs should equip professionals with both technical literacy in AI and field competencies in HUMINT, preparing them to operate in a digitally augmented yet human-centered intelligence environment.

HUMINT Preservation in AI-Dominated Environments

Research should also investigate strategies to preserve and enhance traditional HUMINT methods in the face of increasing automation. As AI takes on more intelligence functions, preserving human judgment, empathy, and ethical reasoning becomes even more critical in fields where machines still lack nuance and cultural sensitivity.

Legal and International Regulatory Frameworks

Finally, scholarly attention should be devoted to international law and policy harmonization surrounding AI use in intelligence. This includes research into treaties, privacy rights, and legal definitions of machine responsibility in surveillance, data handling, and autonomous decision-making.

CONCLUSION

Human Intelligence (HUMINT) and Artificial Intelligence (AI) each offer unique, complementary strengths to modern intelligence operations. HUMINT, rooted in human relationships, cultural understanding, and psychological insight, provides the depth of context, ethical judgment, and strategic nuance often absent in purely technical systems. In contrast, AI enables rapid, scalable data analysis and pattern recognition across enormous information environments, detecting anomalies and predicting behaviors at speeds no human could achieve.

However, neither HUMINT nor AI alone is sufficient to address the full spectrum of modern intelligence challenges. From transnational terrorism and cybercrime to geopolitical instability and state-sponsored misinformation, today's threats are complex, adaptive, and multi-domain. A siloed approach will fall short. The integration of HUMINT and AI into a cohesive, collaborative intelligence architecture is essential for national and global security.

This integration must be grounded in clear ethical frameworks that ensure the responsible use of both human and artificial resources. Transparent oversight mechanisms, privacy safeguards, and equitable data governance are crucial to prevent abuse, discrimination, or loss of public trust. Furthermore, global cooperation will be necessary to establish interoperability, mutual accountability, and shared norms among intelligence partners.

Ultimately, intelligence services must evolve in both capacity and conscience. Investments in human capital, technological innovation, and international alliances will determine whether intelligence operations in the 21st century become tools of collective security—or sources of division and controversy. Balancing the analytical power of AI with the moral compass of HUMINT may well define the future of ethical intelligence.

REFERENCES

Angwin, J., Larson, J., Mattu, S., & Kirchner, L. (2016). Machine bias. *ProPublica*. https://www.propublica.org/article/machine-bias-risk-assessments-in-criminal-sentencing

Bamford, J. (2001). *Body of secrets: Anatomy of the ultra-secret National Security Agency*. Anchor Books.

Brayne, S. (2017). Big data surveillance: The case of policing. *American Sociological Review*, *82*(5), 977–1008. PMID: 38322733

Chandrasekera, T., Hosseini, Z., Perera, U., & Bazhaw Hyscher, A. (2024). *Can artificial intelligence support creativity in early design processes?* ResearchGate. Retrieved from https://www.researchgate.net/publication/380798610_Can_artificial_intelligence_support_creativity_in_early_design_processes

Coll, S. (2004). *Ghost wars: The secret history of the CIA, Afghanistan, and bin Laden, from the Soviet invasion to September 10, 2001*. Penguin Press.

Crandall, R. (2002). *Driven by drugs: U.S. policy toward Colombia*. Lynne Rienner Publishers.

Creemers, R. (2022). China's Social Credit System and the Digital Governance of Behavior. *Information Communication and Society*, *25*(7), 1005–1021.

European Commission. (2021). Proposal for a regulation laying down harmonised rules on artificial intelligence. https://digital-strategy.ec.europa.eu

Fidler, D. P., Pregent, R., & Vandurme, A. (2013). NATO, Cyber defense, and international law. *John's J. Int'l & Comp. L.*, *4*, 1.

Gentry, J. A. (2019). Intelligence Accountability in the United Kingdom. *Intelligence and National Security*, *34*(3), 353–371.

Greenwald, G. (2014). *No place to hide: Edward Snowden, the NSA, and the U.S. surveillance state*. Metropolitan Books.

Hinsley, F. H., & Simkins, C. A. G. (1990). *British intelligence in the Second World War: Volume 4, Security and Counter-Intelligence*. HMSO.

Horne, A. (2006). *A savage war of peace: Algeria 1954–1962*. NYRB Classics.

Human Rights Watch. (2019). *China's algorithms of repression: Reverse engineering a Xinjiang police mass surveillance app.* Human Rights Watch. Retrieved from https://www.hrw.org/report/2019/05/01/chinas-algorithms-repression/reverse-engineering-xinjiang-police-mass

Liberty Human Rights. (2021). *"Face Off: The Lawless Growth of Facial Recognition in UK Policing."* https://www.libertyhumanrights.org.uk

Lowenthal, M. M. (2016). *Intelligence: From secrets to policy* (7th ed.). CQ Press.

Mehrabi, N., Morstatter, F., Saxena, N., Lerman, K., & Galstyan, A. (2021). A survey on bias and fairness in machine learning. *ACM Computing Surveys, 54*(6), 1–35.

Mozur, P. (2019, May 14). *Inside China's Dystopian Dreams: A.I., Shame, and Lots of Cameras. The New York Times.*

Mozur, P. (2019). One month, 500,000 face scans: How China is using AI to profile a minority. *The New York Times.* https://www.nytimes.com

Nilsson, N. J. (2009). *The quest for artificial intelligence: A history of ideas and achievements.* Cambridge University Press.

O'Neil, C. (2016). *Weapons of math destruction: How big data increases inequality and threatens democracy.* Crown Publishing Group.

Pasquale, F. (2015). *The black box society: The secret algorithms that control money and information.* Harvard University Press.

Polyakova, A., & Boyer, S. (2018). The future of political warfare: Russia, the West, and the coming age of global digital competition. *Brookings Institution.* https://www.brookings.edu

Pomerleau, M. (2020). *"NATO Looks to AI for Decision Support and Threat Detection." Defense News.* https://www.defensenews.com

Prados, J. (1996). *Presidents' secret wars: CIA and Pentagon covert operations since World War II.* Ivan R. Dee.

Qiang, X. (2019). The road to digital unfreedom: President Xi's surveillance state. *Journal of Democracy, 30*(1), 53–67. DOI: 10.1353/jod.2019.0004

Roff, H. M. (2019). Artificial intelligence: Power to the people. *Ethics & International Affairs, 33*(2), 127–140.

Russell, S., & Norvig, P. (2016). *Artificial intelligence: A modern approach* (3rd ed.). Pearson.

Singer, P. W., & Friedman, A. (2014). *Cybersecurity and cyberwar: What everyone needs to know*. Oxford University Press.

Tzu, S. (1910). The art of war (L. Giles, Trans.). *London, United Kingdom: Luzac & Co.(Original work published nd).*

Zegart, A. B. (2021). *Spies, lies, and algorithms: The history and future of American intelligence*. Princeton University Press.

Zuboff, S. (2019). *The Age of Surveillance Capitalism*. PublicAffairs.

ADDITIONAL READING

Allen, G., & Chan, T. **(2017).** *Artificial intelligence and national security*. Belfer Center for Science and International Affairs, Harvard Kennedy School. https://www.belfercenter.org/publication/artificial-intelligence-and-national-security

Chen, T. M., & Abu-Nimeh, S. (2011). Lessons from Stuxnet. *Computer*, *44*(4), 91–93. DOI: 10.1109/MC.2011.115

Czosseck, C., Ottis, R., & Ziolkowski, K. (Eds.). **(2011).** *2011 3rd International Conference on Cyber Conflict*. NATO Cooperative Cyber Defence Centre of Excellence.

De Silva, E. and Abeyagoonesekera, A. (2021) "Intelligence and Law Enforcement in the 21st Century." – IGI Global Publishers – Explores various intelligence models and policies.

Ghosh, A., & Rai, A. (2019). The ethics of artificial intelligence and robotics. In *The Stanford Encyclopedia of Philosophy* (Fall 2019 Edition). https://plato.stanford.edu/archives/fall2019/entries/ethics-ai/

Lin, P., Abney, K., & Bekey, G. A. (2011). *Robot ethics: The ethical and social implications of robotics*. MIT Press.

Marr, B. (2020). *Artificial intelligence in practice: How 50 successful companies used AI and machine learning to solve problems*. Wiley.

Russell, S. J., & Norvig, P. (2021). *Artificial intelligence: A modern approach* (4th ed.). Pearson.

Taddeo, M., & Floridi, L. (2018). How AI can be a force for good. *Science*, *361*(6404), 751–752. DOI: 10.1126/science.aat5991 PMID: 30139858

Waltz, E. (2020). Man versus machine: When AI outperforms humans in intelligence analysis. *Nature, 586*(7828), 22–25. DOI: 10.1038/d41586-020-02649-4

Zegart, A. B. (2022). *Spies, lies, and algorithms: The history and future of American intelligence*. Princeton University Press.

KEY TERMS AND DEFINITIONS

Artificial Intelligence (AI): The branch of computer science focused on creating machines or systems capable of performing tasks that typically require human intelligence, such as reasoning, learning, perception, and decision-making.

Autonomous Systems: Technological systems, often powered by AI, that can operate independently without real-time human control, especially in tasks like surveillance, data analysis, and threat detection.

Big Data Analytics: The process of examining vast, complex datasets to uncover hidden patterns, correlations, and other insights relevant to intelligence operations and decision-making.

Cognitive Computing: A subset of AI designed to simulate human thought processes in complex problem-solving through the use of self-learning algorithms and natural language processing.

Cyber Intelligence: Information derived from monitoring, analyzing, and understanding digital networks and behaviors, often used to identify threats and support cybersecurity efforts.

Ethical Governance: A framework of policies, values, and oversight mechanisms that guide the responsible development and use of technologies such as AI, ensuring compliance with legal and moral standards.

Human Intelligence (HUMINT): Information collected directly from human sources through interpersonal contact, including interviews, observations, and informants, used primarily in security and espionage contexts.

Machine Learning: A method of data analysis that enables computers to learn from and make predictions or decisions based on data patterns without being explicitly programmed.

Operational Security: Measures and protocols used to protect sensitive information and activities from adversaries, ensuring the effectiveness and secrecy of intelligence operations.

Sentiment Analysis: An AI-powered process of analyzing human communication; such as speech or text, to determine emotional tone or intent, often used in evaluating threats or public sentiment.

Chapter 2
Prioritizing Threats:
AHP-Based Assessment of Terrorist Intention and Capability for Intelligence Operations

I Made Wisnu Wardhana
https://orcid.org/0009-0003-4756-9448
Universitas Indonesia, Indonesia

ABSTRACT

Intelligence analysts play a vital role in evaluating terrorist threats, a process that demands objectivity, consistency, and analytical rigor. To move beyond intuition-based assessments and reduce subjective bias, this paper introduces a structured methodology grounded in the Analytic Hierarchy Process (AHP) a decision-making framework developed by Thomas L. Saaty. This approach focuses on two fundamental indicators central to terrorism threat analysis: intention and capability. By assigning weights and ratings to relevant sub-indicators, AHP allows analysts to systematically prioritize persons of interest (POIs) based on quantifiable threat levels. The paper further enhances its practical relevance through a series of illustrative case studies that simulate real-world profiles, demonstrating how limited information can be transformed into actionable intelligence. This research offers a scientifically grounded, scalable model that supports intelligence and law enforcement agencies in making informed, data-driven decisions in the fight against terrorism.

INTRODUCTION

The nature of terrorist operations is highly adaptive, with perpetrators continuously modifying their methods to evade detection by intelligence and law enforcement

DOI: 10.4018/979-8-3693-3522-2.ch002

agencies. This ongoing evolution challenges conventional approaches and demands increasingly sophisticated techniques to identify and disrupt emerging threats. Intelligence and law enforcement bodies must therefore enhance their analytical tools to proactively assess and respond to these threats. One of the primary objectives of such tools is to enable early intervention by strategically identifying and neutralizing individuals or groups with the potential to conduct violent acts. However, assessing the threat posed by a potential terrorist remains a complex task due to the absence of a standardized and operationally reliable framework for evaluating both intent and capability.

To address this analytical gap, the study proposes a structured, scientific method for evaluating terrorist threats using the AHP, a decision-making model developed by Thomas L. Saaty in 1980. This approach introduces a scalable and replicable framework that translates qualitative indicators into quantitative assessments. It begins by identifying two fundamental dimensions of a terrorist threat: intention and capability. Each dimension is further subdivided into measurable sub-indicators—such as behavioural activities, personal and familial backgrounds, access to resources, and technical proficiency. Furthermore, intelligence analysts rate each Person of Interest (POI) on a 1-to-9 scale for each indicator. The weighted scores are then integrated into a risk matrix, classifying individuals into low, medium, or high threat levels. This systematic method enhances the consistency, transparency, and operational utility of threat assessments in dynamic field environments.

While this model presents a significant advancement in operational decision-making, it is crucial to situate it within the broader body of research on terrorist threat assessment. Over the past two decades, numerous scholars and practitioners have explored behavioural indicators associated with terrorist activity particularly those related to intent and capability. However, existing models have often been descriptive, inconsistent across case types, or lacking in empirical validation. The literature remains fragmented, with varying methodologies offering limited guidance for real-time intelligence work. The following review synthesizes key contributions by scholars, outlining the evolution of thought in this domain and highlighting persistent gaps that justify the development of a structured, quantifiable model like the one proposed in this study.

LITERATURE REVIEW

Intention and Capability

Understanding and predicting terrorist acts hinges upon accurately identifying a perpetrator's intention and capability. Across the literature, various conceptual frameworks and methodologies have been developed to discern these two dimensions. This review analyses two key papers Schuurman & Eijkman (2015) and Schuurman et al. (2018) to define terrorist intention and capability.

Based on literatures, Intention refers to an individual's goal-oriented drive to plan, prepare, and execute an act of terrorist violence. It is not a static trait but a situational process that emerges from the interaction between personal experiences, ideological influences, and external frictions such as political grievances or personal trauma. This motivational drive can fluctuate over time and often needs reinforcement through ideological validation or social encouragement. Indicators of terrorist intent may include expressions of desire to commit violence, ideological radicalization (especially toward extremism), or threats made toward specific targets. However, the presence of such indicators alone is not sufficient to predict violence, as many who harbor radical beliefs do not necessarily act on them

Capability, on the other hand, encompasses both the material and cognitive means necessary to execute a terrorist attack. This includes tangible actions such as acquiring weapons, explosives, or technical training, as well as more abstract components like overcoming moral inhibitions or developing operational skills. Capability also implies a belief in one's own effectiveness if individuals do not perceive themselves as able to successfully carry out an attack, their motivation may diminish. Capability can also manifest through social connections that provide access to resources, skills, or legitimization. Observable indicators may range from weapons procurement and reconnaissance to engagement in paramilitary training or bomb-making activities.

To conclude, a threat becomes operationally significant only when intention and capability converge. While many individuals may hold radical views or express hostile rhetoric, the actual risk of violence depends on whether those intentions are supported by actionable means. Therefore, effective threat assessment models must evaluate both dimensions simultaneously and contextually.

While existing literature provides deep conceptual and empirical grounding for understanding terrorist intention and capability, it lacks quantitative prioritization mechanisms and operational tools for real-world threat management. There is a clear need for future research to bridge the divide between robust theoretical models and actionable decision-making frameworks that support intelligence and law enforcement operations.

Analytical Hierarchy Process

The AHP, introduced by Thomas L. Saaty in 1980, is a multi-criteria decision-making method designed to aid in structuring and analysing complex decisions. In the field of counter-terrorism, AHP has emerged as an essential tool to evaluate and prioritize threats, particularly when integrated with other analytical frameworks such as *Social Network Analysis* (SNA) and *Technique for Order Preference by Similarity to Ideal Solution* (TOPSIS). This literature review examines the application and importance of AHP in terrorism assessment by analysing a range of academic studies.

Firstly, the combination of AHP and SNA has been shown to significantly enhance the reliability and interpretability of network-based threat assessments. In their analysis of the 26/11 Mumbai terrorist attack, Choudhary and Singh (2016) integrated AHP with SNA centrality measures to produce a consolidated ranking of 13 terrorist nodes. Their results indicated that this hybrid model was more robust in identifying key actors compared to using SNA metrics independently. Similarly, in a broader application, Choudhary and Singh (2018) examined terrorist organizations operating in India between 2000 and 2003. Using a combined SNA-AHP approach, the study generated a unified ranking of organizations, highlighting how AHP could be used to weigh centrality measures based on expert judgment, thereby resolving inconsistencies found in traditional network analyses.

Furthermore, Fox et al. (2015) extended the application of AHP through a hybrid AHP-TOPSIS methodology to prioritize individual terrorist targets. This model involved deriving decision-maker weights via AHP and applying TOPSIS to rank alternatives. The authors emphasized that AHP provided a structured approach for capturing subjective expert inputs, which were then used in the more quantitatively rigorous TOPSIS phase. The methodology proved effective in handling large datasets and complex variable interrelations inherent in terrorist profiling.

The AHP proves to be an invaluable tool in terrorism assessment due to its capacity to: Consolidate diverse metrics into a unified decision-making framework; Integrate subjective expert knowledge with quantitative analysis; Enhance robustness and transparency in threat prioritization; Support strategic evaluations of counter-terrorism systems; Bridge the gap between qualitative intent and quantitative capability in threat modelling.

Therefore, a significant advancement in terrorism risk analysis is the application of AHP to systematically assess both the intention and capability of terrorist actors. Intention, often abstract and inferred from ideological alignment, history, and communications, can be structured as criteria alongside observable capability indicators such as logistical support, operational sophistication, and weapon access. By constructing a hierarchical model with intention and capability as top-level criteria, AHP allows decision-makers to perform pairwise comparisons and derive weighted scores that reflect both strategic motive and tactical potential. This structured approach enhances the predictive validity of threat assessments, enabling law enforcement and intelligence agencies to prioritize suspects or organizations not solely based on what they have done, but on what they are both inclined and able to do.

METHODOLOGY

This research methodology follows a structured sequence grounded in the AHP to assess terrorism risk through a balance of qualitative insight and quantitative rigor. The process begins with identifying and classifying key indicators and sub-indicators representing both terrorist intention (such as historical behaviour) and capability (such as access to weapons and operational history). These are then organized into a hierarchical model, starting with the primary goal, followed by the criteria categories and their corresponding sub-indicators. Once structured, the methodology proceeds to determine the level of significance of each sub-indicator, allowing analysts to judge the relative importance of each factor. From these comparisons, weight coefficients are calculated, representing the priority level of each sub-indicator. Subsequently, each sub-indicator is scored based on observed data or intelligence assessments, and these scores are multiplied by their respective weights to produce weighted values. The final risk score is obtained by aggregating these weighted values, enabling the classification of threats according to severity.

Hierarchy of Indicators

Based on an extensive literature review and adapted to Indonesia's specific security context, this study adopts two primary indicators for assessing terrorist threats: intention and capability. The first indicator, *intention*, refers to the motivation or ideological commitment of an individual to carry out a terrorist act. This includes a set of sub-indicators that provide insight into the subject's personal background and behavioural patterns. Informed by Indonesian case studies, the selected sub-indicators include daily behaviours (such as physical routines and communication patterns), prior involvement in terrorist activity, and relational networks. Particular attention is paid to whether the individual is a former convict, deportee, or returnee from a conflict zone profile commonly found in Indonesian terrorism cases. Familial ties to known extremists are also analysed, recognizing the recurrent role of kinship networks in sustaining and expanding terrorist cells in the region.[1]

The second core indicator is *capability*, which reflects the individual's operational potential to execute an attack. This encompasses technical skills such as expertise in explosives, proficiency in firearms, and martial arts training. It also includes the individual's financial independence and their access to external support from terrorist networks. In the Indonesian context, group affiliation is especially relevant, as local extremist organizations often provide logistical support, funding, and paramilitary training. The selection of these indicators was informed by patterns observed in domestic counterterrorism investigations and intelligence reports. Together, these elements form the foundation of the hierarchical assessment model illustrated in Figure 1.

Figure 1. Hierarchy of indicators

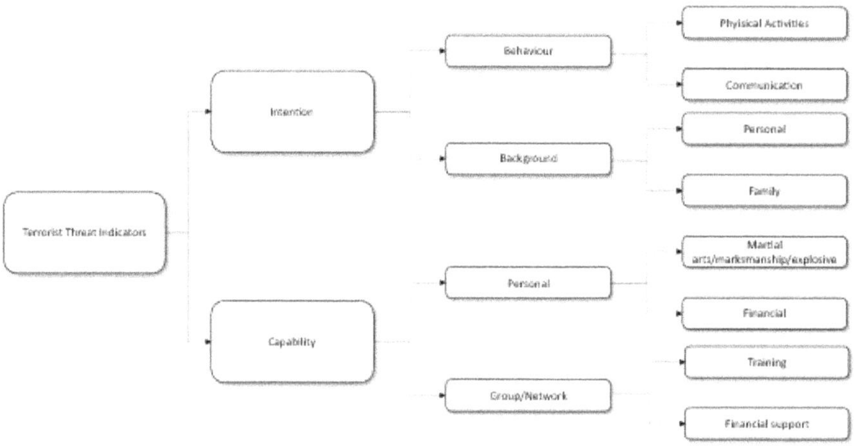

The Framework

Once the relevant indicators and sub-indicators have been identified, the next step is to assign weights to each sub-indicator within its respective category. Using the method developed by Thomas L. Saaty, this process involves determining which sub-indicators hold the greatest significance in assessing the threat. To implement this approach, several key steps must be followed: understanding the level of significance of each sub-indicator, assigning appropriate weights, and applying standardized ratings. These steps form the foundation for a structured and objective threat assessment process.[2]

Level of Significance: A Modified Application of Saaty's Scale

Firstly, comprehending the importance of sub-indicators is essential in evaluating terrorism risk. As previously mentioned, various sub-indicators contribute to assessing both the intent and capability of a terrorist actor. A fundamental question arises: how can we quantify or evaluate these sub-indicators in relation to each other? Which sub-indicator holds more weight in the context of threat assessment? Traditionally, the Analytic Hierarchy Process (AHP) uses Saaty's nine-point scale, which offers fine granularity in expressing preferences ranging from equal importance (1) to extreme importance (9). While this detailed scale allows for nuanced comparisons, it may introduce subjectivity, inconsistency, and cognitive overload when applied in complex or operational environments. To address this, the current study proposes a modified model using only three levels of significance. As illustrated in Figure 2, these levels are: *less significant* (the sub-indicator is less important), *significant* (the sub-indicator is important), and *highly significant* (the sub-indicator is most important). This simplification aims to reduce ambiguity, enhance inter-rater reliability, and streamline decision-making while maintaining enough differentiation to support effective prioritization in terrorism risk evaluation.

Figure 2. Level of significance

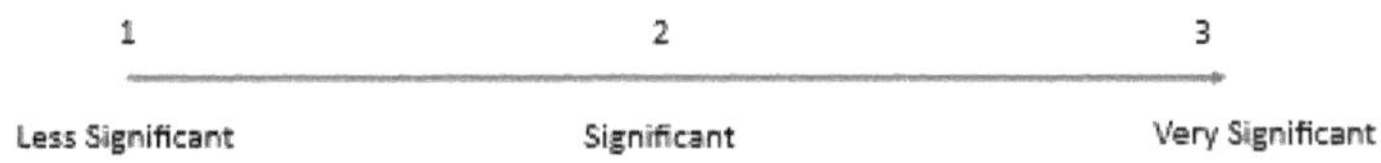

Weighting Sub-indicators

Why is it necessary for the analyst to establish the level of significance? This initial step is directly linked to the subsequent phase assigning weights to the sub-indicators. In principle, the total weight of all sub-indicators should sum to 1.00. For instance, if the intention category consists of four sub-indicators, each would initially carry an equal weight of 0.25. However, in practice, not all sub-indicators hold equal relevance. Some, such as a behavioural indicator, may be deemed more critical than others like familial background. Conversely, an analyst might assign greater importance to familial ties if they provide stronger evidence of an individual's affiliation with a terrorist network. Therefore, establishing the significance level early in the process is essential, as it directly influences the weight and prioritization of each sub-indicator in the overall risk assessment model. To determine the relative weight of each sub-indicator, the following normalization formula is applied:

$$Weight\left(\mathcal{W}_i\right) = \frac{Significance_i}{\sum_{t=1}^{n} Significance_t}$$

$\mathcal{W}_i$: Weight assigned to sub-indicator i

Significance$_i$: Significance score of sub-indicator i
Significance$_t$: Total significance (sum) across all sub-indicators t

Rating Guidance

Finally, each sub-indicator must be evaluated a critical phase that relies heavily on investigative findings related to the suspected terrorist. To ensure a precise assessment and categorization of terrorist threats, this study adopts a nine-point rating scale grounded in defined calculations and methodological criteria. The scale is divided into three distinct categories: (1) *Low level* (ratings 1 to 3), which indicates that the activity is present but poses minimal or no immediate terrorist threat; (2) *Moderate level* (ratings 4 to 5), which reflects a possible connection to terrorist-related actions; and (3) *High level* (ratings 6 to 9), which suggests a strong and significant association with terrorist activities. This structured approach allows for nuanced interpretation while maintaining consistency in threat classification (see Table 1 below).

Table 1. Rating level

Rating Level	Score Range	Description
Low	1 - 3	Activity is present but does not demonstrate a substantial terrorist threat.
Moderate	4 - 5	Activity suggests a possible or emerging connection to terrorist operations
High	6 - 9	Activity shows strong and credible association with known terrorist behaviour.

Scoring

After completing the three preceding stages, the next step involves calculating the weight and rating for each sub-indicator. The objective of this phase is to determine the total score of the target's intention and capability, which reflects the overall threat level. The total threat score for each target, denoted as $\mathcal{S}_i$. $\mathcal{S}_i$ is calculated using the following formula:

$$\mathcal{S}_i = \sum_{t=1}^{n} \mathcal{W}_i \bullet \mathcal{R}_i$$

$\mathcal{S}_i$: Final composite score for indicator t
$\mathcal{W}_i$: Weight of sub-indicator i
$\mathcal{R}_i$: Rating of sub-indicator i

Risk Matrix

After obtaining the total scores for both terrorist intention and capability, the next step is to interpret these results using a risk matrix to determine the threat level posed by the target classified as high, medium, or low risk. While various risk matrices exist, this study adopts and modifies a matrix originally designed for evaluating internal and external risk factors, ensuring consistency with the AHP-based methodology applied in earlier stages. The proposed risk assessment matrix consists of a 3x3 grid with nine cells, mapping the interaction between levels of intention and capability. Each axis represents a gradient from low to high, allowing for a visual representation of the threat posture (see Figure 3).

Figure 3. Risk matrix (Intention and Capability

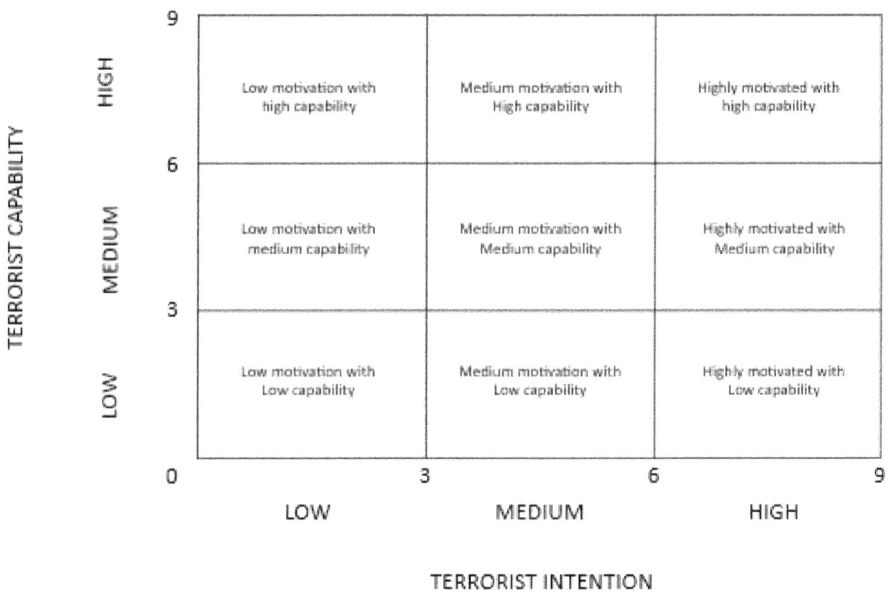

CASE STUDIES: FOUR ILLUSTRATIVE SCENARIOS

To demonstrate the practical application of this framework, the study presents four illustrative scenarios representing different types of terrorist involvement: a bomb maker, a lone actor, a financier, and a social media propagandist. These scenarios are constructed not as actual case studies but as simulated exercises designed to guide analysts in interpreting limited and fragmented information. Each scenario reflects a unique profile and operational role within terrorist ecosystems, thereby covering a broad spectrum of potential threat sources. The aim is to test and exemplify how the AHP-based methodology, in combination with the risk matrix, can be used to assess and classify varying levels of threat based on partial data inputs.

It is important to note that the level of significance and the resulting weights assigned to sub-indicators are not fixed, but vary across each scenario depending on the nature of the threat profile. In this model, the analyst plays a central role in determining the significance level of each sub-indicator, a process that is inherently subjective and context-dependent. For example, a sub-indicator such as financial capacity may carry more weight in the financier scenario than in the lone actor case. While this flexibility allows for tailored assessments, it also introduces variability influenced by the analyst's interpretation and professional judgment. To maintain methodological consistency and transparency, the process of assigning significance levels and calculating weights is explicitly outlined in the methodology section. Analysts are encouraged to review these foundational principles to ensure that the application of the model remains rigorous, replicable, and aligned with the threat environment being assessed.

Case Study 1: Bomb Maker

Scenario: According to intelligence reports, a suspected terrorist (Mr. X) has been frequently observed visiting a chemical supply store. However, there is no confirmed evidence of specific chemical purchases linked to illicit activity. Human intelligence has not conclusively established that these visits are related to terrorism, as Mr. X is also engaged in the legitimate business of buying and selling chemicals. Database records indicate that Mr. X is a returnee from a known conflict zone and is the son-in-law of the leader of a domestic terrorist group. He possesses expertise in explosive manufacturing, skills reportedly acquired during his time in the conflict area. Additionally, Mr. X operates a chemical store that stocks various dual-use chemicals potentially suitable for bomb-making. His affiliated group maintains a gym facility for physical training and manages a fraudulent charity organization used for fundraising.

Case Study 1 Assessment

Based on this information, the analyst proceeds to evaluate the relevant sub-indicators using the rating guidelines outlined in Table 2. The following evaluations are conducted based on the previously established analytical hierarchy, incorporating the defined indicators, assigned significance levels, and the rating guidance presented earlier. This ensures consistency in interpreting the scenarios within the structured AHP-based threat assessment framework.

Table 2. Case study 1 rating

No	Indicator/ Sub-indicator	Intel / information	Rating	Consideration
Intention / Motivation				
1	Daily activity	Mr. X has been frequently observed visiting a chemical store; however, no additional information has been obtained regarding specific item or chemical purchases.	4	Activity suggests a possible or emerging connection to terrorist operations
2	Communication pattern	Human intelligence has not firmly linked chemical purchases to terrorist activity due to the fact that Mr. X is also operating in that buying and selling chemicals.	4	Activity suggests a possible or emerging connection to terrorist operations
3	Personal background	According to the database, Mr. X is a returnee from the battle zone	8	Activity shows strong and credible association with known terrorist behaviour.
4	Family background	Mr. X is the son-in-law of the leader of a domestic terrorist group's leader.	8	Activity shows strong and credible association with known terrorist behaviour.
Capability				
1	Personal Skill	Mr. X has expertise in making explosives.	8	Activity shows strong and credible association with known terrorist behaviour.
2	Self-funding	Mr. X runs a chemical store	4	Activity suggests a possible or emerging connection to terrorist operations
3	Training support	Mr. X 1 has a gym for daily exercise	8	Activity shows strong and credible association with known terrorist behaviour.
4	Financial support	The group operates a fraudulent charity organisation for fundraising.	8	Activity shows strong and credible association with known terrorist behaviour.

As a subsequent step, the analyst should conduct a detailed evaluation of the significance, strength, and overall assessment of Mr. X's intention and capability, as summarized in Table 3 below.

Table 3. Case study 1- intention and capability score

	Significance	Weight	Rating	Score
Intention				
Daily behaviours	3	0,33	4	1,33
Communication Activities	3	0,33	4	1,33
Personal Background	2	0,22	8	1,78
Family Background	1	0,11	8	0,89
	9	1,00		5,33
Capability				
Personal Skill	3	0,27	8	2,18
Self-funding	2	0,18	4	0,73
Training Support	3	0,27	8	2,18
Financial Support	3	0,27	8	2,18
	11	1,00		7,27

Table 3 presents the detailed scoring of Mr. X's intention and capability based on the previously established hierarchy, including the significance levels, weights, and analyst-assigned ratings. Under the *intention* category, four sub-indicators were assessed: daily behaviours, communication activities, personal background, and family background. Each was assigned a significance level, normalized into weights, and rated according to observed intelligence. The cumulative intention score totalled 5.33. Similarly, four sub-indicators were evaluated under the *capability* category: personal skill, self-funding, training support, and financial support. These factors reflect Mr. X's operational readiness and access to resources, resulting in a total capability score of 7.27. These scores are then plotted on a 3x3 risk matrix to determine the overall threat level. The horizontal axis of the matrix represents intention, while the vertical axis represents capability (see Figure 4).

Figure 4. Case study 1- risk matrix

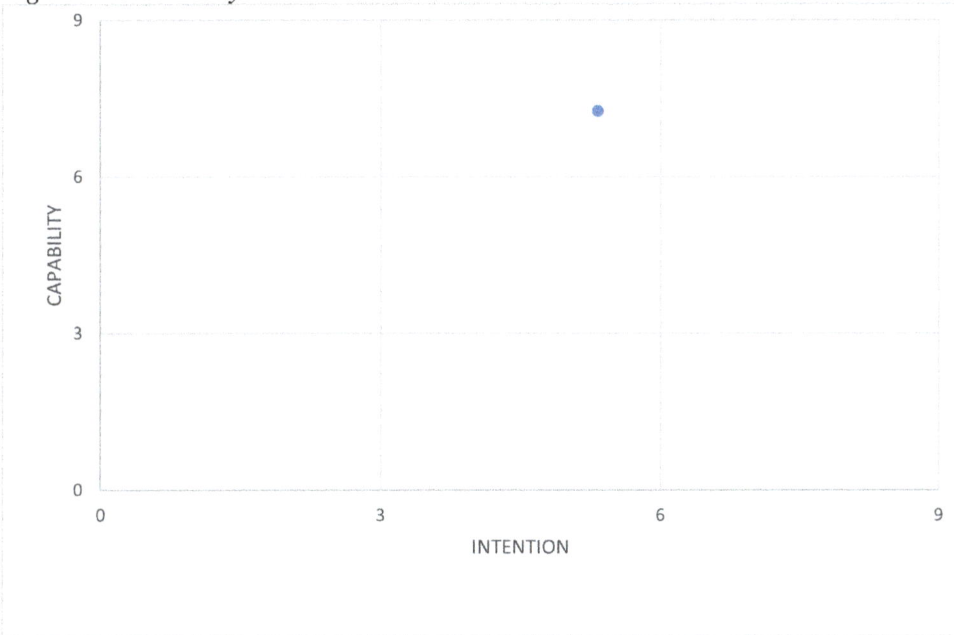

Case Study 1 Risk Assessment and Recommendation:

With an intention score falling within the moderate range and a capability score nearing the high threshold, Mr. X is assessed to fall within the high-risk cell—indicating that he possesses both the motivation and operational means to potentially conduct a terrorist act. Based on this assessment, the analyst recommends acquiring further intelligence to clarify unresolved gaps, particularly regarding the procurement and intended use of dual-use chemicals. Verification of transactional records, surveillance footage, and supplier testimonies could strengthen the evidence base. Additionally, cross-referencing open-source intelligence (OSINT), financial tracing, and communications monitoring may yield critical insights to either confirm or reassess the threat level. This step is essential to ensure that response strategies are proportionate and intelligence-led.

Case Study 2: Lone Actor

Scenario: A known sympathizer of a terrorist group, identified as Mr. Y, was detected searching for bomb-making tutorials during a cyber patrol of social media platforms. Further investigation revealed that Mr. Y is employed as an electrician and possesses the technical skills necessary to construct bomb detonation switches. However, he has no prior criminal record in police or immigration databases, nor any familial connections to known terrorists or affiliations with extremist groups.

Case Study 2 Assessment

Based on the existing scenario and additional findings from the preliminary investigation, a more detailed evaluation of Mr. Y's threat profile is conducted using the structured methodology outlined earlier. This process begins with identifying the relevant sub-indicators under the categories of intention and capability. Each sub-indicator is assigned a significance level based on its relevance to the scenario, which is then normalized into a weight to reflect its proportional importance in the overall assessment. Following this, the analyst assigns a rating to each sub-indicator using the standardized 1–9 scale, reflecting the strength or clarity of observed behaviour or intelligence (See Table 4).

Table 4. Case study 2 - rating

No	Indicator/ Sub-indicator	Intel / information	Rating	Consideration
Intention / Motivation				
1	Daily activity	Mr. Y active on social media and associated with radical activity	8	Activity shows strong and credible association with known terrorist behaviour.
2	Communication pattern	Mr. Y was discovered seeking bomb-making tutorials through cyber patrol on social media	9	Activity shows strong and credible association with known terrorist behaviour.
3	Personal background	No criminal record in police or immigration databases	-	-
4	Family background	No familial ties to known terrorists or affiliations with any groups.	-	-
Capability				
1	Personal Skill	Mr. Y works as an electrician, possesses the expertise to construct bomb switches.	8	Activity shows strong and credible association with known terrorist behaviour.
2	Self-funding	Mr. Y works as an electrician, have the capacity in self-funding	4	Activity suggests a possible or emerging connection to terrorist operations
3	Training support	-	-	-
4	Financial support	-	-	-

Following the completion of the rating phase, the next step involves calculating the weighted scores for each sub-indicator to determine Mr. Y's overall intention and capability levels. This is achieved by multiplying the assigned weight of each sub-indicator by its corresponding rating. The resulting weighted scores offer a quantified measure of the threat each sub-indicator contributes to the overall assessment. These values are then aggregated to produce cumulative scores for both intention and capability. Table 5 below presents a detailed breakdown of this calculation, providing a clear view of how each factor contributes to the final threat profile of Mr. Y.

Table 5. Case study 2- intention and capability score

	Significance	Weight	Rating	Score
Intention				
Daily behaviours	3	0,33	8	2,67
Communication Activities	3	0,33	9	3,00
Personal Background	2	0,22	0	0,00
Family Background	1	0,11	0	0,00
	9	1,00		5,67
Capability				
Personal Skill	3	0,50	8	4,00
Self-funding	3	0,50	4	2,00
Training Support	0	0,00	0	0,00
Financial Support	0	0,00	0	0,00
	6	1,00		6,00

Table 5 summarizes the calculated scores for Mr. Y's intention and capability based on the weighted evaluation of each sub-indicator. Under the *intention* category, the most influential factors were daily behaviours and communication activities, both of which received high ratings due to Mr. Y's active engagement with online bomb-making content. These contributed significantly to the total intention score of 5.67, while personal and family background had no observable influence, resulting in zero scores. In the *capability* category, Mr. Y's personal skill as an electrician was the primary contributor, along with limited self-funding potential, yielding a total capability score of 6.00. Both cumulative scores are then plotted into the 3x3 threat matrix (see Figure 5).

Figure 5. Case study 2 - risk matrix

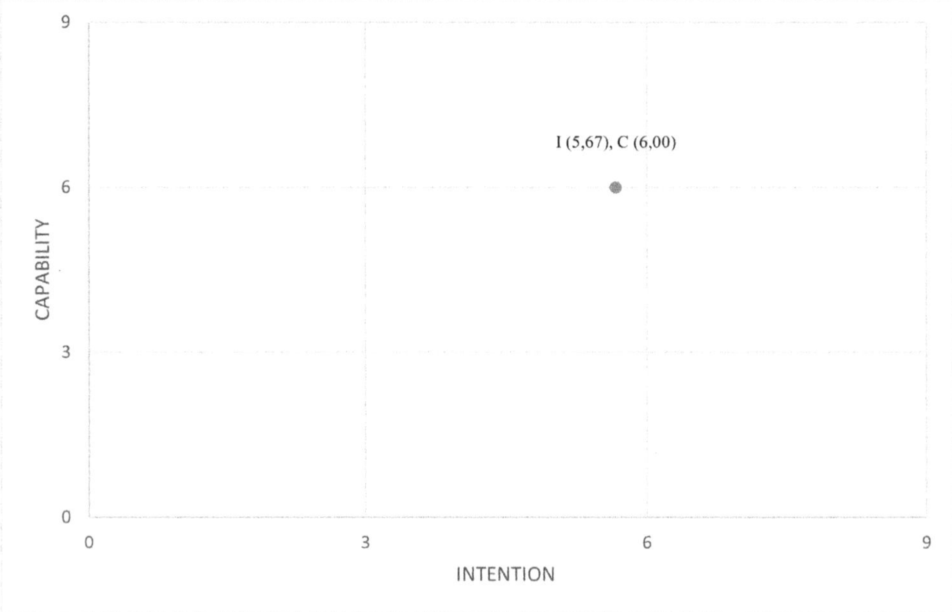

Case Study 2 Risk Assessment and Recommendation:

With an intention score in the moderate-to-high range and a capability score reflecting moderate operational readiness, Mr. Y is positioned within the high-risk cell of the threat assessment matrix. This placement indicates a credible potential for future engagement in terrorist activity and therefore warrants continued monitoring and pre-emptive intervention. However, critical information gaps remain particularly concerning Mr. Y's financial capacity to self-fund any operational efforts. To strengthen the reliability of the threat assessment, it is essential to gather additional intelligence from a variety of sources, including financial records, communication data, social associations, and transactional behaviour. These data points are vital to verify the depth of Mr. Y's capability and to detect any emerging intent indicators. Based on the current analysis, the subject poses a substantial risk due to his technical expertise, behavioural patterns, and demonstrated interest in terrorist methodologies. Without further disruption or intervention, this risk could escalate into a more immediate and actionable threat.

Case Study 3: Terrorist Financier

Scenario: Intelligence reports indicate that Mrs. Z has been regularly attending meetings organized by a known radical group in nearby areas. Further investigation revealed that she has made substantial financial contributions to a front charity believed to be affiliated with the extremist organization. Mrs. Z is a housewife who also runs a small retail shop selling common household items. She has no prior criminal record in law enforcement or immigration databases, nor does she have any known familial connections to terrorist individuals or networks.

Case Study 3 Assessment

Given the emerging behavioural indicators in Mrs. Z's profile namely her regular attendance at radical group meetings and financial contributions to a suspected front charity it becomes essential for the analyst to systematically assess the potential threat she may pose. Although her background appears clean, with no criminal history or familial ties to terrorism, her recent activities warrant closer scrutiny. To evaluate her level of risk objectively, the analyst must apply the established set of indicators, assign significance levels, and use the standardized rating scale to assess both her intention and capability. This process enables the transformation of qualitative observations into quantifiable data, forming a structured basis for identifying the extent of threat and informing appropriate preventative measures.

Table 6. Case Study 3-rating

No	Indicator/ Sub-indicator	Intel / information	Rating	Consideration
Intention / Motivation				
1	Daily activity	Mrs. Z frequently attends meetings of a radical group meetings in nearby areas.	6	Activity shows strong and credible association with known terrorist behaviour.
2	Communication pattern	-	-	-
3	Personal background	She has no criminal record in law enforcement or immigration records	-	-
4	Family background	Mrs. Z is not related to any terrorists.	-	-
Capability				
1	Personal Skill	-	-	-

continued on following page

Table 6. Continued

No	Indicator/ Sub-indicator	Intel / information	Rating	Consideration
2	Self-funding	Mrs. Z is a housewife who also operates a shop that sells common household goods.	2	Activity is present but does not demonstrate a substantial terrorist threat.
3	Training support	-	-	-
4	Financial support	Mrs. Z contributes a substantial sum of money to a sham charity associated with the extreme group.	8	Activity shows strong and credible association with known terrorist behaviour.

In conducting this assessment, the analyst's subjectivity plays a critical role in interpreting the available intelligence and assigning appropriate ratings to each sub-indicator. Given that the data surrounding Mrs. Z's activities such as her participation in radical group meetings and financial contributions may be incomplete or lack direct evidence of operational intent, the analyst must rely on professional judgment guided by contextual understanding and experience. Each sub-indicator is evaluated based on its relevance and clarity within the scenario, and then rated on the standardized scale from 1 to 9. These ratings are combined with the pre-determined weights to calculate the weighted scores for both intention and capability.

Table 7. Case study 3- intention and capability score

	Significance	Weight	Rating	Score
Intention				
Daily behaviours	3	0,33	6	1,98
Communication Activities	3	0,33	0	0,00
Personal Background	2	0,22	0	0,00
Family Background	1	0,11	0	0,00
	9	1,00		1,98
Capability				
Personal Skill	3	0,27	0	0,00
Self-funding	2	0,18	2	0,36
Training Support	3	0,27	0	0,00
Financial Support	3	0,27	8	2,18
	11	1,00		2,55

Table 7 presents the weighted scoring of Mrs. Z's intention and capability based on the evaluated sub-indicators. Under the *intention* category, her daily behaviours specifically, consistent attendance at radical group meetings received a moderate rating (6) and contributed significantly to the total intention score of 1.98. However, other sub-indicators such as communication activities, personal background, and family background were rated zero, indicating no observable evidence of direct involvement or historical ties to extremist networks. In the *capability* category, Mrs. Z demonstrated a notable level of financial support to a suspected front organization, resulting in a high rating (8) and a weighted score of 2.18. While her self-funding ability received a low score, and other indicators such as personal skill and training support were absent, the overall capability score amounted to 2.55. Together, these findings suggest limited operational capacity but emerging ideological alignment. To determine the overall risk level, these scores must now be visualized in the 3x3 threat matrix, allowing the analyst to map Mrs. Z's position within the broader risk landscape and guide potential follow-up actions.

Figure 6. Cases study 3 - risk matrix

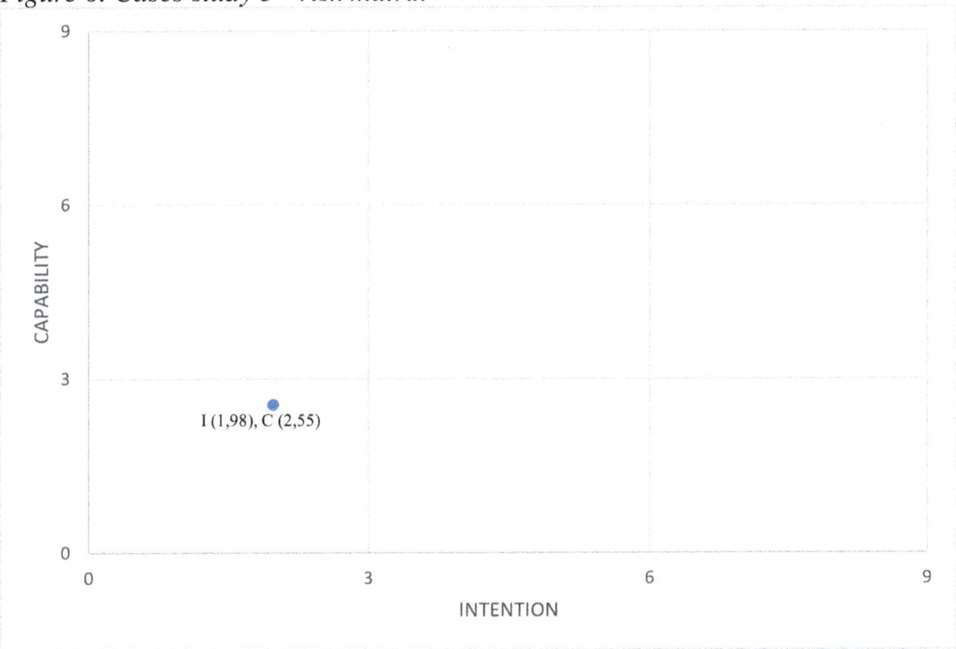

Case Study 3 Risk Assessment and Recommendation:

Mrs. Z demonstrates low levels of both intention and capability to carry out a terrorist attack, with respective scores of 1.98 and 2.55. However, her financial activity warrants further scrutiny. As the owner of a retail business, Mrs. Z may possess the means to contribute funds to extremist causes, potentially serving as a financier within the broader network. Although her operational involvement appears minimal, the financial support provided to a suspected front charity suggests a possible enabling role that should not be overlooked. To accurately assess her funding capacity and potential risk, additional information is required particularly in relation to her financial transactions, business revenue streams, and charitable contributions. Gathering intelligence from a variety of sources, including financial institutions, transaction monitoring systems, open-source data, and human intelligence, is essential to fill existing gaps in the assessment and ensure a comprehensive evaluation of her threat profile.

Case Study 4: Online Propaganda

Scenario: Ms. A has been identified as actively disseminating radical content through social media platforms, including the sharing of extremist posters and videos within online groups. She is characterized as an introverted individual with limited or no known social affiliations. Ms. A is currently unemployed and resides with her family, with no evidence of independent income or operational involvement.

Case Study 4 Assessment

Given Ms. A's observable behaviour in disseminating radical content online, the analyst must proceed with assessing her threat profile by applying the relevant sub-indicators. Each indicator should be rated using the established significance levels and standardized rating scale to evaluate the extent of her intention and capability based on current intelligence. This step is essential to quantify her potential risk and inform subsequent threat classification (See Table 8).

Table 8. Case study 4 - rating

No	Indicator/ Sub-indicator	Intel / information	Rating	Consideration
Intention / Motivation				
1	Daily activity	Ms A is classified as an introverted individual with no social connections.	-	-
2	Communication pattern	Ms. A is engaging in social media propaganda by sharing radical content, such as posters and videos with the social media group.	8	Activity shows strong and credible association with known terrorist behaviour.
3	Personal background	-	-	-

continued on following page

Table 8. Continued

No	Indicator/ Sub-indicator	Intel / information	Rating	Consideration
4	Family background	-	-	-
Capability				
1	Personal Skill	Online propaganda	9	Activity shows strong and credible association with known terrorist behaviour.
2	Self-funding	Ms. A is unemployed and resides with her family.	1	Activity is present but does not demonstrate a substantial terrorist threat.
3	Training support	-	-	-
4	Financial support	-	-	-

Following the analyst's assignment of ratings to each sub-indicator, the next step involves calculating the weighted scores to quantify Ms. A's overall levels of intention and capability. This is done by multiplying the weight of each sub-indicator by its respective rating, producing a set of weighted values that reflect the strength of each factor in the threat assessment. These scores are then summed within each category intention and capability to generate cumulative values that provide a clearer, data-driven picture of Ms. A's potential risk (See Table 9).

Table 9. Case study 4 - intention and capability score

	Significance	Weight	Rating	Score
Intention				
Daily behaviours	3	0,33	0	0,00
Communication Activities	3	0,33	8	2,67
Personal Background	2	0,22	0	0,00
Family Background	1	0,11	0	0,00
	9	0,50		2,67
Capability				
Personal Skill	3	0,60	9	5,40
Self-funding	2	0,40	1	0,40
Training Support	0	0,00	0	0,00
Financial Support	0	0,00	0	0,00
	5	0,50		5,80

Table 9 presents the calculated scores for Ms. A's intention and capability based on weighted sub-indicator ratings. In the *intention* category, the only significant contribution came from her active engagement in online communication activities, resulting in a score of 2.67, while other indicators such as daily behaviours, personal background, and family background were rated as non-threatening. In contrast, her *capability* score reached 5.80, driven largely by her strong personal skills in digital media or content creation evident from her effective dissemination of radical propaganda. Though she lacks financial resources and external training support, her technical proficiency significantly elevates her capability score. When visualized on the 3x3 threat matrix, Ms. A fall into the moderate-risk cell, where relatively low ideological commitment is coupled with a higher capacity to influence or mobilize others. This positioning highlights the need for targeted monitoring, particularly of her online activity, as she could act as a key vector for spreading extremist narratives (See Figure 7).

Figure 7. Case study 4 -risk matrix

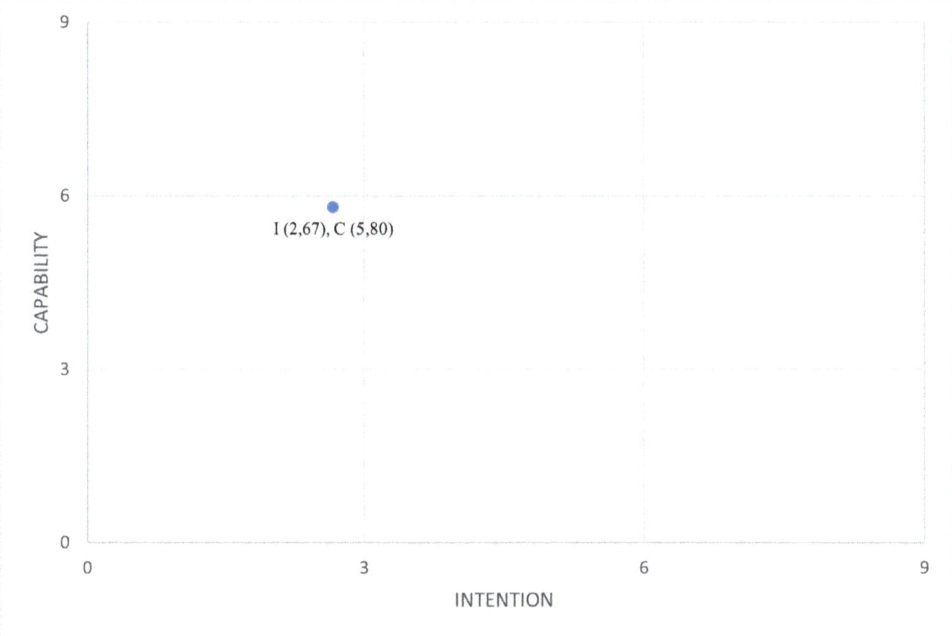

Case Study 4 Risk Assessment and Recommendation:

Ms. A's intention score of 2.67 indicates a relatively low likelihood of directly engaging in an attack. However, her elevated capability score driven by strong personal skills in digital media suggests a significant potential to influence others through online propaganda. While she may not present an immediate operational threat, her role as an ideological amplifier cannot be overlooked. Given her capacity to disseminate radical content that could inspire or incite others, ongoing monitoring of her online activities is recommended. Additionally, further intelligence is required to strengthen the case profile particularly regarding her digital networks, potential links to extremist communities, and the origin of the content she circulates. This information will be critical for assessing whether her activities remain within the bounds of ideological expression or escalate into facilitation of terrorism.

IMPLEMENTING THREAT ASSESSMENT METHOD IN PRACTICE

By applying the four scenarios presented, the analyst is able to compile a structured list of targets or persons of interest (POIs). This list includes the calculated intention and capability scores for each individual, along with a summary of their contextual background. Such a method is critical for enabling analysts to identify which POIs possess both the motivation and the operational capacity to plan and execute a terrorist attack. It supports a comparative risk analysis and helps prioritize monitoring and intervention efforts based on objective threat indicators (see Table 10).

Table 10. Person of interest's assessment

POI	Intention	Capability	POI's Status
Mr. X	5,33	7,27	Mr. X demonstrates a moderate level of intention to carry out an attack, with a score of 5.33, but exhibits a high level of capability, scoring 7.27.
Mr. Y	5,67	6	Mr. Y demonstrates a moderate level of motivation to carry out an attack, with a score of 5.67, and possesses a high level of capability due to his expertise in constructing bomb switches. However, his financial capacity remains uncertain and should be further examined as a potential limiting or enabling factor.
Mrs. Z	1,98	2,55	Mrs. Z exhibits low levels of both intention and capability to carry out an attack, with scores of 1.98 and 2.55, respectively. However, her financial capacity warrants attention, as her ownership of a business suggests the potential to provide funding and possibly serve as a key financier for a terrorist group.
Ms. A	2,67	5,8	Ms. A, with an intention score of 2.67, demonstrates a low likelihood of directly executing an attack. However, given her digital competence, she possesses the capability to engage in online propaganda that could influence or incite others to commit acts of terrorism.

Figure 8 below illustrates an alternative method for visualizing the identification of individuals classified as persons of interest (POIs). The risk matrix serves as an effective tool for pinpointing POIs who exhibit both high capability and high intention those most likely to pose an immediate threat. This visualization becomes particularly valuable when monitoring a large volume of subjects, ranging from hundreds to potentially thousands. By leveraging this matrix, analysts and surveillance teams can efficiently prioritize targets, ensuring that resources are focused on individuals who represent the greatest potential risk.

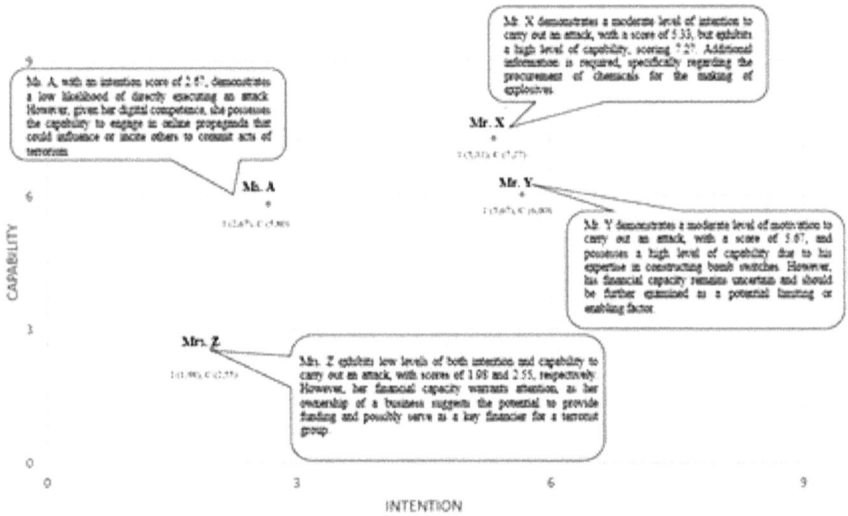

Figure 8. POI risk matrix

CONCLUSION

The growing complexity of terrorism threats in the digital age necessitates more structured and adaptive analytical tools for accurate and actionable assessments. Drawing from both existing literature and practical application, this paper demonstrates the relevance and effectiveness of the AHP as a strategic decision-making tool for terrorism threat assessment. AHP's strength lies in its ability to deconstruct abstract concepts such as *intention* and *capability* into measurable sub-indicators, assign them relative weights based on expert judgment, and generate objective scores through a repeatable process. When integrated with a visual 3x3 threat matrix, AHP further enhances clarity in identifying and prioritizing persons of interest (POIs) across a spectrum of potential threats.

While numerous sources and frameworks contribute valuable insights into terrorism analysis, this study introduces a structured and scalable alternative that not only enables prioritization but also facilitates consistency in evaluating subjects with limited available intelligence. Recognizing that each jurisdiction may present unique contextual variables, this approach allows flexibility in adapting indicator sets while maintaining a clear methodological sequence. The step-by-step process outlined in this paper provides analysts with a practical framework to move from qualitative observations to quantifiable risk profiles.

The illustrative case studies covering various roles such as bomb-makers, lone actors, financiers, and propagandists demonstrate the model's feasibility in real-world contexts, especially when only fragmentary information is accessible. These scenarios underscore the importance of interagency cooperation, particularly between analysts and surveillance operators, to enrich data collection and validate initial assessments. Such collaboration is crucial for refining the understanding of a subject's evolving intent and operational readiness.

Ultimately, the integration of AHP into terrorism risk assessment contributes significantly to intelligence-led decision-making. It promotes transparency, adaptability, and precision three pillars essential for anticipating threats and preventing acts of violence. As terrorism continues to evolve, so too must the tools we use to detect and disrupt it. This study offers a foundational step in that direction, with practical implications for both field operations and strategic threat management.

REFERENCES

Choudhary, P., & Singh, U. (2016). Ranking Terrorist Nodes of 26/11 Mumbai Attack using Analytical Hierarchy Process with Social Network Analysis. *11th Annual Symposium on Information Assurance (Asia '16).* Albany.

Choudhary, P., & Singh, U. (2018). *Ranking Terrorist Organizations Network in India Using Combined Sna-Ahp Approach. International Journal of Recent Technology and Engineering*. IJRTE.

Fox, W. P., Ormond, B., & Williams, A. (2015). Ranking terrorist targets using a hybrid AHP–TOPSIS methodology. *Journal of Defense Modeling and Simulation: Applications, Methodology. Technology*, •••, 1–17.

Saaty, T. L. (1980). *The Analytic Hierarchy Process: Planning, Priority Setting, Resource Allocation*. McGraw-Hill International Book Company.

Schuurman, B., Bakker, E., Gill, P., & Bouhana, P. (2018). Lone Actor Terrorist Attack Planning and Preparation: A Data-Driven Analysis. *Journal of Forensic Sciences*. PMID: 29059713

Schuurman, B. W., & Eijkman, Q. A. (2015). Indicators of Terrorist Intent and Capability: Tools for Threat Assessment. *Dynamics of Asymmetric Conflict.*

KEY TERMS AND DEFINITIONS

Analytic Hierarchy Process (AHP): A multi-criteria decision-making framework that assigns weights to indicators to evaluate complex scenarios

Risk Matrix: A visual assessment tool that plots weighted scores to categorize threats into low, medium, or high-risk levels.

Threat Prioritization: The process of ranking and categorizing potential terrorist threats based on risk assessment.

ENDNOTES

1 It is recommended that intelligence agencies develop context-specific indicators and sub-indicators tailored to their national priorities and threat landscape. Incorporating relevant case studies is advisable to enhance the accuracy and applicability of the assessment framework.

2 The assessment of each sub-indicator relies heavily on the analyst's subjectivity and judgment. To ensure the effectiveness of this model, it is essential that the analyst has a thorough understanding of the core principles of the Analytic Hierarchy Process (AHP), including the logic behind pairwise comparisons, consistency ratios, and the normalization of significance weights. A misinterpretation of these elements can lead to skewed results, potentially underestimating or overestimating an individual's threat level. Moreover, analysts should be trained to balance qualitative insights with quantitative scoring, especially when dealing with limited or fragmented intelligence. Regular calibration sessions, peer reviews, and the use of scenario-based training can enhance consistency and reduce bias in the application of this methodology. Ultimately, the integrity of the model depends not only on the structure of the tool itself but also on the competence and objectivity of those who apply it.

Chapter 3

Islamic Political Thought in Historical Perspective: Classical Foundation and Contemporary Extremism in South Asia

Sinduja Umandi W. Jayaratne
https://orcid.org/0009-0006-3607-6666
Bandaranaike Centre for International Studies, Sri Lanka

ABSTRACT

This chapter offers a historical and conceptual exploration of Islamic political thought, with a focus on its evolution and contemporary manifestations in South Asia. The chapter highlights the expansion and background in Islamic governance during different caliphates and the regional adaptation of it during the Mughal empire. It also reflects on the colonial influence in South Asia and how it impacts to the emergence of reformist thinkers such as Syed Ahmad Khan and Muhammad Iqbal. Special attention is paid to the ideological contributions of Maulana Abul A'la Maududi, showing how modern extremist movements in South Asia have reinterpreted and occasionally distorted his vision of Islamic governance, which was first framed within democratic and nonviolent principles. This chapter provides insights into the origins and development of political Islam and violent extremism in the region by illustrating the intricate relationship between traditional Islamic political ideals and contemporary political realities through a historical and analytical lens.

DOI: 10.4018/979-8-3693-3522-2.ch003

INTRODUCTION

Islamic political thought is a diverse and dynamic intellectual tradition that has had a significant impact on government, legislation, and political identity throughout the Muslim world. It proposes a picture of political order based on the Quran, Hadith, and early Islamic history, with divine sovereignty (Hakimiyyah), justice (Adl), consultation (Shura), and communal welfare (Maslaha) as essential foundations (Esposito, 1998; Khatab, 2006). Islamic political ideology is theocratic, emphasizing the need for legitimate power to align with divine will (Laski, 1919; Maksimović & Milosavljević, 2018).

This tradition has evolved significantly over the centuries, responding to internal theological discussions as well as external sociopolitical difficulties. From the example of the Prophet Muhammad and the Rashidun Caliphate to the imperial complexity of the Umayyad, Abbasid, and Ottoman empires, Islamic political thinking has continuously adjusted to evolving situations while maintaining its fundamental principles (Kennedy, 2023; Lapidus, 2002). The colonial era further damaged Islamic governance systems, resulting in intellectual resistance and reformist reactions that attempted to combine Islamic ideals with modern political demands (Brown, 1993; Silverstein, 2004).

In the modern era, particularly since the mid-twentieth century, Islamic political thinking has resurfaced in the form of political Islam or Islamism movements that seek to apply Islamic law and Islamic governance in the modern nation-state (Roy, 1996). While some of these movements have engaged in peaceful political campaigns, others have used violent measures to accomplish their goals. Thinkers like as Maulana Abul A'la Maududi, whose political theology established the groundwork for several Islamist groups in South Asia, have played a crucial role in this intellectual renaissance. Although Maududi advocated for a gradual, nonviolent approach to Islamic reform, violent extremist groups have used his works to justify insurrection and terrorism (Zaidi, 2009).

This chapter gives a thorough examination of Islamic political thinking, following its evolution from classical Islamic administration to modern political ideas that impact Muslim-majority states today. Special emphasis is placed on the South Asian context, where Islamic political principles have both inspired inclusive statecraft and been twisted to fuel extremist violence. This chapter uses historical research and critical reflection to explore the intricacies of Islamic political thinking and its ongoing importance in influencing political ideologies and violence in the world.

ISLAMIC POLITICAL THOUGHT AND ITS EXPANSION

Islamic political thought has played a leading role in Muslim societies and global political discourses. Stemming from the Prophet Muhammad's teachings and some foundational Islamic texts such as the Quran and Hadith, Islamic political philosophy provides a distinctive governance framework based on religious precepts. Contrary to secular political ideologies, Islamic political thought interweaves religion and politics into the proposition that divine guidance must direct governance (Esposito & Voll, 1996). This was extended through successive stages, first through the early empires of Islam, the classical caliphs, and up to the contemporary era, where Islamic movements tried to rework these ideas against the challenge of the times.

Islamic political thought is wrapped around Islamic theology. It finds the root of its foundational texts in the Quran and Hadith regarding governance (Sudarmanto & Aulia, 2022). The Quran, believed to be the literal word of God, provides principles of justice, morality, and social equality as central to governance (Esposito, 1998). The Hadith, or sayings of the Prophet Muhammad, offers further guidance on political issues based on the importance of leadership, accountability, and justice. For example, Hadith 34 of 40 Hadith Shah Waliullah states, "The leader of the people is their servant." This explains that the leader is there to serve the people[1].

According to Sayyid Qutb in his book 'Milestone', the concept 'Hakimiyyah' means that God alone has the right to legislate or govern, considering God the sovereign (Khatab, 2006). Human beings, including those who happen to be rulers, are charged to govern but are supposed to do so per divine guidance with the totality of Islamic law based on the Quran and Hadith. Likewise in Christianity, in Islam also the ultimate sovereignty rests with God, known as Allah in Islam, and human leaders are mere stewards required to rule in concert with divine law, or Shaia[2] (Maksimović & Milosavljević, 2018). On the contrary, in secular systems, sovereignty belongs to the people, thereby becoming a characteristic of the modern nation-state (Laski, 1919)

Another fundamental concept in Islamic political thought is Shura or consultation. The Quran advises that Muslims should conduct their affairs through consultation (Quran, 42:38). This has been interpreted as a means of participatory governance in which the ruler is bound to consult a body of advisors or the community itself before making decisions (Lewis, 1993). For example, Article One of the Shura Council Law of Saudi Arabia states, "And following His Messenger Peace Be Upon Him (PBUH) in consulting his Companions and urging the (Muslim) Nation to engage in consultation. The shura council shall be established to exercise the tasks entrusted to it, according to this Law and the Basic Law of Governance while adhering to the Quran and the Path (Sunnah) of his Messenger (PBUH), maintaining brotherly ties and cooperating unto righteousness and piety."[3] Also, the concept of Ijma, or consensus, in Islamic political thought plays a crucial role in shaping governance. While 'Shura' describes consultation, 'Ijma' describes the Muslim community coming to a consensus on a specific matter. Both these notions are related in that they are supposed to be manners through which governance will reflect the people's will, even in a theocracy[4].

Following the death of the Prophet Muhammad in 632 CE, the Muslim community fell under the rule of the Rashidun Caliphs, or the 'Rightly Guided' Caliphs: Abu Bakr (reigned 632–634), Umar (reigned 634–644), Uthman (reigned 644–656), and Ali (reigned 656–661) (El-Hibri, 2010). These first four caliphs formed governance based on Islamic values such as justice, consultation, Shura, and the rule of law, also called Sharia(Lapidus, 2002). The Rashidun Caliphate was the model of Islamic polity wherein the ruler's legitimacy depended upon his piety, justice, and adherence to the Islamic code the Rashidun period also laid the groundwork for Islamic political expansion when Muslim armies spread Islam throughout the Arabian Peninsula and parts of African Maghreb, Persia, and parts of the Byzantine Empire (Refer to map 1 for territorial expansion of Rashidun Caliphate). There was a concurrent increase in Islamic political institutions and legal systems across the expanded territories (Kennedy, 2023).

Figure 1. Map Depicting the Territory of Rashidun and Umayyad Dynasty

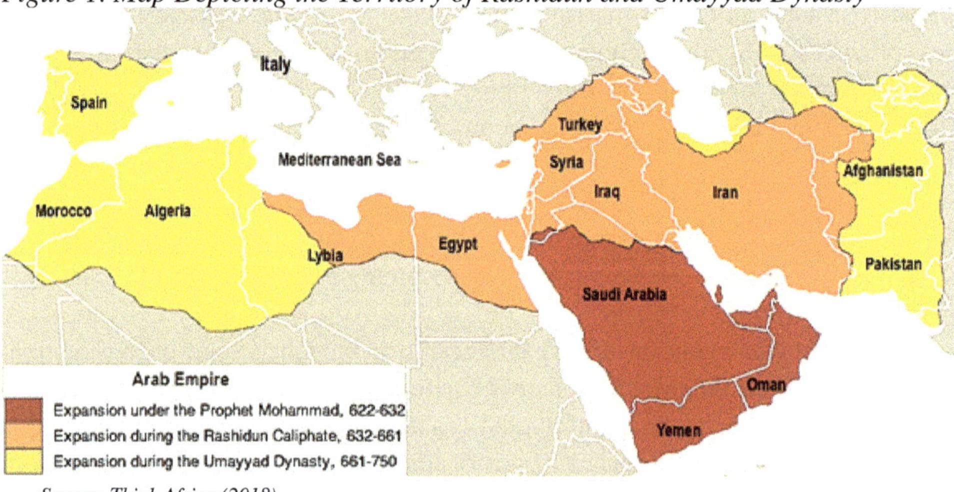

Source: Think Africa (2018)

The Bayt al-Mal, or the Islamic welfare state instituted during the period of the Rashidun (under Umar al-Khattab, the second rightly guided Caliph), was responsible for collecting and distributing wealth to help the poor and the needy (Abdullah, 2012). This redistribution of wealth, combined with the principles of charity and justice, means that rulers are to govern for the benefit of the community (Ummah) and not for the benefit of the elites.

With the end of the Rashidun Caliphate, Islamic political thought continued to expand under the Umayyad and Abbasid Caliphates. The Umayyads ruled from 661 to 750 CE and extended Islamic governance across North Africa, Spain, and Central Asia (Refer to map 1 for territorial expansion of Rashidun Caliphate) (Fenwick, 2020). Despite often being regarded for their autocratic rule, the Umayyads developed taxation, administration, and law systems, which contributed to the institutionalization of Islamic political thought. The Abbasids then superseded the Umayyads.

The Abbasids' contribution to Islamic civilization was primarily intellectual and cultural (Rusydi et al., 2023). With the beginning of the Abbasid Caliphate from 750 until 1258 CE, writings on Islamic political philosophy expanded immensely. The works of scholars such as Al-Farabi and Al-Mawardi on governance, justice, and the role of the caliph go into detail. For instance, al-Mawardi argued that the caliph was meant to be both a political and a religious leader who should take up the responsibility for upholding law and order in ensuring the well-being of members of the community (Maghfiroh, 2023). With this, the combination of religion and politics emerged as one of the characteristics of Islamic authority.

Another significant chapter in the history of the expansion of Islamic political thought is that of the Ottoman Empire, 1299–1924 (Muttaqin et al., 2020). The Ottomans were to rule over extensive parts of Europe, the Middle East, and North Africa, developing a highly complex system of governance in which Islamic law combined with pragmatic administrative practice (Lapidus, 2002). Adorned with the title of caliph, the Ottoman sultans posed as the defenders of Islam. However, their political system was more flexible than earlier caliphates, with the inclusions of local governance and legal pluralism. Indeed, the Ottomans played a significant role in the evolution of Islamic legal theory, notably in criminal and commercial law.

The developments within Islamic political thought in the modern era have been defined by colonialism and the struggle for independence in Muslim-majority countries. During colonial rule, Muslim societies were subjected to various Western political systems at the hands of European powers, which often had a marginalizing effect on Islamic law and governance. The influence of Islamic legal institutions in Egypt gradually weakened due to British colonial administration (1882–1956). Egypt had a solid Sharia-based legal system during Ottoman rule, with Sharia courts religious courts handling criminal cases, inheritance, divorce, and marriage. When the British took over, they built a dual legal system that included mixed courts, which are civil courts in the Western form (Brown, 1993). The marginalization of Sharia law by the colonial legal system contributed to a deep sense of alienation among Muslim Egyptians, who viewed the new legal structure as an imposition of foreign values that were at odds with Islamic traditions. By the time Egypt gained independence in 1952, the integration of Western legal principles had already weakened the foundational role of Sharia in governance and everyday life.

Moreover, one of the most explicit instances of colonial cultural pressure was the French assimilation policy in Algeria. By pushing Algerians to embrace the French language, dress, and habits, the French aimed to reshape Algerian society in their image (Silverstein, 2004). Islamic customs were discouraged or openly prohibited in public places, such as women's veiling and men's traditional attire. Additionally, the French promoted secular officials who were more accessible to subjugate French authority to weaken the influence of Islamic religious leaders. The Islamic response, by political thinkers such as Jamal al-Din al-Afghani[5] (1838-1897) and Muhammad Abduh[6] (1849-1905), advocated the restoration of an Islamic polity. They said Islam is not opposed to modernity, and as such, Muslim societies should retrieve their political autonomy by recourse to Islamic principles. These ideas thereby served as the bedrock upon which anti-colonial movements in the so-called Muslim world had been founded. From Egypt to India to Algeria, Islamic political thought also became a rallying cry for independence, wherein leaders employed principles of justice, sovereignty, and self-determination from Islamic law.

Another expansion of Islamic political thought occurred in the 20th century with the rise of political Islam, popularly called 'Islamism'. The Islamist movements are determined to see the establishment of Islamic states governed by Sharia law; they oppose secularism and Western influence on politics in Muslim-majority countries (Roy, 1996). As a result, one of the most potent Islamist thinkers, such as Sayyid Qutb, became a founding member of the Muslim Brotherhood in Egypt. Qutb, especially in his book 'Milestones,'[7] called for nothing less than a return to Islamic governance and the rejection of all Western political mechanisms. He believed that the modern world was in a state of 'Jahiliyyah' and that only through the application of the Sharia could true justice be realized (Qutb, 2006). Therefore, various Islamist movements started to be widely established in the 1970s and 1980s and, most importantly, after the Iranian Revolution of 1979. Having the Islamic Republic under Ayatollah Khomeini as an end product, the Iranian revolution showed that Islamic political thought could be a practical aspect of modern politics while rejecting the influence of Western governing and social principles. It also showcased the possibility of establishing and governing a state with Islamic principles and laws. It can be argued that such notions in political Islam have echoed in the contemporary period, where terror organizations such as Al-Qaeda and the Islamic State (IS) have attempted to create the so-called 'Caliphate' under the influence of political Islam.

ISLAM IN SOUTH ASIA

Figure 2. Map Depicting the Malabar Coast in India

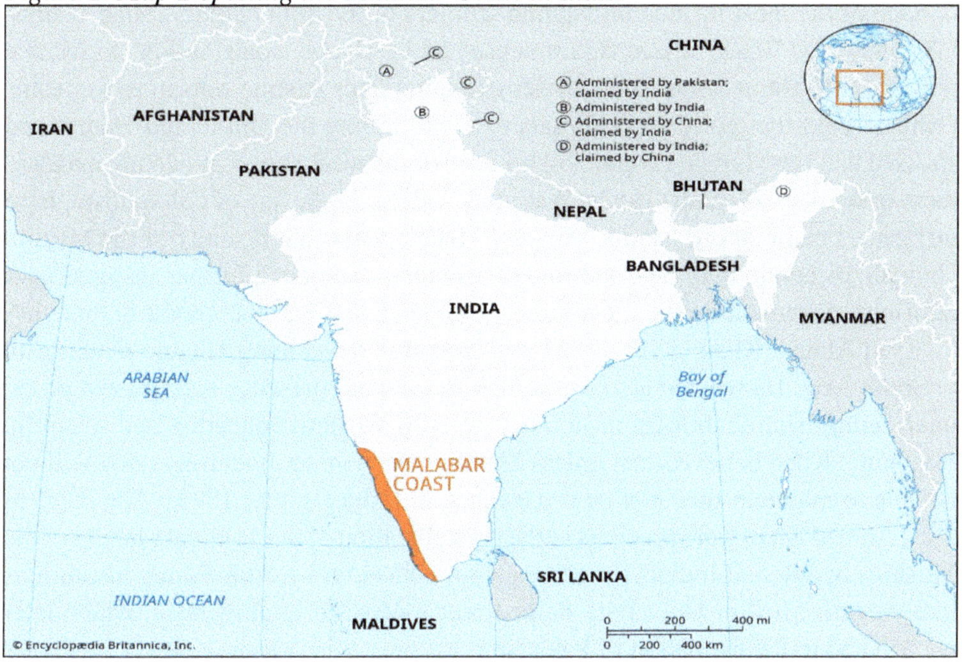

Source: Encyclopedia Britannica

Islam first appeared in South Asia through trade routes and missionary activities along the Malabar Coast in the 7th century. The political arrival of Islam in this region became pronounced with the establishment of the Delhi Sultanate in 1206 (Nossov, 2006). This initiated, for the first time, Islamic rule over India, whereby rulers combined Islamic governance principles with prevailing Indian practices. As Eaton (2006) argued, Sultanate political thought was a mix of Islamic law with local governance structures, leading to a specific political culture. Noticeably, the concept of justice (`adl) and, subsequently, the role of the ruler as the 'shadow of God on Earth' was strongly propagated, which then defined political and religious authority.

The Mughal Empire epitomised the golden age of South Asian Islamic political thought from 1526 to 1857 (Mahajan, 2023). Emperor Akbar founded a policy which mixed Islamic law with local tradition, managed to practice religious tolerance, and combined a syncretic political philosophy under the term 'Sulh-i-kul' or 'peace with all.' (Richards, 1993). Such pluralism and inclusion represented a significant development in South Asian Islamic political thought in this approach toward governance. Akbar's politics also generated debates amongst Muslim scholars. The inflexible Ulema, for example, aired their views against Akbar's policy; the latter's views denied Sharia its central role in governance. Theologians such as Sheikh Ahmad Sirhindi[8] (1564–1624) resisted Akbar's religious tolerance and wished to revert to an era of strict Islamic principles (Ahmad, 1966).

One of the most influential Islamic scholars of the 18th century, Shah Waliullah Dehlawi (1703-1762), made immense and invaluable contributions to Islamic political thought in South Asia, thereby shaping later Islamic reform movements. Dehlawi held that political governance should follow the Quran and Hadith and stressed that the Mughal Empire fell because of the weaknesses in Islamic management principles (Metcalf, 1982). Waliullah's ideas, in the age of colonialism, have influenced many future Islamic thinkers. His emphasis on the unity of the Muslim Ummah, or community, and the role of Islamic governance further inspired later reformist movements in the subcontinent Deobandi and Barelvi schools of thought[9].

Syed Ahmad Khan (1817-1898) was crucial in developing Islamic modernism in South Asia. He reacted against the British colonial presence and insisted on reinterpreting Islamic thought as compatible with Western education and scientific reasoning. Khan believed that unless Muslims open up to modernity, they will not be able to maintain their political relevance in India (Hardy, 1973). The ideas of Syed Ahmad Khan were precious in the crystallization of the political identity of the Muslims in colonial India. His advocacy for education by establishing institutions like Aligarh Muslim University helped rear a Muslim intelligentsia, which later contributed to the formation of Pakistan.

The philosopher and poet Sir Muhammad Iqbal (1877-1938) was highly instrumental in formulating the connotation of an Islamic state in the Indian subcontinent. Iqbal supported the revival of Islamic political thinking because Islam is dynamic and evolves with time due to changing historical variables (Iqbal, 2013). Iqbal was a staunch believer in pan-Islamism and a supporter of the formation of a separate state for Muslims. An infinite belief in the compatibility of Islam with modernity marked Iqbal's thought. He believed that Islamic principles could be molded into their purest form to meet the needs of the modern world.

NEXUS BETWEEN NAUDUDI'S IDEOLOGIES AND VIOLENT EXTREMISM IN SOUTH ASIA

The Jamaat-e-Islami, founded by Maulana Abul A'la Maududi in 1941, is one of the most influential Islamic movements in South Asia, significantly impacting Islamic political thought across the Muslim world. Islamic political thought underwent significant changes in the 20th century, especially in response to colonialism, modernization, and the secularization of Muslim societies. One of the most prominent figures in this intellectual transformation was Maulana Abul A'la Maududi

(1903–1979). Maududi founded the Jamaat-e-Islami (JI) in 1941 in British India, aiming to establish an Islamic state based on Islamic laws and governance (Lone, 2018). His writings and political activism significantly influenced the landscape of Islamist movements in South Asia and globally (Nasr, 1996).

Maududi also introduced the concept of jihad as a means of establishing an Islamic state. Unlike radical Islamists who later advocated for a violent form of jihad, Maududi initially promoted a peaceful struggle and self-improvement (jihad e-akbar) focused on education, moral reform, and gradual transformation (Zaidi, 2009). In fact, "Maududi ruled out the option of the use of physical force to bring about a revolution in an Islamic state" (Marath, 2021). During the investigations of the Easter Sunday Attacks in Sri Lanka, it was revealed that the Sri Lanka Jamaat-e-Islami Student Movement (SLJISM) was involved in the Buddha statue discretion in Mawannalla in 2018. The two main suspects, Sadiq Abdul Haq and Shahid Abdul Haq, who were involved in the incident, were immersed in the ideology of the creation of an Islamic State and, therefore, had been supportive of the preachings of Zaharan Bin Hashim, who was the alleged mastermind of the Easter Sunday Attacks in 2019[10].

Although Maududi strongly condemned insurrection against Muslim authorities who lacked basic Islamic understanding and legitimacy, militant organizations have utilized his ideologies to justify violence. For example, the Tehrik-i-Taliban Pakistan[11] (TTP) has used Maududi's reasoning to identify Pakistani administrations as apostate regimes worthy of overthrow (Abbas, 2015). Similarly, Lashkar-e-Taiba's[12] (LeT) doctrinal leaders, particularly Zaki-ur-Rehman Lakhvi and Hafiz Saeed, have used Maududi's divide between 'Dar al-Islam' and 'Dar al-Harb'[13] to portray India as a legitimate location to wage jihad (Rana, 2008).

Islamist groups in Bangladesh, like Jamaat-e-Islami (Bangladesh) and its former student wing, Islami Chhatra Shibir, have spread Maududi's views while participating in politically motivated violence, particularly against secularist and minority targets (Riaz, 2004).

Maududi's impact on violent extremism cannot be understood without reference to South Asia's broader sociopolitical situation. His writings found popularity in circumstances where political repression, identity problems, and social marginalization provided an ideal environment for radical ideas. The Afghan Jihad (1979-1989), which was supported by the US, Saudi Arabia, and Pakistan, aided in the fusing of Maududian ideology with militant jihadism, resulting in the formation of hybrid jihadist networks (Weinbaum, 1991).

Critics believe that Maududi's stark contrast between Islam and secularism promotes prejudice and leads to political violence. His rejection of pluralism and democratic institutions has been linked to sectarianism and intellectual authoritarianism (Nasr, 1996). However, reformist Islamic scholars such as Javed Ghamidi and Wahiduddin Khan have questioned Maududi's theocratic views, pushing for a more inclusive and spiritually based vision of Islam in the public realm (Ghamidi, 2001; Khan, 2009; Saleem, 2010).

Maududi's contributions to Islamic political thinking have left a lasting and divisive mark on South Asia. While he was not a militant, his vision of Islamic administration, jihad, and divine sovereignty established an effective intellectual framework that was embraced by a number of violent extremist organizations. The use of his ideas for militancy highlights the complicated link between philosophy, political situation, and violent activism. Decoding this intellectual heritage is critical to combating extremism and fostering a different, peaceful views of Islam in the region.

CONCLUSION

Islamic political thought, rooted in the foundational teachings of the Quran and Hadith, has evolved through dynamic historical experiences ranging from the classical Caliphates to modern nation-states. Across centuries, Islamic governance has taken on diverse forms, shaped by theological debates, colonial disruptions, and modern political challenges. From the inclusive and pluralistic visions of the Mughal Empire and the Ottoman administrative sophistication to the anti-colonial reformism of thinkers like Iqbal and Syed Ahmad Khan, Islamic political theory has displayed an ability to adapt while remaining anchored in its core principles of justice, consultation (shura), and divine sovereignty (hakimiyyah).

However, the contemporary period has witnessed a significant ideological transformation, wherein political Islam or Islamism has emerged as a force of both reform and radicalism. While figures like Maududi contributed immensely to the intellectual revival of Islamic governance, their writings have also been reinterpreted and radicalized in ways that fuel violent extremism. In South Asia, the selective adoption of Maududi's teachings by groups such as the Tehrik-i-Taliban Pakistan, Lashkar-e-Taiba, and certain factions of Jamaat-e-Islami illustrates how political thought can be distorted under specific socio-political and sectarian pressures.

This chapter has traced the multifaceted journey of Islamic political thought from its classical ideals to its contemporary challenges such as Islamist violent extremism. It has shown that while the tradition offers a robust framework for ethical governance and social justice, it is vulnerable to misinterpretation when co-opted by actors seeking power through violence. Understanding this intellectual lineage and its contextual applications is essential not only for scholars of political thought but also for policymakers, religious leaders, and civil society actors working to counter extremism and reclaim Islam's ethical-political legacy for peace, pluralism, and human dignity.

REFERENCES

Abbas, H. (2015). *The Taliban Revival: Violence and Extremism on the Pakistan-Afghanistan Frontier*. Yale University Press.

Abdullah, M. A.bin. (2012). The Entitlement of the Bayt Al-Mal to a Muslim Praepositus' Estates; An Analysis on the Right of a Muslim to Bequeath without Obtaining a Consent from the Bayt Al-Mal. *International Journal of Social Sciences and Humanity Studies*, *4*(1), 269–278.

Ahmad, A. (1966). *Studies in Islamic Culture in the Indian Environment*. Oxford University Press.

Brown, N. J. (1993). The Precarious Life and Slow Death of the Mixed Courts of Egypt. *International Journal of Middle East Studies*, *25*(1), 33–52.

El-Hibri, T. (2010). *Parable and Politics in Early Islamic History: The Rashidun Caliphs*. Columbia University Press.

Esposito, J. L. (1998). *Islam and Politics*. Syracuse University Press.

Esposito, J. L., & Voll, J. O. (1996). *Islam and Democracy*. Oxford University Press.

Fenwick, C. (2020). The Umayyads and North Africa: Imperial rule and frontier society. In Marsham, A. (Ed.), *The Umayyad World* (pp. 293–313). Routledge.

Ghamidi, J. A. (2001). *Meezan*. Al-Mawrid Institute of Islamic Sciences.

Hardy, P. (1973). *The Muslims of British India*. Cambridge University Press.

Iqbal, M. (2013). *The Reconstruction of Religious Thought in Islam (1930)*. Stanford University Press.

Kennedy, H. (2023). *The Prophet and the Age of the Caliphates: The Islamic Near East from the Sixth to the Eleventh Century*. Routledge.

Khan, W. (2009). *The Prophet of Peace: Teachings of the Prophet Muhammad*. Penguin Press.

Khatab, S. (2006). *The Political Thought of Sayyid Qutb: The Theory of Jahiliyyah*. Routledge.

Lapidus, I. M. (2002). *A History of Islamic Societies*. Cambridge University Press.

Laski, J. H. (1919). *Authority in the Modern State*. Yale University Press.

Lewis, B. (1993). *Islam and the West*. Oxford University Press.

Lone, R. A. (2018). Jamaat-i-Islami: Ideology. *International Journal of Research in Social Sciences*, *8*(5), 792–798.

Maghfiroh, M. (2023). Al Mawardi's Social Contract Theory. *Journal of Islamic Studies and Humanities*, *8*(2), 142–157.

Mahajan, M. (2023). Islam and the Mughal Empire in South Asia: 1526-1857. *Education About Asia*, *28*(1), 37–46.

Maksimović, A., & Milosavljević, Z. (2018). Sovereignty in Islam: A reflection of tradition and contemporariness in modern political systems. *Vojno Delo*, *70*(8), 38–46.

Malabar Coast. (n.d.). Britannica. Retrieved June15, 2025, from https://www.britannica.com/place/Kerala/Resources-and-power

Marath, M. M. (2021). Abul A'la Maududi and Sayyed Qutb on Revolution: A Comparative Analysis. *Al-Az vā*, *32*(47), 43–50.

Metcalf, B. D. (1982). *Islamic Revival in British India: Deoband, 1860-1900*. Princeton University Press.

Muttaqin, M., Azra, A., Saepudin, D., Jabali, F., Lubis, A., & Fakih, Z. (2020)... *The Rise and Fall of Ottoman Empire and How It Fits Ibnu Khaldun's Theory.*, *11*(2). Advance online publication. DOI: 10.4108/eai.20-10-2020.2305158

Nasr, S. V. R. V. R. (1996). *The Vanguard of the Islamic Revolution: The Jama'at-i Islami of Pakistan*. University of California Press.

Nossov, K. S. (2006). *Indian Castles 1206-1526: The Rise and Fall of the Delhi Sultanate*. Osprey Publishing.

Qutb, S. (2006). *Milestones*. Maktabah Publications.

Rana, M. A. (2008). *Jihadi Print Media in Pakistan : An Overview Jihadi Print Media in Pakistan : An Overview*. Pak Institute for Peace Studies.

Riaz, A. (2004). *God Willing: The Politics of Islamism in Bangladesh*. Rowman & Littlefield Publishers.

Richards, J. F. (1993). *The New Cambridge History of India, Volume 1, Part 5: The Mughal Empire*. Cambridge University Press.

Roy, O. (1996). *The Failure of Political Islam*. Harvard University Press.

Rusydi, I., & Saepudin, D., &Murodi. (2023). The Golden Age of Islamic Intellectuals and The Development of Science During the Abbasid Dynasty. *Tafkir: Interdisciplinary Journal of Islamic Education*, *4*(4), 599–609.

Saleem, S. (2010). *Islam : A Comprehensive Introduction*. Al Mawrid.

Schimd, A. P. (2014). *Violent and Non-Violent Extremism: Two Sides of the Same Coin?* The International Centre for Counter-Terrorism (ICCT). https://icct.nl/sites/default/files/2023-01/ICCT-Schmid-Violent-Non-Violent-Extremism-May-2014.pdf

Silverstein, P. A. (2004). *Algeria in France: Transpolitics, Race, and Nation*. Indiana University Press.

Sudarmanto, E., & Aulia, T. Z. (2022). Principles of Good Governance in Quranic's Perspective. *International Journal of Islamic Thought and Humanities*, *1*(2), 79–90.

Weinbaum, M. G. (1991). Pakistan and Afghanistan: The Strategic Relationship. *Asian Survey*, *31*(6), 496–511.

Zaidi, M. (2009). A Taxonomy of Jihad. *Arab Studies Quarterly*, *31*(3), 21–34.

KEY TERMS AND DEFINITIONS

Extremism/violent extremism: "Extremism refers to the holding of political, ideological, or religious beliefs that are significantly outside the accepted norms of society, often characterized by intolerance toward opposing views and a willingness to use violence or undemocratic means to achieve one's goals." (Schimd, 2014) It usually entails opposition to democratic values like freedom of speech, human rights, and religious freedom, as well as absolutist views and a rejection of pluralism. In the context of this chapter, it refers to the use of violence by Islamist organizations that use radical interpretations of Islamic political concepts, such as Maududi's ideas, to defend their actions.

Hakimiyyah: The idea that God (Allah), not people, is the ultimate sovereign. It suggests that political power must be used in accordance with divine law.

Islamic Political Thought:_A collection of concepts about government: political power, and statecraft that are drawn from Islamic theology and jurisprudence (Qur'an, Hadith, and academic interpretations). Both traditional theories and contemporary modifications in Muslim societies are included.

Jamaat-e-Islami: An Islamic political party founded by Maududi in 1941 aiming to establish an Islamic state through education and social reform. Its ideological offshoots have been implicated in violent extremism.

Maulana Abul A'la Maududi: An Islamic philosopher who founded Jamaat-e-Islami in the 20th century. Although his writings established the ideological foundation for Islamic rule, radical organizations in South Asia later misrepresented some of his ideas.

ENDNOTES

[1] It can be assumed that this concept of leadership has influenced the 'servant-leadership' by Robert K. Greenleaf in the in the 1970s.

[2] Sharia is more than criminal and civil law, it includes economic policy guidelines, social welfare, and behavioral ethics. It insists that the rulers be just, accountable, with justice, Adl, as one of the cardinal virtues of Islamic governance.

[3] Refere the Saudi Arabian Shura Council website, https://www.shura.gov.sa/wps/wcm/connect/ShuraEn/internet/Laws+and+Regulations/The+Shura+Council+and+the+rules+and+regulations+job/Shura+Council+Law/

[4] A theocracy is an oligarchic society in which religious leaders rule in the name of a divine power, and religious law serves as the foundation for the legal and political systems. In a theocracy, the state's legitimacy and governance are inextricably linked to a specific religion, and policies are frequently defended using religious doctrine.

[5] Muslim politician, political agitator, and journalist Jamāl al-Dīn al-Afghānī was born in Asadābād, Persia (now in Iran), in 1838, and died in Istanbul, Ottoman Empire [now in Turkey], on March 9, 1897. His belief in the strength of a resurrected Islamic civilization against European dominance had a significant impact on the evolution of Muslim thought in the 19th and early 20th centuries.

[6] Mu ammad ʿAbduh was a religious scholar, jurist, and liberal reformer who spearheaded the late 19th-century movement in Egypt and other Muslim countries to revive Islamic teachings and institutions in the contemporary world. He was born in the Nile delta region of Egypt in 1849 and died close to Alexandria on July 11, 1905. He challenged the rigidity of Muslim ritual, doctrine, and familial ties while serving as Egypt's muftī (Islamic legal adviser), implementing reforms in Islamic law, administration, and higher education despite conservative opposition. Among his works were a commentary on the Qurʾān and the "Treatise on the Oneness of God."

[7] The book 'Milestones' which was written by Sayyid Qutb was first published in 1964.

[8] Shaykh Ahmad Sirhindi was born in the little town of Sirhind, which is two hundred kilometres northwest of Delhi. He was inducted into three Sufi lineages: the Chishtiyya, the Qadiriyya, and the Suhrawardiyya. He was also a

brilliant religious teacher and the leader of a Sufi lodge. His encounter with Muhammad Baqi billah (d. 1603), a Central Asian Naqshbandi shaykh, marked a sea change in his life. After three months, Sirhindi came back to Sirhind with complete authorization to spread the Naqshbandi lineage's teachings. The majority of Baqi Billah's followers acknowledged Sirhindi as the primary heir three years after his death.

9 The Barelvi School of Thought is a Sunni Islamic revivalist movement that began in the late nineteenth century on the Indian subcontinent. It emphasizes devotion to the Prophet Muhammad (PBUH), adherence to traditional Sufi traditions, and strong respect for saints and shrines. Ahmed Raza Khan Barelvi (1856-1921), a well-known Islamic scholar from Bareilly, Uttar Pradesh, India, is the inspiration for the movement.

10 The information was retrieved during an informal discussion with Security Force individual in Sri Lanka. Due to security reasons the name of the security force individual is not disclosed in this chapter.

11 Tehrik-i-Taliban Pakistan (TTP) is a group of Islamist militants formed in 2007 to establish Sharia in Pakistan and resist Western alliances. Drawing inspiration from Deobandi Islamism, TTP has links with Al-Qaeda and the Afghan Taliban. Known for deadly attacks, TTP targets civilians, security forces, religious minorities, and educational institutions. Despite claims of political negotiation, TTP remains a formidable internal security threat in Pakistan.

12 Lashkar-e-Taiba (LeT), a prominent Islamist militant group in South Asia, emerged in the late 1980s with Salafi-Jihadism roots and close ties to Pakistan's security establishment. Founded by Hafiz Muhammad Saeed and Zafar Iqbal, LeT has primarily focused on India, particularly Jammu and Kashmir, but has ambitions beyond South Asia. LeT justifies its operations by labeling secular and democratic states as oppressive and illegitimate, framing its jihad as defensive warfare.

13 Maududi's concept of Dar al-Islam (abode of Islam) and Dar al-Harb (abode of war) reflects his broader political theology, which emphasizes God's sovereignty (hakimiyyah) and the need to construct an Islamic state regulated by Sharia. Unlike classical Islamic jurists, who traditionally defined Dar al-Islam and Dar al-Harb in terms of ruling authority and Muslim security, Maududi reinterpreted these categories in ideological and revolutionary terms. Dar al-Islam, according to Maududi, is more than just a country ruled by Muslims; it is governed by divine law, with fully Islamic legal, political, and social. In contrast, any state even one ruled by Muslims that fails to fully apply Sharia

is effectively Dar al-Harb, because it rejects God's sovereignty and accepts man-made rules, which Maududi compares with jahiliyyah (ignorance of divine guidance).

Chapter 4
Extremism in the UK: Historical Roots, Contemporary Challenges, and Policy Responses

Kavindu Peiris
https://orcid.org/0009-0006-3607-6666
University of Westminster, UK

Sinduja Umandi W. Jayaratne
Bandaranaike Centre for International Studies, Sri Lanka

ABSTRACT

In the modern world, radicalization is a serious danger to societal cohesion, global security, and fundamental human rights, making it one of the most contentious issues. Its subtle effects could affect different groups, leading to the rise of radical beliefs and violent crimes that jeopardize the foundation of a democratic society. The UK has become a leader in the fight against radicalization due to its unwavering pursuit of security and resilience. It employs a variety of strategic approaches to stop the spread of extremist ideologies and shield its citizens from the dangers of violent extremism (VE). In this context this research aims to identify the rising threat of extremism in UK and understand how global trends of violent extremism are affecting the security in UK. At the same time, this research is also conducted to analyze the counter violent extremism (CVE) approaches/measures of UK to mitigate the threat of rising violent extremism in the country. Finally. this research would recommend how to minimize the gaps in the existing CVE approaches in UK.

DOI: 10.4018/979-8-3693-3522-2.ch004

INTRODUCTION

The United Kingdom (UK), widely seen as a stable liberal democracy[1], has not been immune to extremism. Historically, the UK witnessed sectarian violence during the Northern Ireland conflict (commonly known as The Troubles, 1969-1998), when nationalist and unionist paramilitary groups committed acts of terrorism, killing over 3,500 people (English, 2003). In recent decades, the United Kingdom has experienced both Islamist and far-right extremism. The 7/7 London bombings of 2005, carried out by British-born Islamist extremists, stunned the nation and prompted enhanced counterterrorism measures. Meanwhile, the rise of far-right organizations such as the English Defence League[2] (EDL) and Britain First[3] has fueled anti-immigrant and Islamophobic views (Goodwin, 2011). Political polarization over Brexit has also resulted in increased extreme language and frequent violence, demonstrating how socio-political instability can fuel extremist tendencies even in long-standing democracies like the UK.

Within such context, this chapter explores how radical concepts have evolved historically in Britain, examine their present revival, and evaluate the government's policy responses. The analysis will argue that although radicalism in the UK has changed over time, a few fundamental themes such as immigration, identity, and economic insecurity have remained important motivators. Government initiatives, on the other hand, have had to adjust to this shifting environment, especially in light of new digital platforms and global influences.

EVOLUTION OF EXTREMISM IN EUROPE

Throughout Europe's long and complex history, there have been waves of extremism, ranging from religious intolerance and political radicalism to racial supremacy and totalitarian ideology. These radical groups have shaped not just the continent's internal dynamics, but also the course of global history. Extremism in Europe has taken different forms, from the Crusades and the Inquisition to fascism, communism, and contemporary right-wing nationalism, and has thrived in specific sociopolitical and economic contexts. Understanding the historical roots and growth of extremism in Europe is critical to comprehending the continent's political upheavals and current difficulties.

Extremism in Europe first appeared in religious contexts. The Christian Crusades (1096-12enache91), led by the Roman Catholic Church, sought to recover the Holy Land from Muslim dominion. These military battles were characterized by bloodshed, religious zeal, and a deeply ingrained 'us versus them' mentality (Menache, 2010). Religious intolerance also fueled the Spanish Inquisition (1478-1834), during which the Catholic monarchy, with the Church's support, tortured Jews, Muslims, and accused heretics before executing them (Kamen, 1999). These early examples demonstrate how religious extremism justified murder, persecution, and exclusion in the name of spiritual purity and divine purpose.

By the 19th century, religious fanaticism had given place to nationalistic and ideological extremism. The Napoleonic Wars[4], and the subsequent restructuring of Europe by the Congress of Vienna (1815), provided a favorable environment for political radicalism. Nationalist movements, such as those in Italy and Germany, mobilized people based on their ethnicity and cultural superiority. Though nationalism aided in the reunion of fragmented states, it also laid the groundwork for ethnic exclusion and militarism.

One significant occurrence was the emergence of anti-Semitism in the late 19th century. While Jews had constantly experienced prejudice in Europe, the contemporary form of political anti-Semitism evolved with writings such as Wilhelm Marr's 'The Victory of Judaism over Germanism' (1879), which contended that Jews were a racial and cultural threat to Europe (Pulzer, 1964). These sentiments will later be used by more radical ideologies in the twentieth century.

The development of fascist and Nazi regimes in the early 20th century represented the most catastrophic manifestation of fanaticism in European history. Following World War I[5], Europe witnessed economic downturn, social instability, and dissatisfaction with liberal democracies. In 1919, Benito Mussolini established the Fascist Party in Italy, proposing authoritarianism, nationalism, and militarism as solutions to the country's problems. Mussolini's dictatorship crushed opposition, emphasized imperial goals, and maintained tight ties with the Catholic Church (Eatwell, 1995).

In Germany, Adolf Hitler's National Socialist German Workers' Party[6] (Nazi Party) took advantage of economic hardship, hatred of the Treaty of Versailles, and underlying anti-Semitism. Hitler's ascent to power in 1933 signaled the start of a state-led extremist regime aimed at establishing a racially pure Aryan nation. The Nazi regime imposed dictatorial control, propaganda, and violent persecution, culminating in the Holocaust, a systematic slaughter of six million Jews and millions of others considered undesirable (Bergen, 2016). This time period marks a watershed moment in European extremism, when radical ideology not only penetrated the community but became institutionalized, with disastrous ramifications for Europe and the world.

While right-wing extremism pervaded Western Europe's remembrance of World War II[7], left-wing extremism thrived in Eastern Europe under Soviet control. After the war, the Soviet Union established communist regimes in Eastern Europe, including East Germany, Poland, Hungary, and Czechoslovakia. While ideologically distinct from fascism, these regimes shared some characteristics, including opposition repression, state monitoring, and political purges.

The Stalinist purges, show trials, and forced collectivization resulted in millions of deaths and widespread incarceration in gulags (Conquest, 2007). The Cold War increasingly polarized Europe, with the West viewing communism as a global threat and the East crushing any liberal or democratic tendencies, as evidenced by the harsh crackdowns in Hungary (1956) and Czechoslovakia (1968).

The collapse of the Soviet Union in 1991, followed by the growth of worldwide terrorism after 2001, changed Europe's extremist environment even more. The 9/11 assaults and subsequent Islamist terrorist incidents in Madrid (2004), London (2005), Paris (2015), and Brussels (2016) resulted in an increase in Islamophobic narratives, and populist parties gained popularity by advocating anti-immigrant, anti-Islam, and nationalist agendas (Roy, 2017). Social media and digital platforms also helped to distribute extremist information, radicalizing people across borders and beliefs.

Europe's counter-extremism measures currently primarily consist of punitive security measures, although proactive, restorative tactics are increasingly being used in addition to them. This change reflects the increasing agreement that addressing the underlying causes of radicalization is just as important as addressing its symptoms to avoid it in a sustainable manner. The "EXIT Deutschland" campaign in Germany serves as an example of this paradigm change. EXIT was established in 2000 and provides a systematic mix of social reintegration, psychiatric counseling, and public disengagement to assist individuals who are leaving far-right extremist networks (Koehler, 2015). Its success is noteworthy because it acknowledges the emotional and identity-based appeal of extremism and provides specialized treatment instead of just criminalization.

Likewise, the "Aarhus Model" from Denmark offers solid evidence of the effectiveness of early, multi-agency intervention. The Aarhus strategy, as described by Bertelsen (2015), combines social workers, psychologists, educators, and local police to create customized escape plans for individuals who are at risk of radicalization. The model's strength is its focus on community involvement, conversation, and trust-building values that lower recidivism and avoid alienation. Furthermore, its inclusive design steers clear of stigmatizing certain communities, which is crucial for preserving legitimacy in varied democracies.

Through initiatives, notably Erasmus+, the European Commission has strengthened this preventive approach at the supranational level. Erasmus+ funds civic educational initiatives that foster critical thinking, democratic resilience, and intercultural conversation, with a focus on adolescents, a generation susceptible to online radicalization (Briggs & Feve, 2013). They serve as intellectual counterbalances to the oversimplified, absolutist narratives propagated by extremist organizations rather than being purely educational supplements.

When combined, these instances indicate that the best counter-extremism strategies in Europe strike a balance between social inclusion, psychological rehabilitation, and legal restraint. Repression alone cannot prevent radicalization in the long run, even while punitive action is still required to confront current threats. Policies based on civic education, community empowerment, and human security provide a more comprehensive and possibly more successful response to violent extremism, as demonstrated by the success of EXIT Deutschland and the Aarhus Model.

HISTORICAL EXPERIENCE OF EXTREMISM IN THE UK

In the UK, extremism has a long and complex history. The country's socio-political landscape has been shaped by far-right groups[8], racial tensions, and later, religiously driven extremism. One of the earliest and most notable far-right groups was the British Union of Fascists (BUF), led by Oswald Mosley in the 1930s. Mosley sought to impose authoritarian control over Britain, fueled by his frustration with the economic fallout of the Great Depression and inspired by the fascist regimes of Germany and Italy. Historian Martin Pugh notes that the BUF *"tapped into a sense of national decline and the public's fear of communism"* (Pugh, 2006). The violent clashes between the BUF and anti-fascist groups culminated in the 1936 Battle of Cable Street, one of the movement's most intense street battles. This incident not only highlighted the instability of the period but also foreshadowed the long-lasting presence of far-right ideologies in Britain.

Following World War II, organized far-right groups in the UK saw a decline as the horrors of the Holocaust discredited fascism and anti-Semitism across Europe. However, far-right sentiment resurfaced in the 1960s and 1970s, largely in response to increased immigration from former British colonies. The National Front (NF), founded in 1967, capitalized on public dissatisfaction with immigration, making it a central focus for attracting support. The NF aimed to defend what it termed 'traditional British values' against what it saw as the threat of cultural and ethnic decline. It gained some electoral traction, particularly in London. In 1998, historian Richard Thurlow noted that the NF emphasized a severe kind of racial nationalism, seeing non-White immigrants as adversaries to the British state (Thurlow, 1998). The group organized public demonstrations and disseminated racist propaganda, fostering an atmosphere of racial tension and hostility.

The British National Party (BNP), which sought to modernize the far-right by portraying itself as a respectable political party, had replaced the NF by the 1980s. Its central argument, however, remained centered on anti-immigration laws and white supremacist ideology. In the 2000s, the BNP experienced a brief period of prosperity, gaining seats in councils and even earning a member in the European Parliament in 2009. The growth of the BNP, according to academics such as Matthew Goodwin, was a sign of broader societal anxiety, especially in working-class communities where members were experiencing social and economic marginalization (Goodwin, 2013).

CONTEMPORARY CHALLENGES OF EXTREMISM IN THE UK

The current extremist landscape in the UK is characterized by a complex interplay of ideology, societal dynamics, and technological advancements that have transformed the tactics used by extremist movements. This environment is primarily dominated by two main types of extremism: far-right extremism and Islamist extremism. Each of these presents unique challenges that necessitate a diverse and tailored approach to effectively address them.

Islamist extremism has been a persistent concern since the late 20th century, intensifying significantly after the September 11 attacks and the 2005 London bombings. This ideology advocates for the establishment of a caliphate and promotes the use of violence against those perceived as enemies of Islam, often based on a fundamentalist interpretation of the religion. Research has identified several factors linked to radicalization, including socioeconomic marginalization, political grievances, and a desire for identity and belonging (Hoffman, 2017). The severity of the issue is demonstrated by Home Office data indicating that Islamic extremism is involved in nearly half of all terrorism-related arrests in the UK (2022).

Further, a key aspect of Islamist extremism is its ability to adapt to changing sociopolitical environments. Extremist ideologies can capitalize on regional crises and geopolitical tensions to gain traction, as seen in the rise of groups like the Islamic State of Iraq and Syria (ISIS). For instance, the Syrian civil war served as a significant recruiting catalyst for individuals in the UK who were inspired to support the jihadist cause(Kenyon et al., 2024). The messages of these organizations often resonate with disillusioned young individuals, who may view violence as a practical way to resolve conflicts or achieve a sense of importance. Additionally, the rapid spread of extremist views through social media has made radicalization more accessible than ever.

In the UK, far-right extremism has noticeably resurged, particularly following significant sociopolitical shifts such as the Brexit referendum and rising anti-immigrant sentiment. Extremist organizations like Britain First and the English Defence League (EDL) capitalize on feelings of cultural and economic marginalization. These movements often frame their narratives around the defense of a *"pure"* national identity, portraying minority and immigrant groups as threats to public safety and social cohesion (Mudde & Kaltwasser, 2017). Additionally, the far-right increasingly employs sophisticated online tactics to spread hate speech, recruit supporters, and organize protests. This trend toward digital radicalization presents significant challenges for counterterrorism and law enforcement efforts.

Moreover, the growing acceptance of xenophobic rhetoric in mainstream discourse has also fueled the rise of far-right extremism by legitimizing extreme beliefs. This normalization can be attributed to populist political movements that leverage nationalist sentiments to gain support. Consequently, it has become increasingly difficult to distinguish between acceptable political discourse and radical ideology. According to the Home Office (2024), arrests related to far-right extremism have risen, highlighting a concerning trend that requires immediate attention.

To address these challenges, the UK government has updated its counter-extremism policies to reflect the evolving nature of radicalization. The 2023 response to the Independent Review of Prevent emphasizes a broader definition of extremism, which includes non-violent beliefs that incite hatred and division (Shawcross, 2023) . This approach recognizes that extreme ideologies often operate within legal boundaries, making them difficult to combat using traditional law enforcement methods. However, critics contend that initiatives like Prevent disproportionately target Muslim communities, potentially fueling resentment and leading to further radicalization (Open Society Justice Initiative, 2016).

Additionally, the current political climate has hindered the government's ability to engage constructively with communities affected by extremism. Perceptions of bias in counter-extremism programmes have eroded trust between law enforcement agencies and minority communities. To address this issue, the government must adopt a more inclusive approach that fosters communication with diverse populations to better understand their concerns and challenges. It is crucial to tackle underlying socioeconomic issues such as economic inequality, discrimination, and a lack of opportunities, as these factors often serve as breeding grounds for radicalization. Building resilience against extremist ideologies requires addressing these root causes.

COMPREHENSIVE ANALYSIS OF THE UK'S PREVENTIVE STRATEGIES AGAINST VIOLENT EXTREMISM

Overview of CONTEST Strategy

Since its inception in the early 2000s, the UK's counterterrorism strategy, known as CONTEST, has undergone significant changes. Its primary goal is to combat and reduce terrorist threats to national security. The strategy is built around the 'four Ps': Prevent, Pursue, Protect, and Prepare. Together, these components encompass a range of strategic efforts aimed at addressing various aspects of the terrorist threat landscape (HM Government, 2018). In this context, the preventive action/

measures focused on early intervention and community resilience plays a crucial role in preventing violent extremism. By aiming to stop individuals from becoming radicalized or engaging in extremist activities, preventive action/measures address the root causes of terrorism and strengthens communities that are vulnerable to radicalization. According to the UK government, the purpose of preventative action/measures is to stop people from becoming terrorists or supporting terrorism by providing education and support services. By fostering trust and cooperation within communities, preventive action/measures seek to create an environment where proactive measures can flourish.

According to Counter-terrorism strategy (CONTEST) 2018, one of the key strengths in preventative action/measures is its focus on early intervention and community involvement, which are essential in preventing radicalization before it escalates to violence. For example, the Building a Stronger Britain Together (BSBT) program supports community-led projects aimed at strengthening social cohesion and promoting alternative narratives to reduce the appeal of extremist ideologies. These community-based initiatives provide a culturally sensitive approach to engaging with communities, equipping them with the resources needed to counter radicalization. The multi-agency strategy used in preventative action/measures, particularly through programs like the 'Channel', indicates the UK's commitment to addressing radicalization from many viewpoints. 'Channel' offers tailored interventions to address the specific vulnerabilities of individuals at risk of extremism, whether these stem from psychological, ideological, or personal factors (HM Government, 2023). By focusing on a person-centered approach, the program ensures that individuals are provided opportunities for rehabilitation and reintegration into society, rather than simply being criminalized.

The UK's preventive approach is strengthened by the Prevent Duty, introduced under the Counter-Terrorism and Security Act 2015, which imposes legal obligations on public institutions such as schools, universities, and healthcare providers to actively identify and address signs of radicalization. This framework ensures that a wide range of professionals, from teachers to medical staff, are trained to recognize and respond to potential risks, reflecting a coordinated commitment to prevention across various sectors (HM Government, 2015). By integrating these preventative measures into public institutions, the UK has extended its counterterrorism efforts beyond law enforcement, ensuring that radicalization is addressed at multiple levels of society.

Moreover, the recent focus on combating online radicalization has been a significant advantage. The government's Online Harms White Paper calls for increased accountability from tech companies, recognizing digital platforms as key channels for extremist content. The Counter-Terrorism and Border Security Act 2019 further strengthens this effort by making it illegal to access or share extremist materials online, limiting the free spread of radicalizing content. These measures highlight the UK's adaptive response to the evolving threat landscape, particularly as the internet increasingly serves as a propaganda and recruitment tool for extremists.

The Prevent Strategy has faced both acknowledgment and criticism regarding its objectives and execution. While it emphasizes community involvement and early intervention to prevent radicalization before it escalates to terrorism, one can argue that it raises concerns about discrimination and its impact on civil liberties, particularly the right to free expression. Although the strategy is viewed as proactive and potentially effective in addressing the root causes of extremism, concerns persist about how it balances individual rights with national security.

The Counter-Terrorism and Security Act 2015 introduced provisions that allow for monitoring individuals suspected of terrorism-related activities and enable authorities to issue orders aimed at dismantling extremism. Walker (2016) has highlighted that this legislation has been closely scrutinized by human rights advocates and civil society organizations, who argue that it may violate individuals' rights to privacy and human dignity. Critics assert that the Act's provisions could lead to disproportionate surveillance and restrictions on civil liberties, compromising due process and privacy rights. They contend that, while combating terrorism is crucial, these measures must be balanced carefully to avoid undermining fundamental freedoms.

Community engagement programmes are another component of the UK strategy that has drawn criticism. Although community-based initiatives aimed at countering extremist narratives have been recognized for their potential to build trust and resilience, challenges remain in ensuring that these programs are successful and inclusive of diverse groups (Morgan, 2009). Programmes like Channel Programme and the Prevent Duty exemplify the proactive and comprehensive approach of the UK's counter-radicalization efforts, emphasizing early intervention and support. These initiatives involve various sectors, including education, healthcare, and law enforcement, working together to identify potential threats and intervene before they lead to acts of terrorism.

One significant concern is that the Prevent Strategy may marginalize and alienate Muslim communities. Critics argue that it disproportionately targets Muslim populations, fostering distrust. The Open Society Justice Initiative (2016) asserts that the Prevent Strategy often conflates religious conservatism with extremism, leading to excessive surveillance and bias. However, many individuals have criticized the preventive actions/measures as a method of spying and criminalizing the Muslim population (Awan, 2012).

A statement from the House of Commons Home Affairs Committee in 2016 indicated that many professionals felt unprepared to implement the preventive actions/measures effectively, which has led to inconsistent application and potential human rights violations. During a debate on the Prevent strategy, Naz Shah, the Member of

Parliament for Bradford West highlighted that, "we have seen evidence of mistrust and fear among communities and individuals who feel that Prevent targets specific communities unfairly," suggesting a need for more training and clearer guidelines to ensure the effective execution of the strategy (UK Parliament, 2017). Additionally, criticism of the UK's legislative measures often centers on finding a balance between security and civil liberties. The broad powers granted by anti-terrorism laws, such as monitoring internet activity and detaining individuals without trial, have raised concerns about the erosion of freedom and privacy. The civil rights organization Liberty argues that these measures can be overly extreme and may lead to abuses of power. They contend that *"the government's counterterrorism strategy has often resulted in civil liberties being violated without necessarily increasing security"* (Liberty, 2019).

The Online Harms White Paper in 2019, aimed at countering online radicalization, has also faced scrutiny due to concerns about potential infringements on freedom of speech. The Online Harms White paper 2019 highlight the fact that "terrorist groups use the internet to spread propaganda designed to radicalize vulnerable people, and distribute material designed to aid or abet terrorist attacks. There are also examples of terrorists broadcasting attacks live on social media." While it is essential to remove harmful material, critics argue that maintaining online safety must be balanced with preserving free expression. The new regulatory framework requires organizations to eliminate extremist content and promote alternative narratives to create a safer internet. Critics warn that such actions could suppress free expression and limit the freedom of individuals in the online space (Index on Censorship, 2019).

Thus, it is clear that while early intervention and community involvement are crucial aspects of the UK's preventive strategies particularly the Prevent Strategy, they have notable weaknesses. Concerns such as stigmatization, inadequate implementation of the Prevent Duty, and the challenge of balancing security with civil liberties emphasize the need for ongoing evaluation and adjustment. Counter-radicalization initiatives must be fair, effective, and respectful of individual rights to build public trust and ensure their long-term success. To develop a more comprehensive and effective strategy against radicalization, the UK must continue to refine its approaches, incorporating the perspectives and experiences of individuals from diverse backgrounds.

RECOMMENDATIONS

To effectively combat extremism in the UK, a fundamental rethink of how counter-extremism is conceived, executed, and maintained is essential. The government must prioritize deeply rooted, community-first strategies over top-down, security-led approaches. Funding local community leaders, youth workers, and mental health professionals to serve as the frontline in early intervention is a necessary first step. These trusted individuals are best placed to identify signs of radicalization before they escalate something law enforcement and external organizations often fail to do.

At the same time, preventative education must be embedded in the national curriculum as a core subject rather than treated as optional. Digital literacy, ideological resilience, and critical thinking should be taught from an early age to help young people recognize and resist online grooming, conspiracy theories, and extremist propaganda. Without this foundation, the unregulated digital environment will continue to put future generations at risk.

Regulating digital platforms and artificial intelligence in the spread of extremism is equally urgent. Extremist groups already exploit deepfakes, encrypted messaging, and algorithm-driven targeting to radicalize on a large scale. The government must enforce cooperation from tech companies, invest in publicly accountable AI monitoring tools, and ensure transparency in content regulation without compromising civil liberties. National security cannot be left vulnerable to the tech sector's reluctance to self-regulate.

Public trust in counter-extremism efforts must also be rebuilt. This requires rejecting stigmatizing, ethnically biased practices in favour of collaborative frameworks developed with the communities most affected. Initiatives like Prevent have suffered from a lack of credibility; unless this is addressed, even well-intentioned policies will fall short.

Accordingly, a resilient UK depends more on sustained, intelligent, and socially just prevention than on reactive policing. The risks are no longer theoretical. If radicalization continues to outpace reform, the consequences will be swift and lasting. The government must act decisively, wisely, and with humility before it is too late.

CONCLUSION

The evolution of extremism in the United Kingdom mirrors broader European patterns, reflecting how ideological radicalism adapts to historical, social, and political currents. From the early influence of fascist ideologies in the 1930s to contemporary forms of far-right nationalism and Islamist extremism, the UK has experienced persistent challenges posed by violent and non-violent radical movements. This continuity reveals that while the forms of extremism may shift, core drivers such as identity politics, immigration anxieties, economic marginalization, and geopolitical tensions remain central to their appeal. The British government's evolving counter-extremism strategy, particularly through the Prevent programme, has taken important steps toward community-based prevention and early intervention. However, critiques regarding disproportionate targeting, civil liberties, and the stigmatization of Muslim communities suggest that significant improvements are necessary. To confront extremism effectively, future policy must balance security with inclusivity, transparency, and civil rights. A more resilient and socially cohesive society can only be achieved through sustained engagement, trust-building, and addressing the root causes of alienation that fuel radicalization. The UK's ongoing challenge, therefore, is not only to suppress extremism but also to foster a democratic culture that undermines its very foundations.

REFERENCES

Awan, I. (2012). “I Am a Muslim Not an Extremist”: How the Prevent Strategy Has Constructed a “Suspect” Community. *Politics & Policy*, *40*(6), 1158–1185.

Bergen, D. L. (2016). *War and Genocide: A Concise History of the Holocaust*. Rowman & Littlefield Publishers.

Bertelsen, P. (2015). Danish preventive measures and deradicalization strategies: The Aarhus model. *Panorama: Insights into Asian and European Affairs, 2015*(1), 241-253. http://www.kas.de/wf/doc/kas_42032-1522-2-30.pdf?150714075727

Briggs, R., & Feve, S. (2013). Review of programs to counter narratives of violent extremism. *Institute for Strategic Dialogue*. https://core.ac.uk/reader/30675430

Busher, J. (2016). *The making of anti-Muslim protest: Grassroots activism in the English Defence League*. Routledge.

Clark, C. (2014). *The Sleepwalkers: How Europe Went to War in 1914*. Harper-Collins Publishers.

Conquest, R. (2007). *The Great Terror: A Reassessment* (40th Anniv). Oxford University Press.

Dahl, R. A. (2000). *On Democracy*. Yale University Press.

Eatwell, R. (1995). *Fascism: A History*. Chatto & Windus.

English, R. (2003). *Armed struggle: The history of the IRA*. Pan Macmillan.

Esdaile, C. (2008). *Napoleon's Wars: An International History, 1803-1815*. Viking.

Evans, R. J. (2005). *The Coming of the Third Reich*. Penguin Press.

Goodwin, M. (2011). *New British fascism: Rise of the British National Party*. Routledge.

Goodwin, M. (2013). The Roots of Extremism: The English Defence League and the Counter-Jihad Challenge. *Chatam House*, 16. https://www.chathamhouse.org/publications/papers/view/189767

Government, H. M. (2015). *Counter-Terrorism and Security Act 2015*. https://www.legislation.gov.uk/ukpga/2015/6/contents/enacted

Government, H. M. (2018). *CONTEST: The United Kingdom's Strategy for Countering Terrorism*. https://assets.publishing.service.gov.uk/media/5b23df8f40f0b634d557b020/140618_CCS207_CCS0218929798-1_CONTEST_3.0_WEB.pdf

Government, H. M. (2023). *Channel duty guidance: Protecting People Susceptible to Radicalisation*. https://assets.publishing.service.gov.uk/media/651e71d9e4e658001459d997/14.320_HO_Channel_Duty_Guidance_v3_Final_Web.pdf

Hoffman, B. (2017). *Inside Terrorism* (3rd Editio). Columbia University Press.

Index on Censorship. (2019). *Government's online harms white paper risk damaging freedom of expression in the UK*. https://www.indexoncensorship.org/2019/07/governments-online-harms-white-paper-risk-damaging-freedom-of-expression-in-the-uk/?utm_source=chatgpt.com

Kamen, H. (1999). *The Spanish Inquisition: A Historical Revision*. Yale University Press.

Kenyon, J., Binder, J., & Baker-Beall, C. (2024). Understanding the Role of the Internet in the Process of Radicalisation: An Analysis of Convicted Extremists in England and Wales. *Studies in Conflict and Terrorism*, *47*(12), 1747–1771. https://doi.org/https://doi.org/10.1080/1057610X.2022.2065902

Koehler, D. (2015). De-radicalization and Disengagement Programs as Counter-Terrorism and Prevention Tools. Insights From Field Experiences Regarding German Right-Wing Extremism and Jihadism. *Countering Radicalisation and Violent Extremism among Youth to Prevent Terrorism, 118*, 120–150. https://doi.org/DOI: 10.3233/978-1-61499-470-1-120

Liberty. (2019). *Liberty: Appointment of 'biased' Prevent reviewer beggars belief.* https://www.libertyhumanrights.org.uk/issue/liberty-appointment-of-biased-prevent-reviewer-beggars-belief/

Mazower, M. (2009). *Hitler's Empire: How the Nazis Ruled Europe*. Penguin Publishing Group.

Menache, S. (2010). Love of God or Hatred of Your Enemy? The Emotional Voices of the Crusades. *Mirabilia Journal, 10*(1), 1–20. https://www.revistamirabilia.com/sites/default/files/pdfs/2010_01_01.pdf

Morgan, M. (2009). Book Review: Riedel, B. (2008). The Search for al Qaeda: Its Leadership, Ideology, and Future. Washington, DC: Brookings Institution. *Armed Forces and Society*, *36*(2), 377–380. https://doi.org/https://doi.org/10.1177/0095327X09340755

Mudde, C., & Kaltwasser, C. R. (2017). Populsim. A very short introduction. In *Populism: A Very Short Intoduction*. Oxford University Press.

Open Society Justice Initiative. (2016). *Eroding Trust: The UK's Prevent Counter-Extremism Strategy in Health and Education.* https://www.justiceinitiative.org/uploads/1237d213-a66e-496a-af41-08e11d38e2c4/eroding-trust-execiutive-summary-20161017.pdf

Parliament, U. K. (2017). *Prevent Strategy Volume 620: Debated on Wednesday 1 February 2017.* Hansard. https://hansard.parliament.uk/commons/2017-02-01/debates/B8BE87F9-7E2E-46C5-9E11-DDAD5897E949/PreventStrategy?utm_source=chatgpt.com

Pugh, M. (2006). *Hurrah for the blackshirts!': fascists and fascism in Britain between the wars.* Pimlico.

Pulzer, P. (1964). *The Rise of Political Anti-Semitism in Germany and Austria.* John Wiley & Sons.

Ravndal, J. A. (2018). Explaining right-wing terrorism and violence in Western Europe: Grievances, opportunities and polarisation. *European Journal of Political Research, 57*(4), 845–866. https://doi.org/https://doi.org/10.1111/1475-6765.12254

Roy, O. (2017). *Jihad and Death: The Global Appeal of Islamic State.* C Hurst & Co Publishers Ltd.

Shawcross, W. (2023). *Independent Review of Prevent* (Issue February). https://assets.publishing.service.gov.uk/media/63e26968d3bf7f17385a3421/Independent_Review_of_Prevent.pdf

Thurlow, R. (1998). *FASCISM IN BRITAIN A History 1918–1998* (Revised Ed). I.B.Tauris Publishers.

Walker, C. (2016). Counter-Terrorism and Human Rights in the UK. In Breen-Smyth, M. (Ed.), *The Ashgate Research Companion to Political Violence.* Routledge.

KEY TERMS AND DEFINITIONS

Aarhus Model: A Danish deradicalization programme focused on mentorship and reintegration for individuals vulnerable to extremism.

Anti-Semitism: Prejudice, hatred, or discrimination against Jews as a religious or ethnic group.

British National Party (BNP): A far-right political party in the UK, known for its white supremacist and anti-immigration stances.

British Union of Fascists (BUF): A 1930s UK political group led by Oswald Mosley that aimed to establish authoritarian rule, inspired by fascist regimes in Italy and Germany.

Building a Stronger Britain Together (BSBT): A UK government programme that supports community-led initiatives to strengthen social cohesion and promote counter-narratives to extremism.

Caliphate: An Islamic state led by a religious leader (caliph), often invoked by Islamist extremist groups as an ideological goal.

Channel Programme: A UK initiative under the Prevent strategy offering personalized interventions to individuals at risk of radicalization.

CONTEST Strategy: The UK's counterterrorism framework consisting of four pillars such as Prevent, Pursue, Protect, and Prepare.

Deradicalization: The process by which individuals abandon extremist ideologies and disengage from extremist networks or beliefs.

Disengagement: The act of withdrawing from involvement in extremist activity, which may not include a change in ideology.

English Defence League (EDL): A far-right UK protest movement known for its anti-Islam and anti-immigration views.

Extremism: The holding or promotion of extreme political or religious views that may include advocating violence or undermining democratic systems.

Far-right Extremism: Political ideologies characterized by ultra-nationalism, xenophobia, racism, and anti-democratic beliefs.

Ideological Causes of Terrorism: Underlying belief systems or narratives that justify the use of violence for political or religious goals.

Islamist Extremism: A form of violent extremism rooted in a fundamentalist interpretation of Islam, advocating the use of violence to establish an Islamic state.

Islamophobia: Fear, hatred, or discrimination directed at Muslims or Islam; often overlaps with xenophobia and racism.

Marginalization: The social exclusion of individuals or groups from mainstream society, often cited as a factor in radicalization.

Online Harms White Paper: A UK government policy document that outlines steps to protect users from harmful content online, including extremist material.

Online Radicalization (Digital Radicalization): The process of becoming radicalized through exposure to extremist content via the internet and social media platforms.

Populism: A political approach that appeals to the concerns of ordinary people, often against elites; may be used by extremist groups to build support.

Prevent Duty: A legal obligation under the UK's Counter-Terrorism and Security Act 2015 requiring public institutions to identify and counter radicalization.

Prevent Strategy: One of the four pillars of the UK's CONTEST strategy, aiming to stop people from becoming terrorists or supporting terrorism.

Propaganda: Information, often biased or misleading, used to promote a political cause or point of view commonly used in extremist recruitment.

Radicalization: The mental and social process through which individuals come to adopt extremist ideologies, possibly leading to violence.

Rehabilitation and Reintegration: Strategies that aim to reintegrate former extremists back into society through counseling, education, and social support.

Social Media Recruitment: The use of platforms like Twitter, Facebook, or Telegram by extremist groups to recruit and radicalize individuals.

Surveillance: Monitoring of individuals by government or security agencies as part of counterterrorism efforts; can raise civil liberty concerns.

Terrorism: The unlawful use of violence and intimidation, especially against civilians, in the pursuit of political aims.

Terrorist Narrative: The ideological or emotional story used by extremist groups to justify violence and attract recruits.

Xenophobia: Dislike or prejudice against people from other countries, often a key theme in far-right extremism.

ENDNOTES

1 A liberal democracy is a political system that combines democratic principles with liberal values, focusing on individual rights, rule of law, and separation of powers. It safeguards civil liberties, independent judiciaries, accountable governments, and a free press, making it the most stable and inclusive form of governance in the Western political tradition. (Dahl, 2000)

2 The English Defence League (EDL), a far-right UK protest group, emerged in 2009, claiming to oppose 'Islamist extremism.' Critics argue it promotes Islamophobia, xenophobia, and violent street politics. The group, initially supported by football hooligan networks, has been linked to hate speech, racial tensions, and cultural divisions. (Busher, 2016)

3 Britain First, a far-right political organization in the UK, is known for its anti-Islam and anti-immigration stance. Founded in 2011, it engages in provocative actions, such as 'Christian patrols' and demonstrations outside mosques, claiming to defend British and Christian values. Despite its patriotic branding, Britain First has faced criticism for promoting hate speech and fostering division within communities. (Busher, 2016)

4 The Napoleonic Wars (1803-1815) were series of conflicts triggered by the French Revolution and Napoleon's rise as Emperor. They shaped European political boundaries, military doctrines, and power dynamics. Napoleon's strategic innovations and military reforms led to France dominating continental Europe. The failed invasion of Russia in 1812 weakened French forces. The Congress of Vienna aimed to restore power balance. (Esdaile, 2008)

5 World War I, which began with the assassination of Archduke Franz Ferdinand, heralded a shift in warfare, state centralization, and sociopolitical transformation. The psychological effects of war on both troops and civilians had an impact on cultural memory and political instability. The Treaty of Versailles, signed in 1919, brought the war to a conclusion, but its harsh conditions and revision of borders laid the groundwork for future hostilities. (Clark, 2014)

6 The Nazi Party, a radical nationalist and anti-Semitic movement, emerged after World War I. Initially known as the German Workers' Party, it was rebranded as the NSDAP in 1920 under Adolf Hitler. The party exploited political instability, the Treaty of Versailles, and the Great Depression. By 1933, it established a totalitarian regime, leading to the Holocaust. (Evans, 2005)

7 World War II, a devastating global conflict involving over 30 countries and over 70 million deaths, was triggered by Nazi Germany's aggressive expansionism and the invasion of Poland. The Axis powers sought territorial dominance, while the Allies aimed to restore international order and defeat totalitarianism. The war saw unprecedented casualties, the Holocaust, and the reshaping of global power structures. (Mazower, 2009)

8 Far-right extremism in Europe is a growing concern, characterized by Islamophobia, xenophobia, ethnonationalism, and violent opposition to democratic institutions. It spreads through radical rhetoric, hate crimes, and online incitement. Social media platforms facilitate this spread, targeting Muslim and Jewish communities. Recent incidents highlight the lethal potential of far-right extremism, which exploits societal fears for authoritarian ideologies. European governments are responding to this threat. (Ravndal, 2018)

Chapter 5

Failure to Connect the Dots, 50 Years Later: "Yom Kippur War" (1973) Versus "October 7"

Galit Margalit Ben-Israel
https://orcid.org/0009-0005-3220-4520
Beit-Berl Academic College, Israel

ABSTRACT

Hamas-led attack on Israel (October 7, 2023) was considered to be a spectacular military surprise similar to the "Yom Kippur War" (1973). There are parallel lines to the attack and the war, most of them in the field of intelligence, such as ignoring intelligence reports and failure to connect the dots, i.e., failing to interpret the large amounts of data accumulated in the intelligence division, and identified in the two events, that a war was about to break out. Israeli intelligence also failed in both wars by sticking to the wrong concepts. According to the first case study ("The 1973 War"), the Egyptian and the Syrian armies would not start a war because the Israeli military had remarkably won the "1967 War". According to the second case study (Hamas-led attack on Israel), "Hamas is deterred," and the conflict between Israel and the Hamas organization controlling in Gaza strip, could be contained by Israel. Though both conceptions were incorrect, they prevented political and military decision-makers and heads of the IDF from "reading" the intelligence reports, which explicitly described the most likely option of war and attack in both situations. In the research, a top-tier intelligence agency, the IDF intelligence, failed miserably to connect the dots twice, 50 years apart. In our research, the "Yom Kippur War" and the Hamas-led attack on Israel (October 7, 2023) are compared using a close tables and artificial intelligence.

DOI: 10.4018/979-8-3693-3522-2.ch005

INTRODUCTION

In the realm of national security, the intelligence community serves as the first line of defense against threats both foreign and domestic. Yet, history has repeatedly shown that even the most sophisticated and well-resourced intelligence agencies can fall prey to catastrophic failures. This chapter delves into two such failures in Israeli intelligence: the Yom Kippur War of 1973 and the Hamas-led attack on October 7, 2023. These events, separated by half a century, share striking similarities in their underlying intelligence breakdowns, particularly in the critical process of "connecting the dots" - the ability to synthesize disparate pieces of information into a coherent and actionable intelligence picture.

The Yom Kippur War, which caught Israel off guard on its holiest day, has long been studied as a classic case of intelligence failure. It exposed significant weaknesses in Israel's intelligence apparatus and led to widespread reforms. However, fifty years later, the October 7 attack orchestrated by Hamas echoed many of the same shortcomings, raising critical questions about the nature of intelligence work and the persistent challenges in interpreting and acting upon available information.

This chapter aims to conduct a comprehensive comparative analysis of these two seminal events, focusing on the parallels in intelligence gathering, analysis, and decision-making processes. We will explore how preconceived notions, or "conceptions," can blind analysts and decision-makers to contrary evidence, and how the failure to challenge these conceptions can lead to catastrophic outcomes. The role of organizational culture, cognitive biases, and the psychological aspects of intelligence work will be examined in depth.

By juxtaposing these case studies, we seek to understand: first, the role of cognitive biases and organizational cultures in shaping intelligence assessments: How do ingrained beliefs and institutional norms influence the interpretation of intelligence data? Second, the challenges of interpreting vast amounts of data in the modern intelligence landscape: In an era of information overload, how can intelligence agencies effectively sift through and prioritize critical information? Third, the importance of fostering a culture of critical thinking and "devil's advocate" approaches in intelligence work: How can agencies institutionalize practices that challenge prevailing assumptions and encourage alternative analyses? Fourth, the impact of hubris on decision-making processes at both the intelligence and political levels: How does overconfidence in one's capabilities or previous successes contribute to intelligence failures? Fifth, the evolution of intelligence practices over the past fifty years: What lessons were learned from the Yom Kippur War, and why were they insufficient to prevent the October 7 attack?

This analysis will draw upon a rich body of literature in intelligence studies, cognitive psychology, and organizational theory. We will examine primary sources, including declassified intelligence reports and testimonies, as well as secondary analyses by scholars and practitioners in the field. Through this multifaceted examination, we aim to draw lessons that can inform future intelligence practices, not only in Israel but in intelligence communities worldwide. As we navigate an increasingly complex global security environment, characterized by asymmetric threats, cyber warfare, and rapid technological change, understanding and addressing the root causes of intelligence failures becomes more critical than ever.

The implications of this study extend beyond the specific context of Israeli national security. By illuminating the persistent challenges in intelligence work, we hope to contribute to a broader dialogue on enhancing the effectiveness and reliability of intelligence agencies in safeguarding national security in the 21st century.

REVIEW OF LITERATURE

In the context of "The Role of Intelligence in Countering Violent Extremism," the chapter "Failure to Connect the Dots, 50 Years Later: 'Yom Kippur War' (1973) Versus 'October 7'" explores a critical aspect of intelligence failures that has persisted across decades. This review examines key literature that informs our understanding of these failures, particularly focusing on cognitive biases, organizational structures, and decision-making processes in intelligence analysis.

The Yom Kippur War of 1973 serves as a seminal case study in intelligence failures. Kuperman (2012) provides a comprehensive analysis of the war's lessons for military intelligence, highlighting the dangers of rigid conceptual thinking. Kahana (2002) further explores this theme, contrasting early warning systems with entrenched concepts that hindered accurate threat assessment. Landau and Pfeffer (2017) dig deeper into Israel's pre-war intelligence assessment, uncovering systemic issues that led to misinterpretation of available data.

Cognitive factors play a crucial role in intelligence failures. Festinger's (1957) theory of cognitive dissonance offers insight into why analysts might cling to outdated assessments despite contradictory evidence. Kruglanski and Webster (1996) expand on this with their work on "motivated closing of the mind," explaining how the need for cognitive closure can lead to premature and erroneous conclusions. Heuer (1999) provides a comprehensive examination of the psychology behind intelligence analysis, offering tools to mitigate cognitive biases.

Organizational structures and decision-making processes are equally important. Betts (1978) argues that intelligence failures are, to some extent, inevitable due to the complex interplay of analysis, war, and decision-making. Jervis (2006) examines how political factors can influence intelligence assessments, using the Iraq War as a case study. These insights are particularly relevant when comparing the 1973 and 2023 intelligence failures.

Recent literature has begun to draw parallels between historical and contemporary intelligence failures. Kuperwasser (2024) offers preliminary insights into the October 7, 2023 intelligence failure, highlighting similarities with past events. Kam (2024) explicitly compares the Yom Kippur War and the October 7 attack, extracting lessons that span the 50-year gap.

The work of Janis and Mann on groupthink provides a crucial framework for understanding how collective decision-making can lead to flawed assessments, a factor present in both the 1973 and 2023 cases.

This body of literature underscores the persistent challenges in intelligence analysis and the critical importance of learning from past failures. By examining these works in the context of both the Yom Kippur War and the October 7 attack, we gain valuable insights into the enduring nature of intelligence failures and potential strategies for mitigation.

MAIN FOCUS OF THE CHAPTER

The chapter examines two significant intelligence failures in Israeli history: the Yom Kippur War of 1973 and the Hamas-led attack on October 7, 2023. Despite being separated by 50 years, these events share striking similarities in their underlying intelligence breakdowns. The focus is on the critical process of "connecting the dots" - the ability to synthesize disparate pieces of information into a coherent and actionable intelligence picture.

Both cases highlight how preconceived notions or "conceptions" can blind analysts and decision-makers to contrary evidence. The chapter explores how organizational culture, cognitive biases, and psychological aspects of intelligence work contributed to these failures. It analyzes the challenges of interpreting vast amounts of data in the modern intelligence landscape and the importance of fostering a culture of critical thinking.

The comparative analysis aims to draw lessons that can inform future intelligence practices, not only in Israel but in intelligence communities worldwide. By illuminating these persistent challenges, the chapter contributes to a broader dialogue on enhancing the effectiveness and reliability of intelligence agencies in safeguarding national security in the 21st century.

THE METHODOLOGY

This study combines several methodological approaches to provide a comprehensive and in-depth analysis of the intelligence failures in 1973 and 2023. At the core of the research is a detailed comparative analysis between the two events, which is carried out through the creation of comparison tables that focus on the processes of gathering, analyzing, and evaluating intelligence.

The research incorporates advanced AI tools for text analysis and pattern recognition in historical and contemporary data to deal with large amounts of information.

The study also includes an analysis of specific test cases that were "preliminary signs" in both periods and a comparative literature review examining previous studies on intelligence failures, emphasizing comparing similar historical cases. This combination of qualitative and quantitative research methods makes it possible to provide a comprehensive picture of the causes of intelligence failures and formulate practical recommendations to improve intelligence assessment processes in the future.

Hypotheses:

1. Israeli conceptions preceding the Yom Kippur War (1973) and Hamas' attack (2023) are fundamentally similar, leading to identical intelligence failures.
2. Collecting overt information about potential threats is insufficient; its intelligence value is realized only when "connecting the dots" through correct analysis and synthesis.

CASE STUDIES FOR INTENSIVE EXAMINATION

This research focuses on two pivotal case studies: the Yom Kippur War (1973) and the Hamas-led attack on Israel (October 7, 2023). For each case study, we will first analyze the prevailing atmosphere and zeitgeist leading up to the event. This analysis aims to elucidate the dominant "conception" held by Israeli decision-makers, including both military leadership and political figures. By examining these pre-event contexts, we seek to understand the intellectual and strategic frameworks that shaped Israel's preparedness and response in each instance.

Before "Yom Kippur War" (1973)

The 1948 War, the 1967 War, and the 1973 War were major conflicts that accompanied the early years of the State of Israel's existence.

The period between 1948 and 1973 was marked by continuous tension and intermittent conflicts between Israel and its Arab neighbors.

Following the 1948 Arab-Israeli War, which resulted in Israel's establishment, the country faced ongoing hostility from surrounding Arab states (Morris, 2008). The Suez Crisis of 1956 further strained relations, particularly with Egypt. However, it was the Six-Day War of 1967 that dramatically altered the regional balance of power. Israel's swift victory led to the occupation of the Sinai Peninsula, Gaza Strip, West Bank, and Golan Heights, significantly expanding its territory (Oren, 2002)

In the aftermath of the 1967 War, Israel experienced a period of relative calm and growing confidence. This era, known as the "conception" period, was characterized by a prevailing belief in Israeli military superiority and Arab reluctance to initiate another war (Bar-Joseph, 2005). This confidence, bordering on hubris, would ultimately contribute to Israel's unpreparedness for the Yom Kippur War in 1973. Despite ongoing low-intensity conflicts like the War of Attrition (1967-1970), Israeli intelligence and political leadership largely dismissed the possibility of a full-scale Arab offensive, setting the stage for one of the most significant intelligence failures in the country's history (Blum, 2003).

The Background to the Outbreak of The 1973 War Israel, Egypt, And Syria

After the Six-Day War (1967 War), a sense of security prevailed in Israel, bolstered by the demonstrated strength and capability of the Israel Defense Forces. The fifteenth government of Israel, led by Golda Meir, believed it was not worth relinquishing territories conquered during this war (Bar-Joseph, 2005). Defense Minister Moshe Dayan's statement epitomized this stance: "It is better to have Sharm el-Sheikh without peace than peace without Sharm el-Sheikh" (Morris, 2008).

The Egyptian army's failure in the "War of Attrition" (1968-1970) and the Israeli air force's tactical successes further enhanced the sense of security among Israel's military and political leadership. This confidence was reflected in Prime Minister Golda Meir's statement just days before the Yom Kippur War: "Our situation has never been better" (Blum, 2003).

Conversely, the defeat and loss of territory severely damaged the honor of neighboring Arab countries' leaders, who did not accept Israel's legitimate existence. Failed attempts to erode the Israeli army and economy through the War of Attrition, coupled with unsuccessful political efforts to reclaim these territories, led Arab leaders to conclude that an all-out war was necessary to reconquer lost lands (Oren, 2002.(

In September 1970, Egyptian President Gamal Abdel Nasser died and was succeeded by Anwar Sadat, whom Israel perceived as a weak leader, further bolstering Israeli confidence (Rabinovich, 2004). In 1971-1972, Sadat attempted to initiate American-backed talks for interim arrangements leading to the return of Sinai to Egyptian sovereignty. However, the Israeli government, suspecting Egypt's intentions due to past hostilities, postponed negotiations and continued occupying Sinai (Shlaim, 2001).

Sadat, determined to regain the territories militarily, convinced Syria to participate and worked to strengthen the Egyptian army. He ordered his commanders to prepare operational plans for conquering Sinai or at least initiating a massive military move in part of Sinai to shock Israel (Herzog, 1975).

U.S. Secretary of State Henry Kissinger later described Sadat's war objectives: "At first, no one understood that Sadat was not aiming for victory, but rather for a change in the equilibrium in the negotiations he wanted to open" (Kissinger, 2003). Sadat estimated that the war's shock would allow both sides to show flexibility, which was impossible while Israel considered itself militarily superior.

Egypt and Syria began arming themselves and training with publicly declared intentions for extensive conquests. However, while Syria planned to conquer at least the entire Golan Heights, Egypt's strategy was more cautious, aiming to hold and fortify a strip up to 10 km wide east of the Suez Canal (Rabinovich, 2004).

In terms of international support, Egypt and Syria relied heavily on the Soviet Union, while Israel, after the French embargo of 1967, forged increasingly close ties with the United States (Shlaim, 2001). The eve of the war coincided with a period of détente between the superpowers, leading them to prioritize diplomatic channels where possible (Kissinger, 2003).

The "Yom Kippur War" (1973)

The Yom Kippur War, also known as the October War or Ramadan War, began on October 6, 1973, when a coalition of Arab states, led by Egypt and Syria, launched a surprise attack against Israel (Rabinovich, 2004). The conflict primarily unfolded in the Sinai Peninsula and Golan Heights, lasting until October 28, 1973, when a ceasefire took effect (Herzog, 1975).

The Arab offensive caught Israeli intelligence, headed by Major General Eli Zaira, off guard. Following Israel's decisive victory in the 1967 Six-Day War, the intelligence community had developed a concept known as "the Conception," which failed to anticipate the timing, intensity, and nature of the Arab attack (Bar-Joseph, 2005). Despite initial setbacks and heavy losses, the Israel Defense Forces (IDF) eventually managed to turn the tide, repelling Syrian forces and crossing the Suez Canal to encircle Egypt's Third Army (Morris, 2008).

The Yom Kippur War was characterized by the use of new combat tactics and technologies, reflecting a dynamic strategic approach, particularly by the Egyptian army (Gawrych, 1996). The conflict also served as a proxy battleground in the Cold War, with Arab countries receiving support from the Soviet Union while the United States backed Israel (Shlaim, 2001).

The war had far-reaching political consequences in Israel. It led to the establishment of the Agranat Commission, which primarily blamed the military echelon for the war's failures (Blum, 2003). This resulted in the removal of Chief of Staff David Elazar and Intelligence Chief Eli Zaira. The political fallout contributed to Prime Minister Golda Meir's resignation less than a year after the war and, coupled with an economic crisis, is considered a significant factor in the 1977 political upheaval in Israel (Shlaim, 2001).

"The Conception," as termed by the Agranat Commission, referred to the intelligence assessment formulated by the IDF's Research Division in 1971 regarding Egyptian and Syrian prerequisites for war (Bar-Joseph, 2005). This concept posited two main assumptions: first, that Egypt would not go to war without the capability to neutralize Israel's air force, and second, that Syria would only attack in conjunction with Egypt (Kahana, 2002).

From late 1972 and particularly in the days leading up to the war, there was a discrepancy between intelligence indicating Arab war preparations and the fact that Egypt had not yet achieved the presumed necessary air capability (Bar-Joseph, 2005). Key intelligence officials, including Research Division head Brigadier General Aryeh Shalev and Egypt analyst Lt. Col. Yona Bandman, adhered to "the Conception" until the morning of October 6, maintaining that Egypt and Syria did not intend to go to war (Kahana, 2002).

The failure to provide adequate warning had severe consequences when hostilities commenced. As Chief of Staff David Elazar had predicted, a war without warning and proper preparation was indeed catastrophic for Israel in its initial stages (Blum, 2003).

The Development of the Concept and its Influence

The roots of the perception that Egypt would not initiate war without air superiority can be traced back to late 1968. At a General Staff meeting on November 21, 1968, Air Force Brigadier General Benny Peled estimated that Egypt would make a grave error attempting to cross the Suez Canal without achieving air superiority (Bar-Joseph, 2005). Major General Ezer Weizman, former Air Force commander, concurred with this assessment.

Despite Egypt's construction of a formidable surface-to-air missile array in 1970, which threatened Israeli air supremacy in the canal sector, this fundamental perception persisted (Shlaim, 2001). The concept was further reinforced by intelligence from various sources, including high-level Egyptian informants, suggesting that Egypt itself believed it was unprepared for war without neutralizing Israel's air superiority (Kahana, 2002).

A significant boost to this perception came from Ashraf Marwan (codenamed "the Angel"), who began working for the Mossad in December 1970. Marwan provided minutes of high-level Egyptian and Soviet discussions, indicating that Egypt did not consider itself capable of war until it received sufficient long-range fighter jets (MiG-23s) and "deterrent weapons" (Scud missiles) from the Soviet Union (Black & Morris, 1991).

However, this Egyptian perception changed in the fall of 1972. On October 24, President Anwar Sadat convened the Supreme Council of the Armed Forces and announced that military measures must be taken "with what we have" (Rabinovich, 2004). Despite opposition from senior security officials, Sadat ordered preparations for war without waiting for additional weaponry. He appointed Ahmed Ismail Ali as Minister of War and accelerated preparations for crossing the Suez Canal (Operation Badr) (Gawrych, 1996).

Concurrently, Egyptian Chief of Staff Saad al-Shazali prepared a more limited plan, codenamed "High Minarets," which aimed to keep Egyptian forces within the protective range of their missile array (Pollack, 2002).

Ashraf Marwan informed the Mossad of this decision shortly after the meeting. On December 1, 1972, Israel's political-security cabinet ("Golda's Kitchen") met to discuss the issue. While most participants agreed that Egypt was incapable of launching a full-scale military operation in Sadat's proposed timeframe, Defense Minister Moshe Dayan warned that Egypt might "renew fire, local fire in the trench at the beginning of 1973" (Bar-Joseph, 2005).

Despite these warnings, the head of Military Intelligence adhered to "the Conception," almost entirely ruling out the possibility of a limited Egyptian military move. This adherence to a flawed concept would prove crucial in the lead-up to the Yom Kippur War (Kahana, 2002).

From early 1973, a discrepancy emerged between the Israeli Military Intelligence's (AMAN) basic premise regarding Egypt's inability to launch a full-scale war and the intelligence information indicating Egyptian preparations for such a conflict (Bar-Joseph, 2005). This gap became particularly noticeable in April 1973 when, alongside information about the arrival of a limited number of attack planes from Libya and Iraq, some Mossad sources and King Hussein of Jordan alerted Israel about Egypt's intention to launch a war in mid-May (Kahana, 2002).

An intelligence review from April 18 concluded that the arrival of new planes would not allow Egypt to proceed with a militarily sensible operation. However, research officers estimated that among three options open to the Egyptians - limited raids in Sinai, renewing the war of attrition, or a significant offensive - the latter was deemed most logical despite its risks (Rabinovich, 2004).

At a cabinet meeting on April 18, convened to discuss these intelligence alerts, the head of AMAN stated, "from a logical point of view - it would be a mistake for the Egyptians to start a war" (Bar-Joseph, 2005, p. 157). He assured that Israel would have advance warning of any canal crossing attempt. Other participants, including Mossad chief Zvi Zamir, the Chief of Staff, the Defense Minister, and Prime Minister Golda Meir, assessed the chance of war as higher and agreed on military preparations, codenamed "blue-white alertness" (Shlaim, 2001).

The absence of war in May and the lack of significant warnings during summer 1973 reinforced the notion that Egypt would not go to war before obtaining the required attack aircraft. This perception was clearly expressed by the head of AMAN at a General Staff meeting on September 17: "The Egyptians understand that they cannot present any real military threat today" (Blum, 2003, p. 143).

The influence of this concept reached its peak in a document issued by AMAN on the evening of October 5, 1973, less than a day before the Yom Kippur War began. Despite all signs indicating war preparations in Egypt and Syria, the document stated, "the likelihood that the Egyptians intend to resume fighting is low" (Bar-Joseph, 2005, p. 201).

At a special meeting of the General Staff on Yom Kippur eve, AMAN chief Eli Zeira described the emergency preparedness in Syria and Egypt as a result of fear of an Israeli attack. He concluded, "All the things I have listed do not change AMAN's basic assessment that the likelihood of a war initiated by Egypt and Syria is very low" (Kahana, 2002, p. 95).

Political decision-makers assumed on October 5 that war was not imminent, unaware that the head of AMAN's adherence to the concept had led to a failure to activate crucial warning measures (Herzog, 1975). This adherence to a flawed concept would prove catastrophic in the hours leading up to the Yom Kippur War.

According to the testimony of Zusia Knazar, the head of AMAN's Jordan branch, on October 6, 1973, he insisted that war would break out that day. He ordered his branch to go on high alert at 1:00 p.m., just an hour before the war actually began (Kuperman, 2012). However, even at the dawn of war, Bandman's and Zeira's adherence to the concept was not completely undermined. When Bandman was ordered to write a document summarizing the warning that war was imminent, he refused, instead writing: "We still estimate that the probability of war is low" (Bregman, 2016, p. 112).

The perceptual fixation among the security elite on the morning of October 6, 1973, was vividly illustrated by Michael Harari, commander of the Mossad's Caesarea Unit. Harari arrived at the Kirya (Israel's military headquarters) on Yom Kippur morning to present to Prime Minister Golda Meir the intelligence file codenamed "the agricultural equipment," which the Mossad had prepared for use in the event of war (Katz, 2010). Meir sent Harari to Defense Minister Moshe Dayan, who in turn sent him to Chief of Staff David Elazar.

In the Defense Minister's office, Harari encountered Yeshayahu Ravid, head of Dayan's office, who was examining telex messages and muttering, "It can't be, it's not possible, it goes against the concept." Ravid then asked Harari, "Do you believe him?" presumably referring to Ashraf Marwan, a senior Mossad source who had provided crucial intelligence (Black, 2016). This incident underscores the deep-rooted nature of the conceptual bias that had taken hold within Israel's intelligence community, even in the face of mounting evidence pointing to imminent war (Ginor & Remez, 2017).

Explanations for Adhering to the Concept

Following the Agranat Commission's conclusions, the term "conception" gained a negative connotation. The commission clarified that the root of the problem was not conceptual thinking itself, but rather the "stubborn adherence" of some senior AMAN officials to the perception that Egypt was not ready for war, despite abundant contradictory information (Bar-Joseph, 2005).

While the Agranat Commission didn't investigate all AMAN evaluators' complicity, later studies revealed that several research officers, particularly those in Branch 5 (Syria) led by Lt. Col. Avi Yaari, assessed that Syrian preparations indicated imminent hostilities. However, their opinions were overshadowed by the prevailing concept that Syria would only join a war initiated by Egypt (Kahana, 2002).

One explanation for adherence to a particular concept despite contrary evidence is Leon Festinger's "cognitive dissonance" theory. This theory posits that individuals strive for consistency between their perception of reality and behavior, often reducing contradictions by finding explanations that fit their existing perceptions (Festinger, 1957). In this case, key analysts sought explanations like "exercise" or "fear of an Israeli attack" to rationalize signs of impending war (Kruglanski & Webster, 1996).

Another explanation focuses on the "need for cognitive closure" theory. This theory suggests that individuals with a high need for cognitive closure tend to reach judgments quickly and avoid reopening discussions, even when their conclusions contradict reality. Such individuals often display authoritarian traits, emphasizing clarity and consistency while being impatient with alternative viewpoints (Kruglanski, 1990). The behavior patterns of analysts like Bandman and Zeira align with these characteristics, potentially explaining their reluctance to revise their assessments (Bar-Joseph & McDermott, 2008).

In an attempt to deflect responsibility, Eli Zeira claimed that the "conception" was planted by Ashraf Marwan, whom Zeira alleged was a double agent. However, subsequent investigations have discredited this claim (Black & Morris, 1991). The Agranat Commission determined that AMAN had received ample warning information in the days leading up to the war, which should have led to a heightened assessment of war probability (Shlaim, 2001).

The commission believed that these reports should have prompted AMAN to provide a strict assessment of imminent war, especially after receiving news of the Soviet evacuation. This failure to properly interpret and act on available intelligence remains a critical aspect of the Yom Kippur War's intelligence failure (Bregman, 2016).

Lessons Learned

The Agranat Commission's conclusion that "stubborn adherence" to the concept was the primary reason for the costly surprise necessitated finding solutions, which were mainly organizational (Bar-Joseph, 2005).

Until the Yom Kippur War, the Israel Defense Forces (IDF) monopolized intelligence evaluation in Israel. As part of the war's lessons, evaluation was decentralized, with assessment bodies established in the Mossad (Intelligence Division) and the Foreign Ministry (Political Research Department) (Kahana, 2002).

A control department (also known as "Ipcha Mistabra" or The Devil's Advocate Unit) was established in the IDF's Intelligence Division. Its role is to present alternative interpretations to the central assessment and question its basic assumptions (Kuperman, 2012).

Additionally, the Intelligence Division was separated from the Intelligence Corps, with the latter headed by a Chief Intelligence Officer subordinate to the head of AMAN (The Israeli Military Intelligenc). This change aimed to focus AMAN on strategic warning without the distraction of day-to-day logistics and organizational matters (Bregman, 2016).

Zvi Zamir, former head of Mossad, argued, "There is nothing wrong with a body like the IDF having a concept in the sense of an overall vision. The problem is not the concept itself but the adherence to it and the refusal to examine it in light of accumulated facts and data. A concept must not become sacred but must be dynamic, continuously tested, and updated" (Shlaim, 2001, p. 318).

However, researcher Ephraim Kam contends that these solutions do not adequately address the problem, arguing that each includes inherent failures that may sometimes exacerbate the situation (Kam, 1988). Kam suggests that organizational changes alone cannot fully prevent conceptual failures in intelligence analysis.

GLOBAL SHIFTS AND ISRAEL'S TRANSFORMATION: FROM THE YOM KIPPUR WAR TO THE EVE OF OCTOBER 7 (1973-2023)

Between 1973 and 2023, the world and the Middle East underwent profound transformations. This period witnessed a transition from modernity to postmodernity (Harvey, 1989), and a shift from a bipolar world dominated by the USA and USSR to a unipolar world led by the USA, with rising powers like Russia and China (Krauthammer, 1990). The late 20th century saw the emergence of "small wars" involving terrorist and guerrilla organizations against nation-states (e.g., Al Qaeda, ISIS, Hezbollah, Hamas) (Kaldor, 2012). The September 11, 2001 attacks serve as a metaphor and signpost for this historical change (The 9/11 Commission Report, 2004).

Concurrently, major powers engaged in invasions of sovereign countries: the USSR invasion of Afghanistan (1979) (Braithwaite, 2011), the US-led coalition in the Gulf War (1991) (Freedman & Karsh, 1993), the US invasion of Afghanistan (2001) (Fitzgerald & Gould, 2009), and the US-led invasion of Iraq (2003) (Ricks, 2006). These events reshaped the global geopolitical landscape and had far-reaching implications for international relations and security.

In the Middle East, Israel experienced significant events that altered its security and diplomatic position. These included two Palestinian intifadas (1987, 2000) (Pearlman, 2011), which were uprisings against Israeli occupation in the West Bank and Gaza Strip, often spilling into Israel proper. Israel was also involved in two wars in Lebanon: the First Lebanon War (1982) and the Second Lebanon War (2006) (Harel & Issacharoff, 2008). On the diplomatic front, Israel made significant strides, signing peace agreements with Egypt (1979) and Jordan (1994) (Shlaim, 2000), the Oslo Accords with the PLO (1993, 1995) (Beilin, 1999), and most recently, the Abraham Accords (2020) (Guzansky & Marshall, 2020). These agreements marked substantial shifts in Israel's relationships with its neighbors and the broader Arab world, reshaping the region's diplomatic and security dynamics.

THE "HAMAS IS DETERRED": THE DEVELOPMENT OF THE CONCEPT AND ITS INFLUENCE

The "Hamas is deterred" conception, which dominated Israeli strategic thinking in the years leading up to October 7, 2023, was a multi-faceted construct shaped by various factors and actors. This conception, deeply ingrained in Israel's military and political echelons, as well as in public discourse, was built on a combination of intelligence assessments, political narratives, and societal beliefs (Bergman & Hubbard, 2023).

The Israeli Military Intelligence Directorate (Aman) played a crucial role in formulating and reinforcing this conception. Their assessments, based on years of observing Hamas's behavior, suggested that the group was more interested in governing Gaza and improving economic conditions than in initiating a large-scale conflict with Israel (Kershner, 2023). The Israel Defense Forces (IDF) largely adopted this view, integrating it into their operational planning and resource allocation (Cohen, 2023).

Political leadership, particularly under Prime Minister Benjamin Netanyahu, also contributed significantly to this conception. Netanyahu's government frequently touted the effectiveness of Israel's deterrence strategy against Hamas, using it as evidence of their successful management of the security situation (Harel, 2023). This narrative aligned with Netanyahu's broader political agenda, which emphasized stability and economic growth over pursuing a comprehensive solution to the Israeli-Palestinian conflict (Pfeffer, 2021).

The pervasiveness of this conception in Israeli society can be attributed to several factors. Israel's economic success, particularly its booming high-tech sector, fostered a sense of security and superiority (Senor & Singer, 2011). This "Start-Up Nation" mentality, coupled with the relative calm in the years preceding October 7, led many Israelis to believe that the Palestinian issue, particularly in Gaza, was effectively managed (Shavit, 2013).

Moreover, this conception was intertwined with certain Israeli notions about Palestinians, particularly those in Gaza. There was a prevailing belief that economic incentives, such as work permits for Gazans in Israel, would be sufficient to maintain quiet (Thrall, 2017). This perspective, however, overlooked the deeper political and ideological motivations driving Hamas and other militant groups.

The shocking events of October 7, 2023, shattered this conception, exposing the dangers of such ingrained beliefs. The attack revealed a significant intelligence failure and a misreading of Hamas's intentions and capabilities (Bergman, 2023). It also highlighted the risks of complacency and the potential consequences of prioritizing short-term stability over addressing underlying conflicts.

In retrospect, the "Hamas is deterred" conception can be seen as a form of collective hubris, an overconfidence in Israel's military and technological superiority (Levy, 2023). It reflected a wider tendency in Western societies to underestimate the resolve and capabilities of non-state actors, particularly those driven by ideological or religious motivations (Byman, 2011).

The "Hamas is deterred" conception was deeply rooted in the overconfidence of Israel's intelligence community, particularly Aman (Military Intelligence Directorate) and Unit 8200, Israel's signals intelligence unit. This arrogance stemmed from their past successes and led to an over-reliance on technological solutions (Bergman, 2023). The Israeli military and decision-makers placed immense faith in high-tech defensive measures such as the separation wall, the "Roeh-Yoreh" (See-Shoot) system, and the "Tal Shamayim" (Sky Dew) aerostat (Gross, 2023). This techno-centric approach resulted in a dangerous neglect of human intelligence and the insights of field observers, creating blind spots in Israel's security apparatus (Kubovich, 2023).

The conception also erroneously focused Israel's attention northward, towards Lebanon and Hezbollah, viewing them as the primary threat. This misplaced focus diverted resources and attention away from the Gaza Strip, which was considered a managed threat (Issacharoff, 2023). Furthermore, when considering potential Palestinian attacks, the prevailing thought was that they would originate from or target the West Bank (Judea and Samaria), rather than Gaza (Khoury, 2023).

Another critical miscalculation was the classification of Hamas and Hezbollah merely as terrorist organizations, despite evidence suggesting they had evolved into more sophisticated "armies of terror." This underestimation of their capabilities and organization proved catastrophic on October 7 (Cohen, 2023). The Israeli establishment's failure to recognize this evolution reflected a broader inability to adapt threat assessments to changing realities on the ground.

The reliance on signals intelligence and cyber capabilities, while impressive, created a false sense of security. The belief that every communication could be intercepted and every movement tracked electronically led to a dangerous complacency. This over-reliance on technology came at the expense of traditional intelligence gathering methods and human analysis, which might have provided crucial context and insights that technology alone, could not capture (Melman, 2023).

THE YEAR BEFORE THE CATASTROPHE

In 2023, Israel experienced unprecedented internal turmoil centered concerning Prime Minister Benjamin Netanyahu's proposed judicial reforms, widely viewed as an attempt to weaken the country's democratic institutions. This "legal revolution" sparked massive protests across the nation, with hundreds of thousands of Israelis taking to the streets weekly to oppose what they perceived as a coup d'état against Israel's democratic foundations (Kingsley, 2023).

The protests united diverse segments of Israeli society, including a significant movement called "Brothers in Arms," composed of military reservists. Many reservists, including elite air force pilots, declared their intention to refuse voluntary service if the judicial overhaul proceeded, raising concerns about Israel's military readiness (Gross, 2023).

The controversy highlighted the growing influence of the national religious group in Israeli politics, represented by far-right figures such as Itamar Ben-Gvir, Bezalel Smotrich, and others in Netanyahu's coalition. Their push for more conservative policies and greater control over the West Bank fueled resistance from secular and liberal Israelis (Harel, 2023).

Key figures in the judicial reform push included Justice Minister Yariv Levin and Knesset Constitution Committee Chairman Simcha Rothman, who became focal points of public anger. The attempted dismissal of Defense Minister Yoav Gallant by Netanyahu, after Gallant warned about the security implications of the reforms, led to a particularly intense wave of protests.

These internal struggles were closely observed by Israel's enemies. Hamas, Hezbollah, and other hostile entities saw the democratic protests and internal divisions as signs of weakness in Israeli society. The refusal of some reservists to serve and the apparent distraction of the government from security matters were likely interpreted as opportunities by these groups (Issacharoff, 2023).

The protests reached a climax in July 2023 when the government passed a law limiting the Supreme Court's power to strike down government decisions. This move further intensified the divide within Israeli society and raised international concerns about Israel's democratic trajectory (Estrin, 2023).

Throughout this period, the focus on internal political struggles seemingly diverted attention from external threats. The preoccupation with the judicial reforms and the resulting societal rifts may have contributed to a reduced vigilance towards security threats, potentially creating vulnerabilities that Israel's enemies sought to exploit (Cohen, 2023).

This tumultuous political climate, marked by deep societal divisions and a perceived weakening of democratic institutions, formed the backdrop against which the October 7 attack occurred, raising questions about how these internal struggles might have affected Israel's preparedness and response capabilities.

THE HAMAS-LED ATTACK ON ISRAEL (OCTOBER 7, 2023)

In the early hours of October 7, 2023, Hamas launched an assault on southern Israel, capturing military bases, cities such as Sderot and Ofakim, as well as kibbutzim and moshavim. Some of these locations were abandoned after only a few hours, while others resisted for as long as 36 hours. For a limited period, Hamas achieved greater success in its invasion of Israel than any Arab army had in previous Israeli–Arab wars. During the attack, Hamas seized eight military bases in southern Israel, including the Navy base and the Gaza Division bases, among them the Erez crossing point (which Hamas destroyed) and the Nahal Oz post. Israeli soldiers were taken captive, killed, murdered, and butchered after capture, and female soldiers were subjected to rape (UN Human Rights Office, 2023).

The atrocities committed on October 7, including acts of rape, mutilation, and the burning alive of civilians, among them children (at the Nova Festival and in various kibbutzim), closely resembled the brutality of the ISIS organization in the Middle East (Ben-Israel, 2024). As Ben-Israel notes, the pre-modern massacres of ISIS occurred "during the second half of 2014, [when] the 'Islamic State' dominates a huge territory in northeastern Syria and western and northern Iraq" (Ben-Israel, 2018, p. 57). These actions by ISIS and the Islamic State should have served as a warning to Israeli political decision makers about the potential for future events in the region and the likelihood that Hamas would replicate ISIS's barbaric methods of conquest.

The Israeli Gaza Division lost control of the outpost when thousands of Palestinians — some of them unarmed — spontaneously raided nearby kibbutzim and abducted Israeli citizens into Gaza. During the invasion, Hamas employed a range of military and diversionary tactics: at sea, in the air, on land, and in cyberspace (where they disrupted technological systems near the separation wall). Hamas soldiers recorded the assault and occupation of southern Israel using GoPro cameras and broadcast the footage simultaneously on Facebook and Telegram (Gross, 2023).

The Hamas surprise attack on October 7, 2023, exposed critical failures in Israel's technological defenses, earning it the moniker of Israel's "second Yom Kippur" in terms of intelligence surprise (Bergman, R., & Hubbard, 2023). Hundreds of Hamas terrorists breached the border fence on multiple fronts, overwhelming IDF outposts and infiltrating nearby settlements with devastating efficiency (Kershner, 2023).

The IDF's first line of defense, designed to protect the border and adjacent settlements, catastrophically failed. This scenario validated Clausewitz's principle that concentrating sufficient forces at a specific point, with speed and surprise, can effectively destabilize an opponent (Clausewitz, 1832).

The IDF's defense strategy for Gaza relied heavily on a combination of technologies intended to prevent, warn of, or provide initial protection against incursions. This included a multi-layered fence system, observation posts, sniper positions, and infantry bases equipped with armored vehicles (Cohen, 2023). However, on October 7, Hamas terrorists rapidly penetrated these defenses using motorcycles and vehicles.

The IDF's response to the Hamas attack was critically delayed and inadequate. Many units designated to respond to such incursions failed to arrive promptly or at all. This breakdown in the response system left civilians in kibbutzim and other communities to fend for themselves for extended periods, some fighting against the attackers for over 24 hours (Kershner, 2023).

The fighting in the kibbutzim was particularly intense and prolonged. In Be'eri, for instance, residents and a handful of soldiers fought against Hamas militants from

Saturday morning until Sunday evening. Similar scenarios played out in Kfar Aza, Nir Oz, and other communities along the Gaza border. These civilian-led defenses, while heroic, highlighted the absence of timely military intervention (Harel, 2023).

The toll of the October 7 attack was devastating. According to official figures, approximately 1,200 Israelis were killed, including over 300 soldiers and security personnel. More than 240 people were taken hostage, including civilians and soldiers. The number of wounded exceeded 5,000, with many suffering severe injuries (Israel Ministry of Foreign Affairs, 2023).

The attack also revealed significant failures in Israel's intelligence and early warning systems. Despite some low-level warnings in the days leading up to October 7, the scale and coordination of the Hamas assault caught Israel's military and intelligence establishments completely off guard (Bergman, 2023).

This catastrophic event not only resulted in immediate loss of life and trauma but also shattered Israel's sense of security and raised serious questions about its military preparedness and intelligence capabilities. The aftermath has led to calls for a comprehensive reevaluation of Israel's defense strategies, particularly in relation to its border with Gaza (Cohen, 2023).

1. Key technological failures included:

First, Roeh-Yoreh" (See-Shoot) system: This remote-operated machine gun system, controlled by female observers, was disabled by Hamas drones (Gross, 2023). Second, Chief of Observations: The surveillance camera network, operated by female observers, was neutralized by anti-tank missiles (Kubovich, 2023). Third, Anti-drone measures: Despite the known threat of drones since at least 2010, the IDF failed to implement effective countermeasures (Melman, 2023). Fourth, Inductive fence: The advanced border fence, designed to alert upon contact, was breached in multiple locations without triggering an adequate response (Issacharoff, 2023). Fifth, Control system: Hamas successfully paralyzed the front command and control system in the Gaza Strip sector, raising questions about the flow of information to higher command levels (Bergman, 2023). The attack highlighted the dangers of over-reliance on technology and the neglect of traditional security measures. It also exposed gaps in manpower deployment, with reduced staffing due to the Sukkot holiday and Shabbat (Harel, 2023). This catastrophic failure of Israel's technological defenses underscores the need for a comprehensive review of security strategies and the integration of both high-tech and traditional defensive measures.

2. The failure of these leaders to correctly interpret the situation stemmed from several factors:

1. Overreliance on the "conception" that Hamas was deterred and focused on economic issues rather than military confrontation.

2. A dismissal of tactical warnings in favor of strategic assessments that discounted the possibility of a major Hamas offensive.
3. Confirmation bias, where incoming information was interpreted to fit existing beliefs about Hamas's intentions and capabilities.
4. Possible complacency due to the perceived effectiveness of Israel's technological defenses and intelligence gathering capabilities (Cohen, 2023).

One of the most troubling aspects of this intelligence failure was the disregard for warnings from women soldiers serving as observers along the Gaza border. In the hours leading up to the attack, several of these observers reported suspicious activity, including unusual gatherings of Hamas fighters and equipment near the border fence. However, their reports were largely ignored or dismissed by their superiors (Gross, 2023). This dismissal of front-line observations in favor of higher-level assessments represents a critical breakdown in the intelligence chain. The observers, with their direct view of the situation on the ground, were uniquely positioned to detect anomalies. The failure to heed their warnings highlights a systemic problem where tactical intelligence was undervalued compared to strategic assessments (Kubovich, 2023).

The events of October 6-7 reveal a multi-layered failure of imagination, interpretation, and action among Israel's top security officials. Their inability to piece together the available intelligence and recognize the impending threat led to one of the most significant security lapses in Israel's history (Melman, 2023).

TABLES COMPARING THE YOM KIPPUR WAR (1973) AND HAMAS'S ATTACK ON ISRAEL IN OCTOBER 7, 2023

Table 1. Basic information

Criterion	Yom Kippur War (1973)	2023 Hamas Attack + Israel-Hamas War
Dates/Period	October 6-25, 1973	October 7, 2023 - Ongoing
Location	Sinai Peninsula, Golan Heights	Southern Israel, Gaza Strip
Who against Who	Egypt and Syria (+Iraq and Jordan) versus Israel	Hamas (and other Palestinian militant groups) versus Israel
Names of War	Yom Kippur War, October War, Ramadan War	Operation Al-Aqsa Flood (Hamas), Operation Swords of Iron (Israel)
Number of Fronts	Two (Egyptian and Syrian)	One (Gaza Strip, with potential for expansion)

Table 2. Strategic and intelligence aspects

Criterion	Yom Kippur War (1973)	2023 Hamas Attack/Israel-Hamas War
Strategy	Surprise attack to reclaim lost territories	Surprise attack to break status quo, take hostages and to sow fear and terror among Israelis
Proxy Powers	Soviet Union (Egypt/Syria), United States (Israel)	Iran (Hamas), Various international supporters
Intelligence Failure	Misinterpreting enemy intentions, adherence to "The Concept"	Underestimating Hamas capabilities, adherence to deterrence concept
The Devil's Advocate	Insufficient challenging of prevailing assumptions	Apparent lack of effective contrarian analysis
Group Think	Belief in Israeli military superiority	Belief in effective deterrence of Hamas

Table 3. Leadership and military

Criterion	Yom Kippur War (1973)	2023 Hamas Attack/Israel-Hamas War
Prime Minister	Golda Meir	Benjamin Netanyahu
Key Ministers	Moshe Dayan (Defense)	Yoav Gallant (Defense)
Key Generals	David Elazar (Chief of Staff), Zvi zamir, director of Mossad, and Eli Zeira, head of Aman	Herzi Halevi (Chief of Staff), Aharon Haliva the head of Aman, Ronen Bar director of Shabak, David Barnea, director of Mossad
Army Weapons	Tanks, aircraft, artillery	Advanced missile defense, cyber capabilities, precision munitions

Table 4. Impact and aftermath

Criterion	Yom Kippur War (1973)	2023 Hamas Attack/Israel-Hamas War
Casualties	Israel: ~2,500-2,800; Arab forces: ~8,000-18,000	Israel: A total of 1,145 Israelis and foreigners were murdered, most of them babies, children, women, and the elderly. A total of 301 soldiers, 55 police officers, and 10 Shin Bet agents were involved in the operation; Palestinian: 11,000+ (numbers may have changed)
Vulnerable Areas Exposed	Northern Israel, Sinai defenses	Southern Israel border communities
Protests	Post-war protests in Israel	Worldwide protests both pro-Israel and pro-Palestinian
Foreign Visits After Attack	U.S. Secretary of State Henry Kissinger	U.S. President Joe Biden, various world leaders

continued on following page

Table 4. Continued

Outside Volunteers	Limited	International volunteers, especially from Jewish diaspora communities
Zeitgeist	End of post-Six Day War euphoria	Shattered sense of security, debate on Israeli-Palestinian conflict
Holy Days	Attack on Yom Kippur (Jewish) and Ramadan (Muslim) + Saturday	Attack near end of Sukkot (Jewish holiday) = Simchat Tora + Saturday
Heroism	Individual soldier stories of bravery	Civilian and military acts of heroism during and after the attack

FINDINGS

1. Persistent Conceptual Blindness: Both the 1973 Yom Kippur War and the 2023 Hamas attack demonstrate a recurring pattern of adherence to flawed conceptions. In 1973, it was "the Conception" that Egypt and Syria wouldn't attack without specific prerequisites. In 2023, it was the belief that "Hamas is deterred." These entrenched beliefs led to misinterpretation of intelligence and a failure to adequately prepare for potential attacks.
2. Overreliance on Technology: The 2023 attack revealed a dangerous overreliance on technological solutions for border security and intelligence gathering. This echoes the 1973 war's faith in Israel's air superiority. In both cases, the focus on technological advantages led to neglect of other crucial aspects of defense and intelligence.
3. Dismissal of Contradictory Intelligence: In both events, there was a pattern of dismissing or misinterpreting intelligence that contradicted the prevailing conceptions. In 1973, warnings from sources like King Hussein and Ashraf Marwan were downplayed. In 2023, reports from border observers were ignored. This highlights a persistent problem in intelligence analysis and decision-making.
4. Influence of Recent Success and Complacency: The 1973 war came after Israel's decisive victory in 1967, leading to overconfidence. Similarly, the relative calm and economic prosperity preceding the 2023 attack fostered a sense of security. This complacency contributed to the underestimation of threats in both cases.
5. Failure to Adapt to Evolving Threats: In both instances, there was a failure to recognize the evolving capabilities and strategies of adversaries. The 1973 war showed a misunderstanding of Egypt and Syria's military developments, while the 2023 attack revealed an underestimation of Hamas's capabilities and intentions.

6. Impact of Internal Political Climate: The political context played a significant role in both events. While the specifics differ, internal political considerations and divisions influenced military and intelligence assessments in both 1973 and 2023.
7. Psychological Factors in Intelligence Analysis: Both cases demonstrate the impact of cognitive biases, such as confirmation bias and the need for cognitive closure, on intelligence analysis. These psychological factors contributed to the misinterpretation of available information.
8. Organizational Structures and Communication: In both events, there were issues with how intelligence was communicated and acted upon within organizational structures. The 2023 attack particularly highlighted problems with the flow of information from tactical to strategic levels.
9. Lessons Not Fully Learned: Despite the reforms implemented after the 1973 war, including the establishment of devil's advocate units and diversification of intelligence assessment bodies, similar failures occurred in 2023. This suggests that organizational changes alone are insufficient to prevent intelligence failures.
10. The Human Element in Intelligence: Both events underscore the critical importance of human intelligence and analysis. The 2023 attack, in particular, highlighted the dangers of marginalizing human observations in favor of technological systems and high-level assessments.

These findings reveal striking parallels between the intelligence failures of 1973 and 2023, suggesting persistent challenges in intelligence analysis, military preparedness, and strategic thinking. They underscore the need for continuous reevaluation of intelligence practices, the importance of challenging prevailing conceptions, and the necessity of balancing technological advancements with traditional intelligence methods and human analysis.

CONCLUSION

Persistent Conceptual Blindness

Both the 1973 Yom Kippur War and the 2023 Hamas attack demonstrate a recurring pattern of adherence to flawed conceptions. In 1973, it was "the Conception" that Egypt and Syria wouldn't attack without specific prerequisites. In 2023, it was the belief that "Hamas is deterred." These entrenched beliefs led to misinterpretation of intelligence and a failure to adequately prepare for potential attacks.

Overreliance on Technology

The 2023 attack revealed a dangerous overreliance on technological solutions for border security and intelligence gathering. This echoes the 1973 war's faith in Israel's air superiority. In both cases, the focus on technological advantages led to neglect of other crucial aspects of defense and intelligence.

Dismissal of Contradictory Intelligence

In both events, there was a pattern of dismissing or misinterpreting intelligence that contradicted the prevailing conceptions. In 1973, warnings from sources like King Hussein were downplayed. In 2023, reports from border observers were ignored. This highlights a persistent problem in intelligence analysis and decision-making.

Influence of Recent Success and Complacency

The 1973 war came after Israel's decisive victory in 1967, leading to overconfidence. Similarly, the relative calm and economic prosperity preceding the 2023 attack fostered a sense of security. This complacency contributed to the underestimation of threats in both cases.

Failure to Adapt to Evolving Threats

In both instances, there was a failure to recognize the evolving capabilities and strategies of adversaries. The 1973 war showed a misunderstanding of Egypt and Syria's military developments, while the 2023 attack revealed an underestimation of Hamas's capabilities and intentions.

Impact of Internal Political Climate

The political context played a significant role in both events. While the specifics differ, internal political considerations and divisions influenced military and intelligence assessments in both 1973 and 2023.

Psychological Factors in Intelligence Analysis

Both cases demonstrate the impact of cognitive biases, such as confirmation bias and the need for cognitive closure, on intelligence analysis. These psychological factors contributed to the misinterpretation of available information.

Organizational Structures and Communication

In both events, there were issues with how intelligence was communicated and acted upon within organizational structures. The 2023 attack particularly highlighted problems with the flow of information from tactical to strategic levels.

Lessons Not Fully Learned

Despite the reforms implemented after the 1973 war, including the establishment of devil's advocate units and diversification of intelligence assessment bodies, similar failures occurred in 2023. This suggests that organizational changes alone are insufficient to prevent intelligence failures.

The Human Element in Intelligence

Both events underscore the critical importance of human intelligence and analysis. The 2023 attack, in particular, highlighted the dangers of marginalizing human observations in favor of technological systems and high-level assessments.

REFERENCES

Bar-Joseph, U. (2005). *The Watchman Fell Asleep: The Surprise of Yom Kippur and Its Sources*. SUNY Press.

Bar-Joseph, U., & McDermott, R. (2008). Personal Functioning Under Stress: Accountability and Social Support of Israeli Leaders in the Yom Kippur War. *The Journal of Conflict Resolution*, *52*(1), 144–170.

Beilin, Y. (1999). *Touching Peace: From the Oslo Accord to a Final Agreement*. Weidenfeld & Nicolson.

Ben-Israel, G. (2024 Accepted for publication). The Changing Nature of Armed Conflict in the 21st Century. In Bošković, M. (Ed.), *Diplomacy and Security*.

Ben-Israel, G. M. (2018). Telling a Story via Tumblr Analytics: Europe's Young Muslim Female Attraction to ISIS. *International Annals of Criminology*, *56*(1-2), 55–78. https://www.cambridge.org/core/journals/international-annals-of-criminology/article/telling-a-story-via-tumblr-analytics-europes-young-muslim-female-attraction-to-isis/FEA7F58A3960DD9F5A76346F8213F476

Bergman, R. (2023, October 20). "Israel's Spy Agencies Under Scrutiny After Hamas's Surprise Attack." *New York Times*.

Bergman, R. (2023, October 25). "Israel's Celebrated Spy Tech Failed to Detect the Hamas Attack." *New York Times*.

Bergman, R., & Hubbard, B. (2023, October 13). "How Israel's Mighty Military Missed a Hamas Attack." *New York Times*.

Betts, R. K. (1978). Analysis, War, and Decision: Why Intelligence Failures Are Inevitable. *World Politics*, *31*(1), 61–89.

Black, I. (2016). *Enemies and Neighbors: Arabs and Jews in Palestine and Israel*. Atlantic Books.

Black, I., & Morris, B. (1991). *Israel's Secret Wars: A History of Israel's Intelligence Services*. Grove Press.

Blum, H. (2003). *The Eve of Destruction: The Untold Story of the Yom Kippur War*. HarperCollins.

Braithwaite, R. (2011). *Afgantsy: The Russians in Afghanistan, 1979-89*. Oxford University Press.

Bregman, A. (2016). *Israel's Wars: A History Since 1947*. Routledge.

Byman, D. (2011). *A High Price: The Triumphs and Failures of Israeli Counter-terrorism*. Oxford University Press.

Clausewitz, C. V. (1832). On War. Translated by Michael Howard and Peter Paret, 1976. Princeton University Press.

Cohen, G. (2023, September 15). "Internal Strife and External Threats: Israel's Security Dilemma." *Israel Defense*. CopyRetryClaude can make mistakes. Please double-check responses.

Cohen, G. (2023, October 15). "IDF's Faulty Conception: How the Military Misread Hamas' Intentions." *Haaretz.*

Cohen, G. (2023, October 22). "Anatomy of an Intelligence Failure: From Conception to Catastrophe." *Israel Defense.*

Cohen, G. (2023, October 25). "Israel's Defense Doctrine Under Scrutiny After October 7." *Haaretz.*

Cohen, Y. (2023, October 20). "From Terror Groups to Terror Armies: Israel's Fatal Misreading of Hamas and Hezbollah." *Israel Defense.*

Estrin, D. (2023, July 24). "Israel passes law that critics say weakens its democracy." *NPR.*

Festinger, L. (1957). *A Theory of Cognitive Dissonance*. Stanford University Press.

Fitzgerald, P., & Gould, E. (2009). *Invisible History: Afghanistan's Untold Story*. City Lights Publishers.

Freedman, L., & Karsh, E. (1993). *The Gulf Conflict 1990-1991: Diplomacy and War in the New World Order*. Princeton University Press.

Gawrych, G. W. (1996). *The 1973 Arab-Israeli War: The Albatross of Decisive Victory. Combat Studies Institute*. U.S. Army Command and General Staff College.

Ginor, I., & Remez, G. (2017). *The Soviet-Israeli War, 1967-1973: The USSR's Military Intervention in the Egyptian-Israeli Conflict*. Oxford University Press.

Gross, J. A. (2023, March 6). Reservists Expand Protest, Say They Won't Volunteer if Judicial Overhaul Passes. *Times of Israel.*

Gross, J. A. (2023, October 11). Hamas filmed its massacres, and made sure the world would see them. The Times of Israel. https://www.timesofisrael.com/hamas-filmed-its-massacres-and-made-sure-the-world-would-see-them/

Gross, J. A. (2023, October 12). Amid intel failure, questions arise over efficacy of IDF's Gaza barrier. *Times of Israel.*

Gross, J. A. (2023, October 25). The Unheeded Warnings: Border Observers' Testimonies Reveal Missed Signals. *Times of Israel.*

Guzansky, Y., & Marshall, Z. A. (2020). The Abraham Accords: Immediate Significance and Long-Term Implications. *Israel Journal of Foreign Affairs, 14*(3), 379–389.

Harel, A. (2023, February 15). "The Rise of Israel's Religious Right." *Haaretz.*

Harel, A. (2023, October 8). "Netanyahu's Gaza Policy Collapses, Taking Israel's Sense of Security With It." *Haaretz.*

Harel, A. (2023, October 15). "The 30-Hour Battle for Kibbutz Be'eri." *Haaretz.*

Harel, A. (2023, October 20). "IDF's Top Brass: A Night of Fatal Misjudgments." *Haaretz.*

Harel, A., & Issacharoff, A. (2008). *34 Days: Israel, Hezbollah, and the War in Lebanon*. Palgrave Macmillan.

Harvey, D. (1989). *The Condition of Postmodernity*. Blackwell Publishers.

Herzog, C. (1975). *The War of Atonement: The Inside Story of the Yom Kippur War*. Weidenfeld & Nicolson.

Heuer, R. J. (1999). *Psychology of Intelligence Analysis*. Center for the Study of Intelligence, Central Intelligence Agency.

Issacharoff, A. (2023, September 1). "How Israel's Enemies View the Judicial Reform Crisis." *The Jerusalem Post.*

Issacharoff, A. (2023, October 9). Israel's Misdirected Focus: How Hezbollah Obsession Left Gaza Underestimated. *Times of Israel.*

Issacharoff, A. (2023, October 18). The Conception That Blinded Israel's Security Establishment. *Times of Israel.*

Jervis, R. (2006). Reports, Politics, and Intelligence Failures: The Case of Iraq. *The Journal of Strategic Studies, 29*(1), 3–52.

Kahana, E. (2002). Early Warning versus Concept: The Case of the Yom Kippur War 1973. *Intelligence and National Security, 17*(2), 81–104.

Kaldor, M. (2012). *New and Old Wars: Organised Violence in a Global Era*. Polity Press.

Kam, E. (1988). *Surprise Attack: The Victim's Perspective*. Harvard University Press.

Kam, E. (2024). From Yom Kippur to October 7: Lessons in Intelligence Failures. *Strategic Assessment*, *27*(1), 41–54.

Katz, Y. (2010). *A Voice Called: Stories of Jewish Heroism*. Gefen Publishing House.

Kershner, I. (2023, October 10). "Israel's Vaunted Intelligence Service Faces a Reckoning." *New York Times.*

Kershner, I. (2023, October 12). "As Hamas Attacked, Israeli Soldiers Were Absent." *New York Times.*

Kershner, I. (2023, October 15). "Israel's Intelligence Chiefs Face Scrutiny Over October 7 Failures." *Haaretz.*

Kershner, I. (2023, March 27). "Netanyahu Fires Defense Minister Who Opposed Judicial Overhaul." *New York Times.*

Khoury, J. (2023, October 14). "Israel's Strategic Blindness: Why Gaza Was Overlooked in Favor of West Bank Threats." *Haaretz.*

Kingsley, P. (2023, July 24). "Israel's Judicial Overhaul Crisis: What to Know." *New York Times.*

Kissinger, H. (2003). *Crisis: The Anatomy of Two Major Foreign Policy Crises.* Simon & Schuster.

Krauthammer, C. (1990). The Unipolar Moment. *Foreign Affairs*, *70*(1), 23–33.

Kruglanski, A. W. (1990). Lay Epistemic Theory in Social-Cognitive Psychology. *Psychological Inquiry*, *1*(3), 181–197.

Kruglanski, A. W., & Webster, D. M. (1996). Motivated Closing of the Mind: "Seizing" and "Freezing". *Psychological Review*, *103*(2), 263–283. PMID: 8637961

Kubovich, Y. (2023, October 18). "Israeli Military's Overreliance on Technology Contributed to Intel Failure, Officials Say." *Haaretz.*

Kubovich, Y. (2023, October 28). "When the Watchers Were Ignored: The Role of Border Observers in the October 7 Debacle." *Haaretz.*

Kuperman, R. D. (2012). The Yom Kippur War and Lessons for Military Intelligence. *Journal of Intelligence History*, *11*(2), 184–203.

Kuperwasser, Y. (2024). The October 7 Intelligence Failure: Preliminary Insights. *Israel Journal of Foreign Affairs*, *18*(1), 1–15.

Landau, E. B., & Pfeffer, A. (2017). Israel's Intelligence Assessment before the Yom Kippur War: Digging Deeper. *The Journal of Intelligence History*, *16*(2), 112–128.

Levy, Y. (2023, October 13). "From Hubris to Humiliation: How Israel's Military Superiority Crumbled." *Haaretz.*

Melman, Y. (2023, October 16). "The Hubris of Tech: How Israel's Intelligence Community Lost Touch with Reality." Haaretz.

Morris, B. (2008). *1948: A History of the First Arab-Israeli War.* Yale University Press.

Oren, M. B. (2002). *Six Days of War: June 1967 and the Making of the Modern Middle East.* Oxford University Press.

Pearlman, W. (2011). *Violence, Nonviolence, and the Palestinian National Movement.* Cambridge University Press.

Pfeffer, A. (2021). *Bibi: The Turbulent Life and Times of Benjamin Netanyahu.* Basic Books.

Pollack, K. M. (2002). *Arabs at War: Military Effectiveness, 1948-1991.* University of Nebraska Press.

Rabinovich, A. (2004). *The Yom Kippur War: The Epic Encounter That Transformed the Middle East.* Schocken Books.

Ricks, T. E. (2006). *Fiasco: The American Military Adventure in Iraq.* Penguin Press.

Senor, D., & Singer, S. (2011). *Start-up Nation: The Story of Israel's Economic Miracle.* Grand Central Publishing.

Shavit, A. (2013). *My Promised Land: The Triumph and Tragedy of Israel.* Spiegel & Grau.

Shlaim, A. (2000). *The Iron Wall: Israel and the Arab World.* W. W. Norton & Company.

Shlaim, A. (2001). *The Iron Wall: Israel and the Arab World.* W.W. Norton & Company.

Thrall, N. (2017). The Only Language They Understand: Forcing Compromise in Israel and Palestine. Metropolitan Books. Israel Ministry of Foreign Affairs. (2023, November 1). *"October 7, 2023 Hamas Terror Attack: The Toll."* National Commission on Terrorist Attacks upon the United States. (2004). *The 9/11 Commission Report.*

UN Human Rights Office. (2023, November 30). *UN experts condemn atrocities by Hamas, call for immediate release of all hostages*. https://www.ohchr.org/en/press-releases/2023/11/un-experts-condemn-atrocities-hamas-call-immediate-release-all-hostages

KEY TERMS AND DEFINITIONS

Analysis: The critical process of examining and synthesizing raw intelligence data to identify patterns, assess threats, and provide actionable insights to decision-makers.

Connecting the dots: The critical intelligence process of synthesizing disparate pieces of information into a coherent and actionable picture, which failed catastrophically in both 1973 and 2023 despite abundant warning signs.

Data: Raw intelligence information collected through various sources that require proper analysis and interpretation to transform into actionable intelligence, as demonstrated by the misinterpreted warning signs preceding both attacks.

Hamas-led attack on Israel: The October 7, 2023, surprise assault that breached Israel's Gaza border defenses, resulting in over 1,200 Israeli deaths and 240 hostages, representing one of the most significant intelligence failures in Israeli history.

Hubris: The dangerous overconfidence in technological superiority and past military successes that blinded Israeli leadership to emerging threats in both 1973 (after the 1967 Six-Day War victory) and 2023 (believing in the effectiveness of high-tech border defenses and deterrence strategies).

Intelligence: The systematic collection, analysis, and interpretation of information about potential threats or adversaries to inform decision-making and strategic planning.

The "Yom Kippur War" (73'): The October 1973 surprise attack by Egypt and Syria that caught Israeli intelligence completely off-guard due to adherence to flawed strategic conceptions, serving as a parallel case study to the 2023 intelligence failure.

The conception: A deeply entrenched strategic belief or assessment that becomes so institutionalized it prevents analysts from properly evaluating contradictory evidence, as demonstrated by Israel's pre-1973 belief that Egypt wouldn't attack without air superiority and the pre-2023 assumption that "Hamas is deterred."

The Devil's advocate: An institutionalized contrarian analysis unit established after the Yom Kippur War to challenge prevailing intelligence assessments and present alternative interpretations to prevent conceptual blindness.

Chapter 6
Countering Violent Extremism With Science and Intelligence:
Countering Violent Extremism

Tehmina Aslam
University of Lahore, Pakistan

ABSTRACT

After the Cold War ended in 1991, extremism surged, seeking expression through violence, while science advanced to embrace Artificial Intelligence (AI), creating intelligent machines. AI blends software and machines, with computers as a fundamental form and robots as advanced versions. In Pakistan, using robots in the field is both novel and costly. This study explores how science and intelligence can counter violent extremism at the induction, training, and action levels of terrorists and their organizations. Through structured, open-ended interviews with Punjab's counter-terrorism officials, the study found five key insights. First, a hide-and-seek dynamic exists between violent perpetrators and counter-efforts. Second, human intelligence remains vital, but AI's potential in thwarting terrorism is significant. Third, combining science and intelligence in AI offers an edge. Fourth, as extremism evolves, counter-terrorism must outpace it with advanced AI integration. Finally, cost remains a major barrier. The study concludes that upgrading counter-terrorism with AI is crucial.

DOI: 10.4018/979-8-3693-3522-2.ch006

INTRODUCTION

The Cold War (1945-1991) kept the world divided along ideological lines: pro-democracy and pro-communism. The conflict continued consuming lives and resources till the war in Afghanistan became unaffordable economically by the Soviet Union under the banner of the Union of Soviet Socialist Republics (Bobbitt, 2002). The United States and allies won the war.

In 1991, the end of the Cold War not only liberated people from the ideology-based global division, but it also drew people's attention to their local parochial submerged disagreements (Sassen, 1996; Jones, 2002). Especially in the developing countries, many ethnic groups woke up to the reality that, without their will, their ancestral lands had been divided along political or religious lines to carve out new countries, which had joined the United Nations in or after 1945. This is how the post-1991 era got awash with claims based on irredentism. With that, history witnessed a conflict within a country (such as the Yugoslavia war in 1991-2001), a direct conflict between two countries (Iraq-Kuwait conflict in 1990) or a conflict between an ethnic group and a country (such as Kurds who have been trying to reclaim their ancestral land from Iran, Iraq, Syria and Turkey). Since then, the Middle East has been a cesspool of conflicts, under one ruse or the other. The conflict may die under an international or regional assertiveness, but it donates life in the meantime to extremism and violence.

Similarly, after 1991, the disappearance of the global ideological conflict gave space to local ideological conflicts, especially when the term ideology personified religion, to which Islam was no exception (Hasnat, 2008). Islamic fundamentalist groups emerged not only to claim victory in repulsing the pro-communist ideology to its point of origin, but also to assert their version of Islamic ideology on their native lands (Synnott, 2009; Akram, 2012). Pakistan bore the brunt of the latter phenomenon, especially when the proclaimed version of the Islamic ideology declared its exclusiveness, to give rise to a sectarian conflict, called the Sunni-Shia conflict (Jones, 2002; Kapur, 2002; Rashid, 2013). The conflict may vanish under the State's domineering assertion, but it bestows life in the meantime on extremism and violence.

Related to violent extremism, Pakistan's experience is that, after 1991, Pakistan has been experiencing extremism and violence rolled into one, violent extremism, which has been an instrument of policy in the hands of militants (Bobbitt, 2008). The gory incident of 9/11 added fuel to the proverbial fire. The war on terrorism began, and Pakistan contributed to it (Khan, 2013). Several militant groups sought birth both inside Pakistan and in the northwestern tribal belt bordering Afghanistan. Pakistan's loss of control over the tribal belt exacerbated the calamity. Pakistan had to develop a counter-terrorism strategy, which was protected by law and supported by technology, which cost Pakistan profoundly in terms of dollars (Nadeem, 2012).

The year 2004 witnessed the first missile strike (launched by the forces of the United States stationed in Afghanistan) through a drone on the Wana (South Waziristan) in the tribal belt of Pakistan in June and in its wake the same year witnessed the first suicide vest blown up to consume lives (Harrison, 2009; Almeida, 2012). Many analysts tried to establish a link between drone strikes and terrorism (Chisti, 2012; Hassan, 2012; Jahangir, 2013). The suicide vest had been brought from Iraq. Afterwards, suicide blasts became a norm, part of global suicide terrorism (Pape & Feldman, 2010). In August 2021, all foreign forces left Afghanistan after handing over power to the Afghan Taliban.

Pakistan had to buy metal detectors and walk-through gates to detect the presence of a suicide bomber. Similarly, Pakistan had to raise a counter-terrorism department which would fight against militant groups and which could defuse improvised suicide vests and bombs, though Pakistan still relies on human intelligence to thwart an act of violent extremism manually by engaging militants in combat (Malik, 2008; Husain, 2012). Recently, Pakistan has developed its drones to get an aerial view of the target area inhabited by militants. There is a scope for the application of science and intelligence, both security and artificial intelligence, to counter violent extremism.

RESEARCH QUESTION

The study aimed to understand in what ways science and intelligence can be used to counter rampant violent extremism at the level of induction, training, and action of a terrorist and a terrorist organization in South Punjab (Pakistan), especially after 9/11.

Sub-Research Questions

The objectives of the study were four:

1. To find out how science and intelligence can be used to counter violent extremism at the level of the induction of an individual into the extremist ideology and an extremist militant organisation?
2. To understand what measures science and technology can take to interfere in the training of a would-be terrorist who could also be a suicide bomber?
3. To identify the role of science and technology in thwarting the actions of a terrorist and a terrorist organization promoting violent extremism?

4. To analyse the scope for the Artificial Intelligence used by the security forces, especially the police in South Punjab (Pakistan), in countering violent extremism?

RESEARCH METHODOLOGY

Research is a planned inquiry undertaken to evaluate a given event closely (Blaster, 2004). Research also constructs new knowledge, which is not known before, and which applies to real life (Gay, 1990). To do this research, out of the two methods of research (qualitative and quantitative), the qualitative method was chosen to generate and analyse the collected data (Bordens & Abbott, 2008). Qualitative research is interpretivist in nature, and it is subject to the interpretation of the researcher (Lavrakas, 2008). Interviews of officials of counter-terrorism and related departments were conducted (Weiss, 1995). Interviews of those who were rehabilitated from the influence of violent extremism (especially in South Punjab) were also conducted.

In this study, secondary sources of data collection were used (Walliman, 2011). To do that, books and journals were read, and notes were taken down (Adler & Clark, 2008). A literature review was also done to find out not only the contrasting themes but also gaps in the literature to be filled (Best & Kahn, 2006). It was done to make the paper worth reading for the readers and be productive for the policymakers.

RESEARCH LIMITATIONS

As the topic is quite broad, the area under study would be limited to meeting the aim of the study, which is limited to understanding the ways science and intelligence can be used to counter rampant violent extremism at the level of induction, training and action of a terrorist and a terrorist organization in functional in South Punjab (Pakistan) especially after 9/11. The cut date of 9/11 has been considered for the sake of brevity. The reason is that Pakistan had been facing militancy coming from Afghanistan after the end of the Cold War in 1991. Moreover, militants from South Punjab are mostly the ex-fighters (or their ideological descendants) who fought the Afghan war against the Soviet forces from 1979 to 1989. Before 9/11, they were active in the realm of sectarianism (Sunni-Shia conflict), but after 9/11, they joined hands with al-Qaeda and the Taliban to launch attacks on Pakistan (Rana & Gunaratna, 2007; Zaidi, 2013).

LITERATURE REVIEW

In simple words, extremism is related to thought (or belief), whereas violence is linked to behavior (or action). Extremism is linked to one's religious, social, political, ethnic, or racial thoughts or beliefs, whereas violence is linked to one's behavior or actions in society (Koomen & Pligt, 2016). To elaborate, extremism can fuel violence. Motivation is considered an important prelude to violence. Fields from which an extremist derives motivation are mostly religious beliefs and political thoughts, or a mix of both. These could also be ethnic or racial ones. (Taji-Farouki & Nafi, 2004) Moreover, one theme can motivate an individual to do an extremist act in a different field. For instance, religiously motivated individuals may become politically extremist. Similarly, a racially motivated individual can express their extremist sentiments socially (Ahmed, 2012). Examples of violent extremists include Islamic fundamentalists, far-right racists, ethnic extremists, and political activists (Rogers, 2016). They usually air their violent narratives to persuade people who are vulnerable and marginalized in society or the political system. Terrorists seek moral justification for their acts. It could be the right to self-determination in the political realms, it could be ethnic nationalism in the realm of irredentism, and it could be *jihad* (a holy war) to achieve certain ends (Woodward, 2010).

The word countering entails both prevention and intervention methods (approaches), which are meant for minimizing the risk of violence by extremist (militant) groups resorting to violence (Boucek, 2008). Pakistan made dialogue part of its counter-terrorism strategy to give terrorists a fair chance to lay down their weapons (Shapiro & Fair, 2010). The strategy followed by the program of de-radicalization and offering them space to join the mainstream (Noor, 2013). Nevertheless, this strategy could not work effectively and sufficiently. The reason was simple: extreme violence could be individuals who are rigid in their thoughts.

Countering requires a multidisciplinary approach or solution to extreme violence (Boucek, 2008). Science and technology are part of the multifaceted approach to counter violent extremism, especially when the threat emanates from stolen nuclear weapons in the case of smart nuclear devices, improvised conventional bomb (or nuclear bomb) explosions, and radiological dispersion devices (Dunn & Perry, 2008).

The use of science and intelligence stands at the crossroads of multiple disciplines governing the world. Science and intelligence can both work in unison. Both can be used to intervene at the juncture where an individual desires or tries to join an extremist group, when the terrorist group is known and designated.

Science is already serving the counter-terrorism efforts of human beings. Pakistan is taking such measures (Rafique & Manan, 2019). For instance, a developing country such as Pakistan, as observable in daily life, has been using metal detectors, walkthrough gates, and fingerprint recognition facilities to identify or recognize an individual suspected of violent extremist affiliations or activities. Similarly, Pakistan has acquired the ability to run drones and take aerial images of suspected hideouts of militants (Siddiqui, 2023). Furthermore, though at a limited level, Pakistan has also been using forensic science facilities such as DNA fingerprinting and electronic face detection (facial recognition system) to recognize a suspected individual (Mateen & Tariq, 2019; Asif, 2023). For spying, Pakistan lacks electronic facilities. Instead, Pakistan relies mostly on human intelligence, which could be an insider who could tip security forces off, or after extracting information from a captured militant. Nevertheless, Pakistan's premier spy agency acquired software to tap into the internet traffic via underwater cables to have a digital espionage capacity, in the form of a huge data collection tool (News Desk, 2015).

Nevertheless, AI is the best example of a combination of scientific innovation and applied intelligence, particularly when talking in the context of automating decision-making and pattern analysis. In its curx AI is a manifestation of the intelligence characterized by man-made machines run by man-made software (Russell & Norvig, 2010). The AI is a product of computer science with the ability to perform specific cognitive tasks such as image recognition, behavior prediction, and pattern detection. However, in totality, AI does not emulate humans completely; rather, it replicates human-like functions deductively rather than inductively in specially well-defined domains (Chen & Chen, 2022). The AI is a field that combines computer science with machines (called robots) to perform the assigned work, including translation from one language to another and interpreting languages, which is otherwise a human faculty to do (Russell & Norvig, 2010). To elaborate, software is installed in either a computer or a computer-controlled robot to perform assigned tasks, which could be on par with those of an intelligent human being.

The AI is used in different ways. For instance, the AI is used to collect data and analyse it (Schroeter, 2020). The speed of the AI is more than that of human beings, but its way to do so is dictated (installed through software) by human beings. The AI is meant to assist human beings in saving their time and energy. The AI has shown its utility in certain sports such as chess, badminton, and Scrabble, competing with human beings. Similarly, the AI has made its mark in the virtual world of gaming on computers (Russell & Norvig, 2010).

In the realm of countering violent extremism, AI can be used to recognize patterns and navigate the online noise which are specific to violent extremism (Schroeter, 2020). If data has to be analysed, what factors lead an individual to resort to violent extremism or get affiliated with one such extremist group, the AI is the best tool to analyse the data. Similarly, the AI can be used to study traits in criminals in jails to find out the chances of relapsing into crime once they get released to restart terrorist acts. Similarly, the AI can be used to study the traits found common amongst individuals resorting to violent extremism. There is potential for the application of AI to counter terrorism online (United Nations, 2021; Rashid, 2023).

Nevertheless, the AI comes with limitations. For instance, the AI simulates human intelligence fed through software, and not beyond that. Moreover, the AI may not sound an alarm if individuals are radicalized online (Schroeter, 2020). Similarly, terrorists can also use the AI against a state to achieve their terrorist objectives (McKendrick, 2019).

DISCUSSION

In this study, two cities of South Punjab (Pakistan) were focused on: Jhang and Sargodha, and interviews with rehabilitated terrorists and counter-terrorism experts were conducted. Jhang and Sargodha remained a focus of attention, as religious extremism encompassing sectarian violence had been rampant here since the early 1990s. To address the aim of the study, the discussion section is divided into five parts.

1. Countering the Induction of an Individual

As the word "countering" includes methods (approaches), spanning both prevention and intervention, to minimize the risk of terrorism (Boucek, 2008), any method (or approach) to minimize the chances of the induction of an individual into an extremist religious ideology would lower down the potential for resorting to violent extremism. It is now known that various factors such as poverty, ignorance, illiteracy, bigotry, marginalization, and mental aberration make an individual, especially at a young age, amenable to joining an extremist ideology engendering an extremist militant organization.

Anwar Raheem (a former terrorist, who was rehabilitated to normal life) says:

I was ignorant of the word sectarianism. I was driven to this nuisance by my friends. After I dropped out of school in the 9th class, my company of friends convinced me to attend the gatherings of a local religious organization. Gradually, I became a regular visitor and attendee. Initially, I felt mental satisfaction by listening to the sermons, but later on I got involved in the activities of the organization bordering on violence as a religious duty.

At a young age, seeking a purpose in life has been one of the major driving factors to resorting to religious extremism and violence. This point single-handedly remained a major challenge to counter violent extremism in South Punjab. Besides fighting against sectarian ideology-driven militants, the Punjab's counter-terrorism department also initiated plans to check the induction of the youth into extremist militant organizations. One of the first methods used was human intelligence by deploying hired informers working under various garbs to penetrate extremist organizations. Informers did two things: first, they foretold any extremist militant planning or attack, and second, they alerted on new entrants, along with supplying information on their whereabouts.

Ansar Dar, an official of the counter-terrorism department, says:

Years ago, when we started operations, it took us some time to penetrate the sectarian organizations inclined to militancy to understand their working and planning, besides forecasting their next step and even target. However, we did it successfully through human intelligence, which saved not only the lives of our people (working on counter-terrorism) but also our time. Informers informed us about new entrants who could be potential offenders in the future. We neutralized them socially. Retrospectively, I can say, if we had better scientific facilities such as CCTV cameras, aerial drones, and geo-fencing services, we could have performed better and earlier.

Whereas the importance of human intelligence is undeniable, when an informer penetrates a given organization, the availability of the help of scientific gadgets can enhance the work of the informer manifold. It simply means that human intelligence (in the shape of inside informers) is important, but equally important are scientific equipment to complement the informer or to verify the information being provided.

Compared to South Punjab, Central Punjab is better managed in terms of sectarian or extremist violence. In Lahore, the main city of Central Punjab, a project named Punjab Safe Cities Authority began its functioning, offering surveillance of the city through its services, including CCTV cameras and deterrence to crime and violence through the collection of electronic evidence in order to create the fear of being accountable. The project was established under the Punjab Safe Cities Ordinance 2015 to establish, develop, and maintain an integrated command, control, and communication system for the police in major cities of the province of Punjab for public safety (Punjab Safe City Authority, 2015). The success of this project in Lahore has convinced the authorities to expand it to other cities of Central Punjab and also to the cities of South and Northern Punjab, to cover the main cities of the province of Punjab.

2. Interfering in the Training of a Would-be Terrorist (or a Suicide Bomber)

Whereas extremism is linked to one's thoughts or beliefs, violence is linked to one's acts in society (Koomen & Pligt, 2016). Terrorists seek moral justification for their acts, especially taking refuge in religion in the name of a holy war (Woodward, 2010). Causing interference in the training of a potential terrorist (or a suicide bomber) is more effective than other methods used to counter extremism. Training relies on three ingredients: a trainer, arms, and a training place. The challenge comes from neighbouring foreign lands such as Afghanistan, where extremist organizations have sought sanctuaries and from these organizations get modern weapons, which render local law enforcement agencies incapable of fighting back. For instance, a sectarian Sunni organization called Sipahe Sahaba Pakistan (SSP), founded by Maulana Haq Nawaz Jhangvi and cohort on 6 September 1985 in Jhang (Punjab) to turn Pakistan into a Sunni state and suppress the influence of the Shia sect, developed its link with the Tehrek-e Taliban Pakistan (TTP) and al-Qaeda (Haqqani, 2013). Pakistan's security forces faced stiff resistance in rooting out the SSP because of its associates like the TTP and al-Qaeda embracing a similar sectarian ideology and offering training, arms, and a place (for training and hiding) to the SSP across the border in the lawless region of Afghanistan. A subsidiary challenge emanated from improvised devices ready to explode, mostly as suicide vests worn by suicide bombers.

Zubair Alam, an official of the counter-terrorism department, says:

A major challenge to Pakistan's internal peace comes from the lawless region of Afghanistan, which is a sanctuary of criminals and fugitives selling drugs to get money and buy weapons from black markets in Central Asia. These weapons are used against Pakistan's security forces inside Pakistan. To add fuel to the proverbial fire, the US and NATO forces left behind light weapons intact while vacating Afghanistan in mid-2021. The criminals have got hold of that stock and have been offering training to Pakistan's sectarian groups like Sipahe Sahaba Pakistan and other extremist groups working under the umbrella of Tehreek-e-Taliban Pakistan.

In the past, Pakistan launched military operations such as Zarb-e-Azb to quell terrorism in the border area lining Afghanistan, but Pakistan could not go beyond the border. Further, Pakistan raised bomb defusing units to meet the challenge of improvised bomb explosions. All such efforts could not yield results to quell the wave of terrorism.

Compared to the past, on June 23, 2024, Pakistan has initiated operation Azm-e-Istehkam and has been using drone technology to get access to the border areas with rugged terrain, inaccessible easily to monitor for potential hideouts and training camps in Afghanistan (Basit, 2024). Although this venture has raised the question of respecting or not the border sanctity of a sovereign Afghanistan, the debate is open to conclusion: whether or not Pakistan has a legitimate right to peace being disrupted by terrorists seeking refuge in Afghanistan. Nevertheless, aerial drones have helped Pakistan security forces to get images of hideouts and training camps in Afghanistan (Baghwan, 2022).

Pakistan still lacks technology encircling and preventing a suicide bomber from exploding. A provision of any such technology can help Pakistan fight against the menace of suicide bombing better.

3. Thwarting the Action of a Terrorist or a Terror-Sponsoring Organization

Hitherto, Pakistan has used various tactics to control terrorism. Prime importance has been given to thwarting the action of a terrorist or a terrorist organization bent on promoting violent extremism. For instance, to give terrorists a chance to lay down their weapons and join the normal tenor of life, Pakistan made dialogue part of its counter-terrorism strategy (Shapiro & Fair, 2010). For those who assented to dialogue and subsequent harmony to join the mainstream of society, they were offered a program of de-radicalization (Noor, 2013). Nevertheless, this strategy remained successful partially, as it could not entice most deviants to normalcy.

Abdul Kareem (a former extremist, who assented to rehabilitation) says:

In the company of my religious brethren, every thorn in life was pleasant. I never lamented a day for joining the TTP [Tehreke-Taliban Pakistan], because it aimed at turning Pakistan into an Islamic State. The Islamic State was the goal of the formation of Pakistan.

When brains are washed for achieving an ideal, the unripe youth becomes the first victim. Though the concept of an Islamic State has been defined in the Constitution of Pakistan (as an Islamic Republic), the influence of the Middle East refuses to spare Pakistan. The Pakistanis are impressed by radical Islamic movements in the Middle East; they are refusing to consider the meaning of an Islamic Republic equal to the concept of an Islamic State (Ziring, 2014). This is where all efforts to rehabilitate religious extremists conceptually fail.

Usman Alvi, an official of the counter-terrorism department, says:

In the 1960s, Pakistan started sending its labour force, which was unskilled or semi-skilled, to the Middle East, enjoying the presence of oil under its soil. The semi-illiterate labour class sent back not only foreign currency to enhance Pakistan's foreign exchange, but they also sent back the Middle-Eastern concepts of Islamic radicalism. It was after 9/11 that the Middle East decided to reform itself to embrace democracy and capitalism, thereby opening its society to the world. This sudden change of strategy has backfired in producing reactionary elements resisting the change. Some of such elements are also influencing Pakistani society to resist any progressive change.

On the one hand, there is a down pouring of radical ideas from the Middle East failing Pakistan's efforts to counter radical thoughts and terrorism, whereas on the other hand, there are all out efforts to de-radicalize the Middle East by introducing reforms, infusing liberalism and creating respect for science and technology (Palmer & Holtz, 2023). Pakistan has been waiting patiently for the trickle-down effect of democratic liberalism and associated respect for science and technology (shunning archaic, unqualified thoughts and unsubstantiated rituals) being embraced by most

Middle Eastern countries as a norm. That is, unless science and technology take root in Pakistani society, all efforts to thwart terrorism or acts of terrorists would meet partial success.

4. Scope for Artificial Intelligence to Counter Violent Extremism

Competition between religious extremists to disturb the even tenor of life, to impose their version of ideology, and for a peace-loving state to keep up with homeostasis is continuing. Man has deployed science to defeat bigotry and the consequent terrorism. Science as a counter-terrorism strategy is a fascinating idea. With the advent of Artificial Intelligence (AI), efforts of science to fight against terrorism have been bolstered (United Nations, 2019). Pakistan is no exception to this development (Rafique & Manan, 2019). The scope of applying AI to counter violent extremism is immense, especially in a developing country like Pakistan.

Sardar Naveed Khan (a former terrorist, who assented to rehabilitation) says:

During the war on terror, the major technology that annoyed us, who were in a hideout in a region of Afghanistan bordering Pakistan, was drones laden with missiles hovering over our heads. The threat of imminent death terrified us, even though we otherwise were ready to fight to the death. Drone strikes caused deaths, and we lost our comrades and their families who had taken shelter alongside.

Using drones and associated technology to locate and destroy an enemy target has drawn attention from counter-terrorism experts in Pakistan to the importance of science-based informers and executors, instead of overly relying on human-based exploits. Consequently, starting from basics, Pakistan has deployed metal detectors, walkthrough gates, and thumb-mark recognition facilities (biometrics) to recognize an individual to sift through human data to distinguish conformists from non-conformists.

AI has revolutionized the world in the realm of technology with its ripple effect spreading on all spheres, be as security, peace, surveillance, and even geopolitics. When talking particularly about surveillance AI systems for such purposes are under the phase of development, yet their partial use has been executed and materialized to monitor public spaces for suspicious behavior through video feeds, facial recognition, and pattern analysis. Other than monitoring, AI surveillance systems are widely used for threat identification and mitigation. In countries like China and the US, AI-powered CCTV systems are used to flag suspicious individuals posing a threat. However, such systems heavily rely on datasets and databases like the Global Terrorism Database (GTD) and Interpol facial image datasets (INTERPOL, n.d.; Mozur, 2020)

In a developing country like Pakistan, the scope for using AI is immense. Pakistan has started using (though at a limited level owing to scarcity of resources) the electronic fact detection/recognition system to identify a suspect (Mateen & Tariq, 2019; Asif, 2023). Similarly, the AI can analyze patterns in data obtained from phone calls, social media activity, and other information-gathering sources to predict probable terrorist attacks (Mathur, Broekaert & Clarke, 2024).

Ansar Dar, an official of the counter-terrorism department, says:

Artificial Intelligence (AI) can be best used for surveillance and monitoring a crowd for any anomaly. Monitors (and cameras at public places) run by relevant software can spot suspicious behavior and objects to rule out any potential threat. Some foreign countries have been using AI for risk analysis, in case human assessment fails. Another area is cybersecurity. The AI can identify gaps which make a system prone to cyber-attacks from hostile forces called cyber criminals, whether from within or outside the country, to spoil a system or to steal data.

Nevertheless, the downside of the scope for the use of AI is that it can also fall into the hands of terrorists who would use it to facilitate their cause and spoil the counter-terrorism efforts of a country (Nelu, 2024).

5. Cost-effectiveness of Artificial Intelligence – A Major Inhibitory Factor

Though the term Artificial Intelligence (AI) was coined by computer scientist John McCarthy of Stanford University in 1956, AI has taken the world by storm in recent years. Primarily, the AI is a man-made software operating or running a machine on its own. Developing software and then constructing a machine are both costly, at least presently, when the field of AI is both expanding and competitive.

Usman Alvi, an official of the counter-terrorism department, says:

The counter-terrorism department in Pakistan may seek the help of office-based AI and not the AI function in the field. The reason is that using AI in the field is quite costly. A time may come when such robots are produced in a large number to make them cheap to buy.

For a developing country like Pakistan, cost-effectiveness is a major concern. High price of the AI is a major inhibitory factor when drawing a comparison between using the AI in an office for collecting and processing data and deploying a robot in the field for accomplishing desired tasks (Data Solutions, 2024). The same point is applicable to counter-terrorism.

The discussion above reflects how cost is a driving factor, making it an urgency for cost-benefit analysis. This is so because if, in particular, we talk about an AI surveillance system, it costs between $5,000 to $100,000. Moreover, integration of AI has the potential to further increase the cost. This high cost comes with benefits like round-the-clock monitoring, faster threat identification, and reduced human resource demands

CONCLUSION

Science and Artificial Intelligence (AI) can be used to counter violent extremism at the level of induction of an individual into a terrorist outfit, training of a would-be terrorist (or a suicide bomber), and thwarting the action of a terrorist or a terror-sponsoring organization. Further, the scope for the application of AI is both wide and immense in counter-violent extremism. However, for a developing country like Pakistan, the main limiting factor is the price of the AI. Pakistan can use a cost-effective AI device inside offices, and Pakistan may not use a costly device like robots, which can work in the field, even if against terrorism. In the future, when competition between market forces may bring the price down, Pakistan may buy and use AI in its efforts to counter terrorism.

Therefore, this study identifies three core forms of intelligence contributing to counter-terrorism: (1) Security Intelligence, such as surveillance, informants, and investigative training; (2) Biological or Human Intelligence, referring to human decision-making and instinct; and (3) Artificial Intelligence, involving software-based tools capable of learning from data and recognizing patterns. These forms often work in tandem for example, AI can flag a threat, security intelligence can investigate it, and human reasoning can decide the final action.

REFERENCES

Adler, E. S., & Clark, R. (2008). *Invitation to Social Research.* Taj Press.

Ahmed, K. (2012). *Sectarian War: Pakistan's Sunni-Shia Violence and its Links to the Middle East.* Oxford University Press.

Akram, M. (2012). "Terrorism and the Taliban." *DAWN.* Retrieved from: https://www.dawn.com/news/756516/terrorism-and-the-taliban [Last accessed: 27 January 2024].

Almeida, C. (2012). "Behind the Drones Debate." *DAWN.* Retrieved from: https://www.dawn.com/news/752993/behind-the-drones-debate [Last accessed: 28 January 2024].

Asif, C. (2023). "Punjab Police Launch AI-Powered System to Track Criminals." *DAWN.* Retrieved from: https://www.dawn.com/news/1766810 [Last accessed: 29 January 2024].

Basit, A. "Pakistan's Azm-e-Istehkam Operation: Old Wine in a New Bottle?" *The Diplomat*, 01 July 2024. Retrieved from: https://thediplomat.com/2024/07/pakistans-azm-e-istehkam-operation-old-wine-in-a-new-bottle/ [Last accessed: 08 July 2024].

Best, J. W., & Kahn, J. V. (2006). *Research in Education.* Pearl Offset Press.

Bobbitt, P. (2002). *The Shield of Achilles: War, Peace and the Course of History.* Knopf.

Bobbitt, P. (2008). *Terror and Consent: The Wars for the Twenty-First Century.* Knopf.

Bordens, K. S., & Abbott, B. B. (2008). *Research Designs and Methods: A Process Approach* (7th ed.). McGraw-Hill Companies.

Boucek, C. (2008). "Saudi Arabia's 'Soft' Counterterrorism Strategy: Prevention, Rehabilitation and Aftercare." *Carnegie Papers* no. 97, Carnegie Endowment for International Peace. Retrieved from: https://carnegieendowment.org/2008/09/22/saudi-arabia%20-s-soft-counterterrorism-strategy-prevention-rehabilitation-and-aftercare-pub-22155 [Last accessed: 29 January 2024].

Chen, H. (2022). *Robert, and Chelsea C. Chen. Artificial Intelligence: An Introduction for the Inquisitive Reader.* Chapman and Hall.

Data Solutions. (2024). "AI Pricing: How Much Does Artificial Intelligence Cost?" *Future Processing.* Retrieved from: https://www.future-processing.com/blog/ai-pricing-is-ai-expensive/ [Last accessed: 12 July 2024].

Dunn, L. A., & Perry, J. L. (2008). *Next Generation Weapons of Mass Destruction and Weapons of Mass Effects: Terrorism.* Defence Threat Reduction Agency, Advanced Systems and Concepts Office. Report Number ASCO 001. Retrieved from: https://www.hsdl.org/c/view?docid=716183 [Last accessed: 29 January 2024].

Gay, L. R. (1990). *Educational Research: Competencies for Analysis and Application* (3rd ed.). MacMillan Publishing Company.

Haqqani, H. (2013). *Magnificent Delusions: Pakistan, The United States, and an Epic History of Misunderstanding*. Public Affairs.

Harrison, S. S. (2009). Global Terrorism: US Policy after 9/11 and Its Impact on the Domestic Politics and Foreign Relations of Pakistan. In Jetly, R. (Ed.), *Pakistan in Regional and Global Politics*. Routledge.

Hasnat, F. (2008). Afghanistan's Unremitting Crises and Its Repercussions on Pakistan. In Hasnat, S. F., & Faruqui, A. (Eds.), *Pakistan: Unresolved Issues of State and Society*. Vanguard Books.

Husain, J. (2012, October). The Scourge of Terrorism. *Nation (New York, N.Y.)*, *16*, •••. Retrieved January 29, 2024, from https://nation.com.pk/columns/16-Oct-2012/the-scourge-of-terrorism

Jahangir, A. (2013). "Militancy and Drones." *DAWN*. Retrieved from: https://www.dawn.com/news/1018571/militancy-and-drones [Last accessed: 29 January 2024].

Jones, O. B. (2002). *Pakistan: Eye of the Storm*. Vanguard Publisher.

Kapur, A. (2002). The Aftermath of 11 September: Changing Geo-Political Equations and Indo-US Relations. In Kapur, A. (Ed.), *India and the United States in a Changing World*. Sage Publications.

Khan, H. (2013). "Pakistan's Contribution to Global War on Terror after 9/11." *Current Affairs Digest*, 24-48. Retrieved from: https://www.ipripak.org/wp-content/uploads/2014/02/art3hidw13.pdf [Last accessed: 1 February 2024].

Koomen, W., & Van Der Pligt, J. (2016). *The Psychology of Radicalization and Terrorism*. Routledge.

Lavrakas, P. J. (2008). *Encyclopedia of Survey Research Methods*. SAGE Publications.

Malik, H. (2008). *US Relations with Afghanistan and Pakistan*. Oxford Press.

Mateen, M. R., & Tariq, A. (2019). Increasing Acceptability of Forensic DNA Analysis in Pakistan. *Egyptian Journal of Forensic Sciences*, *9*.

Mathur, P., Broekaert, C., & Clarke, C. P. (2024). "The Radicalization (and Counter-Radicalization) Potential of Artificial Intelligence." *ICCT Publications*. Retrieved from: https://www.icct.nl/publication/radicalization-and-counter-radicalization-potential-artificial-intelligence [Last accessed: 10 July 2024].

McKendrick, K. (2019). "Artificial Intelligence and Counterterrorism: Limitations, Opportunities, and Risks." *International Security Department*, Chatham House Institute. Retrieved from: https://imctc.org/en/eLibrary/INTReports/Documents/Report-Issu-09-EN.pdf [Last accessed: 29 January 2024].

Nadeem, A. H. (2012). "Countering Terrorism with National Consensus." *The Express Tribune*. Retrieved from: https://tribune.com.pk/story/413410/countering-terrorism-with-national-consensus/ [Last accessed: 28 January 2024].

Nelu, C. (2024). "Exploitation of Generative AI by Terrorist Groups." *ICCT Publications*. Retrieved from: https://www.icct.nl/publication/exploitation-generative-ai-terrorist-groups [Last accessed: 10 July 2024].

News Desk. (2015). "ISI Sought Data Collection Tools, Claims Report." *DAWN*. Retrieved from: https://www.dawn.com/news/1196023 [Last accessed: 29 January 2024].

Noor, S. (2013, August). From Radicalization to De-Radicalization: The Case of Pakistan. *Counter Terrorist Trends and Analyses*, *5*, 16–19.

Palmer, A., & Holtz, M. (2023). "The Islamic State Threat in Pakistan: Trends and Scenarios." *Center for Strategic and International Studies*. Retrieved from: https://www.csis.org/analysis/islamic-state-threat-pakistan-trends-and-scenarios [Last accessed: 12 July 2024].

Pape, R. A., & Feldman, J. K. (2010). *Cutting the Fuse: The Explosion of Global Suicide Terrorism and How to Stop It*. University of Chicago.

Punjab Safe Cities Authority. Head Office in Lahore. Retrieved from: https://psca.gop.pk/about-us/ [Last accessed: 12 July 2024].

Rafique, N., & Manan, A. "Countering Measures of Terrorism in Pakistan." *Pakistan Journal of Humanities and Social Sciences Research*, Vol. 2 (December 2019). Retrieved from: https://journals.wumardan.edu.pk/papers/06%20Naila.pdf [Last accessed: 29 January 2024].

Rana, M. A., & Gunaratna, R. (2007). *Al-Qaeda Fights Back Inside Pakistani Tribal Areas*. Pakistan Institute for Peace Studies.

Rashid, Q. (2013). "Ethno-Sectarian Conflict in Pakistan." *The Daily Times*. Retrieved from: https://dailytimes.com.pk/87315/ethno-sectarian-conflict-in-pakistan/ [Last accessed: 27 January 2024].

Rashid, W. (2023). Using Artificial Intelligence to Combat Extremism. *Pakistan Journal of Terrorism Research*, *5*, 2.

Rogers, P. (2016). *Irregular War: ISIS and the New Threat from the Margins*. I. B. Tauris.

Russell, S. J., & Norvig, P. (2010). *Artificial Intelligence: A Modern Approach* (3rd ed.). Pearson Education.

Sassen, S. (1996). *Losing Control? Sovereignty in an Age of Globalization*. Columbia University Press.

Schroeter, M. (2020). "Artificial Intelligence and Countering Violent Extremism: A Primer." *The Global Network on Extremism and Technology* (GNET), *International Center for the Study of Radicalisation* (ICSR), King's College London. Retrieved from: https://gnet-reports.s3.eu-west-2.amazonaws.com/GNET-Report-Artificial-Intelligence-and-Countering-Violent-Extremism-A-Primer_V2.pdf [Last accessed: 29 January 2024].

Shapiro, J. N., & Fair, C. C. (2010, Winter). Understanding Support for Islamist Militancy in Pakistan. *International Security*, *34*, 79–118.

Siddiqui, T. (2023). "The Rise of Pakistan's Drones: How They Are Changing the Game in Kashmir, India and the South Asian Region." *South Asia Press*. Retrieved from: https://southasiapress.org/2023/09/21/the-rise-of-pakistans-drones-how-they-are-changing-the-game-in-kashmir-india-and-the-south-asian-region/ [Last accessed: 29 January 2024].

Synnott, H. (2009). *Transforming Pakistan: Ways Out of Instability*. Routledge Publications.

Taji-Farouki, T., & Nafi, B. M. (2004). (Eds.). *Islamic Thought in the Twentieth Century*. New York: I.B.Tauris.

United Nations. (2019). "New Technologies, Artificial Intelligence Aid Fight against Global Terrorism." *Department of Operational Support*. Retrieved from: https://news.un.org/en/story/2019/09/1045562 [Last accessed: 10 July 2024].

United Nations. (2021). *Countering Terrorism Online with Artificial Intelligence: An Overview for Law Enforcement and Counter-Terrorism Agencies in South Asia and South-East Asia*. A Joint Report by UNICRI and UNCCT. United Nations Office of Counter-Terrorism (UNOCT). Retrieved from: https://www.un.org/counterterrorism/sites/www.un.org.counterterrorism/files/countering-terrorism-online-with-ai-uncct-unicri-report-web.pdf [Last accessed: 29 January 2024].

Walliman, N. (2011). *Research Methods: The Basics*. Routledge.

Weiss, R. S. (1995). *Learning from Strangers: The Art and Method of Qualitative Interview Studies*. The Free Press.

Woodward, B. (2010). *Obama's Wars: The Inside Story*. Simon and Schuster.

Ziring, L. (1984). From Islamic Republic to Islamic State in Pakistan. *Asian Survey*, *24*(September), 931–946.

KEY TERMS AND DEFINISTIONS

Artificial Intelligence (AI): The field of computer science referred to as artificial intelligence (AI) involves with building devices and software that can carry out operations that normally call for human intelligence. Learning, reasoning, problem-solving, decision-making, language comprehension, and pattern recognition are some of these tasks.

Counter-Terrorism: Many counter-terrorism efforts aim to combat terrorism at both the strategic and operational levels. Intelligence gathering, law enforcement, military action, legislative frameworks, community participation, and international cooperation are all used to reduce the threat and consequences of terrorist activity.

De-Radicalization: The process of encouraging people who have embraced extremist ideologies especially those that defend violence to renounce them and reintegrate into society at large is known as de-radicalization. It seeks to alter the way of thinking, feeling, and acting that encourages radical or terrorist actions.

Drone Surveillance: Unmanned Arial Vehicles (UAVs) equipped with a range of instruments, including as high-resolution cameras, thermal sensors, GPS, night vision, facial recognition, and communications intercept devices, are used in drone surveillance, a remote sensing technique, to monitor a specific area. It provides high-altitude, wide-area, and continuous monitoring while posing little risk to human personnel.

Forensic Science: Forensic science bridges the gap between the legal and scientific disciplines. It employs a wide range of scientific disciplines, including biology, chemistry, physics, and digital technology, to examine evidence from crime scenes such as DNA, fingerprints, weapons, digital files, and trace material. The findings are used in counter-terrorism activities, defense cases, criminal investigations, and prosecutions.

Human Intelligence: One of the earliest and most basic methods of obtaining intelligence is Human Intelligence (HUMINT). It refers to information obtained from human sources. To support intelligence analysis, security operations, and decision-making in domains such as national defense, counterterrorism, and law enforcement, insights are gathered from people through direct engagement, observation, or debriefing. In contrast to technical intelligence (such as signals or imagery), HUMINT obtains confidential or concealed data through interpersonal interaction. Spies, informants, undercover agents, interrogators, defectors, and cooperating witnesses may all be involved in this.

Intelligence: Intelligence is the process of collecting, evaluating, and disseminating data necessary for making decisions about foreign policy, law enforcement, military activities, and national security. It aims to provide timely, relevant, and valuable information into threats, opportunities, and opponents.

Violent Extremism: The views and behaviors of people or organizations that support or resort to violence in order to fulfill ideological, religious, political, or social objectives are referred to as violent extremism. It entails intolerance for other people, a rejection of democratic norms, and a readiness to impose an extreme worldview by opposing the status quo through coercion, armed conflict, or terrorism.

APPENDIX 1

Interviews conducted with the following individuals:

1. Former terrorists, who assented to rehabilitation:
    - o Interview of Abdul Kareem (from Sargodha) conducted on 01 July 2024.
    - o Interview of Anwar Raheem (from Jhang) conducted on 03 July 2024.
    - o Interview of Sardar Naveed Khan (from Jhang) conducted on 03 July 2024.
2. Officials of the counter-terrorism department:
    - o Interview of Ansar Dar (an official of counter-terrorism department) conducted on 06 July 2024.
    - o Interview of Usman Alvi (an official of counter-terrorism department) conducted on 07 July 2024.
    - o Interview of Zubair Alam (an official of counter-terrorism department) conducted on 08 July 2024.

Chapter 7
Radicalization and Violent Extremism:
An Analysis of the Belt and Road Initiative

Bhagya Senaratne
https://orcid.org/0000-0003-2631-6444
Bandaranaike Centre for International Studies, Sri Lanka & New York University, Shanghai, China

Asif Fuard
General Sir John Kotelawala Defence University, Sri Lanka & Center for Law and Security Studies, Sri Lanka

ABSTRACT

The Belt and Road Initiative (BRI) is poised to propel a Global China that can reshape the international order. However, the growing threat of radicalization, terrorism, political instability, and the escalation of violence in Afghanistan, Pakistan and China's Xinjiang Uyghur Autonomous Region pose security threats to South and Central Asian states that are beneficiaries of the BRI. This chapter examines the evolution and the complex interplay between three regional terror actors using Afghanistan and Pakistan for their operations, while exploring how they challenge the BRI. By examining the regional security implications of the BRI and its effect on the current trajectory of conflicts in the region examined, this chapter provides an in-depth analysis of the multifaceted issues that prompt regional Islamist terror groups focusing on China's increasing involvement in the region. This analysis highlights the need to understand the drivers of radicalization and violent extremism in the region and the urgent need for effective counterterrorism measures aimed at deterring one of the greatest evolving threats to international security.

DOI: 10.4018/979-8-3693-3522-2.ch007

INTRODUCTION

China's Belt and Road Initiative (BRI) is poised to propel the Asian giant on a trajectory toward becoming a Global China that is a dominant global diplomatic, informational, military, and economic superpower with the potential to reshape the international order. However, the growing threat of radicalization, terrorism, political instability, and the escalation of violence in Afghanistan, Pakistan, and China's Xinjiang Uyghur Autonomous Region (XAR) pose grave security implications to Central and South Asian states that are beneficiaries of the BRI.

Beijing is grappling with challenges stemming from the rising tide of radicalization and violent extremism in the Central and South Asian region, which threaten the progress of the Belt and Road Initiative. A key factor contributing to radicalization and extremism in South and Central Asia is the increase in militancy and conflict, which has been compounded by the situation in China's Xinjiang Uyghur Autonomous Region and its regional expansion through the BRI. China's counterterrorism efforts have involved extensive use of force, resulting in the targeting of the predominantly Uyghur Muslim population in XAR. This has sparked global concern as reports of human rights violations, including mass detention and forced labor, continue to emerge, leading to such grievances creating an avenue for radicalization and violent extremism (UN Office of the High Commissioner for Human Rights, 2022). China's counter terrorism response has led to a concerning trend of Uyghur radicalization, with individuals being indoctrinated as suicide bombers and increasingly joining regional terror groups, such as East Turkestan Islamic Movement (ETIM) and transnational actors, such as Islamic State of Khorasan Province (ISKP).

This chapter delves into the evolution and the complex interplay between regional terror actors that are using both Afghanistan and Pakistan as hubs for their operations, while exploring how these dynamics pose significant challenges to China's BRI. By examining the regional security implications of the BRI and its effect on the current trajectory of the conflicts in the Central and South Asian region, this chapter provides an in-depth analysis of the multifaceted issues that have led to regional Islamist terror groups focusing on China's increasing involvement in the region. Moreover, this chapter sheds light on the implications of the radicalization of a section of the Uyghur population, which is reshaping regional security and the broader geopolitical landscape in the Indo-Pacific region. This analysis highlights the need to understand the drivers of radicalization and violent extremism in the region and the urgent need for effective counterterrorism measures aimed at deterring one of the greatest evolving threats to international security. As a qualitative study, we use primary sources including government websites, communiques, and speeches to evaluate official government policies and use a wide range of secondary sources, such as journal articles, media reports from reputed news agencies, reports and publications by reputed think-tanks and international non-governmental organizations.

Accordingly, the chapter consists of six sections, with this introduction falling into the first section of this chapter. Section two consists of a background on the BRI. It is further sub-divided into two sections detailing the significance of Central and South Asia to the Belt and Road Initiative and non-BRI collaborative mechanisms that the People's Republic of China (PRC) government has initiated in the 21st century to address radicalization leading to violent extremism in the Central and South Asian regions. These sections help us situate the argument to understand the implications of radicalization and violent extremism within the context of the BRI. The main focus of the chapter discusses the drivers of radicalization, and the evolving militant threats to the BRI in sections three and four. The implications of the BRI being used by radical and violent extremist groups are examined in the fourth section of this chapter, titled solutions, and recommendations. This analysis further elucidates the ramifications of China's foreign policy, emphasizing the intricate nexus between BRI and the emergence of anti-China terrorism. It explores how China's strategic infrastructural investments and diplomatic engagements under the BRI may inadvertently contribute to radicalization, thereby fostering conditions conducive to anti-China militant activities. The penultimate section elucidates the future research directions of radicalization and violent extremism. Sub-divided into sections, the sub-section on policy recommendations provides five key recommendations for policymakers, while that of research implications and Key Areas for Focus shares avenues for future research in six areas. The conclusion irons out four thoughts: the BRI is an important project for several major extremist groups that want to gain a renewed momentum in their Jihadist struggle, by targeting what is perceived as a new anti-Islamic superpower state; the Belt and Road Initiative facilitates militant and extremist groups' the ability to network with one another; militants attacking foreign nationals and targeting of BRI projects in Central and South Asia has transpired into a diplomatic issue; cross pollination of militant ideologies along with the convergence of China's conflict in Xinjiang has paved the way for an evolving existential threat to regional security and stability.

BACKGROUND: THE BELT AND ROAD INITIATIVE

Chinese President Xi Jinping launched the One Belt-One Road Initiative (OBOR) in two phases: the first, known as the Silk Road Economic Belt, was launched in September 2013 in Astana, Kazakhstan; and the second, known as the 21st Maritime Silk Road, was launched a month later in October 2013 in Indonesia. President Xi proposed the OBOR to promote greater connectivity and cooperation among regions. The Silk Road Economic Belt (or 'the Belt') is a Chinese initiative to improve economic integration and infrastructure across Eurasia, connecting China with Europe aiming to foster growth and partnership with the European Union (EU) (see Ghiasy and Zhou, 2017). 21st Century Maritime Silk Road connects China with the Southeast Asian, South Asian and the African regions.

The projections and plans from the BRI indicated the potential for infrastructure development projects in the fields of energy and ports, connectivity by way of road and railway networks, economic integration, and cultural connectivity could be initiated as well as the ability for other countries to also invest in this region and reap its benefits (State Council, People's Republic of China [PRC], 2015 as cited in Senaratne, 2021).

In 2015, the OBOR was renamed as the Belt and Road Initiative. From its modest beginnings, 150 countries have now partnered with the BRI (Belt and Road Portal, 2023; Nedopil, 2023). In 2023, the BRI celebrated its tenth anniversary. Speaking at the BRI's tenth anniversary event, President Xi stated (as cited in Feingold, 2023):

Over these 10 years, we have endeavoured to build a global network of connectivity consisting of economic corridors, international transportation routes and information highways. ... Covering the land, the ocean, the sky and the internet, this network has boosted the flow of goods, capital, technologies and human resources among countries involved.

The BRI focuses on five priority areas, namely policy coordination, facilities connectivity, unimpeded trade, financial integration, and people-to-people bond (Hu, 2023). China's engagements bilaterally and through the BRI are based on the Five Principles of Cooperation (see Senaratne, 2019 and 2021). John W. Graver (2012, p. 392) observes that:

China's objective in the SA-IOR [South Asia-Indian Ocean Region] is to grow friendly, cooperative relations across many dimensions with all the countries of that region on the basis of mutual benefit, understanding and trust. In the Chinese formulation, this dictum is called the Five Principles of Peaceful Coexistence.

China has lent more that USD 1 trillion and is considered one of the largest creditors (see Tsuji, 2025). Notable among the projects are the China Pakistan Economic Corridor (CPEC) running from China's Kashgar in the Xinjiang Uyghur Autonomous Region to Gwadar in Pakistan, the China–Mongolia–Russia Economic Corridor, the New Eurasia Land Bridge, the Colombo Port City, China-Laos Railway, and Jakarta-Bandung High-Speed Railway.

A global initiative of this magnitude inherently encounters a range of challenges and criticisms in a competitive geopolitical battle ground. The Belt and Road Initiative and its associated projects have been subject to critical scrutiny on several fronts, including facing accusations of debt-trap diplomacy, inadequacies in job creation, issues related to transparency, and deficiencies in technical and institutional cooperation (see Abi-Habib, 2018; Arduino, 2018; Senaratne, 2018; Himaz, 2019; Economic Times, 2023). It has also borne the ire of local populations in places like Cambodia, Myanmar, Nepal, Pakistan, and Sri Lanka for uprooting locals in conducting projects (see Senaratne, 2019; Palmer, 2024[3]). We see an increase in the number of targeted attacks on Chinese nationals in the African continent and in Pakistan leading to diplomatic discord and innovative responses by the PRC government. We discuss these issues at length in later sections of this chapter.

Significance of Central and South Asia to BRI

Central and South Asia are integral to China's Belt and Road Initiative, serving as both a strategic corridor for trade and an arena for geopolitical influence. The geographical proximity to critical markets and resources, coupled with the potential for economic partnerships and regional stability, positions these regions as vital components of China's aspirations of transcending into an unmatched global superpower. However, to leverage these opportunities, China must carefully navigate the complexities of regional politics, economic challenges, and most importantly the regional security landscapes of Central and South Asia. The Central Asia Data-Gathering and Analysis Team (2019) has cataloged 261 projects related to the Belt and Road Initiative across Central Asian countries, reflecting a minimum investment that surpasses US$136 million. The China-Pakistan Economic Corridor, for example, connects China's Xinjiang Province with Pakistan's Gwadar Port, offering a direct maritime route to the Arabian Sea and the western Indian Ocean.

According to Imtiaz Gul (2024), 21 Chinese engineers and technical workers have been killed in Pakistan since 2017. At the time of writing, the latest major attack on a Chinese convoy took place on 6 October 2024 near the Karachi Airport – with escalation of the conflict between Baloch insurgents and the Pakistani military, which has prompted both Beijing and Islamabad to consider a counterterrorism cooperation arrangement, to ensure the security of BRI projects and Chinese personnel that are working in Pakistan (Zaman, 2025). These attacks on Chinese personnel and BRI projects in Pakistan have recently led to China being vocal about security lapses on the part of Pakistan. They have asked that the Pakistani government ensure the safety and security of their nationals and bring the perpetrators to justice. The Chinese Ambassador in Pakistan, Jiang Zaidong stated:

> *security was the biggest constraint to the China-Pakistan Economic Corridor (CPEC) and without safe and sound environment nothing can be achieved. ... It is very unacceptable for us to be attacked twice in only six months and these attacks have also caused causalities. ... Pakistan should severely punish the perpetrators and crack down on all anti-China terrorist groups (as cited in Rana, 2024).*

In response to the above statement by the Chinese envoy, the Pakistan Foreign Ministry spokesperson Mumtaz Baloch (as cited in Gul and Zaman, 2024) stated:

The statement of the Chinese ambassador is perplexing and is not reflective of the diplomatic traditions between Pakistan and China. We will continue to engage with our Chinese brothers to reassure them of Pakistan's complete commitment to their security and well-being in Pakistan.

This has further escalated with China requesting for their troops to be stationed in Pakistan to protect its investments and personnel (Ahmed, 2024; Reuters, 2024). These dynamics in the region require comprehensive analysis and understanding to develop necessary preventive measures. By analyzing the multiple insurgencies in Balochistan, Xinjiang and Afghanistan, the current wave of anti-China terrorism provides a clear indication of how local drivers of Islamist extremism has converged with the geopolitical and regional drivers of extremism.

Non-BRI collaborative mechanisms

The People's Republic of China has been wary of its safety and security since Mao Zedong established it in 1949. "[M]utual respect for territorial integrity and sovereignty" featured strongly in the First Session of the National Committee of the Chinese People's Political Consultative Conference on 29 September 1949 that later influenced the diplomatic relations of the PRC with other countries since its establishment on 1 October 1949 (Ministry of Foreign Affairs, PRC, n.d.). This notion was then expanded and presented during border discussions with the Republic of India, as the Five Principles of Peaceful Co-Existence. They are "mutual respect for each other's territorial integrity and sovereignty (changed to mutual respect for each other's sovereignty and territorial integrity at the Asian-African Conference), mutual non-aggression, non-interference in each other's internal affairs, equality and mutual benefit (changed to equality and mutual benefit in the Sino-Indian joint Statement and Sino-Burmese Joint Statement), and peaceful co-existence" (Ministry of Foreign Affairs, PRC, n.d.). According to Bhagya Senaratne (2019 and 2021), the Five Principles of Peaceful Co-Existence are also enshrined in the Belt and Road Initiative, which was constitutionalized in 2015.

China has been vocal of external threats to its internal stability and the need to safeguard territorial integrity even before they launched the BRI. For example, in 2009 State Councilor Dai Bingguo (as cited in Brown, 2018) stated that China's 'core interests' are: "to maintain its fundamental system and state security; next is state sovereignty and territorial integrity; and third is the continued stable development of the economy and society." They have also been vocal in using the Five Principles of Coexistence.

Shanghai Cooperation Organization (SCO) was initiated in 2001, long before the BRI was conceptualized. Kazakhstan, China, Kyrgyzstan, Russia, Tajikistan, and Uzbekistan founded it to promote peace, and security and stability in the region. It succeeds the Shanghai Five. Currently, the SCO has nine member states, with the inclusion of India, Iran, and Pakistan. It also has three observer states and fourteen dialogue partners (Shanghai Cooperation Organization, 2017). The SCO cooperates with many organizations including the Association for Southeast Asian Nations (ASEAN), Commonwealth of Independent States (CIS) and the United Nations (UN). Established in 2004, the Regional Anti-Terrorist Structure (RATS) which is a permanent organ within the SCO is aimed at coordinating counterterrorism efforts among member states. It aims to fight extremism, terrorism and separatism through joint exercises, intelligence sharing, and coordinated strategies. Since 2023, RATS also pledges to ensure "information security and responding to challenges and threats on the internet" (Norov, 2024). These illustrate the various non-BRI collaborative efforts China has in place to counter threats arising from extremism, separatism and terrorism.

MAIN FOCUS OF THE CHAPTER: DRIVERS OF RADICALIZATION

While the supremacist ideologies based on religious and ethnic identities are central to the influence of violent extremist groups, they are not the sole driver of radicalization (Fuard, 2020). Many Islamists militant groups are inherently political in nature, leveraging religion as a strategic instrument to obscure their true objectives and to cultivate broader public support. Since the end of the Cold War, the exploitation of religious and ethnic identities to legitimize acts of terrorism has become a persistent global security challenge (Hoffman, 1999).

Notably, scholars (Rogers, 2007; Juergensmeyer, 2004) have underscored the role of geopolitical dynamics in shaping religious violent extremism. Empirical evidence further challenges the perception of ideologies, regardless of it being ethno-nationalist, separatist or religious as the predominant driver of extremism. Lydia Wilson, of the Centre for the Resolution of Intractable Conflict, University of Oxford (The Nation, 2015), in her interviews with captured ISIS combatants, observed that the majority exhibited profound ignorance regarding Islamic jurisprudence, militant jihad, and the concept of the caliphate. Similarly, counterterrorism scholar Bruce Hoffman (1997) theorizes that contemporary terrorist actors frequently deploy religious rhetoric as a communicative tool rather than a genuine doctrinal commitment. These scholarly findings dismantle the prevailing notion that ideology singularly underpins religious violent extremism. They instead highlight the multifaceted and often politically motivated nature of such movements.

David Kilcullen's (2009) Accidental Guerrilla Syndrome conceptualizes insurgency as a four-stage process: infection, contagion, intervention, and rejection. Drawing on medical analogies, he parallels insurgency proliferation with disease transmission, a framework followed by the US counterinsurgency efforts. Insurgents first establish themselves in ungoverned spaces, exploiting societal fractures (infection). Their influence expands through legitimacy-building and local support (contagion). Government countermeasures, shaped by strategic priorities, follow (intervention), often triggering population alignment with insurgents in reaction to state actions rather than ideological affinity (rejection).

Four core insurgent tactics, provocation, intimidation, protraction, and exhaustion are pivotal. Provocation incites disproportionate state responses, as seen in the 9/11 attacks, Beslan siege, the Afghan counter insurgency prior to the US withdrawal in 2021 and Pakistan's counterterrorism campaign in Balochistan. Intimidation deters civilian collaboration, while protraction forces prolonged asymmetric warfare, adding further complexities and challenges to counterinsurgency campaigns. Exhaustion imposes unsustainable costs of war, as illustrated by the trillions of dollars in defense expenditure during the US War on terror in the aftermath of the 9/11 attacks.

Clausewitz noted conventional tactics favor states, yet strategic longevity benefits insurgents. Mao Zedong advocated protracted war, arguing, "The first law of war is to preserve ourselves and destroy the enemy." Insurgents dictate a sustainable operational tempo, compelling prolonged attrition that depletes state resources and public resolve. Fuard (2023) has highlighted that the insurgents success is primarily dependent on its ability to remain resilient despite the loss of leaders, combatants and territory which has been exemplified by the Taliban's rise to power in 2021 and the operational endurance displayed by ISKP, Al-Qaeda, ETIM, Tehrik-e-Taliban Pakistan (TTP/ Pakistani Taliban) and Balochistan Liberation Army (BLA), which remains a potent threat to regional security that is further aggravated by China's repressive counterterrorism measures that is coupled with Beijing's plans to advance the BRI.

While all major militant groups that threaten China's interest in the region pursue diverse political goals which differ on religious, ethnic, and nationalistic lines, these groups remain collaborative in their attacks against China due to finding a common enemy. This would help continue their cause by projecting anti-China narratives, which creates a renewed resolve to engage in their jihadist war. Another significant reason that unifies most militant groups in targeting China is the symbiotic relationship that exists amongst these groups (Fuard, 2021). The US withdrawal from Afghanistan in 2021 paved the way for China to fill the ensuing security vacuum in the region, combined with its counterterrorism campaign targeting the Uyghur, have led to such events becoming catalysts that converge transnational and local conflict drivers of radicalization. Paul Gill (2007) while analyzing the radicalization process of Islamist suicide bombers has argued that a ‘catalyst event’ along with a broad socialization process and exposure to propaganda can create the environment for an individual to join a terrorist organization.

Despite Afghanistan experiencing less armed violence in 2022 and 2023 than in the years prior, the persistent humanitarian crisis, the prospect of hunger, worsening economic conditions, and many internal disputes have exacerbated the ongoing hybrid war (International Crisis Group, 2022). The weaponizing of byproducts of war has further redefined Afghanistan’s state of perpetual conflict, leading to the most dominant Jihadist insurgent groups in the country, Taliban, Al Qaeda and ISKP engaging in an ideological and propaganda war (Fuard, 2023). To be successful, they must stay in charge of the informational (propaganda), psychological, social, and political battlespaces. This is because it makes it easier for these insurgent groups to recruit new members, even though they have suffered heavy losses and strategic setbacks (Fuard, 2023).

Afghanistan which has remained in a perpetual state of conflict for over half a century is currently facing a precarious situation with state and non-state actors engaging in hybrid warfare, leading to militant groups in the region regaining a renewed momentum to conduct terror campaigns. The coordinated use of both traditional and non-traditional warfare tools, like political, psychological, diplomatic, informational, cyber, and economic tools, have made militant groups in the region stronger. This has led to a new type of radical militant who sees China as the new enemy (Fuard, 2023). The anti-China rhetoric has become a significant part of these militants’ propaganda arsenal leading to significant radicalization.

The center of gravity of insurgent groups such as ISKP, TTP, ETIM and BLA have shifted from the physical to the online and psychological domains. These conditions further exacerbate an already volatile regional security landscape, which has shown that the sole dependance of a military response would be futile in engaging multidimensional and synchronized threats that emerge in regions plagued by a state of perpetual hybridity (Fuard, 2023). These current dynamics in Afghanistan has further created avenues for neighboring central Asian states, such as Tajikistan, Turkmenistan, Kyrgyzstan, and Uzbekistan facing a trend, which is leading to nationals from these countries becoming susceptible to radicalization by groups such as ISKP and ETIM.

Therefore, to effectively counter the current wave of terrorism and insurgency in the Central and South Asian region, Beijing and its allies should consider countering the current anti-China radicalization by comprehending the distinct drivers of each major militant group threatening the BRI. Based on the current threat perception and conflict trajectory within the region, specific structural and contextual drivers of radicalization influence major anti-China militant groups such as ETIM, ISKP and BLA.

ETIM

ETIM is also known as the Turkish IM. Over the past few decades, the group has evolved into a significant player in the global jihadist landscape, and has specifically targeted China's geopolitical and domestic interests, including conducting attacks on infrastructure linked to the Belt and Road Initiative. A complex interplay of local, regional, and global factors, which can be broadly categorized into ethnic and religious identity, political grievances, external influences, and strategic objectives have influenced the radicalization of ETIM, which has led to a separatist insurgency in Xinjiang province. ETIM has been able to form strategic alliances with several terror groups including ISKP and has been using central Asian states and the Afghan-Pakistan region in order to conduct its campaign against China in Xinjiang. China's counterterrorism measures along with mass detention and destruction of places of worship of the Uyghur have further exacerbated radicalization.

Baloch Liberation Army (BLA)

Balochistan is the largest and most impoverished province in Pakistan, which is grappling with persistent poverty and high unemployment, which are symptomatic of horizontal inequalities and the disproportionate distribution of resources. The BLA has increasingly focused its insurgency against China, particularly targeting its investments and personnel linked to the China-Pakistan Economic Corridor (see Arduino, 2018). The radicalization of the BLA against China is driven by a complex interplay of economic exploitation, marginalization, forced demographic changes, militarization, political exclusion, and external geopolitical factors. China has become the primary target not only because of its economic presence but also due to its perceived role in empowering Pakistan's military suppression of Baloch national self-determination. As CPEC deepens, radicalization within Baloch insurgent groups is expected to intensify, leading to a sustained campaign of anti-China terrorism in the region and regular clashes with the Pakistani military.

Perceived threat to cultural and ethnic identity of the Baloch population due to mounting fears regarding the influx of Chinese workers and other non-Baloch populations into Balochistan as part of CPEC projects has led to fears among the Baloch community of becoming a minority in their own land, which is further escalating the conditions for radicalization.

Islamic State of Khorasan Province

ISKP which is the Afghan affiliate of the Islamic State (ISIS), has evolved into the most lethal transnational jihadist group by surpassing the ISIS Central and Al-Qaeda. The IS Afghan affiliate's transnational capabilities is exemplified by the multiple transnational terror attacks targeting Chinese nationals engaged in BRI projects and the 2024 attack on a concert which was held at Crocus Hall in Russia, which led to 145 people being killed and 551 people being injured (Amnesty International, 2024; BBC, 2024). ISKP which is operating in Afghanistan and using the Afghan-Pakistan border to conduct its attacks against the Taliban and in Pakistan has shown signs of the group gaining momentum following the US withdrawal from Afghanistan in 2021. ISKP has remained resilient due to its ability to conduct hybrid warfare operations by exploiting the militant landscape in the region. ISKP has further intensified its propaganda campaigns focused on radicalizing and recruiting foreign nationals including Uyghur from China's Xinjiang province and has even used Pakistan's insurgency in Balochistan as part of its propaganda rhetoric is linked to targeting what is perceived as Chinese expansionism. Even though ISKP's primary objective is to establish a pan-Islamist caliphate in Afghanistan, its drivers for radicalization have focused on leveraging ethnic divisions, sectarian and separatist conflicts in the region, which will undoubtedly pave the way for the transnational terror group to recruit thousands of Muslims who are faced with persecution, polarization, economic hardships, and protracted internal conflicts. This added a new layer to the regional security complexities stemming from the BRI as ISKP has been successful in attracting thousands of Uyghurs.

Table 1 illustrates the drivers of radicalization of the major anti-China terror groups in the region ETIM, BLA and ISKP.

Table 1. Drivers of Radicalization

Radical group	Motives
ETIM	• Historical grievances and political exclusion which have led to a call for national-self-determination as China annexed the region • ETIM's radicalization lies in the deep-rooted ethnic and religious identity of the Uyghur people, who are a Turkic-speaking Muslim minority in China, based in the Xinjiang region. • Suppression of Uyghur culture and religion as part of China's counter terrorism strategy. • Human rights abuses including the detention of millions of Uyghurs who are in Chinese internment camps. • The BRI's expansion has exacerbated local resentment among Uyghurs, as the project has been associated with the forced assimilation of Uyghurs into China's broader national economic and security projects. • Global jihadist discourse which is creating the conditions for ETIM to collaborate with transnational terror groups such as ISKP and Al Qaeda, and regional terror groups such as TTP and BLA. • Regional conflict dynamics and the ability to use Afghanistan and the Afghan-Pakistan border as a launchpad to conduct offensives against China and their interests. • Geopolitical factors
BLA	• Economic disenfranchisement and rising unemployment have created minimum opportunities for local Baloch people. • Displacement of a section of the local population in Balochistan due to CPEC projects. • Perceived exploitation of natural resources by the Federal government and BRI projects. • Lack of opportunities for the Baloch community in BRI projects. • Perceived political marginalization and lack of representation. • Environmental degradation and livelihood disruption. • Militarization and increased security in BRI projects. • Human rights abuses by the state combined with excessive counterinsurgency measures. • Deepening resentment against Chinese influence in Pakistan's historic Gwadar Port. • The vibrant militant landscape which is fueling radicalization and militancy. • Strategic Targeting of Chinese nationals and interests, which the BLA aims to internationalize their struggle to draw global attention to their grievances.
ISKP	• Ideological Drivers of resurrecting its caliphate in Afghanistan. • China's mass internment and re-education policies targeting Uyghur Muslims in Xinjiang have been framed by ISKP as acts of oppression against Islam, justifying retaliatory jihad. • ISKP propagates the notion that the Chinese Communist Party (CCP) is inherently anti-Islamic and that its atheistic governance structure is a direct threat to Islamic values • ISKP's global jihadist narratives seeks to position itself as a protector of persecuted Muslims worldwide, using China's Uyghur policies as a recruitment tool to attract fighters from Central Asia, the Middle East, and the Uyghur diaspora. • ISKP has been critical of China-Taliban relations due to its ongoing conflict with the Taliban which is considered an apostate regime • China's BRI in Afghanistan and Pakistan is perceived by ISKP as neo-colonialism. • ISKP is motivated to strategically position itself as the most dominant transnational jihadist terror group by attacking China, for the group to differentiate itself from rival jihadist groups like the Taliban and Al-Qaeda, which have shown increasing pragmatism in dealing with Beijing. • Regional conflicts and ethnoreligious fault-lines. • Geopolitical rivalries and influences that have enabled ISKP to inadvertently precipitate radicalization and recruitment of combatants, while motivating lone wolf and inspired networks • The tactical and strategic drivers behind ISKP's radicalization and recruitment strategy focuses on; a). Recruitment of Uyghur and Central Asian fighters leveraging anti-China propaganda, b). Expanding its operational reach by attacking Chinese targets to elevate its status among global jihadist networks, attracting foreign fighters and funding, c). Disrupting regional stability by undermining China's efforts to stabilize Afghanistan under the Taliban, thereby creating an environment conducive to its insurgency.

Source: FPRI, 2019; Russel and Berger, 2020; Soliev, 2021; Basit, 2022; Fuard, 2023

The Evolving militant threats to the BRI

The increasing number of attacks on Chinese personnel and projects demonstrates that Afghanistan and the Afghan-Pakistan border regions have evolved into a catalyst which is threatening the BRI and China's interest in the Central and South Asian regions. Initially, China's concerns regarding Islamist radicalization and terrorism were internal due to its conflict with ETIM in Xinjiang province, which consist of predominantly Uyghur Muslims. China's expanding global footprint through the BRI has made it a target for terrorist activities both domestically and internationally (Byman, 2019).

Domestically, Xinjiang has experienced violence driven by ethno-nationalist separatism which has transpired into a low intensity insurgency conducted by ETIM. Continuous repressive counterterrorism measures adopted by Beijing including the construction of internment camps which has imprisoned 1.8 million Uyghurs, Kazakhs, and other Turkic minorities (as of 2017) has further exacerbated radicalization amongst the Uyghur population (Zenz, 2020). The repression of Uyghur Muslims in Xinjiang has further created a rallying point for regional and transnational extremist groups that are able to leverage China's conflict in Xinjiang by radicalizing and recruiting a steady flow of combatants that would target China and BRI projects in Pakistan, Afghanistan and Central Asia. This has created an avenue for an internal conflict to take a transnational dimension that poses the potential of destabilizing the BRI and Beijing's influence in the region.

Outside of Xinjiang, Chinese nationals and projects are targeted in countries participating in the BRI from multiple militant groups that view China's BRI projects as encroachments. The convergence of the internal conflict dynamics in Xinjiang with China's expansion into the Central and South Asian region through the BRI have shaped the conditions for China to become the latest target of multiple Islamist terror groups.

ETIM has shown signs of evolving from its local militant roots into an Islamist separatist group that has a transnational reach, due to its ability to develop strategic alliances with multiple militant groups that threatened China's influence (UN Security Council, 2024). The Security Council (2024) report has indicated that ETIM has been collaborating with Hay'at Tahrir al-Sham (HTS) in conducting operations against Syrian Forces under the Assad regime. ETIM has established a significant operational presence within Syria, particularly in the provinces of Idlib, northeastern Latakia, northern Hama, and western Aleppo. ETIM's alliance with Hay'at Tahrir al-Sham, which includes engaging in joint military offensives against Syrian government forces in Idlib and Aleppo, has also resulted in benefits from financial and logistical support provided by HTS, which enables it to sustain its operations and expand its influence in the region (UN Security Council, 2024). The group's transnational operations have been part of their propaganda campaigns and have specifically targeted Muslim women, advocating for their participation in terrorist activities and have also commenced a drive of radicalization with the aim of creating a new breed of lone wolf and inspire networks that would target China. Following the fall of the Assad Regime, ETIM fighters in Syria have turned their guns towards China by openly threatening to take its fight to liberate Xinjiang (Economist, 2025). In 2017, Imad Moustapha, the Syrian Ambassador to China, stated that there were 5,000 Uyghur militants in Syria.

With the end of the Assad regime, the newly formed Syrian administration, led de facto by Ahmed al-Sharaa, has undertaken a significant restructuring of its military leadership, appointing fifty new officials. Notable, among these appointees are six foreign fighters, including individuals linked to ETIM. China has voiced strong apprehensions over this development, particularly regarding the elevation of ETIM members within Syria's senior military ranks (Decan Herald, 2025). This further indicates that ETIM is strengthening its transnational network, which would create further concerns for China.

UN reports indicate that approximately five hundred fighters from the East Turkestan Islamic Movement form a significant component of the Taliban's forces in Badakhshan province, alongside Tajik, Uzbek, Hazara, and Chechen militants, rather than the Pashtun majority. Strategically positioned, Badakhshan connects northern Afghanistan to China's Xinjiang region via the Wakhan Corridor (Gupta, 2021). While the Taliban have historically maintained close ties with ETIM, their northern ranks are primarily composed of non-Pashtun groups, including Uyghurs. Any Taliban-led persecution of ethnic minorities could drive these factions to align with the anti-Taliban militant groups. Intelligence assessments from Afghanistan and Türkiye further suggest that ETIM militants, fearing potential Taliban crackdowns and extradition to China's Ministry of State Security (MSS) will lead to a shift in allegiance to the Islamic State of Khorasan Province.

While the Afghan Taliban have maintained a cooperative relationship with China, their ability, or willingness, to prevent ETIM from operating within Afghanistan remains uncertain. The Taliban's territorial control is far from absolute, as evidenced by the continued presence of ISKP cells. Furthermore, their historical policy of offering sanctuary to ideologically aligned Islamist groups, on the condition that they do not conduct external attacks, suggests a degree of ambiguity in their stance towards ETIM.

This raises the possibility that ETIM could re-establish a presence in Afghanistan and the Afghan-Pakistan border of the Wakhan corridor bordering Xinjiang, either with tacit acceptance or independently of Taliban control. If such a scenario unfolds, the group could emerge as a major threat to the China-Pakistan Economic Corridor. In this regard, ETIM's potential operational trajectory to a certain extent resembles that of the Balochistan Liberation Army, which has leveraged Afghan territory as a staging ground for attacks on CPEC infrastructure and Chinese personnel.

The collaboration between ISKP and ETIM is driven by mutual interests, with ISKP benefiting from ETIM's experienced Uyghur militants and ETIM leveraging ISKP's operational capabilities. The partnership manifests in several ways: a) operational collaboration between the two groups has led to ETIM fighters joining ISKP ranks, particularly in Afghanistan's Badakhshan and Nuristan provinces, which border China, b) ISKP has provided training, resources, and logistical support to ETIM operatives, c) conducting Joint operations, including attacks targeting Chinese nationals and projects, d) ISKP has integrated ETIM's anti-China rhetoric into its propaganda campaigns, reinforcing narratives of Islamic oppression in Xinjiang, e) the ideological synergy between the two groups has facilitated recruitment among Uyghur and Central Asian jihadists, f) the December 2022 attack on a hotel in Kabul housing Chinese nationals was attributed to ISKP, with intelligence suggesting ETIM involvement, further indicating ISKP leveraging from the internal conflict in Xinjiang and China's counterterrorism measures.

ISKP has strategically employed suicide bombings and attacks on minority communities, particularly Shia and Sufi Muslims, to deepen sectarian divisions. The attack on Gozar-e-Sayed Abad, a prominent Shia Mosque in Kunduz on 8 October 2021, resulted in over fifty fatalities and 143 injuries. A week later, a similar attack on a Kandahar Shia Mosque killed sixty-five. These incidents underscore ISKP's objective of inciting sectarian conflict, mirroring ISIS Central's tactics in Iraq, with the aim of resurrecting its pan-Islamist caliphate in Afghanistan (The Express Tribune, 2021; Fuard, 2021).

The perpetrators of these attacks reflect ISKP's strategy of constructing symbolic narratives. The Kunduz bomber was identified as a Uyghur from China, while one of the Kandahar bombers was a Baloch from Pakistan. By recruiting individuals from insurgency-affected or marginalized groups, ISKP seeks to foster a perception of the Islamic State caliphate as the sole recourse for grievances in Central and South Asia. This aligns with the group's broader objective of targeting China, leveraging narratives surrounding the Baloch insurgency, exacerbated by China's Belt and Road Initiative, and the repression of Uyghur Muslims in Xinjiang (The Guardian, 2021; The Times of India, 2021).

The growing threat of multidimensional operations conducted by multiple militant groups that are using the Afghan-Pakistan border region, which includes the strategic Wakhan corridor, has led to Beijing seeking continuous reassurances from the Taliban regime in Kabul and the Pakistan government to counter the growing threat. Apart from the most notable threat posed by ETIM, ISKP, TTP and more obscure networks such as Tehreek-e-Jihad Pakistan (TJP), Chinese nationals and BRI projects have increasingly become targets of BLA which is an ethno-nationalist separatist group that is operating in Balochistan, located in the Southwest of Pakistan (Hussain, 2024). Unlike the other major militant groups which pose a threat to Chinese interests in Pakistan that adhere to a Salafi jihadist ideology, BLA has been pursuing an ethno-nationalist separatist goal. While Pakistan has attracted a significant amount of anti-China terrorism stemming from multiple militant groups that pursue diverse political goals, after a lapse of five years, in December 2024, both countries conducted a joint counterterrorism exercise in Rawalpindi (China Military Online, 2024). This comes in the wake of multiple attacks and threats from BLA on Chinese nationals, including the 2024 October Karachi Airport bombing that led to the killing of two Chinese nationals and the 2024 March suicide bombing which killed five Chinese engineers at the Dasu Dam in the Khyber-Pakhtunkhwa region (Associated Press, 2024)

The escalating violence in Balochistan and TTP strongholds has led to increased military deployments to protect BRI projects. However, these measures have strained Pakistan's resources and complicated its relations with local communities and fueling diplomatic tension between Beijing and Islamabad. Despite many of these militant groups which have targeted China and the BRI following diverse political agendas and ideologies, a symbiotic relationship exists between them which has led these militant groups to collaborate to counter a new enemy.

The Baloch Liberation Army has progressively transitioned into a hybrid insurgent entity, adept at simultaneously leveraging local popular support and garnering political endorsement to advance its separatist agenda. This evolution exemplifies a complex interplay of ideological motivations, socio-political dynamics, and strategic calculations, whereby insurgent groups not only undertake militant activities but also cultivate legitimacy and influence through political means.

The recent escalation of tensions between India and Pakistan a geopolitical rivalry with profound regional repercussions has further compounded China's strategic calculus in Pakistan, particularly within the context of Balochistan. China's growing economic and strategic interests in the region exemplified by the China-Pakistan Economic Corridor—have rendered Beijing increasingly attentive to stability and security concerns therein. Meanwhile, the BLA has explicitly articulated its support for Indian backing, even extending overt diplomatic overtures to the Indian government. Reports indicate that the insurgent group has sought recognition from India by proposing the establishment of an embassy in New Delhi, to legitimize their aspirations for statehood and to reposition themselves as a formal political actor within the broader regional framework. Such a development carries significant geostrategic implications; it complicates the regional security landscape and could challenge existing power balances. Notably, China's regional influence traditionally solidified through its alliance with Pakistan may be undermined if Indian support for the BLA facilitates the consolidation of a more autonomous separatist movement in Balochistan. This scenario exemplifies a state of perpetual hybridity, characterized by using multidimensional strategies by actors engaged in protracted conflict. Hybrid strategies often encompass both kinetic (military) and non-kinetic (political, diplomatic, informational) tools, fostering intricate linkages between state and non-state actors. The employment of insurgent groups and terrorist organizations as instruments or proxy forces within broader geopolitical objectives underscore a strategic paradigm where non-state actors and state actors would have mutual interests.

Consequently, Pakistan's ongoing military setbacks in Balochistan, compounded by mounting insurgent activity and external support for separatist factions, could significantly alter regional dynamics particularly if India exploits these developments to advance its own strategic interests. This multi-layered conflict environment underscores the necessity of understanding hybrid threats not merely as a tactical approach but as a fundamental axis of contemporary geopolitics. It exemplifies how actors within prolonged insurgencies deploy diverse methods ranging from asymmetric warfare to diplomatic maneuvers to influence state behavior and regional stability. Ultimately, such a hybrid landscape engenders complex nexus points between state and non-state entities, reflecting a broader trend towards multifaceted and interconnected conflict dynamics in the South and Central Asian regions.

SOLUTIONS AND RECOMMENDATIONS

Since the Taliban's resurgence and the subsequent overthrow of the Kabul regime of Ashraf Ghani in 2021, Afghanistan has reemerged as a focal point in the 'great game' of geopolitical contestation that has drawn the attention of both superpowers and regional state actors. The enduring state of conflict in Afghanistan and Pakistan has facilitated the convergence of local and transnational militant objectives with political agendas, resulting in a complex link between state and non-state entities engaging in hybrid war (Fuard, 2023). The deployment of hybrid warfare strategies by these actors has introduced a novel dimension to the ongoing conflict, presenting a significant challenge to peace and stability in the Central and South Asian regions, which is a key component of China's broader geopolitical strategy that is implemented through the BRI (Fuard, 2023).

After ISIS Central was defeated in Iraq and Syria, ISKP, the Afghan branch of the international terrorist group, said it wants to expand beyond Afghanistan. This fits with its goal of restoring its short-lived pan-Islamist Caliphate, which used to control large areas of Iraq and Syria (Fuard, 2021). A 2018 report by the United

Nations Security Council notes a significant migration of foreign terrorist fighters (FTFs) from countries such as Algeria, France, Russia, Tunisia, and Central Asia to Afghanistan as ISIS Central faced territorial losses and a depletion of combatants (UN Security Council, 2018). This migration presents substantial regional security concerns in Central and South Asia, posing a specific challenge to the BRI in the wake of the vacuum created by the withdrawal of the United States and NATO forces in 2021 from Afghanistan.

A key factor that would enable China to annex its hegemony in the Central and South Asian regions is dependent on its close alliances with Pakistan and Afghanistan. China's growing influence in the region is paving the way for militancy in Pakistan and Afghanistan, which has evolved into a catalyst that is driving anti-China terrorism, leading to BRI projects becoming the latest targets for Islamist and ethno-nationalist separatist militant groups. This further gives rise to the potential for state actors to engage in multidimensional operations that fall within the realm of hybrid warfare. In such a context rival state actors would be able to take advantage of anti-China Islamist extremist and separatist groups to destabilize the BRI plans in the region.

Currently, the number of attacks targeting Chinese personnel that are working in BRI related projects in the region has intensified since the Taliban take over in 2021. While China is grappling with its own internal insurgency against ETIM in Xinjiang province which consists of a predominant Uyghur Muslim community, Beijing is further challenged by transnational terror groups such as ISKP and Al Qaeda that have been using anti-China rhetoric to radicalize and recruit a new breed of Islamist militants from China's Uyghur population. Similarly, regional ethno-nationalist separatist militant groups, such as BLA have been targeting Chinese nationals and BRI projects in Pakistan which has led to tension in China-Pakistan relations. These militant groups continue their insurgency by using both Pakistan and Afghanistan as safe havens to target China's personnel and their projects.

The attacks on Chinese BRI projects have prompted the Chinese government to recruit and establish their own private security contractors to safeguard their "projects, citizens, and diplomats" (Nantulya, 2020). China has been employing security contractors in several African countries, such as Kenya, Zimbabwe, and Guinea. Reuters (2024) reports that China is considering their own security contractors to Pakistan since the two attacks on Chinese personnel in March and October 2024. It further reports that

> *The attacks, and Islamabad's failure to deter them, have angered China, which has pushed Pakistan to begin formal negotiations or a joint security management system. ... A written proposal...forwarded to Pakistani security agencies for review, mentioned a clause allowing the dispatching of security agencies and military forces into each other's territory to assist in counter-terrorism missions and conduct joint strikes. ... Pakistan has asked China for help in improving its*

intelligence and surveillance capabilities instead of direct involvement. (Reuters, 2024)

ISIS's propaganda targeting China traces back to 2015, with intensified efforts following the Taliban's assumption of power. Recent online propaganda by ISKP underscores China's significance, manifested in attacks on Chinese interests, such as the Kabul hotel bombing in December 2022 and the January 2023 suicide bombing at the Ministry of Foreign Affairs in Kabul. This heightened focus may be attributed to Afghanistan's favorable environment for jihadist activities, facilitating collaboration with groups like the ETIM. Emerging reports highlight substantial collaboration between ISKP and ETIM, posing challenges for China's engagement in Afghanistan under the BRI framework amid escalating security concerns (Kelemen, 2023).

India's foreign policy has changed as a Taliban government supported by China and Pakistan consolidates its power, aiming to forge important partnerships with Central Asian countries. Afghanistan continues to be strategically important to both India and Pakistan because of the ongoing conflicts and tensions between the two countries (Dormandy, 2007). Reducing Pakistan's power in Afghanistan and opposing China's influence in the region are the main drivers of India's geopolitical activities in that country. India's larger objective to protect its national interests includes these strategic imperatives centered on Afghanistan. Beijing's crucial role as a major financial benefactor and a check on Indian supremacy in the region is a major factor in China's geopolitical goals in Afghanistan, which are closely aligned with those of Pakistan.

Three main strategic goals drive China's involvement with the Taliban: preventing terrorism in Xinjiang that stems from ETIM, which is primarily made up of Chinese Uyghur Muslims; investing in mineral resources and other business endeavors; and broadening the BRI's reach to establish regional dominance (Russel and Berger, 2020). In China's Xinjiang province, which borders Mongolia, Russia, Kazakhstan, Kyrgyzstan, Tajikistan, Afghanistan, Pakistan, and India, the ETIM, an ethnic Uyghur terrorist group with strong ties to ISKP, uses Afghanistan as a base to plan terrorist attacks and low-intensity conflicts. China succeeded in getting the Taliban to fight ETIM militants and stop them from using Afghanistan as a safe haven for their activities. Recently, ETIM operatives and Uyghur Chinese suicide bombers have aligned with ISKP, perpetrating numerous deadly attacks targeting Chinese nationals in Afghanistan and Pakistan. Through extensive aid packages and economic inducements to Afghanistan, China aims to wield considerable influence over the Taliban. The China-Pakistan nexus will be fortified by China's substantial financial resources and Pakistan's close ties with the Taliban, forging a robust alliance with shared interests deeply embedded in Afghanistan's affairs. Nonetheless, the relationship between China and Pakistan faces internal challenges, notably concerning

BRI initiatives in Balochistan, which has intensified the conflict between Baloch militants and Pakistani authorities.

To win over tribal groupings and jihadist networks, ISKP has been engaging in its own tribal forms of diplomacy, much like the Taliban. The ISKP has already received the support of other jihadist organizations from the region and Pakistan, making them a strong candidate to challenge the Taliban's internal rule in Afghanistan. By forming partnerships with local jihadist networks and gaining a sizable following in rural Afghanistan, ISKP will aim to expand its base of support internationally. This is a result of regional strife, particularly in areas like the Duran line, which separates Afghanistan and Pakistan; the Baloch insurgency in Pakistan; and the conflict in Xinjiang province, which has caused many Uygur Muslims to join ETIM and collaborate with ISKP. Criticizing the Taliban for its partnership with China through an anti-China campaign that has significantly radicalized Uyghur Muslims is how ISKP is energizing their base of support.

The Belt and Road Initiative is already facing many challenges and criticism related to financial and environmental concerns. Its ability to foster and facilitate, either intentionally or unintentionally, radicalization and violent extremism in the Central and South Asian regions is a concern for not only these regions but to the world at large as it infringes on global peace and security. As the ability for regional terror actors to use the BRI network and resources for violent extremism creates major security implications, it is important that causes are identified and preventive measures are taken before a major calamity strikes the Central and South Asian regions (see Senaratne, 2021).

The attack on Chinese personnel provides an indication of the regional security implications Beijing is facing in advancing its BRI plan. While Afghanistan is currently faced with multiple conflicts which has led to it becoming the latest political battleground, the Afghan-Pakistan border region serves as a catalyst that could destabilize the region primarily due to the hybrid warfare engaged by both state and non-state actors–posing the threat to advancing China's BRI in the region.

FUTURE RESEARCH DIRECTIONS

The escalating wave of anti-China terrorism in South Asia, particularly in Pakistan and Afghanistan, represents a complex security challenge with profound regional and global repercussions. As both Pakistan and Afghanistan grapple with internal conflict and instability, the threat posed by insurgent groups targeting Chinese interests most notably in Balochistan and bordering regions necessitates comprehensive policy and research responses.

Policy Recommendations

This paper provides five key recommendations for policymakers. First, strengthening regional security cooperation. Since regional cooperation is crucial, South and Central Asian states should establish robust channels for intelligence sharing, joint counterterrorism operations, and border security measures. This cooperation must transcend political differences to address vulnerabilities and track insurgent movements effectively. Second, addressing the root causes of insurgency. Policy efforts must extend beyond security measures to address socio-economic grievances fueling insurgency, especially in Balochistan and eastern Afghan regions. Governments need to invest in sustainable development, education, and political inclusion to mitigate grievances exploited by insurgent groups to recruit and operate. Third, engaging China in diplomatic and security dialogues. Given China's stake in stability and economic investments in the region, Beijing should be actively involved in regional security dialogues. BRI states need to develop joint strategic frameworks that include counterterrorism, infrastructure protection, and risk-assessment components. Four, enhancing counterterrorism capacity. Regional countries should bolster their counterterrorism capacity, including specialized training, intelligence infrastructure, and law enforcement collaboration. International assistance through organizations like the United Nations and regional security alliances can support these capacity-building efforts. Five, developing a comprehensive conflict resolution approach. Long-term peace and stability depend on addressing underlying political conflicts, including autonomy demands in Balochistan and factions in Afghanistan. Diplomatic engagement aimed at conflict resolution and reconciliation is essential for sustainable peace.

Research Implications and Key Areas for Focus

This paper conducted research on radicalization and violent extremism in the context of the BRI. It was exploratory research that primarily used secondary data. Therefore, there are avenues for future research in six areas: first, research to deepen the understanding of insurgent networks. This could focus on mapping insurgent networks, funding sources, recruitment patterns, and cross-border links. This type of research would contribute to understanding the operational capabilities regional and transnational groups have, thereby enhancing predictive and preventive measures. Second, examining the role of external state and non-state actors. Investigating how foreign governments, intelligence agencies, and ideological groups support or influence insurgent activities will reveal vulnerabilities and points of intervention. This includes exploring links with elements in Afghanistan, Iran, or other neighboring states. Analyzing Socio-Political Drivers is the third area this chapter identifies as possible research in the future. Conducting in-depth research into local grievances, economic disparities, political exclusion, and identity issues in Balochistan and bordering Afghan regions is necessary to develop contextual solutions and counter-radicalization strategies. Research to develop early warning systems. This type of research should aim to create sophisticated early warning mechanisms using intelligence, social media analysis, and ground reports to anticipate attacks and disrupt insurgent plans before they materialize. Fifth, contributing to developing understanding of hybrid threats is another possible area for research. Currently states and non-state actors are increasingly engaging in hybrid warfare strategies and their success in remaining resilient despite losses is due to their capabilities of engaging in non-kinetic operations. Lastly, mapping out the drivers of extremism which are fueling anti-China terrorism and threatening BRI.

CONCLUSION

This chapter explored the evolution and the complex interplay between regional terror groups that are using Afghanistan as a hub for operations and examined the implications of those dynamics towards China's mega diplomatic and economic project, the Belt and Road Initiative. The PRC has invested US$ 1 trillion into the BRI, making it the world's largest lender to developing countries. The Belt and Road Initiative is proposed to foster regional connectivity, economic growth and people-to-people exchange. In doing so, it also connects and provides easy access to militant and extremist groups to also network with one another. Connecting countries and their people also means that those with malicious intentions too can benefit from these global initiatives.

The chapter mentioned that the BRI is a massive investment and that 150 countries are now partnering with it. This is extremely useful for extremists that want to call attention to their existence and their motives. Therefore, attacks on projects that are considered part of the Belt and Road Initiative will continue to grow. Multiple attacks on Chinese convoys and nationals in Pakistan in 2024 exemplifies this. Insiders with sensitive and confidential information, who sympathize with these militant groups will also support them with intelligence. Therefore, host countries of BRI projects need to prioritize their national security so that they are sensitive to this issue.

Militants attacking foreign nationals has become a diplomatic issue, further escalating regional insecurities. Thus, ensuring the safety and security of foreign nationals, in this case Chinese working overseas, becomes a priority of those foreign governments. The lack of attention in this regard would anger the PRC government and its people and would lead to the deterioration of bilateral diplomatic ties. This is currently the case for Pakistan, as it attempts to overcome the damage the BLA militants have caused to its bilateral relations with China.

This has resulted in China using private security contractors to ensure the longevity and safety of their projects and people. The use of these private security contractors has created a national security risk for the host state. This will create a vicious cycle of mistrust in the host state, the Chinese financing, that of BRI projects, and foreign direct investment (FDI) as a whole. Therefore, it is imperative that host states ensure that they are able to provide security for the foreign nationals and the FDI in their countries.

Since unstable countries such as Afghanistan and Pakistan are situated in the Central and South Asian regions, it becomes the region's responsibility to ensure that they maintain regional security. Lack of attention in this regard would mean that militant and extremist groups will flourish in these countries and use them as safe havens to conduct their training and operations. Since China is involved in Afghanistan, it has a role to play in ensuring that the Taliban insurgents do not cross borders into Xinjiang and vice versa. Cross pollination of militants and their ideas would be detrimental to regional security and stability.

REFERENCES

Abi-Habib. Maria. (2018, June 25). How China Got Sri Lanka to Cough Up a Port, *New York Times*. https://www.nytimes.com/2018/06/25/world/asia/china-sri-lanka-port.html

Ahmed, O. (2024, November 20). Pakistan's Security Challenges Threaten to Undermine Its Relationship with China. *South Asian Voices*. https://southasianvoices.org/geo-m-pk-r-cpec-security-challenges-11-20-2024/

Amnesty International. (2024). *Russia 2024*. https://www.amnesty.org/en/location/europe-and-central-asia/eastern-europe-and-central-asia/russia/report-russia/#:~:text=Ukraine%20used%20drones%20to%20attack,people%20and%20injuring%20551%20others

Arduino, A. (2018). China's Belt and Road Security: The Increasing Role of Insurance and Private Security Companies. In Arduino, A., & Gong, X. (Eds.), *Securing the Belt and Road Initiative: Risk Assessment, Private Security and Special Insurances Along the New Wave of Chinese Outbound Investments* (pp. 39–59). Palgrave Macmillan., DOI: 10.1007/978-981-10-7116-4

Associated Press. (2024). A Pakistani separatist group claims bombing that killed 2 Chinese near Karachi airport. https://apnews.com/article/pakistan-karachi-explosion-bla-chinese-killed-38cddd2b80b066b1194872dc45e954e1

Basit, A. (2022). ISKP's evolving propaganda against Chinese imperialism. *Jamestown*. https://jamestown.org/program/iskps-evolving-propaganda-against-chinese-imperialism/

BBC. (2024, April 09). *What we know about attack on a Moscow concert hall*. https://www.bbc.com/news/world-europe-68645755

Belt and Road Portal. (2023, June 21). About Us. https://eng.yidaiyilu.gov.cn/p/0T4ND13J.html

Brown, K. (2018). The Belt and Road: Security Dimensions. *Asia Europe Journal*, *16*, 213–222. DOI: 10.1007/s10308-018-0514-9

Byman, D. (2019). IS CHINA PREPARED FOR GLOBAL TERRORISM? XINJIANG AND BEYOND. *Brookings*. https://www.brookings.edu/articles/is-china-prepared-for-global-terrorism/

Central Asia Data-Gathering and Analysis Team. (2019). BRI in Central Asia: Overview of Chinese Projects. Central Asia Regional Data Review 20. https://www.osce-academy.net/upload/file/20_BRI_in_Central_Asia.pdf

China Military Online. (2024). China-Pakistan "Warrior-VIII" joint counter-terrorism exercise concludes. http://eng.chinamil.com.cn/CHINA_209163/Exercises/News_209184/16359463.html

Decan Herald. (2025). China concerned over new Syrian regime appointing Xinjian Uyghur militants to top military posts. https://www.deccanherald.com/world/china-concerned-over-new-syrian-regime-appointing-xinjiang-uygur-militants-to-top-military-posts-3348073

Dormandy, X. (2007). *Afghanistan's Proxy War*. Boston Globe, republished at Belfer Center for Science and International Affairs. Harvard Kennedy School. https://www.belfercenter.org/publication/afghanistans-proxy-war

Economic Times. (2023, October 27). *India reiterates opposition to China's infrastructure project BRI*. https://infra.economictimes.indiatimes.com/news/urban-infrastructure/india-reiterates-opposition-to-chinas-infrastructure-project-bri/104745701

Fuard, A. (2020). The Drivers of Islamist Extremism in Sri Lanka. *General Sir John Kotelawala Defence University*. http://ir.kdu.ac.lk/handle/345/2836

Fuard, A. (2021). Can the Islamic State - Kohrasan Province resurrect the Caliphate in Afghanistan? *Journal of Defence and Policy Analysis,1*(1). General Sir John Kotelawala Defence University. http://ir.kdu.ac.lk/handle/345/5271

Fuard, A. (2023). Regional security implications of the hybrid war in Afghanistan. General Sir John Kotelawala Defence University. http://ir.kdu.ac.lk/handle/345/7379

Ghiasy, R., & Zhou, J. (2017). *The Silk Road economic belt: Considering security implications and EU-China cooperation prospects*. Stockholm International Peace Research Institute.

Gill, P. (2007). A Multi-Dimensional Approach to Suicide Bombing. *International Journal of Conflict and Violence, 1*(2), 142–159. DOI: 10.4119/ijcv-2750

Gul, I. (2024, October 12). Karachi attack: watershed in Sino-Pak relations? *The Express Tribune*. https://tribune.com.pk/story/2502214/karachi-attack-watershed-in-sino-pak-relations

Gupta, S. (2021). ETIM may shift to ISKP with Taliban-China alliance over Xinjiang. Hindustan Times. https://www.hindustantimes.com/world-news/etim-may-shift-to-iskp-with-taliban-china-alliance-over-xinjiang-101630304620049.html

Himaz, R. (2019). Challenges associated with the BRI: A review of recent economics literature. *Service Industries Journal*, *41*(7–8), 512–526. DOI: 10.1080/02642069.2019.1584193

Hoffman, B. (1997). The confluence of international and domestic trends in terrorism. *Terrorism and Political Violence*, *9*(2), 1–15. DOI: 10.1080/09546559708427399

Hoffman, B. (1999). *Inside Terrorism*. Columbia University Press.

Hu, P. (2023, June 26). What is the BRI? *The Belt and Road Portal*. https://eng.yidaiyilu.gov.cn/p/0N4P7CF0.html

Hussain, A. (2024). March of 'terror': Pakistan Grapples with deadly attacks on China interests. Al-Jazeera. https://www.aljazeera.com/news/2024/3/29/march-of-terror-pakistan-grapples-with-deadly-attacks-on-china-interests

International Crisis Group. (2022). *Afghanistan's security challenges under the Taliban*. https://www.crisisgroup.org/asia/south-asia/afghanistan/afghanistans-security-challenges-under-taliban

Juergensmeyer, M. (2004). *Terror in the Mind of God: The Global Rise of Religious Violence*. University of California Press.

Kelemen, B. (2023). China's Clouded Future in Afghanistan. *The Diplomat*. https://thediplomat.com/2023/02/chinas-clouded-future-in-afghanistan/

Kilcullen, D. (2009). *The Accidental Guerrilla*. Oxford University Press.

Ministry of Foreign Affairs. PRC (n.d.). China's Initiation of the Five Principles of Peaceful Co-Existence. *Ministry of Foreign Affairs, The People's Republic of China*. https://www.mfa.gov.cn/eng/zy/wjls/3604_665547/202405/t20240531_11367542.html

Nantulya, P. (2020, October 8). Chinese Security Contractors in Africa. *Carnegie Endowment for International Peace*. https://carnegieendowment.org/research/2020/10/chinese-security-contractors-in-africa?lang=en

Nedopil, C. (2023). "Countries of the Belt and Road Initiative"; *Shanghai, Green Finance & Development Center*, FISF Fudan University. www.greenfdc.org

Norov, V. (2024, January 25). Shanghai Cooperation Organization is playing an important role in ensuring regional security and stability. *Shanghai Cooperation Organization.* https://eng.sectsco.org/20240125/1244550.html#:~:text=Since%20its%20establishment%20in%20Tashkent%2C%20in%202004%2C,as%20combating%20drug%20trafficking%20in%20the%20region

Rana, S. (2024, October 30). Chinese envoy miffed at CPEC security lapses. *The Express Tribune.* https://tribune.com.pk/story/2506203/chinese-envoy-miffed-at-cpec-security-lapses

Reuters. (2024, November 13). China pushing to deploy its own security staff to protect its own citizens in Pakistan: Report. *Times of India.* https://timesofindia.indiatimes.com/world/china/china-pushing-to-deploy-its-own-security-staff-to-protect-citizens-in-pak-report/articleshow/115235966.cms

Rogers, M. B. et al., (2007, June). *The Role of Religious Fundamentalism in Terrorist Violence: A Social Psychological Analysis.* DOI: 10.1080/09540260701349399

Russel, D. R., & Berger, B. H. (2020). *Weaponizing the Belt and Road Initiative* (Report). Washington D.C.: The Asia Society Policy Institute. https://asiasociety.org/sites/default/files/2020-09/Weaponizing%20the%20Belt%20and%20Road%20Initiative_0.pdf

Senaratne, B. (2018). *Diplomats' Role in Strengthening China's Overseas Image: A Case Study of Sri Lanka. China International Studies 71.* China Institute of International Studies.

Senaratne, B. (2019). *China's Future Relations in the South Asian Region: A Study from a Neoclassical Realist Approach. Defence & Security Journal, 4. Sapugaskanda.* Defence Services Command & Staff College.

Senaratne, B. (2021). 21st Century Maritime Silk Route: Preventive Diplomacy as a Mechanism to Mitigate Future Security Implications. In Ni, H., Abeyratne, S., Siriwardena, L., & Zhou, G. (Eds.), *Lion Dragon Dance: Practice and Reflection on the People-to-People Dialogues in China and Sri Lanka* (pp. 112–128). Zhejiang University Press.

Shanghai Cooperation Organization. (2017, January 17). General information. *Shanghai Cooperation Organization.* https://eng.sectsco.org/20170109/192193.html

Soliev, N. (2021, October 30). Why Is the Islamic State in Afghanistan's Propaganda Targeting China? *The Diplomat.* https://thediplomat.com/2021/10/is-the-islamic-state-in-afghanistan-targeting-china/

The Economist (2025). Militant Uyghurs in Syria threaten the Chinese government. https://www.economist.com/china/2025/01/09/militant-uyghurs-in-syria-threaten-the-chinese-government

The Express Tribune. (2021). *At least 55 killed in Afghanistan mosque attack.* https://tribune.com.pk/story/2323867/at-least-55-killed-in-afghanistan-mosque-attack

The Guardian. (2021). *Protest in Pakistan erupts against China's belt and road plan.* https://www.theguardian.com/environment/2021/aug/20/water-protests-in-pakistan-eruptagainst-chinas-belt-and-road-plan

The Times of India. (2021). *Attack by Uyghur suicide bomber affects China's investment.* https://timesofindia.indiatimes.com/world/south-asia/attack-by-uyghur-suicide-bomber-affectschinas-investment-plans-in-afghanistan/articleshow/87036074.cms

Tsuji, C. (2025, February 6). Belt and Road Initiative. *Britannica.* https://www.britannica.com/topic/Belt-and-Road-Initiative

UN Office of the High Commissioner for Human Rights. (2022). *OHCHR Assessment of human rights concerns in the Xinjiang Uyghur Autonomous Region, People's Republic of China.* https://digitallibrary.un.org/record/3985699?v=pdf

UN Security Council. (2024). *S/2024/556.* https://documents.un.org/doc/undoc/gen/n24/191/91/pdf/n2419191.pdf

Wilson, L. (2015). What I Discovered From Interviewing Imprisoned ISIS Fighters. *The Nation.* https://www.thenation.com/article/archive/wh at-i-discovered-from-interviewing-isisprisoners/

Zaman, S. (2025), Islamabad, Beijing pledge counterterrorism cooperation for security of Chinese workers in Pakistan. *Voice of America.* https://www.voanews.com/a/islamabad-beijing-pledge-counterterrorism-cooperation-for-security-of-chinese-workers-in-pakistan/7965181.html

Zenz, A. (2020). China's Own Documents Show Potentially Genocidal Sterilization Plans in Xinjiang. *Foreign Policy.* https://foreignpolicy.com/2020/07/01/china-documents-uighur-genocidal-sterilization-xinjiang/

KEY TERMS AND DEFINITIONS

Baloch Liberation Army: A militant group which is based out of Pakistan's Balochistan Province that gained traction due to persistent poverty, high unemployment, and inequal development.

Belt and Road Initiative: A diplomatic tool of the People's Republic of China that focuses on connectivity and regional development.

Central Asia: A region comprising five countries: Kazakhstan, Kyrgyzstan, Tajikistan, Turkmenistan, and Uzbekistan, that often share history, culture, and geography. They were former Soviet republics.

China Pakistan Economic Corridor: A billion-dollar Chinese infrastructure development project that links China's western regions to the Arabian Sea.

East Turkestan Islamic Movement: A Uyghur Islamist organization that seeks to establish an Islamic state in the Xinjiang region of China. It is also known as the Turkistan Islamic Party.

Islamic State of Khorasan Province: The Afghan affiliate of the Islamic State (ISIS), which has evolved into the most lethal transnational jihadist group, surpassing the ISIS Central and Al-Qaeda.

Shanghai Cooperation Organization: Initiated in 2001, Kazakhstan, China, Kyrgyzstan, Russia, Tajikistan, and Uzbekistan founded the organization to promote peace, and security and stability in the region.

South Asia: A region at the southern-most tip of Asia comprising Afghanistan, Bangladesh, Bhutan, India, Maldives, Nepal, Pakistan, and Sri Lanka.

Xinjiang Uyghur Autonomous Region: An autonomous region in northwest China, which home to many ethnic minority groups, including the Turkic Uyghur people.

Chapter 8
Cyber Security Threats, Cyber Terrorism, Cyber Warfare

Pankaj Bhambri
https://orcid.org/0000-0003-4437-4103
Guru Nanak Dev Engineering College, Ludhiana, India

Alex Khang
https://orcid.org/0000-0001-8379-4659
Global Research Institute of Technology and Engineering, USA

ABSTRACT

The chapter delves into the multifaceted landscape of cyber threats, emphasizing the critical need for robust security measures in the face of escalating cyber terrorism and warfare. Beginning with an exploration of the evolving nature of cyber threats, the chapter elucidates the various forms of cyber-attacks that pose significant risks to individuals, organizations, and nations alike. From phishing and malware to sophisticated state-sponsored cyber espionage, the arsenal of cyber threats continues to expand, underscoring the urgency for proactive defense strategies. The chapter delves into the intricacies of cyber terrorism, highlighting how malicious actors leverage digital tools to instill fear, disrupt critical infrastructure, and sow chaos in society. It underscores the imperative for advanced security frameworks capable of mitigating the impact of cyber terrorism and safeguarding against its devastating consequences.

DOI: 10.4018/979-8-3693-3522-2.ch008

INTRODUCTION

Cyber assaults, network security, and information present intricate challenges that extend into novel domains for national security as well as public policy. The concept of cyber terror is based on the idea that as states and key infrastructure increasingly rely on networks of computers for their functioning; new weaknesses are introduced, creating a significant vulnerability in the electronic realm (Singh et al., 2005). An adversarial nation or faction could exploit these weaknesses to infiltrate an inadequately protected computer network and impair or perhaps disable vital operations. A considerable portion of the research on cyber-terrorism operates under the assumption that the susceptibility of computer networks and critical infrastructures are equivalent and that these susceptibilities pose a substantial threat to national security. Considering the novelty of computer network technology and its quick integration into economic activities, it is not surprising that these assumptions exist. Upon closer examination of the interconnections between computer networks and key infrastructures, as well as their susceptibility to attacks and the subsequent impact on national security, it becomes evident that the generally accepted view of vulnerability is incorrect. While this article does not conduct a comprehensive appraisal, a cursory examination indicates that although several computer networks are very susceptible to attacks, only a limited number of essential infrastructures share the same level of vulnerability.

Strategies focusing on targeting vital civic infrastructures have been under discussion for over eight decades (Petrović, 1999). Furthermore, it is necessary to analyze cyber attacks in the context of regular infrastructure malfunctions. There is a wealth of data available on power outages, airline delays, and communications interruptions that occur as part of daily operations. By analyzing the repercussions of these routine failures, we can assess the impact of cyber-warfare and cyber-terrorism. Furthermore, it is necessary to assess the level of reliance that infrastructure has on networks of computers and the extent of redundancy that already exists within these systems. Regarding cyber-terrorism, it is essential to analyze the utilization of cyber weapons within the framework of terrorists' political objectives and reasons and assess the likelihood of cyber weapons accomplishing these goals. Upon initial examination, these elements indicate that computer vulnerabilities in networks pose a growing and significant issue for businesses, but their impact on national security is exaggerated. Modern industrial societies possess a greater level of resilience than what may initially be seen. Figure 1.1 depicts the various types of cyber-attacks. Here, each category is represented by icons corresponding to the type of attack.

Figure 1. Main cyber-attack types

Complex infrastructures, particularly in major market economies, are highly dispersed, varied, redundant, and capable of self-repair, making them less susceptible to attacks than a superficial evaluation might imply. Cyber attacks are consistently less efficacious and less disruptive than physical assaults in all instances. Their sole benefit lies in their cost-effectiveness and logistical simplicity compared to a physical assault.

ROUTINE FAILURE VERSUS CYBER ATTACK

National security is faced with a fresh set of challenges due to the safeguarding of critical infrastructure. Multiple actors are involved. The emphasis is placed on technologies and services that are intended for use by civilians and businesses. The significance of military might is diminished. The extent of these emerging issues is contingent upon our definition of national security and the criteria we establish for tolerable harm. No country will tolerate any form of attack on infrastructure or disruption of services, whether from a legal or humanitarian standpoint. By aiming to avoid any disruption of electric energy or water delivery due to cyber-attacks, we have established an exceptionally rigorous security benchmark. Nevertheless, in terms of strategic military analysis, attacks that fail to diminish national capabilities lack significance. From this standpoint, if a cyber-attack fails to result in damage beyond the level of ordinary interruptions encountered by any economy, it does not provide an urgent or substantial threat to national security.

At a national scale, numerous systems that are responsible for essential infrastructure services often experience frequent failures at either the system or local level, resulting in customers being deprived of service for extended periods, ranging from hours to days. To instill fear, accomplish strategic objectives, or produce a discernible impact, cyber-terrorists would have to launch coordinated attacks on several targets concurrently, sustaining them for extended durations. It is highly unlikely that hackers, terrorist groups, or nation-states would be able to carry out multiple sustained attacks on critical infrastructure. This is especially true for nation-states, as the risk of being discovered and facing universal condemnation for an act of war far exceeds the limited benefits gained from cyber assaults on infrastructure.

CYBER SECURITY THREATS

Cybersecurity is dependent on the vigilance and decision-making of humans as they organize, manage, and use computer networks and the internet. Multiple endeavors have been undertaken to address the difficulty of evaluating cyber security, resulting in the creation of various frameworks. Nevertheless, the frameworks face various challenges despite their initial smooth operation throughout the development phase. The restrictions arise from various factors, including the emergence of new technology and limitations in facilities. Security concerns are frequently seen as a compromise between the need for security and the advantages offered by other factors (Singh et al., 2021).

The National Initiative for Cybersecurity Education (NICE) framework is a collaborative effort between multiple government agencies, led by the National Institute of Standards and Technology (NIST). The agency's primary areas of interest include raising awareness, providing cyber security education, offering training programs, and facilitating professional development opportunities. Pleasant Developed the Cybersecurity Workforce Framework. This paradigm emphasizes the importance of acknowledgment during the process of instruction. Furthermore, it achieves a safe cyber architecture as specifically stated within the given environment. Furthermore, the framework has failed to include the escalating emergence of new technologies, which exacerbates the issues posed by cyber security risks. The scholars also emphasize the importance of having sufficient cybersecurity standards and procedures, which should be regularly evaluated. The researchers also note that the frameworks do not encompass the components of threats that exploit vulnerabilities. Therefore, it is necessary to address risk management strategies in order to mitigate these risks. Furthermore, the authors suggest that there is a lack of cybercrime legislation to effectively address the actions of criminals. An efficient security strategy can collaborate with modeling business operations.

Cybersecurity refers to a collection of strategies, protocols, and behaviors aimed at safeguarding computers and personal information from a range of malicious attacks. Every organization has a Cyber-safety Program policy, PPM 310–22, that mandates all devices connected to the company's electronic communications network to adhere to specific security criteria. As mandated by the system, the majority of departments provide annual reports that outline their degrees of compliance. Additionally, there are other resources available to support academics, staff, and students in meeting the requirements for cyber-safety. Cybersecurity dangers can arise from viruses, hackers, identity thieves, and spyware. The malware infiltrates the PC via email attachments and file sharing (Bose et al., 2021). A single infected machine has the potential to disrupt all computer networks. Hackers are individuals who gain unauthorized access to a computer system from a remote place. These individuals employ a computer to distribute unsolicited bulk messages or malicious software, or engage in other actions that result in computer dysfunction. When it comes to detecting thieves, individuals who gain unlawful access to personal information such as social security and financial account details are classified. Spyware refers to software that clandestinely attaches itself to downloaded programs, collecting data on internet activities and surreptitiously transmitting personal information without the user's awareness. Furthermore, neglecting to safeguard personal information and user's computer might result in many repercussions for a corporation, in addition to the concern mentioned earlier. The consequences include loss of access to the campus computer network, exposure of confidential information, disruption of integration and access to valuable University data, potential lawsuits related to personal electronic data, loss of public trust, missed opportunities, internal conflict, and possible employment termination. Multiple research have been undertaken to investigate the process of filtering email viruses. Previous research has examined many spam detection approaches and identified an effective, accurate, and reliable process for detecting spam. The existing applications utilized by different anti-spam technologies are regarded static, meaning they can be easily bypassed by making slight modifications to the messages. In order to accomplish this, the spammer would assess the existing anti-spam techniques and identify the strategies to manipulate. In order to effectively tackle spam, it is crucial to implement a new technique. This novel technique must fully counteract the evolving strategies employed by spammers. It must also possess the ability to adjust to the specific organization it is safeguarding, as the solution resides in Bayesian mathematics. The study findings revealed the efficacy of certain spam detection methods and highlighted the various challenges connected with spam. Multiple studies have indicated that it is not possible to completely eliminate spam. However, we may successfully reduce its impact by employing the Bayesian technique, which outperforms other strategies in terms of limiting spam. Furthermore, previous studies have also investigated a range of issues related to spam and the methodologies and strategies used for spam filtering. The various techniques used to identify inbound spam include Bayesian analysis, Blacklist/Whitelist, Keyword checking, and Mail header analysis (Bakshi et al., 2021). The various spam filtering techniques include Distributed Adaptive Blacklists, Rule-based Filtering, Bayesian Classifier, K Nearest Neighbors, Support Vector Machine (SVM), and Content-based Spam Filtering Techniques such as Neural Networks, Multi-layer Networks, Search Engine Techniques, Genetic Engineering Techniques, and Artificial Immune System Techniques. The study findings indicate that numerous filtering strategies rely on text categorization methods. However, no methodology can assert to offer a perfect solution with a 0% rate of false positives and false negatives. There are numerous research opportunities available for the classification of multimedia and text messages.

CYBER WARFARE

Wars have been an integral aspect of human existence since the beginning of recorded time.

The collective knowledge gained from repeated acts of devastation has led to the development of several measures aimed at mitigating the atrocities of war. These include the establishment of global institutions, the formulation of international treaties that regulate the permissible conduct during warfare, the creation of humanitarian aid organizations, and the implementation of a judicial system to prosecute individuals responsible for war crimes (Kuzhaloli et al., 2020). Due to the novelty of cyberspace and its divergence from the fundamental principles of the physical world, a precise definition of the idea of cyber war has not yet been established. In Israel, there have been ongoing conversations for at least ten years over the topic of war in the information age, computer warfare, and information warfare. Twenty Cyber threats can be categorized based on the nature of the action and the extent of the resulting harm. The following is a suggested taxonomy, organized in a descending order of severity.

A deliberate assault on multiple non-military locations resulting in tangible harm.
The intentional disturbance and assault on vital national information infrastructures, resulting in tangible harm.
Disruption and assault on military objectives within the state's independent borders.
Sabotage and assault on military objectives beyond the jurisdiction of the nation's sovereign territory.
Incorporation of inactive offensive instruments, such as a Trojan horse or logic bomb, which are probable indications of premeditation for an assault.
Illicit behavior, corporate espionage.
Utilization of dual-use weapons: collection of intelligence, exploration of shared security weaknesses, conducting penetration tests.

The activities include conducting a propagandist media campaign and engaging in the misuse and defacement of official websites. The challenge in understanding cyber warfare arises from the complex and intricate nature of the notions of assault, defense, and violence in the realm of cyberspace. To ascertain whether a cyber strike is a component of a war, certain characteristics need to be scrutinized: a. Is the activity being carried out by a nation state, and if so, what is its organizational basis and geographic origin? b. Results: Was the attack capable of causing damage, and did it indeed result in damage and casualties? c. Complexity level: Was the attack characterized by intricate planning and the utilization of coordinated resources typically accessible to nation-states? Given the current characteristics of cyberspace, it is exceedingly challenging to address these inquiries, let alone provide satisfactory responses that might inform the development of public policy.

Deterance

Researchers in political science, security studies, game theory, economics, and psychology are actively engaged in advanced study on the topic of deterrence. Up to now, the world has effectively managed the threat of nuclear weapons that have the potential to annihilate the planet by relying on deterrence strategies centered on guaranteed response. Nevertheless, the Cold War strategy of nuclear deterrence is completely unworkable in the realm of cyber warfare, primarily because to the current configuration of cyberspace (Kaur and Bhambri, 2019). This configuration renders it exceedingly difficult to definitively attribute an attack and swiftly determine the origin and identity of the assailant. Implementing deterrence by inflicting significant consequences on the attacker is highly challenging; therefore, any form of deterrence in the realm of cyberspace must rely on stopping the attacker from achieving their goals. Investing in targeted research on deterrence is crucial for mitigating threats to national security.

DIFFERENCES BETWEEN THE TERMS CYBERCRIME AND CYBERTERRORISM

Currently, there exist numerous definitions regarding cyber crime & cyber terrorism. There has been some disagreement on whether the phrases "cybercrime" and "cyber terrorism" are synonymous with each other. However, some authors argue that these two concepts are synonymous, while others disagree with this definition and propose two distinct definitions. From a worldwide perspective, the most significant definitions are those that are utilized to develop the language of the United States. However, to differentiate between the phrases "cybercrime" and "cyber terrorism" in the next paragraphs, it is essential to highlight their differences. It is essential to provide a precise definition of the term "cyber terrorism," and officials are actively encouraging this. The primary objective of cyberterrorism is to infiltrate specific institutions' systems to cause violence and inflict damage, such as financial loss and property destruction. This is done to destabilize the targeted country and weaken its security. Actors known as hackers engage in cybercrime, driven by either personal fun or a competitive desire for greater individual accomplishment. Additionally, they may pursue financial gain or other objectives. Hackers, who are frequently associated with terrorist organizations such as Al Qaeda, ETA, IRA, etc., engage in cyber activities to achieve specific political objectives (Ottis & Lorents, 2010). In addition, certain authors delineate distinctions between hackers based on their motivations. Hackers who engage in attacks for pleasure might be categorized as ordinary criminals, whereas cyber terrorists should be classified as a distinct and severe form of criminal activity (Guice and Duffy, 2000). Cyber terrorists can target specific strategic locations that are of great importance to certain countries. However, this does not imply that their attacks are limited in scope and cannot have a broader impact to accomplish their desired objectives. For instance, a potential target of cyber terrorists may be an electrical plant that provides electricity to residents living near it. Engaging in this form of attack, cyber terrorists can have a significant impact across a broad spectrum with few resources (Schudel and Wood, 2000). If the chain of energy supply is disrupted by this type of attack, it will have an impact on the daily routine of citizens in meeting their vital demands (Petrović R. S., 2001). Another instance of cyber terrorism involves the hacking of hospital computer systems to alter medical prescriptions, resulting in harm to patients by administering incorrect medication. According to Petrović R. S. (2001), this terrorist act has the potential to affect anyone, making them a victim. The key distinction between cyber crime & cyber terrorism lies in their shared utilization of computers or ICT as a weapon to carry out acts of terrorism or criminal activities.

Weapons of Mass Annoyance

An in-depth analysis of various scenarios involving assaults on vital infrastructures provides a more precise understanding of the strategic or national security implications of cyber-attacks. Dams utilized for storing water and power generation are frequently identified as potential targets for cyber attacks. According to a recent article in The Washington Post, unidentified "U.S. analysts" assert that an intruder might potentially cause harm to people and property by gaining control over floodgates in a dam or substations managing 300,000 volts of electricity using virtual methods. The water delivery infrastructure in the USA is highly vulnerable to cyber-attacks. The United States has a total of 54,064 distinct water systems. Several water delivery systems in the United States, including those in major cities, still depend on technologies that are resistant to network intrusions. In the United States, there have been instances where a community's supply of water has been disrupted for several days, typically due to flooding (Forno, 1998). However, these incidents have not caused fear or complete immobilization. If a terrorist were to discover a weakness in the supply of water that could be used to temporarily disable the water supply of a city, this vulnerability may be utilized to amplify the impact of an assault physically by preventing firefighters from accessing water. Typically, a digital assault that would go unnoticed in the usual chaos of everyday life could have significant amplifying effects if carried out at the same time as a physical strike.

Analyzing the similarities and differences between aerial with cyber attacks on dams that generate electricity can be used as a means of assessing the level of cyber threats. At the onset of the Second World War, the British Royal Air Force executed a bold assault on the dams located in the Ruhr region, which served as a primary supplier of electricity for German industrial operations (Horrigan, 2004). The raid achieved its objective as the dams were ruptured by explosive devices, resulting in a temporary disruption of the power supply in the area.4 An analogous cyber assault took place when a juvenile hacker allegedly breached the computer controls of a dam in the U.S. Southwest, albeit no disruption of service or bodily harm was inflicted. Neither strike caused paralyzing harm or a significant drop in electrical power. Between the two incidents, the online assault was somewhat ineffective as it did not result in any tangible harm and could be categorized more as a nuisance rather than a danger. The airborne assault caused tangible destruction that required restoration.

The sole benefit of a cyber assault is its cost-effectiveness, as it requires only a teenager and a desktop computer, rather than the deployment of important aircrews and pricey planes. Several investigations indicate that cyber-terrorists are capable of disabling the electrical power supply. The U.S. power grid is an attractive target due to its critical importance. However, it is a complex network consisting of numerous backup structures that are designed to handle routine system failures and disruptions. The national power system is a complex network including more than 3,000 public and private firms and cooperatives that are closely interconnected. These 3,000 power suppliers utilize a diverse range of information technologies to manage their power generation and transmission controls. To significantly interrupt the power supply, a hacker or a large number of hackers would have to identify flaws in several systems. However, even in such a scenario, the resulting attack may only cause a few hours-of-service disruption (Clarke, 1996). During Congressional declarations, NERC officials have stated that in recent years, there have been no instances of viruses or massive Denial of Service assaults causing interruptions in the U.S. electrical grid.7 Although industry sources may occasionally present an excessively positive outlook, it is a fact that electric system disruptions have been primarily caused by fallen trees, while no disruptions have been caused by cyber-attacks (Freeh, 1998). The Information Assurance Group of the National Security Telecommunication Advisory Panel conducted a risk assessment and determined that the most significant danger to the electric power infrastructure is physical destruction. Electronic intrusion, although still a very minor hazard, is emerging in comparison to this. The United States has conducted a significant experiment on the consequences of disrupting electricity supplies, as demonstrated by California's encounter with 'deregulation' in the previous year. California's attempts to deregulate the electricity market led to extended periods of power outages and intermittent reductions in power supply throughout the state. Deregulation posed a greater threat to the electrical system than any potential cyber-terrorist strike. The California regulation event had a discernible economic impact, but it was not severe enough to cause significant damage or instill fear in the American population. In 1999, widespread power outages had a significant impact on millions of individuals as well as resulted in substantial financial losses for electrical power customers due to disrupted company operations and reduced productivity (Advocat, 2005). The disruptions occurred due to a rise in electricity consumption caused by prolonged hot weather conditions. Unlike the State government of California or hot weather conditions, there have been no instances of blackouts in the United States that can be attributed to hackers or cyber-terrorists.

A commonly mentioned cyber-threat is the deliberate disruption of national air traffic systems, which can lead to flight cancellations, the suspension of air transport services, and pose risks to passengers and crew members (Singh et al., 2004). Currently, computer networks cannot remotely control aircraft, therefore making it impossible to allow a cyber-attacker to gain control of an aircraft. Aircraft continue to employ pilots who are extensively trained to operate the aircraft in the event of an emergency. In a similar vein the Federal Aviation Authority is not dependent exclusively on computer networks to oversee aviation traffic, nor does it rely on the Internet for its communications.

The extensive human engagement in the management and decision-making process for the aviation industry significantly mitigates the likelihood of any cyber assault. During a typical month, the occurrence of storms, electrical outages, and programming problems routinely leads to a significant amount of disruption in flight operations. Pilots as well as air traffic control officers are familiar with unforeseen disruptions and have adjusted their procedures to mitigate the impact. Airlines and travelers are familiar with and anticipate a significant level of disturbance in the system.

Every month, it is customary for fifteen thousand to twenty thousand flights in the USA to experience delays or cancellations. A cyber assault that undermined the air traffic network would result in delays and inconvenience, but it wouldn't be considered a threat to national security.

The Federal Aviation Administration (FAA) possesses a total of 90 significant computer systems and operates on nine distinct communications networks. These networks depend on outdated equipment and employ proprietary software, which makes it challenging for unauthorized individuals to breach. This may elucidate the reason why the limited number of recorded attacks has not had an impact on aviation traffic (Copeland, 2000).

During a documented occurrence, a juvenile hacker disrupted the local telephone line in a part of New England, resulting in the cessation of operations at a control tower of a small airport and the inability to activate the runway lights. Despite the interruption lasting 6 hours, there were no incidents reported at the airport. On separate occasions, the computer networks at FAA headquarters were breached, enabling hackers to disclose unpublished information regarding airport passenger screening operations. Additionally, a hacker successfully gained access to an FAA mail server. None of these instances led to any interruption in air travel. Paradoxically, if security measures are not given adequate attention, modernization could potentially heighten the vulnerability of the FAA. An internet attack that occurred recently exemplifies the inherent weaknesses that can be exploited through cyber attacks. The attack lasted for one hour. Due to the attacks, eight out of the thirteen systems were taken offline. The attack was imperceptible and had no impact on

Internet users. The assault on the world of DNS did not perceptibly diminish the performance of the Internet. The majority of DNS data required for the everyday functioning of the Internet is maintained locally and refreshed regularly. Only a small number of requests necessitate aid from the primary servers. In addition, the existence of thirteen servers (with five remaining unaffected by the attack) indicates a level of redundancy that implies the DNS servers are not vulnerable to internet weaknesses.

Following the DNS attack, a significant number of Internet users in the western part of the USA saw significant delays as their service provider encountered routing issues caused by programming faults. Contrary to the attack, this DNS outage caused a genuine disruption in service, but it did not impact national security (Arquilla and Ronfeldt, 1993). Although the Internet has certain potential weak areas that could lead to widespread disruption, it was specifically created to be a resilient and decentralized communication network that can continue functioning even in the event of a strategic nuclear attack.

The development of packet switching and Internet protocols enabled the preservation of communication even in the event of node removal inside the network (Rana and Bhambri, 2024). Additionally, the Internet was specifically built to automatically reroute around any damage, ensuring uninterrupted communication. In addition, computer networks depend on a robust infrastructure of high-capacity telecommunications systems that are generally resistant to cyber-attacks. The implementation of novel communication technologies also improves the ability to endure and persist. Wireless and satellite connections offer additional backup for landline systems. Currently, the majority of industrialized nations possess the capability to utilize three or four distinct methods of communication, resulting in a far more resilient system compared to ten years ago. However, similar to different infrastructures, it is a resilient target.

In the United States, there is not a unified 911 system. Instead, there are numerous local systems, each employing distinct technologies and protocols. There has been no instance of a big city's 911 system being compromised via hacking. It is potentially feasible to inundate the system by dispatching a large number of email messages, urging individuals to dial 911 for crucial information. This method was employed during the 1997 United States cyber exercise known as “Eligible Receiver”. This type of approach often has limited effectiveness, usually only being successful once. However, when combined with a bombing or another physical attack, it can significantly enhance the impact of a terrorist event, acting as a 'force multiplier'.

Computer networks have become increasingly crucial for manufacturing and economic activity, but they also pose new risks such as cyber crime and corporate espionage. Nevertheless, there is conflicting information regarding the susceptibility of industrial processes to cyber attacks. In the year 2000, a virus infiltrated and affected a total of 1,000 computer systems within Ford Motor Company. Ford had an influx of 140,000 tainted email messages over three hours, prompting the company to promptly halt its network operations (Shanmuga and Bhambri, 2024). The organization experienced a nearly week-long interruption in its email service. However, Ford stated that the rogue program seems to have only caused minimal irreversible harm. All 114 factories of the manufacturer remained operational, as reported by the company. The computerized engineering drawings and other technical data remained unaltered. Ford continued to publish information for dealers and automobile component providers on its designated websites. Companies now indicate that the protective measures they have implemented have reduced the impact of viruses that were initially highly destructive, rendering them only insignificant annoyances.

Cyber attacks are frequently portrayed as a menace to the armed forces, and the web has significant ramifications for spying and warfare. Information warfare encompasses a variety of actions, with cyber strikes being maybe the least significant among them. Although information operations and information dominance have become crucial components of effective military campaigns, no country has exposed its military personnel to a situation where they rely on computer networks that are susceptible to external attacks. This significantly restricts the efficacy of cyber weapons, which are codes transmitted across computer networks. The numerous claims concerning military networks of computers being compromised often fail to specify if these networks are utilized for essential military operations. It is important to note that these attacks did not lead to the cancellation of any sorties or cause any casualties. Likewise, it is improbable that a foreign entity employing cyber weapons would be successful in its attempt to hinder the departure of a carrier war group from the United States. A recent assault conducted by a British cybercriminal did not compromise any secret data nor cause any disruption to military activities.

INDIA'S IT INFRASTRUCTURE

India's record in the IT sector is varied, despite achieving success in software development. This is mostly due to outdated technical infrastructure and insufficient investment in the communications sector. Based on a recent scholarly analysis, the growth of the Internet relies on the presence of several elements such as the telecommunications infrastructure, networking engineers and users, networking and user gear, and government guidance. The subsequent paragraphs delineate India's IT infrastructure across these four aspects.

Infrastructure: India's telephone network infrastructure has traditionally been constrained in terms of its scale and dependability. Despite continuous advancements, the sub-continent still lacks a fiber optic infrastructure for high-speed data connections. In addition, VSNL, the governmental monopoly in international telecommunications and domestic Internet access, has artificially increased the expense of IT services. According to a report published in 2001, a sluggish-speed dial-up subscription can cost $200 per year for 500 hours of usage.

Engineers: The Indian government has a longstanding history of endorsing technical education. The sub-continent is a major source of engineers and scientists for export. One source states that Silicon Valley has a large number of Indian millionaires, and American immigration regulations have provided Indians with a greater advantage. India's internationally competitive computer software business is mostly driven by small groups of experienced engineers who operate independently.

Networking and end-user hardware: Historically, the IT manufacturing sector in India has had a certain level of protection. In regards to computer hardware with peripherals, the manufacturing sector saw modest growth in the 1990s. This was mostly due to minimal expansion in the home market and the inability of manufacturers with limited production capacity to compete effectively. Foreign investors faced difficulties when they tried to get into the Indian market due to New Delhi's inadequate intellectual property protection.

Government leadership: Before the early 1990s, the progress of the IT field in New Delhi was hindered by the sluggishness of the government bureaucracy and other obstacles, which put it behind neighboring countries like China. Capitalizing on India's abundant pool of skilled professionals in the computer and engineering sectors, the government made strategic investments in software technology parks along with other initiatives throughout the early 1990s to stimulate the growth of intellectual property. These endeavors, backed by state governments that prioritize reform, established a policy framework that fosters growth.

QUANTUM COMPUTING

The progress in computer capabilities has resulted in a gradual shift from traditional computing to quantum computing. Quantum computing signifies a substantial shift from traditional computing (Anand and Bhambri, 2018). Quantum computers may perform complex calculations at a speed that is 100 million times quicker than ordinary computers by utilizing the 'superposition' property of a qubit. The qubit possesses the distinct ability to discern between two states (such as 0 or 1, true or false, black or white) and also handles values that lie between these two states. Quantum computers differ from classical computers in that they make use of quantum bits, or qubits, instead of binary bits (0s and 1s), to process data. These qubits utilize the fundamental principles of quantum mechanics, namely superposition and entanglement. This allows them to assess intricate calculations at speeds that cannot be achieved by their classical counterparts. This remarkable skill, however, is accompanied with substantial cybersecurity ramifications. The manner in which mathematical operations are executed can be altered. This facilitates the execution of an unlimited array of calculations while simultaneously considering all possibilities.

Classical cryptography mostly depends on the computational complexity of specific mathematical issues. The primary problem revolves around the vulnerability of existing encryption techniques. Contemporary encryption methods, such as ECC and RSA, rely on the computational complexity of mathematical issues such as discrete logarithms and integer factorization. on instance, the RSA encryption scheme, which is extensively employed in Cryptography, relies on the computational complexity of factoring big numbers on classical computers. Modern cryptography categorizes cryptosystems into two distinct types based on the method used to encrypt a message: asymmetric and symmetric key schemes (Bhambri and Gupta, 2018). Asymmetric key schemes, also known as public key schemes, involve the use of two distinct keys for each party involved in the exchange of secrets. Messages are encrypted using a public key. The received messages are decrypted using the corresponding private key. Symmetric key systems utilize a single key for both encryption and decryption techniques. The RSA cryptosystem is widely employed as an asymmetric key cryptosystem technique.

Quantum computers have enhanced computing capability and advanced processing capacity, enabling them to potentially surpass current computers in breaking cryptography systems and solving issues at a far faster rate. Consequently, making current encryption methods obsolete. A quantum computer executing Shor's algorithm has the capability to accurately factorize big integers, thereby compromising RSA encryption. This issue has led to the development of post-quantum cryptography. Cybersecurity and encryption were employed in response to the imperative to safeguard the information present in cyberspace. Nevertheless, the emergence of quantum computing has significantly disrupted the traditional functioning of cybersecurity and cryptography, resulting in considerable challenges. While various publications have been written on research undertaken in this field, there are still restrictions and constraints in thoroughly reviewing the current method of using quantum computing for this purpose. The key features of Quantum Information include the quantum no-cloning theory, quantum teleportation, the principle of uncertainty, and the hidden properties of quantum information (Bhambri et al., 2019).

All of these measures are adopted and employed to counteract cyber communication threats, which can be either active or passive in nature. The theory of quantum no-cloning describes the properties of quantum information, including the inability to delete or create exact copies of an unknown quantum state. Cloning refers to the process of generating an identical quantum state in a separate system without any discernible differences. Research has demonstrated that the replication of quantum systems by machines is not feasible. The idea of undeleting ensures that any harmful or deletion-related impact caused by an adversary on quantum information would leave behind a trace in secure communication. The removal of an arbitrary duplicate of a quantum state is prohibited by the linearity of quantum theory, as stated in the Nature publication. In the process of quantum teleportation, the sender obtains classical information by measuring the initial quantum state. The sender distributes this information through traditional communication methods. The quantum information that was not extracted by the sender in the measurement is still remaining. The transmission of the item to the recipient occurs subsequently through measurement. The principle of uncertainty is commonly referred to as Heisenberg's uncertainty principle. The concept was first proposed by the German physicist Heisenberg in 1927. The uncertainty principle is based on the concept that it is fundamentally impossible to precisely pinpoint the position of a particle in a micro-environment. The particle's presence is typically associated with varying probabilities in different locations. Quantum information possesses distinct qualities that classical information lacks, which are found in its hidden attributes. More precisely, the local measurement operation is unable to obtain the quantum code information when it is in the entangled state. This information can only be revealed through a joint measurement.

Quantum encryption is an advanced technique used to secure the transmission of information. It relies on the principles of quantum mechanics. This technique employs quantum bits, sometimes known as "qubits", instead of conventional binary bits, to perform data encryption and decryption. Quantum encryption utilizes the principle of entanglement, where two particles become connected in such a way that their states are immediately influenced by each other, regardless of the distance between them. The notion of sharing the key for encrypted data decryption using entangled particles is utilized in Quantum Key Distribution (QKD). Any attempt to disrupt the particles triggers a modification in their condition, thereby alerting the intended recipients of a potential violation. Quantum cryptography offers a multitude of advantages. Quantum encryption offers an unparalleled level of protection due to its interference invulnerability. The sophistication of quantum cryptography renders existing encryption systems inconsequential due to the progress of emerging standards. The present encryption methods used in quantum encryption setups make it highly challenging to instantly detect breaches, man-in-the-middle attacks, and eavesdropping. In the realm of cybersecurity and encryption, eavesdropping refers to a cyberattack when a malevolent individual disrupts, intercepts, and intrudes into encrypted communication without the consent of the persons involved in the conversation. The primary goal is to illicitly acquire confidential data, such as login passwords, personal information, or encryption keys. The interference caused by an external entity disrupts the state of the particle and notifies both the transmitter and receiver of the attempted attack, as it is challenging to detect a quantum system without causing disturbance.

CONCLUSION

The worldwide web is a novel phenomenon, and unfamiliar entities can sometimes evoke a greater sense of fear than their actual nature warrants. Many first assessments of cyber threats along with cyber security seem to adopt a pessimistic outlook. There is no imminent danger or threat to national security, and the effectiveness of cyber weapons in undermining a country's power or instilling fear in its populace is limited. The examples outlined in this paper indicate that governments possess greater strength and adaptability than what was first believed by early theories of cyberterrorism. To comprehend the susceptibility of crucial infrastructures to cyber attacks, it is imperative to conduct a comprehensive evaluation of each targeted infrastructure. Based on this preliminary evaluation, it appears that the infrastructures of major industrial nations are resilient against cyber attacks. Terrorist organizations or foreign military forces may attempt to carry out cyber attacks; however, they tend to be dissatisfied with the outcome. Nations possess greater resilience than initially acknowledged by early analysts of cyber-terrorism and cyber-warfare, and the impact of cyber attacks is comparatively less severe than that of physical attacks. The occurrence of Digital Pearl Harbors is highly improbable. Infrastructure systems, due to their frequent encounters with failures, exhibit a higher level of adaptability and efficiency in restoring services than initially anticipated by analysts. Cyber attacks, unless they are coupled with a simultaneous physical assault that causes bodily harm, have a brief duration and are not successful. While the potential dangers of cyber-terrorism and cyber-warfare may be exaggerated, the significance of espionage and cybercrime may not be properly recognized by many onlookers.

The susceptibility of critical assets to cyber attacks is not fixed and can be influenced by three factors. The prevalence of vulnerability may escalate as civilizations transition to a ubiquitous computing environment, where an increasing number of daily tasks are automated and dependent on remote computer networks. The shift towards increased dependence on networks is inevitable due to the cost-effectiveness of Internet communication protocols, but also opens up new opportunities for access. If countries do not effectively balance their transition towards increased networking and reliance on Internet protocols with measures to enhance network security, strengthen law enforcement, and ensure the resilience of critical infrastructures, these changes will result in heightened vulnerabilities. From a wider security standpoint, countries currently encounter a variety of vague threats to their security that are challenging for conventional national security methods to address. The boundaries separating domestic and international, public and private, or the military and police are becoming less distinct, and the characteristics and demands of national security are undergoing fast transformation. The primary consequences of these shifts in cyber security are the necessity for national policy to adapt to the increasing interconnection between economies and prioritize collaboration among nations to overcome cyber threats.

REFERENCES

Advocat, J. (2005). *"Internet clinical trials: examining new disciplinary experiments in health care", Monash University* (Vol. 7). Anthropology Matters Journal.

Arquilla, J., & Ronfeldt, D. (1993). Cyberwar is Coming. *Comparative Strategy, Taylor & Francis, 12*(2), 141–165.

Bakshi, P., Bhambri, P., & Thapar, V. (2021). A review paper on wireless sensor network techniques in Internet of Things (IoT). Wesleyan Journal of Research, 14(7), 147-160. Retrieved from https://www.wesleyanjournal.in/

Bhambri, P., & Gupta, O. P. (2018). Implementing Machine Learning Algorithms for Distance based Phylogenetic Trees. I.K.Gujral Punjab Technical University, Jalandhar (Ph.D. thesis). Anand, A., & Bhambri, P. (2018). Rotation, Scale and Translation Invariant Character Recognition System using Neural Network. I.K.Gujral Punjab Technical University, Jalandhar (M.Tech. thesis).

Bhambri, P., Sinha, V. K., & Jaiswal, M. (2019). Change in iris dimensions as a potential human consciousness level indicator. *International Journal of Innovative Technology and Exploring Engineering, 8*(9S), 517–525. DOI: 10.35940/IJITEE.I1082.0789S19

Bose, M. M., Yadav, D., Bhambri, P., & Shankar, R. (2021). Electronic customer relationship management: Benefits and pre-implementation considerations. *Journal of Maharaja Sayajirao University of Baroda, 55*(01(VI)), 1343–1350.

Clarke, R. (1996), "Information Technology & Cyberspace: Their Impact on Rights and Liberties", Mietta's, The Australian National University, Melbourne.

Copeland, E. Thomas, (2000) "The Information Revolution and National Security", Strategic Studies Institute, U.S. Army War College.

Forno, F. R. (1998) "Hidden threats and vulnerabilities to information systems at the dawn of a new century", Emergency Net News, 11/22, http://www. emergency.com/techthrt.htm

Freeh, J.L. (1998) "Threats to US national security: Congressional statement", FBI, January 28

Guice, J., & Duffy, R. (2000). *The future of the internet in science*. USRA Research Institute for Advanced Computer Science, NASA Ames Research Center.

Horrigan, B. J. (2004) "How Americans Get in Touch With Government", Pew Interne&American Life Project, www.pewinternet.org

Kaur, J., & Bhambri, P. (2019). Design of Paddy Crop Prediction Technique based on K-Mean, Naïve Bayes, KNN and SVM Classifiers. I.K. Gujral Punjab Technical University, Jalandhar (M.Tech. thesis).

Kuzhaloli, S., Devaneyan, P., Sitaraman, N., Periyathanbi, P., Gurusamy, M., & Bhambri, P. (2020). Invention titled "IoT based Smart Kitchen Application for Gas Leakage Monitoring" (Application No. 202041049866A). Published on 27th November 2020 (Issue No. 48/2020, Page No. 59674). Retrieved from http://ipindia.nic.in/writereaddata/Portal/IPOJournal/1_4929_1/Part-1.pdf

Ottis, R., & Lorents, P. (2010) "Cyberspace: Definition and Implications", In *Proceedings of the 5th International Conference on Information Warfare and Security*, Dayton, OH, US, 8-9 April.

Petrović, R. S. (1999). *"Globalno informaciono ratovanje", Zbornik radova (CD-ROM), YU INFO 99*. Kopaonik.

Petrović R. S., (2001) "Neki aspekti nacionalne bezbednosti u informacionom dobu, Nauka, Tehnika, Bezbednost (NTB)", Rad po pozivu, UDC: 681.324; 65.012.8, Godina XI, Broj 1, str. 7-27.

Rana, R., & Bhambri, P. (2024). Healthcare Computational Intelligence and Blockchain: Real-Life Applications. In P. Bhambri, S. Rani, & M. Fahim (Eds.), Computational Intelligence and Blockchain in Biomedical and Health Informatics (pp. 155-168). CRC Press, Taylor & Francis Group, USA. DOI: DOI: 10.1201/9781003459347

Schudel, G., & Wood, B. (2000), "MODELING BEHAVIOR OF THE CYBER-TERRORIST", In Proceedings of a Workshop "Research on Mitigating the Insider Threat to Information Systems - #2", RAND Corporation.

Shanmuga, S. M., & Bhambri, P. (2024). Pulmonary and Lungs Nodule Classification using Deep Learning. In P. Bhambri, S. Rani, & M. Fahim (Eds.), Computational Intelligence and Blockchain in Biomedical and Health Informatics (pp. 320-332). CRC Press, Taylor & Francis Group, USA. DOI: DOI: 10.1201/9781003459347

Singh, P., Singh, M., & Bhambri, P. (2004). Interoperability: A problem of component reusability. In International Conference (Abstract Book) (p. 60). Presented at the "Emerging Technologies in IT Industry" at PCTE, Ludhiana on November 27, 2004.

Singh, P., Singh, M., & Bhambri, P. (2005). Embedded systems. In U.G.C. Sponsored National Seminar (pp. 10-15). Presented at the "Embedded Systems" seminar at KMV, Jalandhar held during January 24-25, 2005.

Singh, S., Lal, Y., Bhambri, P., Kumar, A., & Dhanoa, I. S. (2021). Advancements in social data security and encryption: A review. *Natural Volatiles and Essential Oils*, *8*(4), 15353–15362.

KEY TERMS AND DEFINITIONS

Advanced Persistent Threats: Advanced Persistent Threats (APTs) are long-term, focused cyberattacks in which an unauthorized user, typically a nation-state or organized cybercriminal group, gains access to a network and remains concealed for an extended period of time in order to steal data or compromise systems.

Cyber Defence Mechanisms: Both proactive and reactive strategies are used in cyber defense mechanisms to identify, stop, respond to, and recover from cyber-attacks. Information systems' confidentiality, integrity, and availability (CIA) are guaranteed by these mechanisms.

Malware: Malware is any software that is intended to damage, disrupt, steal, or gain unauthorized access to computer systems, networks, or data. Cybercriminals utilize it to exploit, control, or harm systems and users.

Quantum Cryptography Applications: Applications of quantum cryptography are the real-world applications of cryptographic methods based on the ideas of quantum mechanics, particularly the behavior of particles at the quantum level, to guarantee data security and secure communication. The security of quantum cryptography is derived from the fundamental laws of physics, as opposed to classical cryptography, which depends on mathematical complexity.

Quantum Key Distribution: Quantum Key Distribution (QKD) is the process of using quantum states, usually photons, to create and distribute a shared secret key between two parties, Alice and Bob. Messages can then be encrypted and decrypted using the key. Since it is impossible to measure a quantum system without disturbing it, the fundamental security of QKD is based on the laws of quantum physics, which allow for the detection of any eavesdropping (Eve).

Threat Intelligence Analysis: Threat intelligence analysis is a systematic review of threat data, including signs of compromise, tactics, methods, and procedures, or commonly known as TTPs, in order to understand the capabilities, intentions, and activities of threat actors. The goal is to generate actionable intelligence that helps organizations successfully prevent, identify, and counter risks.

Chapter 9
Attribution:
Challenges in Cyber Terrorism and Cyber Security Preparedness

Aishwarya Majumdar
https://orcid.org/0009-0001-3495-4414
Delhi High Court, India

Pranjal Chaturvedi
https://orcid.org/0009-0007-0993-9005
Allahabad High Court, India

Bhupinder Singh
https://orcid.org/0009-0006-4779-2553
Sharda University, India

ABSTRACT

Amidst the evolving technological landscape and readily available tools and high speed internet, there exists a remarkable propensity for technology to be employed with wisdom, misused with malevolence, or catastrophically unleashed. The stark illustration of such catastrophic misuse is the realm of 'Cyber Terrorism. The very mode through which terror is sown is undergoing a profound transformation in the present era, one that is destined to further evolve in the future. Acknowledging technology is neutral, and the use of technology depends on the person using it, serious challenges are standing tall, which need significant notice and venturing. This chapter explores the evolving threat of cyber terrorism, and examines the cyber security preparedness to combat cyber terrorism. Through the exploration in real world incidents and attribution techniques it explores the intricate landscape of attributing cyber terrorism; it accentuates the crucial role of attribution in context of national and international cyber security.

DOI: 10.4018/979-8-3693-3522-2.ch009

INTRODUCTION

The terror landscape is changing from being foot on ground the terror actions are going online. It has turned more severe due to it being face and figure less. The future of inflicting terror is inextricably tied to the cyber domain, and cyber terrorist activities will happen in cyber space, a boundless space where territorial constraints or national borders do not apply (Cheng et al., 2021). Even the Intelligence agencies or the agencies in business of providing cyber security can't claim to be completely secured and past real world experiences of cyber terrorism (Muhlhoff, 2021) (Saltz et al., 2019). Even they are susceptible to crafty cyber-attacks and one of such system of communication is internet (Hoijtink & Planque-van Hardeveld, 2022) (Dean, 2024). The unprecedented proliferation of the internet, exemplified by rapidly enhancing and advancing Information and Communication Technology, has connected the world through an invisible chain (Utami et al., 2022). The dependence on Information and Communication Technology has increased many folds. Today we place reliance on Technology for our daily chorus (Zhang et al., 2022). This technology plays role in regulating Stock Market, Supreme Court Rosters, Water or Food Distribution System, Electronic Governance, Cashless Economy, Integrated Banking System, etc. (Baker & Robinson, 2020). The technology fostering interconnected system facilitates economic efficiency in governance and affects all social, political and economic dimensions of life. This chapter also examines the cyber security alacrity and preparedness by state and non-state actors (Aziz & Andriansyah, 2023).

Figure 1. shares the Landscapes of Introduction Split Section (Source- Original)

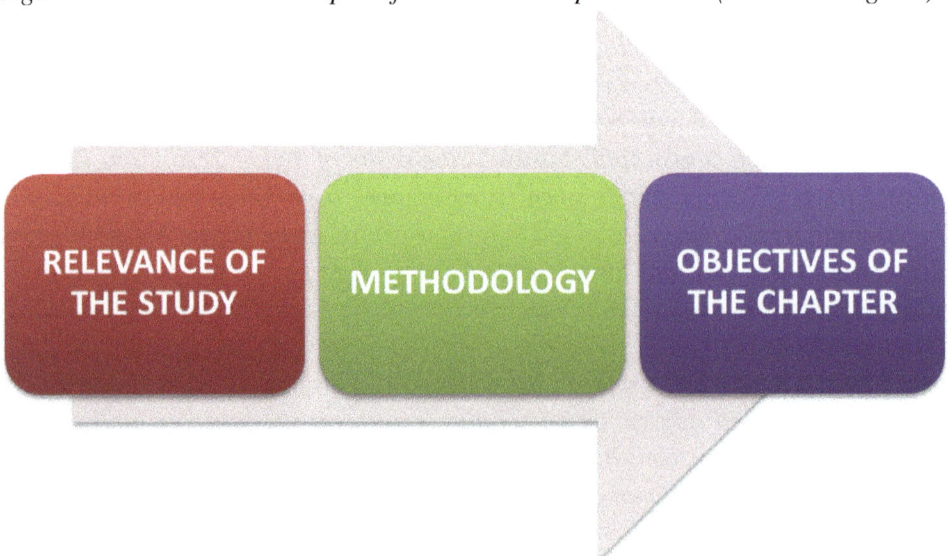

RELEVANCE OF THE STUDY

Internet as a technology is neutral. It is the person whose hands are equipped with technology and tools determine how to make use of it (Burrell, 2024). Carrie P. Snow wonderfully says it, "*Technology is a queer thing. It brings you great gifts with one hand and it stabs you in the back with the other*". In the joinery of human evolution, the human beings have seen most production and most destructive use of technology. Technology is a paradoxical entity (Attaran & Deb, 2018). It bestows remarkable gifts, and on the other, it has the capacity to betray and cause harm (Brotcke, 2022). When humans use Internet productively, humans have succeeded in making world a global village and bring people together through communication medium on the contrary we can also see cyber offences. Such misuse of Internet is Cyber Terrorism (Alnajim, et al., 2023). Terrorism aims at instilling fears in mind of people, vis-à-vis disrupting political activities of state (Abebe et al., 2020). Proficient attribution serves as the core arena in guaranteeing the culpability of malefactors, instilling deterrence against future attacks, and fortifying the protection of critical infrastructure and sensitive information (Hagendorff, 2019).

METHODOLOGY

Doctrinal Method of Research through legal reasoning and rational deduction. The researcher has gone through various law Reports, Government data, News Reports, Government Websites, Case Laws.

OBJECTIVES OF THE CHAPTER

This chapter has the following objectives to:

- recognizing and classifying cyberterrorism threats and their possible effects on public safety, vital infrastructure, and national security (Dash et al., 2022).
- talk about how hard it is to assign blame for cyberattacks to particular persons or organizations. This discussion could cover topics like anonymity, false flag operations, and the technological challenges involved in tracking down the origin of an attack (Britz, 2024).
- entail assessing the level of cybersecurity readiness that public institutions, commercial enterprises, and other stakeholders currently possess. It may also point out weaknesses in defensive systems and offer suggestions for strengthening them (Tyagi et al., 2020).

- analyze these frameworks. It would evaluate how effectively these frameworks handle the dangers that exist today and identify any areas where they might need to be reinforced or modified (Cao et al., 2021).
- offer useful suggestions on how to reduce the danger of cyberterrorism and raise general cybersecurity readiness for decision-makers, cybersecurity experts, and businesses. This might involve cooperative projects, training courses, and technological solutions (Williams & Burnap, 2023).

Figure 2. expresses the Objectives of the Chapter (Source- Original)

HACKTIVISM, CYBER CRIME AND CYBER TERRORISM: DIFFERENCES

NATO defines cyber-terrorism as "*a cyber-attack using or exploiting computer or communication networks to cause sufficient destruction or disruption to generate fear or to intimidate a society into an ideological goal.*" The most accepted notion of cyber-terrorism is defined by the FBI which defines it as, "a *premeditated, politically motivated attack against information, computer systems, computer programs, and data which results in violence against non-combatant targets by sub-national groups or clandestine agents.*"

Hacktivism is a non-violent means to disrupt private or institutional activity either through utilizing technologically ambiguous or illegal means. Cyber Criminals are those who use Internet space to commit crimes (Yarkoni & Westfall, 2024). In Cyber Terrorism either the Cyber Tools are used coupled with conventional forms of terrorism or Cyber Space is itself used as a means to instill fear in a large number of people and target people at large, State and Organizations of National Importance, in furtherance of securing political ends (Zhang et al., 2022). In Cyber Crime or Hacktivism generally, the subject is an individual or institution, without intentions to compromise state sovereignty whereas Cyber Terrorism aims at intimidating or coercing the government or its people and challenging the state sovereignty as the ultimate target (Lee & Shin, 2023).

The Department of State faced a network breach that resulted in the unapproved extraction of a significant volume of data by foreign entities (Li et al., 2020). If Chinese or Russian intelligence agents were to physically trespass onto the State Department's grounds, forcibly bypass security personnel, and clandestinely remove physical documents overnight, it would unquestionably be regarded as an act of warfare. However, in the domain of cyberspace, these incidents often go relatively unnoticed (Henke & Jacques Bughin, 2023).

Cyber terrorism holds a profound allure for those who engage in such activities. This appeal extends multiple advantages to terrorists, affording them the means to target even the most fortified computer resources, residing within High-Security Zones, all while maintaining a cloak of anonymity and confidentiality. Entities like ISRO, RBI, AIMS, and nuclear plants become potential targets (Bao et al., 2022). This clandestine approach significantly mitigates the risk of exposure, as cyber terrorists possess the ability to swiftly change locations and erase any trace of their operations, often operating without the need for state support (Odinet, 2024).

In stark contrast to conventional terrorism, cyber terrorism offers cost-effective and time-efficient means of wreaking havoc (McKendrick, 2019). Gone are the days when terrorists had to invest heavily in training, the procurement of weapons and explosives, and actions that inevitably raised red flags on surveillance radars. In this virtual realm of operations, they can transcend the confines of the physical world and unleash very real threats, all while remaining elusive (Varma et al., 2022).

MAJOR INCIDENTS OF CYBER ATTACKS AT GLOBALLY

An American Think Tank, The Center for Strategic and International Studies has recorded more than 800 'Eight Hundred incidents of Cyber Attacks' on Government,

Government Agencies, Defence, and High-Tech Companies (Gangadharan, 2021). Cyber threats have proliferated globally, with government bodies, agencies, defense institutions, and advanced technology companies emerging as prime targets (Tippins et al., 2021). These episodes have given rise to profound concerns regarding the safeguarding of sensitive information and essential infrastructure (Ducas & Wilner, 2024). There are several significant instances of cyber attacks in recent years that have impacted these domains (Lui & Lamb, 2023).

SolarWinds Hack (2020): Among the most prominent recent cyber-attacks, the SolarWinds breach affected numerous government agencies and high-tech corporations (Schmitt, 2020). Believed to be the work of Russian actors, this breach exploited the Solar Winds software supply chain, compromising the systems of over 18,000 organizations, including various U.S. government departments (Zhang et al., 2020). This incident underscored the susceptibility of software supply chains and the potential for state-sponsored actors to exploit them (Nassar & Kamal, 2021).

Office of Personnel Management (OPM) Data Breach (2015): The OPM breach serves as a prime example of a cyber-attack targeting a government agency (Tene & Polonetsky, 2022). In this case, Chinese hackers gained access to OPM's databases, compromising the personal data of more than 20 million present and former federal employees. The breach exposed sensitive background investigation information, raising concerns about the possibilities of espionage and identity theft (Grimm et al., 2021).

Stuxnet (2010): Stuxnet was an exceptionally sophisticated worm that specifically targeted Iran's nuclear facilities, particularly its uranium enrichment centrifuges (Dhoni & Kumar, 2023). While its origins remain the subject of speculation, there is widespread belief that it was a collaborative effort between the United States and Israel. This cyber-attack set a precedent for employing malware as a tool in international conflicts and espionage, with a specific focus on undermining critical infrastructure (Kordzadeh & Ghasemaghaei, 2022).

NotPetya (2017): NotPetya, a ransomware attack, wreaked havoc on various high-tech and defense firms. This malware camouflaged itself as ransomware but carried a destructive payload that wiped data from infected systems (Sambasivan et al., 2021). Its rapid spread impacted companies like Maersk, Merck, and even Ukraine's power grid. This incident shed light on the perils of ransomware and its potential to cause widespread disruption.

Ukraine Power Grid Cyber-attack (2015 and 2016): In December 2015 and again in December 2016, Ukraine's power grid experienced cyber-attacks resulting in extensive power outages. Attributed to Russian hackers, these events exposed vulnerabilities in critical infrastructure systems. The 2016 attack, in particular, affected hundreds of thousands of people, showcasing the potential of cyber attacks to disrupt essential services (Passas, 2023).

Equifax Data Breach (2017): While not a state agency, Equifax is a widely known and reliable credit reporting agency, which occupies a critical role in the U.S. financial system. In year 2017, Equifax fell prey to attackers resulting to a substantial data breach, revealing the personal information of 147 million Americans (Zhang et al., 2023). The data breach had wide implications for the national security and highlighted the need for more robust data protection measures in United States (Katyal, 2019).

Figure 3. Major Incidents of Cyber Attacks at Globally (Source- Original)

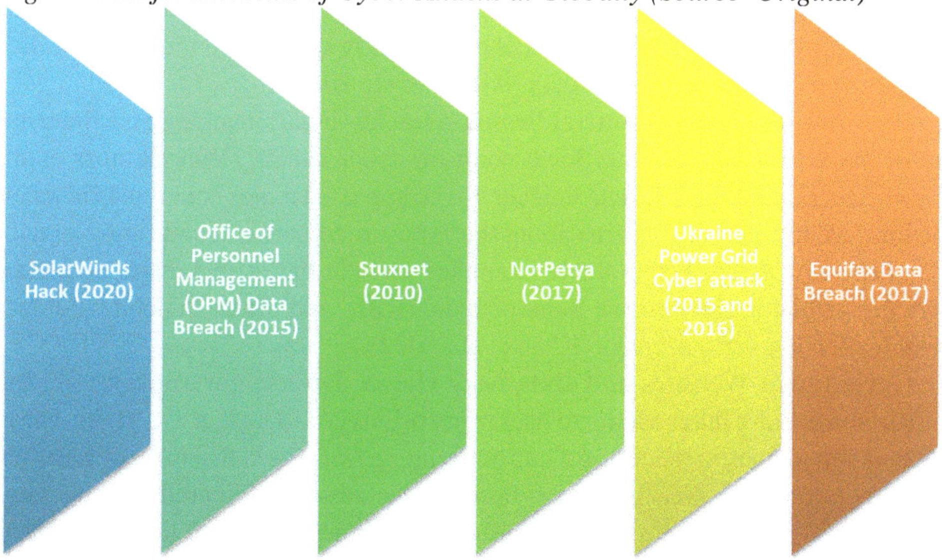

MAJOR INCIDENTS OF CYBER ATTACK IN INDIA

Kudankulam Nuclear Power Plant Malware Infection (2019): In year 2019, a malware infection was detected and reported at the Kudankulam Nuclear Power Plant (Tamil Nadu) (Irfan et al., 2023). Though the plant's operator asserted that the malware affected only administrative systems and did not compromise any vital operational infrastructure, the incident prompted concerns regarding the security of India's nuclear facilities (Selbst & Barocas, 2024). This incident also highlights, that the Critical Infrastructure, as Nuclear Power Plants, having large potency are also under attack by attackers (Daugherty & Wilson, 2023). The information's associated with Critical Infrastructures and Data of such institutions regarding their operations are not only important for a nation but has global importance and any such data breach may have global ramifications (Swiakowska, 2020).

Indian Space Research Organization (ISRO) Cyber Espionage (2017): The Reports surfaced in year 2017, indicating that Indian Space Research Organization had been targeted by a cyber espionage (spying) campaign, which was attributed to a North Korean group (Berk et al., 2021). The Trojan Malware, "*XtremeRAT*", was detected in server. This Malware was detected in Telemetry of ISRO that provides tracking support for all satellite and launch vehicle of ISRO. In year 2018, The Indian and French Security researchers, claimed that hackers could have taken control of Space Research Organizations, and command rocket launches. ISRO itself stated that sensitive data was not breached; but the event rightly spotlighted the susceptibility of crucial space technology and data (Asharf et al., 2023).

Data Breaches and Financial Sector Attacks: India's banking and financial sector has also been a primary focal point for cyber-attacks (Vinayakumar et al., 2024). Several high-profile data breaches have impacted major banks and financial institutions, instigating concerns about the exposure of personal and financial data of millions of customers. Notable examples include the 2016 breach of India's banking regulator, the Reserve Bank of India (RBI), and the 2016 debit card data breach affecting various banks (Khan et al., 2022).

Government Websites and Databases Hacks: Diverse government websites and databases have fallen victim to hacker intrusions (Al-Garadi et al., 2020). These incidents encompass a spectrum of attacks, ranging from the defacement of websites to more severe data breaches. Such occurrences have underscored the necessity for improved security measures within the digital infrastructure of the government (Elhoseny et al., 2021).

Ongoing Border Disputes: India has been facing persistent border disputes with neighboring nations, i.e. China and Pakistan. The disputed are now not limited to Cross Border Firing with Pakistan or Military Standoff with China (Kimbugwe et al., 2021). These disputes have extended into the realm of cyberspace, with state-affiliated hacking groups purportedly engaging in cyber espionage campaigns targeting the Indian Government, Critical Infrastructure, and Military Entities (Saheed & Arowolo, 2021). China is a hostile neighbor, and post Indo- China Galwan Valley, military standoff, China has gone cyber offensive against India, targeting Crucial Institutions The objectives of these attacks are to gather intelligence, Privacy Breach and attain a strategic advantage.

To mitigate these cyber security challenges, organizations are allocating vast resources to implement advanced cyber security measures, leverage threat intelligence, and engage in international cooperation to construct effective responses to cyber threats. Any country singlehandedly can't claim to be, in a situation to defend Cyber Space (Waheed et al., 2020).

CYBER TERRORISM: REALITY OR EXAGGERATION

The recent trend shows the indirect involvement of computer networks to facilitate the end of terrorism, by terrorist organizations (Gao et al., 2023). As of now directly any specific computer or network has not been proven subject to cyber target, to subdue Political Power of any existing Political Authority (Government) (Sarker, 2021). In generalized manner computer attacks can't be regarded as terrorist activity and largely termed as cyber terrorism, as it levels the identity of terrorist on the attackers. Terrorism and Organized Crime both have a common element of it being organized. But the driving force behind Terrorist Organization is political motive, backed by religious, social, cultural, linguistic or any other cause (Bout et al., 2021).

Cyberterrorism is currently one of the most controversial and debated issues in contemporary security discourse. As the world becomes more and more deeply networked through the Internet, concerns about online terrorism have mounted as well. Simply put, cyber terrorism implies the use of IT to inflict harm or damage to a society, economy and way of life of a country. Critics say "cyber terrorism" is routinely sensationalized, used by the media and lawmakers to scare the public and justify draconian surveillance. But the fact is that cyberspace is an emerging arena for hostile activities that have the potential for catastrophic effects similar to traditional terrorism.

This threat has been demonstrated in real-life events. Consider, for example, the cyberattacks in 2007 against Estonia that shut down banking, media and government services, or the Stuxnet worm in 2010 that was designed to cripple Iranian nuclear facilities: evidence that digital tools can become weapons of strategic sabotage. Terrorist groups have made greater use of cyberspace for propaganda, recruitment and planning, muddying the waters between cybercrime and terrorism. But skeptics also highlight the absence of major cyber-attacks causing physical damage or deaths, arguing that the menace is being overhyped. Most of what passes for cyber terrorism are better described as cybercrime, hacktivism, or state-sponsored cyber warfare - rather than what we traditionally call terrorism. This lack of definition is exacerbated by a lack of consensus worldwide on what cyber terrorism actually is. Indeed, many governments and international groups use the term freely, blurring it with espionage or online dissent. But the possibility of cyber terror can't be ignored. Expanding technology in industries such as healthcare, transportation, defense, and energy opens the door for bad actors. A well-planned cyberattack could result in mass disruption, financial chaos or even threaten lives, if, say, hospital systems or air traffic controls are attacked.

While the level of cyber terrorism has not yet reached that of conventional terrorism, its potential for causing great harm is real and it is growing. The question is how to separate real threats from exaggeration, build resilient cyber defenses and create international cooperation. Instead of considering cyber terrorism as an over exaggerated propaganda, a pragmatic attitude towards it as an emerging phenomenon will prominently contribute. It is a real thing, albeit one that gets exaggerated in the public imagination. They must also advance the structures for detection, prevention and indeed for attribution, as cyber capabilities advance. Regardless of whether or not cyber terrorism has actually occurred in catastrophic form, its potential as a weapon of contemporary terrorism is clear and requires sober and substantial consideration. Whereas, in Organized Crimes the driving for is financial gain or material benefit. The criminals do not challenge the sovereignty of political authority whereas in terrorist activity, the state sovereignty is under challenge (Aqeel et al., 2022).

The terrorist activity and acts of organized crime may overlap, especially when terrorist organizations are in a pursuit to make financial arrangements, but even this financial arrangement is to fund and finance political goals (Zhang et al., 2021). The other major distinction between terrorism and organized crime is by the definitional understanding, Organized Crime cannot be committed by single individual, it requires structured group of three or more persons, whereas there is no such number of people are required to commit terrorist, activity (Reddy et al., 2022). The organized criminal groups can also adopt tactics adopted by terrorists, to further their operational aims by spreading large scale violence (Oladipo et al., 2021). At times Organized Crime Groups and Terrorist Organizations' can also come together and form alliance, to foster their objectives resulting in transmigrating in affairs of one another (Jagannath et al., 2022).

As of now, terrorists cannot terrorize a nation by merely using a computer network, but it does not mean they can't attain it shortly, in a technologically advancing world. We can also look at the facts as:

In *Anuradha Bhasin v. Union of India, (2020)*, the honorable Supreme Court has observed that modern terrorism is being propagated through the internet and by using technology in the following manner:

Modern terrorism heavily relies on the internet. Operations on the internet do not require substantial expenditure and are not traceable easily. The internet is being used to support fallacious proxy wars by raising money, recruiting and spreading propaganda/ideologies. The prevalence of the internet provides an easy inroad to young impressionable minds.

In the *Foundation for Media Professionals v Union Territory of Jammu and Kashmir*, 2020, the Union Territory of Jammu and Kashmir submitted before the Supreme Court of India that the Pakistani Military in its "Green Book 2020" has called for information warfare on Kashmir, after the revocation of special status of Jammu and Kashmir.

The reports suggest that Al-Queda used Internet resource to enhance, the secrecy of documents (Spaulding & Mohaisen, 2018). Even today the documents recovered from Al-Queda are not completely decrypted. Terrorist organizations have adopted technology to recruit members from countries that have their cult members (Ahmad et al., 2021). Khalid Sheikh Mohammed, the alleged orchestrator of the 9/11, World Trade Center attacks, is said to have employed internet chat applications to communicate with at least two of the individuals involved in the airline hijackings. Cyber Terrorism is no more a national problem, rather is Trans National Problem (Altaie & Hoomod, 2022).

CYBER TERRORISM AS A CHALLENGE AND PREPAREDNESS

Being one of the world's most extensive and interconnected nations, India remains susceptible to cyber-attacks that could target critical infrastructure, disrupt essential services, or jeopardize national security (Javeed et al., 2022). Nevertheless, India is far from complacent; it has undertaken substantial measures to elevate its state of preparedness and strengthen its defensive capabilities (Malik et al., 2022).

India has adopted policy of zero tolerance against all form of terrorism; hence India has made Cyber Terrorism punishable under Section - 66F of the Information Technology Act, 2000, with the punishment of Imprisonment till life (Rudenko et al., 2022). India also established the Indian Computer Emergency Response Team, under Section 70B (1) of Information Technology Act, 2000 to take safety measures and ensure cyber safety in India (Tayfour et al., 2023).

A noteworthy initiative in this endeavor is the establishment of the National Cyber Coordination Centre (NCCC), functioning as a central hub for real-time evaluation of cyber threats and the orchestration of coordinated responses. The NCCC promotes information sharing and collaboration between government entities and the private sector, fostering a more robust reaction to cyber threats (Gokulakrishnan et al., 2023).

CHALLENGES IN THE DIRECTION OF CYBER SECURITY PREPAREDNESS ENSURING SAFETY OF CYBER-SPACE

India has youth population, but Indian population is not exploring new domains and upcoming arenas with the pace it should do. Measures to Ensure Prevention of Cyber Attack and Terrorism as *"Prevention is better than Cure"*, this is the gospel in respect of Cyber Space. Nobody can absolutely restrict cyber-attacks and cyber-attack is the undeniable reality of the day. What at the most can be done is to take adequate and appropriate preventions and such preventions as to be steps ahead of cyber attackers. For cyber security, more and more filtering layers can be created and such layers should be impenetrable. No layers could be absolutely secure. Nevertheless, layers should be strong enough to prevent and if any layers is targeted, immediate alarm should be there, so the institution can do incident management (Arora et al., 2024). To ensure better cyber security mechanism and secure cyber space vis-à-vis to fortify India's cyber preparedness, India needs to adopt three stages defense mechanism with utmost alacrity as-

Figure 4. displays the Three Stage Defense Mechanism (Source- Original)

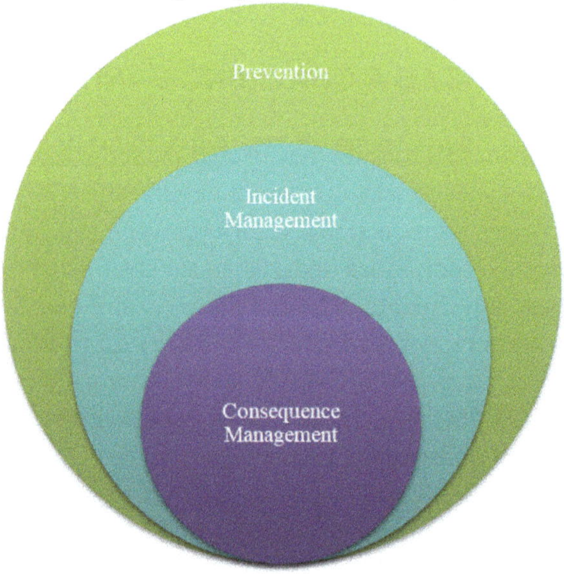

Prevention: Prevention should be the primary step and it should have a robust cyber security prevention system. It can be secured by having efficient alert mechanism, in case of any cyber intrusion. To prevent cyber terrorism the Public at large and Government employees need to be cyber literate (Bordeanu, 2024). The employees working in technologically critical institutions must be trained and sensitized about dealing with and preventing electronic infiltration. The devices should be made more electronically secure (Inuwa & Das, 2024). There are some devices with high-security efficiency, taking the examples of devices running on IOS that are safer in comparison to Android OS, though even Apple has claimed that IOS devises are facing hacking threats in India. The Security of the device should be the primary concern. This will increase the cost and might reduce efficiency and effectiveness but in the future with Research and Development, it is going to make technical advancement and will reduce cost as well (Khansadurai et al., 2024).

To enable the organization to resume regular activities as soon as feasible, recovery primarily focuses on the restoration of IT assets. This is a comparatively passive part of the defense (Xiao, 2024). But the response phase concentrates on finding and punishing the guilty parties as well as learning from the event to improve the organization's defense capabilities going forward. This is an example of a more proactive defense (Shang, 2024). There are some tasks falling under the recovery phase may encompass as:

1. The destruction or deactivation of adversarial or broken entities.
2. Carrying out a damage assessment to identify what has been damaged or compromised and what has not.
3. Putting in place an automated or semi-automatic procedure for the effective assessment and distribution of available resources.
4. The restoration of essential functions is a top priority.
5. Restoring systems to their pre-attack or pre-incident condition while protecting any relevant evidence.

CONCLUSION AND FUTURE DIRECTIONS

The rapidly evolving technological landscape, including advances in artificial intelligence and quantum computing, presents both novel challenges and opportunities. India must adapt to these technological strides, leveraging them for security while remaining vigilant against potential misuse. India's preparedness against cyber terrorism represents an ongoing journey. It mandates perpetual vigilance, innovation, and adaptability. This is a shared responsibility encompassing the government, private sector, and individuals alike. Together, we can fortify our digital frontier and shield our national interests from the looming threat of cyber terrorism.

As per the India Threat Landscape Report by Singapore-based cyber security firm *Cyfirma* 2023, state sponsored cyber attacks against India went up by 278% between March 2021 - September 2023. This report also highlighted that “India is the most targeted country globally, facing 13.7 per cent of all cyber-attacks in the world”. Honorable Minister of State (MoS), Electronics and Information Technology (MeitY), Rajeev Chandrasekhar, during a parliamentary session in February, 2023 revealed that a staggering 13.91 Lakh cyber security incidents hit India in year 2022.

The cyber terrorism is a reality, and government, intelligence agencies and our law and order enforcement agencies must accept and embrace his truth as soon as possible, and should make every attempt to thwart, mitigate and investigate such attacks. In the arena of cyberspace, it must bear in mind that proactively, collaborative efforts and the capacity to adapt to emerging threats constitute the linchpins of success. India's commitment to securing its digital future is evident in its journey to fortify its defenses against the specter of cyber terrorism. In the ever-changing landscape of cyber security, preparedness remains our foremost defense. A vigilant citizenry and proactive security agencies can reduce the intensity of cyber-attacks.

REFERENCES

Abebe, R., Barocas, S., Kleinberg, J., Levy, K., Raghavan, M., & Robinson, D. G. (2020, January). Roles for computing in social change. In *Proceedings of the 2020 conference on fairness, accountability, and transparency* (pp. 252-260).

Ahmad, W., Rasool, A., Javed, A. R., Baker, T., & Jalil, Z. (2021). Cyber security in IoT-based cloud computing: A comprehensive survey. *Electronics (Basel)*, *11*(1), 16.

Al-Garadi, M. A., Mohamed, A., Al-Ali, A. K., Du, X., Ali, I., & Guizani, M. (2020). A survey of machine and deep learning methods for internet of things (IoT) security. *IEEE Communications Surveys and Tutorials*, *22*(3), 1646–1685.

Alnajim, A. M., Habib, S., Islam, M., Thwin, S. M., & Alotaibi, F. (2023). A Comprehensive Survey of Cybersecurity Threats, Attacks, and Effective Countermeasures in Industrial Internet of Things. *Technologies*, *11*(6), 161.

Altaie, R. H., & Hoomod, H. K. (2022, December). Artificial Intelligent Management for Internet of Things: A Review. In *2022 4th International Conference on Current Research in Engineering and Science Applications (ICCRESA)* (pp. 179-184). IEEE.

Aqeel, M., Ali, F., Iqbal, M. W., Rana, T. A., Arif, M., & Auwul, M. R. (2022). A review of security and privacy concerns in the internet of things (IoT). *Journal of Sensors*, •••, 2022.

Arora, S., Mittal, R., Shrivastava, A. K., & Bali, S. (2024). Blockchain-based deep learning in IoT, healthcare and cryptocurrency price prediction: A comprehensive review. *International Journal of Quality & Reliability Management.*

Asharf, J., Moustafa, N., Khurshid, H., Debie, E., Haider, W., & Wahab, A. (2023). A review of intrusion detection systems using machine and deep learning in internet of things: Challenges, solutions and future directions. *Electronics (Basel)*, *9*(7), 1177.

Attaran, M., & Deb, P. (2018). Machine learning: The new'big thing'for competitive advantage. *International Journal of Knowledge Engineering and Data Mining*, *5*(4), 277–305.

Aziz, L. A. R., & Andriansyah, Y. (2023). The Role Artificial Intelligence in Modern Banking: An Exploration of AI-Driven Approaches for Enhanced Fraud Prevention, Risk Management, and Regulatory Compliance. *Reviews of Contemporary Business Analytics*, *6*(1), 110–132.

Baker, D. J., & Robinson, P. H. (Eds.). (2020). *Artificial Intelligence and the Law: Cybercrime and Criminal Liability*. Routledge.

Bao, Y., Hilary, G., & Ke, B. (2022). Artificial intelligence and fraud detection. *Innovative Technology at the Interface of Finance and Operations, I*, 223–247.

Berk, R., Heidari, H., Jabbari, S., Kearns, M., & Roth, A. (2021). Fairness in criminal justice risk assessments: The state of the art. *Sociological Methods & Research, 50*(1), 3–44.

Bordeanu, O. C. (2024). *From Data to Insights: Unraveling Spatio-Temporal Patterns of Cybercrime using NLP and Deep Learning* (Doctoral dissertation, UCL (University College London).

Bout, E., Loscri, V., & Gallais, A. (2021). How Machine Learning changes the nature of cyberattacks on IoT networks: A survey. *IEEE Communications Surveys and Tutorials, 24*(1), 248–279.

Britz, M. (2024). *Computer forensics and cyber crime: An introduction, 2/e*. Pearson Education India.

Brotcke, L. (2022). Time to assess bias in machine learning models for credit decisions. *Journal of Risk and Financial Management, 15*(4), 165.

Burrell, J. (2024). How the machine 'thinks': Understanding opacity in machine learning algorithms. *Big Data & Society, 3*(1), 2053951715622512.

Cao, L., Yang, Q., & Yu, P. S. (2021). Data science and AI in FinTech: An overview. *International Journal of Data Science and Analytics, 12*, 81–99.

Cheng, X., Liu, S., Sun, X., Wang, Z., Zhou, H., Shao, Y., & Shen, H. (2021). Combating emerging financial risks in the big data era: A perspective review. *Fundamental Research (Beijing), 1*(5), 595–606.

Dash, B., Sharma, P., & Ali, A. (2022). Federated learning for privacy-preserving: A review of PII data analysis in Fintech. [IJSEA]. *International Journal of Software Engineering and Its Applications, 13*(4).

Daugherty, P. R., & Wilson, H. J. (2023). *Human+ machine: Reimagining work in the age of AI*. Harvard Business Press.

Dean, J. (2024). *Big data, data mining, and machine learning: value creation for business leaders and practitioners*. John Wiley & Sons.

Dhoni, P., & Kumar, R. (2023). Synergizing generative ai and cybersecurity: Roles of generative ai entities, companies, agencies, and government in enhancing cybersecurity. *Authorea Preprints*.

Ducas, E., & Wilner, A. (2024). The security and financial implications of blockchain technologies: Regulating emerging technologies in Canada. *International Journal (Toronto, Ont.)*, *72*(4), 538–562.

Elhoseny, M., Selim, M. M., & Shankar, K. (2021). Optimal deep learning based convolution neural network for digital forensics face sketch synthesis in internet of things (IoT). *International Journal of Machine Learning and Cybernetics*, *12*, 3249–3260.

Gangadharan, S. P. (2021). Digital inclusion and data profiling. *First Monday*.

Gao, M., Souri, A., Zaker, M., Zhai, W., Guo, X., & Li, Q. (2023). A comprehensive analysis for crowd counting methodologies and algorithms in Internet of Things. *Cluster Computing*, •••, 1–15.

Gokulakrishnan, S., Chakrabarti, P., Hung, B. T., & Shankar, S. S. (2023). An optimized facial recognition model for identifying criminal activities using deep learning strategy. *International Journal of Information Technology : an Official Journal of Bharati Vidyapeeth's Institute of Computer Applications and Management*, *15*(7), 3907–3921.

Grimm, P. W., Grossman, M. R., & Cormack, G. V. (2021). Artificial intelligence as evidence. *Nw. J. Tech. & Intell. Prop.*, *19*, 9.

Hagendorff, T. (2019). From privacy to anti-discrimination in times of machine learning. *Ethics and Information Technology*, *21*(4), 331–343.

Henke, N., & Jacques Bughin, L. (2023). The age of analytics: Competing in a data-driven world.

Hoijtink, M., & Planqué-van Hardeveld, A. (2022). Machine learning and the platformization of the military: A study of google's machine learning platform TensorFlow. *International Political Sociology*, *16*(2), olab036.

Inuwa, M. M., & Das, R. (2024). A comparative analysis of various machine learning methods for anomaly detection in cyber-attacks on IoT networks. *Internet of Things : Engineering Cyber Physical Human Systems*, •••, 101162.

Irfan, M., Elmogy, M., & El-Sappagh, S. (Eds.). (2023). *The impact of AI innovation on financial sectors in the era of industry 5.0*. IGI Global.

Jagannath, A., Jagannath, J., & Kumar, P. S. P. V. (2022). A comprehensive survey on radio frequency (rf) fingerprinting: Traditional approaches, deep learning, and open challenges. *Computer Networks*, *219*, 109455.

Javeed, D., Gao, T., Khan, M. T., & Shoukat, D. (2022). A hybrid intelligent framework to combat sophisticated threats in secure industries. *Sensors (Basel)*, *22*(4), 1582. PMID: 35214481

Katyal, S. K. (2019). Private accountability in the age of artificial intelligence. *UCLA Law Review. University of California, Los Angeles. School of Law*, *66*, 54.

Khan, A. R., Kashif, M., Jhaveri, R. H., Raut, R., Saba, T., & Bahaj, S. A. (2022). Deep learning for intrusion detection and security of Internet of things (IoT): Current analysis, challenges, and possible solutions. *Security and Communication Networks*, •••, 2022.

Khansadurai, A. M., Veluchamy, A. D., Balasubramani, S., & Balasubramaniyan, K. (2024). Crime Rate Prediction using Cyber Security and Artificial Intelligent.

Kimbugwe, N., Pei, T., & Kyebambe, M. N. (2021). Application of deep learning for quality of service enhancement in internet of things: A review. *Energies*, *14*(19), 6384.

Kordzadeh, N., & Ghasemaghaei, M. (2022). Algorithmic bias: Review, synthesis, and future research directions. *European Journal of Information Systems*, *31*(3), 388–409.

Lee, I., & Shin, Y. J. (2023). Machine learning for enterprises: Applications, algorithm selection, and challenges. *Business Horizons*, *63*(2), 157–170.

Li, L., Zhao, T., Xie, Y., & Feng, Y. (2020). Interpretable machine learning based on integration of nlp and psychology in peer-to-peer lending risk evaluation. In *Natural Language Processing and Chinese*

Lui, A., & Lamb, G. W. (2023). Artificial intelligence and augmented intelligence collaboration: Regaining trust and confidence in the financial sector. *Information & Communications Technology Law*, *27*(3), 267–283.

Malik, R., Singh, Y., Sheikh, Z. A., Anand, P., Singh, P. K., & Workneh, T. C. (2022). An improved deep belief network ids on iot-based network for traffic systems. *Journal of Advanced Transportation*, •••, 2022.

McKendrick, K. (2019). Artificial intelligence prediction and counterterrorism. *London: The Royal Institute of International Affairs-Chatham House, 9.*

Mühlhoff, R. (2021). Predictive privacy: Towards an applied ethics of data analytics. *Ethics and Information Technology*, *23*(4), 675–690.

Nassar, A., & Kamal, M. (2021). Ethical Dilemmas in AI-Powered Decision-Making: A Deep Dive into Big Data-Driven Ethical Considerations. *International Journal of Responsible Artificial Intelligence*, *11*(8), 1–11.

Odinet, C. K. (2024). Consumer bitcredit and fintech lending. *Alabama Law Review*, *69*, 781.

Oladipo, I. D., AbdulRaheem, M., Awotunde, J. B., Bhoi, A. K., Adeniyi, E. A., & Abiodun, M. K. (2021). Machine learning and deep learning algorithms for smart cities: a start-of-the-art review. *IoT and IoE driven smart cities*, 143-162.

Passas, N. (2023). Cross-border crime and the interface between legal and illegal actors. *Security Journal*, *16*, 19–37.

Reddy, Y. H., Ali, A., Kumar, P. V., Srinivas, M. H., Netra, K., Achari, V. J., & Varaprasad, R. (2022). A Comprehensive Survey of Internet of Things Applications, Threats, and Security Issues. *South Asian Res J Eng Tech*, *4*(4), 63–77.

Rudenko, R., Pires, I. M., Oliveira, P., Barroso, J., & Reis, A. (2022). A Brief Review on Internet of Things, Industry 4.0 and Cybersecurity. *Electronics (Basel)*, *11*(11), 1742.

Saheed, Y. K., & Arowolo, M. O. (2021). Efficient cyber attack detection on the internet of medical things-smart environment based on deep recurrent neural network and machine learning algorithms. *IEEE Access : Practical Innovations, Open Solutions*, *9*, 161546–161554.

Saltz, J., Skirpan, M., Fiesler, C., Gorelick, M., Yeh, T., Heckman, R., & Beard, N. (2019). Integrating ethics within machine learning courses. [TOCE]. *ACM Transactions on Computing Education*, *19*(4), 1–26.

Sambasivan, N., Arnesen, E., Hutchinson, B., Doshi, T., & Prabhakaran, V. (2021, March). Re-imagining algorithmic fairness in india and beyond. In *Proceedings of the 2021 ACM conference on fairness, accountability, and transparency* (pp. 315-328).

Sarker, I. H. (2021). Machine learning: Algorithms, real-world applications and research directions. *SN Computer Science*, *2*(3), 160. PMID: 33778771

Schmitt, M. (2020). Artificial intelligence in business analytics, capturing value with machine learning applications in financial services.

Selbst, A. D., & Barocas, S. (2024). The intuitive appeal of explainable machines. *Fordham Law Review*, *87*, 1085.

Shang, Y. (2024). Detection and Prevention of Cyber Defense Attacks using Machine Learning Algorithms. *Scalable Computing: Practice and Experience*, *25*(2), 760–769.

Spaulding, J., & Mohaisen, A. (2018, October). Defending internet of things against malicious domain names using D-FENS. In *2018 IEEE/ACM Symposium on Edge Computing (SEC)* (pp. 387-392). IEEE.

Tayfour, O. E., Mubarakali, A., Tayfour, A. E., Marsono, M. N., Hassan, E., & Abdelrahman, A. M. (2023). Adapting deep learning-LSTM method using optimized dataset in SDN controller for secure IoT. *Soft Computing*, •••, 1–9.

Tene, O., & Polonetsky, J. (2022). Big data for all: Privacy and user control in the age of analytics. *Nw. J. Tech. & Intell. Prop.*, *11*, 239.

Tippins, N. T., Oswald, F. L., & McPhail, S. M. (2021). Scientific, legal, and ethical concerns about AI-based personnel selection tools: A call to action. *Personnel Assessment and Decisions*, *7*(2), 1.

Tyagi, A. K., Aswathy, S. U., & Abraham, A. (2020). Integrating blockchain technology and artificial intelligence: Synergies perspectives challenges and research directions. *Journal of Information Assurance and Security*, *15*(5), 1554.

Utami, S. H., Purnama, A. A., Hidayanto, A. N., Utami, S. H., Purnama, A. A., & Hidayanto, A. N. (2022). Fintech Lending in Indonesia: A Sentiment Analysis, Topic Modelling, and Social Network Analysis using Twitter Data. *International Journal of Applied Engineering & Technology*, *4*(1), 50–56.

Varma, P., Nijjer, S., Sood, K., Grima, S., & Rupeika-Apoga, R. (2022). Thematic Analysis of Financial Technology (Fintech) Influence on the Banking Industry. *Risks*, *10*(10), 186.

Vinayakumar, R., Alazab, M., Srinivasan, S., Pham, Q. V., Padannayil, S. K., & Simran, K. (2024). A visualized botnet detection system based deep learning for the internet of things networks of smart cities. *IEEE Transactions on Industry Applications*, *56*(4), 4436–4456.

Waheed, N., He, X., Ikram, M., Usman, M., Hashmi, S. S., & Usman, M. (2020). Security and privacy in IoT using machine learning and blockchain: Threats and countermeasures. *ACM Computing Surveys*, *53*(6), 1–37.

Williams, M. L., & Burnap, P. (2023). Cyberhate on social media in the aftermath of Woolwich: A case study in computational criminology and big data. *British Journal of Criminology*, *56*(2), 211–238.

Xiao, P. (2024). Malware Cyber Threat Intelligence System for Internet of Things (IoT) Using Machine Learning. *Journal of Cyber Security and Mobility*, 53-90.

Yarkoni, T., & Westfall, J. (2024). Choosing prediction over explanation in psychology: Lessons from machine learning. *Perspectives on Psychological Science*, *12*(6), 1100–1122. PMID: 28841086

Zhang, A., Lipton, Z. C., Li, M., & Smola, A. J. (2023). *Dive into deep learning*. Cambridge University Press.

Zhang, J., Pan, L., Han, Q. L., Chen, C., Wen, S., & Xiang, Y. (2021). Deep learning based attack detection for cyber-physical system cybersecurity: A survey. *IEEE/CAA Journal of Automatica Sinica, 9*(3), 377-391.

Zhang, X., Liu, L., Lan, M., Song, G., Xiao, L., & Chen, J. (2022). Interpretable machine learning models for crime prediction. *Computers, Environment and Urban Systems, 94*, 101789.

Zhang, Y., Xiong, F., Xie, Y., Fan, X., & Gu, H. (2020). The impact of artificial intelligence and blockchain on the accounting profession. *IEEE Access : Practical Innovations, Open Solutions*, *8*, 110461–110477.

Zhang, Z., Al Hamadi, H., Damiani, E., Yeun, C. Y., & Taher, F. (2022). Explainable artificial intelligence applications in cyber security: State-of-the-art in research. *IEEE Access : Practical Innovations, Open Solutions*.

KEY TERMS AND DEFINISTIONS

Advanced Persistent Threat (APT): A long-term and targeted attack in which an intruder gets into a network and stays there, generally stealthily, for some time, with government backing a common claim.

Attribution: The process of determining who is the responsible party for a cyberattack, either an individual, group or nation-state. Attribution is difficult for a variety of reasons and can be technical, political, or for time constraints, specifically used for litigation.

Critical Infrastructure: National security, economic activity, public health, or safety systems and assets e.g., power, communications, and water infrastructure that are vulnerable to attacks in cyber terrorism.

Cyber Hygiene: A series of practices and protocols followed by people and companies to keep digital systems healthy and enhance cybersecurity replacing software or using strong passwords, for example.

Cybersecurity Preparedness: An organization's or nation's state of preparedness and capacity to effectively prevent, detect, respond to, and recover from cyber incidents, including policies, technologies, education and awareness, and integrated incident management capabilities.

Cyber Terrorism: Engaging in terrorist activity, including attacks against critical infrastructure, spreading fear, and/or political or ideological objectives, using the internet or digital technologies.

False Flag Operation: False flag is a surreptitious action carried out in order to deceive in such a way as to create the appearance that it was done by someone other than the attacker.

Incident Response Plan: The arranged plan that details how a corporation identifies, responds to, and recovers from cyber-attacks or breaches to reduce harm and resumed regular services.

Threat Intelligence: Information gathered and analyzed about ongoing and potential attacks that organizations can use to predict, prevent and mitigate cyber-security threats.

Zero-Day Vulnerability: An unpatched software vulnerability in a product that attackers are leveraging either to access or control systems.

Chapter 10
Ethical Implications of Artificial Intelligence in Countering Violent Extremism

Aamer Hayat khan
https://orcid.org/0009-0001-3340-885X
Shah Abdul Latif University, Khairpur, Pakistan

ABSTRACT

This chapter explores the ethical dimensions of using Artificial Intelligence (AI) in countering violent extremism (CVE), highlighting its transformative impact on intelligence, security, and public policy. As AI becomes integral to surveillance, predictive analysis, and decision-making processes, states face the dual challenge of enhancing national security while upholding democratic values and human rights. The author critically examines the tension between state control and individual freedoms in the age of algorithmic governance, where the boundaries of privacy, freedom of expression, and ethical responsibility are increasingly blurred. Through a discussion of regulatory frameworks, including the EU AI Act, the chapter argues for a balanced approach that legitimizes AI in CVE while ensuring robust safeguards and ethical accountability. It ultimately calls for the development of international norms and adaptive legal structures to prevent misuse and foster trust in AI-driven security mechanisms.

DOI: 10.4018/979-8-3693-3522-2.ch010

INTRODUCTION

The concept of violent extremism in the modern world has transformed into a complex phenomenon that is far from being solved with each passing day. It is an inclusion of socio-political issues in inequality and historical enmity and altogether is a challenge posed at the world resulting in extremist acts and consequences. During the past few years, the phenomenon of violent extremism has become even more frequent and intense. From countries like Nigeria, Iraq, Afghanistan, Somalia, and all the way to Pakistan, terror attacks have been recorded, resulting in around 26000 fatalities (Institute for Economics & Peace, 2022).

To solve this pertinent issue, AI has recently been identified as a possible innovative solution as far as the management of this much-needed reform is concerned. AI capacity to handle large volumes of data, its pattern recognition and other predictive scenarios that can reveal imminent dangers in relation to extremism has made it an important role player. However, this application of AI is not without big ethical dilemmas on the use of AI in fighting violent extremism. Some of the issues that are brought by the use of AI technologies includes invasion of privacy, surveillance, and potential abuse by state and non-state actors. Finally, security involves conflict of interest since it always involves the protection of an individual's rights. (Borum, 2011)

It is for this reason that the ethical procedures of AI use in countering extremism are highly contested, because it is believed that the usage of AI might increase problems rather than reducing them. Altogether, using AI in the fight against violent extremism can and should be beneficial, but it has to be done while paying attention to the certain ethical considerations. The upcoming sections of this book chapter will explore the challenge of violent extremism globally, the ethical shortcomings in addressing this challenge worldwide, the philosophies behind the need of ethics for AI, global case studies to learn from, ethical dilemmas of AI in general, and the need for Global collaboration for a successful ethical AI framework. The chapter further provides considerable recommendations, a future outlook and a way forward.

The Global Challenge of Violent Extremism

The phenomenon of violent extremism has transformed into a complex and widespread phenomenon that is being observed in societies of different countries. It is not what is the product of short-lived ideological passion, but is tied up with socio-political issues, inequality, and historical enmity. During the past few years, the phenomenon of violent extremism has become even more frequent and intense. Topping the list of countries with the highest terror-related deaths is Nigeria, Iraq, Afghanistan, Somalia, and Pakistan respectively, as confirmed by the GTI 2022 report that shows that the terrorist attacks have risen by 17 per cent from 2020 resulting in over 26000 fatalities. The GTI also noted that Sub-Saharan Africa and South Asia are still the most affected areas where more than 60 per cent of All Terrorism Civilian Deaths come from (Institute for Economics & Peace, 2022).

The terrorist networks are no longer localized but rather have become a global threat as demonstrated by ISIS and Al-Qaeda which have factors worked on increased technological capabilities to expand their operational reach. These organizations have also been equally spectacular in their ability to respond to changes in geopolitical features availing themselves of social networks whose messages are difficult to track as well as encrypted communication tools meant for spreading propaganda messages, mobilization of supporters and organization of acts of terrorism on different contents (Neumann, 2013). For instance, how ISIS finely utilised Twitter and the company of other social media to solicit foreign fighters exposed in Berger and Morgan (2015) showed more than 46, 000 active ISIS Twitter accounts during the peak digital campaign. This has laid bare the efficiency at which the radical groups use technology in recruiting people and perpetuating the cultures.

It has been worst in Europe, where the effect of the recession hit hard as companies and households struggled to continue their spending spree on preventing violent extremism particularly between 2015 to 2017. The continent has witnessed a surge of jihadist-related activities; with countries like France, Germany and the United Kingdom among the worst affected targets of terror attacks in the past several years. It is very much active as evidenced by the mass killings of the 2015 attacks in Paris where 130 people were killed and fewer than 50 people murdered in the 2017 Manchester Arena bombing. Such events have heightened insecurity amongst the people and have resulted in Installation of strict anti-terrorism measures. Ranstorp, 2016 points out that the background to radicalization in Europe is always set against social and economic, and therefore political exclusion that provides a niche for extremism.

It is for this reason that, counter-terrorism approaches have to adapt to be in a position to eventually accommodate new and emerging trends. AI has recently been identified as a possible innovative solution as far as the management of this much-needed reform is concerned. AI capacity to handle large volumes of data in real-time, analyze them for pattern recognition and other predictive scenarios that can reveal imminent dangers in relation to extremism has made it an important ally at a global level. For instance, programs based on artificial intelligence can be used to detect those extremist views in social media and thus, prevent people becoming involved into violent activities. According to the Counter-Terrorism Internet Referral Unit (CTIRU) of the UK government in 2020, AI technologies were used to counter over 300,000 pieces of terrorist propaganda from various sites which severely hampered the existing ISIS narrative (UK Home Office, 2020).

However, this application of AI is not without big ethical dilemmas on the use of AI in fighting violent extremism. Some of the issues that are brought by the use of AI technologies includes invasion of privacy, surveillance, and potential abuse by state and non-state actors. Finally, security involves conflict of interest since it always involves the protection of an individual's rights. Moreover, as the AI systems get even more progressive in identifying potential threats, there is a high possibility of false positives, whereby law-abiding citizens will be regarded as potential threats to society and therefore receive undue scrutiny and breach of their civil rights (Borum, 2011). Second, due to its 'black box,' or the fact that its work is not fully transparent it creates accountability issues, as there is often uncertainty about particular decisions.

It is for this reason that the ethical procedures of AI use in countering extremism are highly contested. Some people believe that risks of applying AI include attacks of terrorist organizations and the participation of citizens; the advantages are the possibility of avoiding new attacks and saving lives; some people are worried about the perspective of revelation of individual rights and freedoms and about the possibility of the development of new types of tools that will deepen social contradictions. Both Schmid (2011) and scholars such as Horgan (2008) have brought forth the fact that radicalization to extremism is mainly driven by multiple factors and thus any form of intervention, including the one with the involvement of AI, has to be well understood in terms of root causes.

Altogether, using AI in the fight against violent extremism can and should be beneficial, but it has to be done while paying attention to the following ethical considerations. The problem of violent extremism is a global one and it must be solved by using AI in a way that can help advance society's development while at the same time fully maintaining the rights and values of every individual. While pursuing an understanding of how AI can inform this important domain, it is imperative that the discussion stays centered on effectiveness in generating security that does not come at the cost of sacrificing the principles for free and just societies.

Ethics in the Crossfire: Balancing AI's Dual-Use

AI is gradually being used in countering violent extremism where the line between the positive uses of AI and negative utilization is rather blurry. AI technologies are encouraged when it comes to eventuating, identifying and ultimately neutralizing the possible risks from extremists thereby increasing public safety. For instance, the AI systems used in security applications can sort out a large quantity of social media data and behavioral patterns attaining a 90% probability rate of detecting potentially extreme content (Whittlestone et al., 2019; Taddeo & Floridi, 2018).

Such capabilities enable measures that could be taken to avert violence and loss of lives which would have otherwise been fatal.

But the AI is used in surveillance and big data processing, and strong ethical questions on or over-protection and misuse of authority occur. According to the sources in 2022 people complained about the fact that more than 2. As O'Neil noted in 2016, nearly 5 billion people across the globe were exposed to AI-powered surveillance where the processes remained largely opaque and largely unaccountable to the public. The extension of AI technology used in surveillance and tracking of individuals and their data increases the potential of government abuse and unlawful use of collected data which would in turn diminish the people's confidence in the respective government agencies. The ethical issues are further magnified by the fact that many AI systems are opaque, the working, the decision-making processes of the algorithmic systems are not very transparent and therefore, it is very hard to hold someone responsible when things go wrong (Moor, 2006; Bostrom & Yudkowsky, 2014).

Prejudice in AI systems also creates additional obstacles to the use of these technologies for security purposes. It has been proven that when datasets fed to AI algorithms are themselves discriminating the AI algorithms that are produced end up discriminating marginalized groups. For example, the study conducted in 2019 whereby it was detected that facial recognition algorithms of different companies misidentify black people 100 times more than white people while others are involved in discriminating activities; this is the reason why Mitrellstadt and others expelled them in 2016. These biases are not as simple technical errors, they are ethical problems, which are against the concepts of justice and equity.

The boundaries of ethical use of AI are also drawn by the possibility of the application of AI technologies by state and non-state actors. The possibility of turning AI into tools, initially developed for security purposes but then used partly for political oppression or suppression of dissident voices, is one of the most dangerous ethical threats. There is a tendency for technologies that are initially introduced for security reasons are translated into surveillance systems worldwide as indicated by the case of global CCTV and biometric systems (Bryson & Winfield, 2017). For instance, in some authoritarian countries, AI has been employed to police and domesticate citizens' movements and actions which shows a very thin line between security and repression (Wallach & Allen, 2008).

Solving these ethical issues is an applied cross-disciplinary problem-solving process that implicates both ethics and law, as well as relevant technologies as well as the social sciences. Creating secure standards and corresponding ethical frameworks regarding AI employment in security is necessary. These guidelines need to be also based on the principles of openness, non-oppression and justice to make sure that utilization of AI is ethical and does not infringe on standards of human rights

(Floridi, 2013; Taddeo & Floridi, 2018). Applying ethical designs for creating AI systems and systematically reviewing the AI systems developed can prevent possible abuses and therefore lower the perceived threat level from the AI systems among the populace (Whittlestone et al., 2019).

Finally, the utilizable ideal in this anti-terrorism endeavour of artificial intelligence, therefore, has to be that of upholding the provisions of the law, while keeping an eye on the tenets of liberty and democracy, within the broad parameters of safety and security. This approach is crucial in order to make sure that AI technologies are positive and beneficial, supporting democracy as well as creating conditions that are favourable for increasing the level of safety in societies. Indeed, it still requires a keen focus for it is a continuous process for advancing AI in security ensure concerns that every safety measure should not be accompanied by injustice and prejudice to human rights (Moor, 2006; Taddeo & Floridi, 2018).

ETHICAL THEORIES AND FRAMEWORKS ACROSS CULTURES

Diverse Ethical Philosophies in Technology

Ethical concerns that govern Artificial Intelligence (AI) come from different cultural as well as philosophical backgrounds with views on how AI should be designed and used. When comparing Western and Eastern ethical frameworks, African and Indigenous ethical approaches are identified as potentially enriching for more globally sensitive AI ethical frameworks.

Besides, in Western cultures, the primary focus is made on ethical issues regulating individual rights and justice along with the significant influence of enlightenment and deontological ethical models. For instance, according to MacIntyre (1984), the majority of English moral philosophies work through formalized generalizations, that is why the concepts of virtue and traditions of a given community should be considered. This view is especially applicable to AI ethics given that discourses are obsessed with the question of who is responsible for the actions taken by an AI and whether such systems will have the capability to defend human rights. According to European Commission, 82 per cent of European citizens deemed that AI technologies should respect human rights and human dignity and as such AI ethics must thus embrace justice as well as fairness (Floridi, 2014).

For East Asian philosophy especially Confucianism, right and wrong are not quite the same as that of Western philosophy in that it looks at a relation-based ethic that stresses reciprocities, ethical character and the society as opposed to the free-spirited individual. Confucian ethics places emphasis on the role of society and the emphasis on collective behaviors and values, including the intensification of positive social relations that are instilled in AI (Feng & Tan, 2018). This attitude is seen in concepts such as interest in AI governance models adopted in nations such as the People's Republic of China whereby the advancement of AI is usually steered by objectives that seek to first promote social order and harmony. For example, while evaluating the Chinese Social Credit System enforcement based on AI, a program that aims at regulating people's behavior with the use of a credit score as a tool of behavioral modification, I agree with Yun (2019) that such surveillance is rooted in Confucianism as a moral education tool for the construction of the harmonious society though raises ethical issues on privacy and autonomy.

The second important source to consider for the AI/ethics research is the African ethical theories, especially Ubuntu. In this regard, Ubuntu is a respect for people and their welfare and explicitly states 'I am because we are'. This philosophy conflicts the egoism of many modern theories stating that a person's humanity is the result of social relations with other people (Metz, 2007). A study on African technologists reveal that 75% of the respondents agreed that AI's objective should be to enrich human social relations as a way to tackling entrenched public issues for example health and education rather than targeting economic return or personal comfort (Yun, 2019). Ubuntu has been used in AI ethics in the sense that it calls for the creation of technologies that will benefit people as such there are many AI projects being implemented in Africa such as health, education, and governance.

IKS are comprehensive ethical theories which include respect for nature and organisms in that nature. Such systems are sustainable; they are based on reciprocity with focus on members in the human and environmental communities (Capurro and Nagenborg, 2009). For instance, Indigenous peoples of Canada have actively participated in the development of AI technologies with the prospect of the protection of the environment and sustainable growth whereas it is unethical to misuse the given natural resources and damage the environment for the needs of the future generations (Ess, 2009). The report on AI was released by the United Nations wherein the indigenous groups have demanded that AI needs to be more aligned towards sustainable development goals and require technologies that are beneficial not just for people but the environment as well.

Arguing for an intersectional conception of AI ethics, I will show that by including these seemingly ''foreign'' ethical systems, the mainstream Anglo-American conception of AI ethics can be enriched and become more culturally sensitive. Some Western theories are effective for protecting individual freedoms and justice and are complemented by Eastern, African, Indigenous ideas that reflect relational, communal, and ecological contexts that are crucial for the better understanding of ethical artificial intelligence application. In light of this paper, a pluralistic approach to AI ethics devices technologies will uphold and advance the standards of cultures within the global society to develop an equal society. Thus, as the AI grows and progresses, it will be essential to understand and adopt all these diverse ethical notions in order to make AI as positive contribution to humanity and the planet as a whole.

Global Human Rights and AI

The ethical use of AI is highly dependent on the various parts of the world and their take on human rights which in most cases differ with cultural, legal and socio-political considerations. Self-determination, privacy, and data protection are key to the politics of Western nations; hence, human rights frameworks in regulating AI are used for surveillance. For example, the General Data Protection Regulation (GDPR) that exists in the European Union has laid down strict guidelines for data privacy and transparency that seek to guard individuals' data from misuse. Since GDPR came into force in May 2018, it has held over €1 billion to €5 billion in fines against companies for data protection violations and asserting firm support for the protection of individual rights against AI's possible threat (Morley et al., 2020).

On the other hand, in the collectivist cultures that value group rights over the individual's freedom such as the Asia and Middle East regions, AI applications are done in consonance with societal interests including security and harmony. For instance, China has integrated AI into the Social Credit System to monitor the population defined as a social menace for stability within the country and prevent criminal activities or offences while parading a different concept of human rights, which doesn't acknowledge the individual's rights as supreme but that of the state. It is predicted that by 2025 China shall be employing more than 600 million surveillance cameras throughout the country and majority of these cameras shall have facial recognition traits (Zuboff, 2019). As of 2023, China had reportedly deployed more than 500 million surveillance cameras with facial recognition traits (NPR, 2023). Fast forward to 2025, China has around 700 million surveillance cameras deployed all over its cities with facial recognition traits intact (Comparitech, 2023). The increasing use of artificial intelligence in surveillance has posed some ethical questions due to the infringement of people's right to privacy and increases the odds of stifling dissent and how the local laws and culture of a country can affect the ethical usage of AI.

In countries where AI technologies are still in their nascent stage, such as the African and Latin American contexts, concepts of human rights are mostly conditioned by socio-economic imperatives and vision of developmental objectives. AI is being proposed to fight inequality and help improve public services, yet the product is often launched without well-considered ethical controls. For example, AI systems have been approved in Brazil for the more effective distribution of healthcare throughout the country; and even though such applications have provided good results in the overall administration of healthcare, the problem of bias has been found in some of these systems, thus affecting the marginalized groups in society. Eubanks (2018); and Andrejevic, (2014) identified that when AI models were deployed in the decision-making process in the public health department in Brazil it increased the chances of resource allocation towards wealthy regions as compared to the poor regions by 20%. This has implications in development for AI and at the same time there is the drawback of developing a new system which supports AI but at the same time reinvents social injustices.

It can be seen that local customs and legal procedures play a massive role in the governing and utilization of innovations in AI technology. This is perhaps due to their commitment to things like participatory governance and human rights meaning that policymaking in these countries will be more inclined to put much importance on issues to do with transparency and acknowledgment of public participation in the development of policy regarding artificial intelligence. For example, the use of public consultation to shape the national guidelines on the use of AI in Canada so that the use of the technology is in line with the democratic values of the people and their expectations (Latonero, 2018). However, in less democratic nations, the AI policies may reflect national priorities with minimal debate, thereby, possibly excluding ethical aspects from decision-making in favor of state interests. It was also noted that in 2020, only 15 percent of the AI policies existing in authoritarian countries provided for public participation or ethical scrutiny as compared to 65 percent for the democracies (Scharre, 2018).

In other words, the ethical use of AI across the world is not the same project because the priorities and contexts of different countries differ. Recognizing these differences is important for the design of these systems so they can also conform to the norms of global human rights as well as the laws of individual countries across the world. Therefore, entrenching a complex and sophisticated discourse around the ethical AI as it impacts and is adopted in different countries around the world will become a critical necessity in order to ensure that the improvements in Artificial Intelligence create positive impacts on human rights and societal welfare (Boddington, 2017).

AI IN ACTION: REGIONAL STRATEGIES FOR COUNTERING VIOLENT EXTREMISM

AI in the Global North: Case Studies

Artificial Intelligence (AI) is quickly becoming a central component of efforts to combat violent extremism in the Global North comprising North America, Europe, and Oceania. AI technologies are used for collecting large portions of information, detecting the path of radicalization, and producing the potential threat. These initiatives are as much the result of new technologies as they are of the drive to uphold democracy: yet these also present acute ethical questions regarding privacy, fairness and governance.

Closely related to this is how AI is applied in intelligence gathering and monitoring of social media accounts in North America especially in the United States in order to prevent acts of extremism. SOCMINT has been a key aspect in countering extremism since it enables assessment of online media concerning trends at radicalization through the application of machine learning algorithms (Omand, Bartlett, & Miller, 2012). For illustration, the U. S. Department of Homeland Security has integrated artificial intelligence which enables it to peruse millions of tweets on a daily basis and identify possible threats with a level of efficiency of up to 90% (Polanski, 2018). It has contributed to the prevention of many planned attacks among them the detection of a terrorist cell in 2019 that was planning a synchronized attack on several soft targets in California, particularly the Los Angeles region. However, these accomplishments lead to some key moral daunting questions; and these are, this concept of eavesdropping on online exchanges is very invasive with regard to privacy and further fuels biases especially that these technologies that are identified largely affect minoritarian groups (Crawford et al., 2019).

Europe too has employed AI's strength in counter-extremism, especially in the policing mechanism and surveillance systems. Currently, states like United Kingdom and France have incorporated the use of AI in national security especially in developing methods of preventing the emergence of extremism. For instance, they use AI in their so-called Prevent program to analyze digital footprints and make assessments on the risk of radicalization leading to early interventions. This is credited to have de-radicalized over 200 people since 2015 (Taddeo & Floridi, 2018). Nonetheless, predictive algorithms have become the central point of ethical discussions and controversies mostly due to fairness. A research study that was conducted by the European Union Agency for Fundamental Rights revealed that the use of AI-based predictive policing in Europe enhanced the attention on certain ethnic groups by 20% thus resulting in growing concerns about models that cause prejudice and unfair profiling (Binns, 2018) Barocas et al., 2019).

Counter radicalization in the context of Oceania particularly Australia and New Zealand is both securitarian while also respecting democratic liberties. New Zealand was very aggressive in its response to the Christchurch mosque shootings of 2019 when it came up with its strategy of using AI to prevent the circulation of such material. Christchurch Call to Action, initiated by New Zealand's Prime Minister recently highlights how AI can be used for the detection of violent content and its removal from Social Media platforms with the intention that no violent clip should go viral without being stopped in the first place (Polanski, 2018). Such actions prove that in just one year the AI algorithms have been capable of deleting 100,000plus violent content from the internet minimizing the presence of the minds behind acts of terror on the Internet. However, the implementation of these technologies in the same way is fast leading to issues with the technologies overtaking the level of need and a worry of intrusion on First Amendment rights (Heuer Jr., 1999).

In the case studies from the Global North, one can observe the possibilities to apply AI as well as its challenges in preventing violent extremism. Thus, although the use of AI technologies is beneficial for stopping the attacks and destabilizing the groups, the AI solutions provide ethical questions which must be addressed properly. Therefore, the application of AI should also take into account the bearings it will have on security and democracy, and human rights in particular: With the advancement of AI and its use in counter-extremism, Western democracies need to establish a sound ethics provision to govern on the use of these technologies and their implementation is at all times, responsible, accountable and equitable (Müller, 2016). It will be the discourse between technologists, ethicists, policymakers, and the public to determine how best to use AI to protect societies and at the same time, maintain the principles of democracy, which are contained in the human rights Charter.

AI in the Global South: Emerging Practices

In the Global South regions including Africa, Asia and Latin America, the Middle East the use of AI in mitigating acts of terrorism is gradually being embraced. Though these regions respond to particular security issues with the help of AI, these areas also experience specific ethical concerns that arise due to differences in technology availability, inequality, and specific cultural considerations. Some of the current practices evident in those areas explain the benefit of AI innovations and at the same time, explain why those innovations are hard to implement in the developing world.

In Africa, the use of AI to fight terrorism and organized crime has started lately and has been used in countries like Nigeria, Kenya, and Somalia. For instance, a facility of surveillance and data analysis using artificial intelligence has been applied to listen and monitor communication as well as monitor movements of such dangerous groups like Boko Haram /Al-Shabaab. A good example is how Nigeria has been employing the use of CDRs and geolocation data through AI algorithms to track suspected terrorists, and within the last three years, it has arrested over 200 of them (Pujol & Teichmann, 2020). However, these technologies have their ethical concerns, especially in developing nations that have weak governance structures of the laws that regulate their use. Hence, the danger of misuse of AI for political intentions or for putting down rebellions is real, especially where human rights are not respected (Makaya & Moyo, 2019).

In the Asian region, Pakistan and India have applied this technology in the fight against terrorism especially in the Kashmir region and between Pakistan and Afghanistan. Currently, applications of Artificial Intelligence are applied in the surveillance of Social Media platforms where AI identifies and incapacitates rebellious groups. For instance, in 2018, Pakistan's National Counter Terrorism Authority put in place an AI system to analyze social media for radical content; with the latter having led to the resolutely of more than 10,000 pieces of content besides identifying 150 people associated with radicalism (Abbasi & Dhar, 2014). Nevertheless, these technologies successfully applied in these regions raise ethical issues of using AI to exploit privacy and continuing the existing tendencies of socio-political biases in society. In a region that has been rife with ethno-religious conflict that conflicts is likely to escalate and undermine the stability of society, if AI is misused (Mamdani, 2004).

It also presents Latin America to show the region's examples where AI applies to counter extremism, especially in fighting operation crime and Drug trafficking. Some of the countries like Mexico, Brazil among others have adopted the use of AI in the prediction and suppression of violent activities through analyzing data obtained from social media, financial transactions and telecommunications among others. In Mexico, AI algorithms are used in identifying trends in drug cartels thereby destabilizing 12 large drug cartels between 2017 and 2021 (Naim, 2005). However, these initiatives as discussed below are not devoid of some ethical dilemmas. In a socio-economic context where there are clear distinctions as to which category of people enjoys what benefits, applying the use of AI by authorities will only widen the polarization if such a technology is applied inequitably against vulnerable groups. Based on a study conducted by the Inter-American Commission on Human Rights AI-driven surveillance in Latin America has been often associated with discriminating and abusive behavior particularly towards lower-income neighborhoods (Shackelford, 2016).

In the Middle East, the application of AI in counter-extremism intersects with state security strategies. Some of the countries in the Middle East that have endeavored to implement the use of AI technologies include Saudi Arabia, UAE and Egypt particularly in surveillance systems to check on the incidences of extremism. Saudi Arabia for instance employs facial recognition technology in public places to detain suspected militants and the government has postured that utilization of this technology reduced terrorism in Riyadh by 40% between 2015-2019(Fukuyama, 2004). However, such technologies bring about major issues of assails to civil liberties and general apprehensions of AI being applied as a tool in political repression. In authoritarian countries, one may find that AI technologies are used to oppress people's freedom of speech and control society rather than be used against extreme violence only (Makinda, 2007).

The application of AI in the Global South can thus be viewed as a dynamic combination of using advanced technology and encountering numerous ethical issues. With AI, there are opportunities for the increase and improvement of security as well as the crippling of extremism networks However the AI, when applied requires a very sensitive approach because the application may at times increase the conflicts and inequalities. These areas should be approached with appreciation to the technology behind AI and the socio-political and ethical complexities such that AI becomes a cause for augmentation of human security and social justice (Glen & Gordon, 2014, Campbell, 2015)

ETHICAL DILEMMAS AND CHALLENGES FROM A GLOBAL PERSPECTIVE

Algorithmic Bias Across Cultures

Bias in algorithms has emerged as the most significant issue in Artificial Intelligence (AI) cutting across ethnic groups, religions, and minorities in the global society. Due to the AI systems' incorporation into the decision-making procedures in such fields as policing, medical services, and finance, there arises a new form of social injustice whereby the embedded biases in the algorithms widen the existing inequalities and/or develop new discriminative procedures. Fear of dying is alarming and these biases underscore the need for an incorporation of cultures in the relationship between the development and deployment of artificial intelligence.

Algorithmic bias is probably best illustrated by facial recognition algorithms that have often been called out and demonstrate significantly lower accuracy for people of color. Buolamwini & Gebru (2018) discovered through another study that facial recognition software was even capable of producing wrong outcomes for darker skin-toned women, and the error rate was 34 -. Three per cent of the time as opposed to the error frequency of 0. 8% for lighter-skinned men. This large disparity not only shows the racial and gender bias inherent in even today's training data but also has incredibly serious consequences in the real world. In America, there have been several cases where errors made by the facial recognition system have led to the arrest of African Americans which then proceed to court and violate civil rights (Buolamwini & Gebru, 2018). The report by the National Institute of Standards and Technology (NIST) was produced to estimate that these systems are between 5 and 100 times more accurate in misidentifying people of color thus increasing systemic racism in police departments (NIST, 2019).

Some of the advanced visibility policing tools such as the predictive policing algorithms have been known to target black and Hispanic regions in the United States.

As these algorithms are fed historical crime data, these systems learn and become prejudiced, which causes more policing in ''minority areas''. (Eubanks, 2018). AI Now Institute's 2019 analysis revealed that predictive policing tools operated in major U. S cities led to a 30% increase in patrols in Black neighborhoods as compared to a 5% rise in white neighborhoods meaning it worsened the community policing relationship by creating a cycle of fear between the police and Black communities (AI Now Institute, 2019).

It is also important to know that algorithmic bias is still a problem not only in Western countries but can pose many issues in other parts of the world. For instance, in India, automated loan approvals discriminate against Muslim and Dalit applicants based on their religion or tribe. Most of them are rooted from the socio-economic prejudices that exist within datasets that are utilized in the development of these AI systems. A report by the Indian Institute of Technology in 2020 revealed that algorithms being used by most if not all, financial institutions In India were found to have a high tendency to refuse loan applications from people from these marginalized communities by 40% (Suresh & Guttag, 2019).

American Indigenous populations of Latin America are worried that artificial intelligence is being used in hiring processes discriminatively. These AI systems, which are trained from the urban mestizo population, cannot capture indigenous applicant's qualification and experience. A study which involved the use of AI tools in the recruitment process was conducted in 2021 by the Latin American Data Initiative and this showed that indigenous applicants received half the number of calls for interviews than the mestizos once A. I was applied in the recruiting process. This has resulted in less employment of its citizens and the deepening of socio-economic inequalities (Birhane, 2021).

In the context of the Middle Eastern region, AI-based surveillance technologies have resulted in the invasion of the right to privacy and freedom of speech. AI use for policing social media has also become common of late in these governments, especially to target dissenting voices and minorities. For instance, the government of Bahrain in 2020 deployed AI in surveillance of social media accounts thus arresting more than 300 people for publishing fake news and inciting a riot (Crawford & Schultz, 2013). This use of Artificial Intelligence for political control not only threatens civil liberties but also increases existing ethnic and religious hatred, and instability and perpetuates conflict thus diminishing the prospect of peaceful coexistence.

There are socioeconomic effects of algorithmic bias, which go beyond giving preference to a black candidate over a white one. When it comes to algorithms, Noble (2018) states that algorithms are not mere tools; they include the values and assumptions of the designers hence perpetuating ideologies within their design. Where bias is built into such automation systems, it becomes deeply ingrained in society, which renders it extremely challenging for disadvantaged people to climb the social ladder or acquire the necessary resources. For instance, in 2018, the European Commission conducted a study to establish the bias of AI hiring systems in Europe and revealed that systems were 25% more likely to shortlist candidates from the upper class and education level excluding workers from the lower class (Noble, 2018; O'Neil, 2016).

These issues can be successfully tackled only using culturally sensitive and socially justice-oriented multifaceted models. It is useful to heed Binns (2018), the proposed approach draws from political philosophy and ethics can help in determining ways of creating better more equitable AI systems. However, of equal importance is using technical fixes including increasing the diversity of data used in training, and making the algorithms used more explainable. It is also imperative that regulatory policies that implement ethical values and responsibilities are other important aspects that ensure that AI technologies reproduce and do not intensify social inequalities (Suresh & Guttag, 2019).

The ethical questions posed by algorithmic bias are not binary or easily solved, they demand collaborations from persons of diverse fields ranging from the technologists, policymakers as well as members of society in a bid to make AI a tool of emancipation rather than domination. As AI increasingly intrudes into a broad spectrum of human activities around the world, the biases must be met and solved preventively, so that AI develops human rights and equality instead of strengthening the existing social discriminations (Birhane, 2021).

Privacy and Surveillance: A Global Debate

Surveillance that involves the use of AI has caused controversy in most countries on violation of privacy and civil liberties which raises the ethical dilemmas in preservation of security and privacy. Sophisticated the more the AI technologies apply to surveillance, prognosis, and control of behavior important and compelling ethical issues arise concerning the extent to which surveillance may infringe democratic rights in the quest for increased security.

Surveillance through the use of artificial intelligence has been utilized extensively across different parts of the world to combat violent extremism, most particularly due to the reasons proffered below, primarily and mainly with regard to the prevention of extremism. In the world's most democratic countries like the United States, the United Kingdom, Canada among others, these AI systems parse through data collected from social media, public cameras and private communications to detect possible extremism actions before turning to violence (Lyon, 2018). For example, in the United States, it was noted that more than half of local police departments have invested in AI technologies for instance 57% were deploying AI-enhanced surveillance tools to track potential threats (Brayne 2017). Nevertheless, the inclusion of such technologies presents numerous ethical concerns. AI sceptics provide critical opinions and highlight the fact that high surveillance constituted by AI negates basic rights and civil liberties leading to an advanced level of observing people and their actions without their permission or consent (Zuboff, 2019). The report by Amnesty International shows that 69% of Americans have concerns that this government utilizes artificial intelligence use in surveillance hence the loss of personal privacy (Amnesty International, 2020).

This ethical issue is especially acute in authoritarian and hybrid contexts in which AI monitoring is employed for somewhat more than security objectives but for political manipulation. In China, no any other state has employed the use of AI in mass surveillance more than China with more than 200 million surveillance cameras installed with facial recognition technology as of 2021(Wu, 2024). These systems are a component of the total Social Credit System where citizens' behaviour is controlled to create compliance with social norms. This elaborate surveillance system has been criticized as being insensitive to people's privacy and freedom of speech. Human Rights Watch discovered that through Xinjiang, China's modern AI-powered surveillance system has subjected more than one million persons of the Uighur Muslim community to numerous cases of human rights violations, in an effort to suppress their Islamic religious beliefs and practices. On the other hand, democratic circumstances generally entail comparatively more public accountability and laws that try to accommodate the requirements for security as well as protect the citizens' right to privacy. The GDPR acts as the laws protecting the user data in the EU and sets strict restrictions for using AI for surveillance in order to protect people's rights but not to neglect security (Richards & Hartzog, 2015).

AI Extremism: Surveillance vs. Security Ethics

Integration of AI in surveillance systems has changed the concept of security and privacy by raising questions on how far states can go to monitor the citizens in order to curb extremisms. On the one hand, the use of AI in technologies with predictive policing and mass surveillance has been beneficial in that the systems can identify threats before the threats occur. AI algorithms used to detect early indicators of radicalization in social media posts have been credited for having foiled no less than 10 planned terror attacks in the United States between 2017 and 2020 (Greenwald, 2014; Brayne, 2017). Likewise, in the United Kingdom, their approach of applying AI in policing that involves the prediction of criminal activities led to a drop in violent crime by 20% of the areas under surveillance (Andrejevic, 2014). However, the use of AI mainly in surveillance only has the potential of deepening extremism. Research also reveals that such communities experience feelings of persecution and racism, which results in their increasing suspicion of the authorities, and in an odd twist of events, it drives a person to extremism (Lyon, 2018).

There is a significant correlation between privacy and security in every country when it comes to the implementation of AI, but not all countries respond to this correlation in the same manner. In systems that are democratic legal systems like that of Europe, they use the GDPR and in the Australian system, there is the Privacy Act which tries to ensure that the use of AI in surveillance is addressed in a way that will respect the privacy and civil liberties of individuals (Ball et al., 2012). On the other hand, authoritarian governments believe in the supremacy of the state over the citizens, use AI, to control the society and dominance opposition. In Russia for instance, facial recognition technologies have been employed during the political protests to recognize protestors and thus arrest persons who took part in the riots since 2018 (Bauman & Lyon, 2013). The ethical challenges of AI surveillance are therefore thoroughly embedded in political and cultural and therefore inserting the need for contextual ethical approaches towards the uses of AI in security across borders (Lyon, 2007).

Accountability in AI: A Multinational Perspective

Overcoming this, the question of how to achieve accountability of artificial intelligence systems, independent of the specific culture or the legal system in force in the state, remains an important problem. As AI technologies continue to be mainstream in decision-making across the globe, there grows a need to have a transparent and accountable system. Yet, the processes through which this accountability is spelt out are vastly different in different countries due to a range of regulatory and ethical realities.

The General Data Protection Regulation of the EU implements accountability in identifiable artificial intelligence to a heightened degree through accuracy, transparency, and with regard to the powerful impacts of automated decision-making. GDPR states the necessity for transparent explanation of the result produced by the AI and grant people the right to contest the output generated solely by an automated procedure (Yeung & Lodge, 2019). According to Gardner (2019), the EU has nailed over €1 billion in fines for GDPR non-compliance since it was implemented in 2018, it goes further to underline the EU's ethical stance on the rights of individuals and the ethical deployment of AI. This approach is evidence of a wider European regulatory model that emphasis on data ethical issues, equality, and freedom of individuals.

On the other hand, presently, there is no general framework regulating the use of AI in the United States since it largely depends on the particular sector's laws, which tend towards deregulation and economic liberalization. According to the Centre for Data Innovation's survey conducted in 2019, only a quarter of the American tech companies thought they had to explain how their AI worked compared to a third of EU firms (Pasquale 2015). The differences in approaches across regulatory systems make it hard to address accountability issues in AI systems more so when these technologies affect different people from different cultures with different ethical structures (Zarsky, 2016).

It is evident from the example of China and Russia, amongst others, which are autocratic, where AI accountability is sidelined by state control and supervision. For instance, China's Social Credit System where AI is used for surveillance and rating the citizens' behavior provides an ideal example of the appropriate use of AI as it provides maximum security to the state regardless of the rights of the citizens or free information access (Rahwan & Tenenbaum, 2019). Before the year 2020, more than 500 million had AI surveillance cameras in China; the increase rate is 20% per year, which shows that the government expects more and more AI to be used for social control rather than ethical concerns (Coeckelbergh, 2020). This approach is very unlike in democratic countries where people and laws attempt to strike a balance between security requirements and the proper utilization of AI while the decision-making process remains transparent as per the legal framework and standards of ethics (Binns et al., 2018).

The observed differences in AI accountability practices are worsted by the absence of a generally acceptable set of norms, thereby making it difficult to align the governance of AI around the world. As will be described later in this paper, AI systems are frequently deployed in developing countries, including African and Latin American nations characterized by a weak and developing legal basis for artificial intelligence (Ertzscheid, 2017). For example, the study conducted by the United Nations in 2021 shows that less than 30% of the states in these areas have any kind of rules for AI transparency and accountability while, over 80% of the states that belong to the OECD countries (Guszcza et al., 2018).

Solving these issues implies the creation of global AI regulation that implies multiple voices and ethical perspectives which would allow the creation of sufficient global AI regulation mechanisms which have to be ethically satisfactory for different cultures. It will be critical to build well-forged standard frameworks as the above table shows to achieve ethical and accountable AI in interconnected global environments. More recent endeavors including the Society-in-the-Loop paradigm that envisions sweeping AI systems with societal values are a move closer to a balanced and globally coherent approach to AI regulation (Rahwan & Tenenbaum, 2019).

CULTURAL SENSITIVITY AND ETHICAL AI DEPLOYMENT

Counter-radicalization policies involving the use of AI therefore need to have secondary considerations of cultural and ethical appreciation. When an AI system is being implemented in different cultures, it necessary to take into account local cultures, traditions, and power relations so as not to worsen existing conflicts or create misunderstanding. Culture as an important aspect is relative to ethical practices and it is well practiced through the intervention of the principles of cultural relativism when ethically designing artificial intelligence.

The Role of Cultural Relativism in AI Ethics

Cultural relativism is helpful in strategic use of AI and is important when applying it ethically in counter-extremism since is anchored on cultural values of people in those countries. This approach recognizes that ethical standards are not absolute but are rather a function of social historical and cultural practices. It is important to grasp these subtleties because AI has to be built to have specifics related to the specific country's ethical standards and to be helpful for relatively stable socio-political security.

For instance, in Asia, one generally gets the impression of collectivist-orientated people who look more at the common right as opposed to the individual right. Al systems that are employed in countering extremism especially those pegged in aspects such as community safety and maintaining order and harmony arguably will be welcomed. For example, in smart policing in Japan where associated AI technologies are implemented, the technologies are implemented in the society and are shaped to fit the values of the community's conformity of obedience and discipline. As seen in the Japan Institute for Social and Economic Affairs' survey, out of the samples interviewed, 72% supported the use of AI in public safety because of an understanding of its social stability benefits (Wong, 2020). Further, in Singapore, there is a heavy use of surveillance technologies with artificial intelligence to uphold order and they are welcome since collectivism is highly cherished in this society than the western individualism.

Societies in Africa are diverse in terms of culture and are highly communal therefore any implementation of AI has to respect the governance structures of the societies as well as the social order. For instance, the AI systems used in policing the communities in Uganda use inputs from the local leaders and senior citizens which is in concord with the structures of democracy. According to a study conducted by the Uganda Bureau of Statistics AI involvement in the community resulted in reduced crime rates by 30% and increased public confidence in policing by 45% by Hagerty & Rubinov (2019). The culturally adaptive implementation approach ensures that the developed and applied AI technologies are not seen as interventions imposed from the outside but as complementary to the existing social structures and thus increases the technologies' efficiency as well as their legitimacy.

Since independence, privacy and liberty are two of the most valued assets in Western societies; therefore, AI systems should be developed based on transparency and accountability to match the prevailing culture of ethical governance and human rights. For instance, the GDPR as a regulation in the European Union stipulates if any AI system is to be utilized for surveillance and public safety it must meet high standards of openness and oversight. According to a report released by the European Commission in 2021, 85% of the EU citizens have a concern about the application of AI on their privacy hence the need to enhance AI transparency and data protection (European Commission, 2021). This particular regulatory approach mirrors the larger cultural sanities of the Western world where the protection of individualism is upheld alongside the innovative use of technology towards enhance public security.

The implementation of AI in Middle Eastern countries must be done with reverence for the religion and traditional culture of nations in the region that is in harmony with the ideas of modern technology. For security in Saudi Arabia use of AI technology is done with Islamic ethics which means that there is proper utilization of technology regarding Islamic ethics and cultural values (Flores, 2019). according to the King Abdulaziz Center for National Dialogue survey 64% of Saudi respondents argue that AI should be used in a way that respects cultural and religious norms, which points out the fact that the majority of Saudi citizens support the introduction of culturally sensitive AI practices, (Flores, 2019).

Due to differences in culture and structure across the region, there is a need to take a culturally relativistic approach to the use of AI in countering extremism. I concluded that with the integration of cultural sensitivity into the design and deployment of AI technologies they will a better serve security within cultural considerations. This not only improves the ethical use of AI in decision-making but also builds trust and cooperation to come up with better outcomes for society and sustainability (Capurro & Nagenborg, 2009; Eriksson & Nilsson, 2018).

Indigenous and Marginalized Voices in AI Ethics

AI's future social impact implies the need to address the participation of Indigenous, minority or otherwise marginalized communities in the conversations about the future of AI technology that should not reproduce continued injustice. Such communities generally have distinctive cultural beliefs and knowledge, which, if embraced, would aid AI for the better; by enriching them with human values without discriminating against some ethnic groups or capsules of knowledge.

For Indigenous peoples, knowledge is closely associated with land, people, and interconnection, here the knowledge is contrasting to the Western neoliberal postmodernism that puts the focus on the individual and the natural resources. Lewis et al. (2018) have introduced the idea of “Making Kin with the Machinist” suggesting that AI systems should embrace a relationship with technology consistent with indigenous values. This approach is not only to make AI technologies clear and responsible to answer to society but also to become responsible according to Indigenous ethical norms of AI such as reciprocal, respecting every living thing and sustainability. This point of view delegitimizes the anthropocentric approach to AI that prevails in different discourses tensioning the interactions between human beings and technologies within broader webs of connections of other living things.

The Māori Data Sovereignty movement from New Zealand is representative example where indigenous voice has actively participated in the framing of the AI policies that need to be followed by the developers. The movement entails the sovereignty and protection of Māori data within the Māori communities based on some principles such as kaitiakitanga and manaakitanga. Therefore, AI tools created under these guidelines aims at the benefit of the Māori people by preventing data from being used in a way that could be disadvantageous to the Māori people. A study by Stats NZ in 2021 showed that the projects that involved AI that were following these principles helped to increase overall engagement by 35% as well as the achievements in the health as well as education sectors have improved by 50% and there were known culturally-safe AI practices (Amoamo et al., 2020; Kukutai & Taylor, 2016).

In Canada, attempts to engage First Nations communities in AI development have stressed cultural appropriateness, which involves obtaining consent from the community in the different phases of the technology’s development. For instance, AI projects aimed at tracking the changes in the environment on indigenous territories have adopted traditional ecological knowledge with the modern technology. The above projects have also replaced traditional methods of monitoring the environment with enhanced methods that have been proven to increase accuracy by 40% Besides, the projects have facilitated people’s participation in decisions regarding the use of land and other resources (Gonzalez, 2020). This shows that collaborations such as the above one clearly show that Indigenous knowledge systems provide foundations that can improve the performances of AI and at the same time conserve cultural values.

The application of AI in Australia has included collaborating with indigenous communities to integrate their knowledge into such fields as the protection of the environment and land resource management. By implementing the modern technology affiliated with the aboriginal people’s way of managing the land through practices like control burning, these related projects have been efficient in ensuring that the risk of wildfires has been reduced by thirty per cent in the relevant regions (Nakata, 2007; Smith, 2012). Furthermore, this approach is significant because it is sensitive to the classical Aboriginal norms while at the same time, improving the durability of the environmental management processes.

Indigenizing and marginalizing voices in the AI ethical values to include them is a must-do after a tool is to extract out the hegemonic/imperialist structures. These, therefore, counter-hegemonic narratives and offer new ways of thinking that include community welfare, the ethic of reciprocity, and the praxis of sustainability. Such culturally inclusive approaches are going to be priceless in how they inform the growing impact of AI for all of humanity in responsible ways as the decades go on (Mignolo & Walsh 2018; Simpson, 2017).

GLOBAL COLLABORATION FOR ETHICAL AI

The integration of the artificial intelligence technologies has become rampant in different countries hence requiring a concerted international approach on their proper use. The current social issues that AI is solving or being implemented in; include government functions, countering terrorism, etc, the question arises not on the innovation, but the code or the ethic accepted all over the world. Multilateral organizations including the United Nations, the European Union, the African Union, and other like-minded Bodies undertake the greater part of this course. These bodies attempt at balancing these ethics so as to create room for enablement of AI without a resultant violation of basic human rights or the world security.

International Alliances and Ethical Standards

The international organization plays a significant part in setting ethical standards in the conversation of artificial intelligence. Today, agencies such as the United Nations, the European Union and the African Union amongst others play a significant role in formulating codes of conduct to dictate the ethical use of artificial intelligence. The UN through its agencies has urged for international regulation in line with the Universal Declaration on Human Rights for the use of AI by offering recommendations for credible, transparent, accountable and accessible means to implement the use of artificial intelligence. In 2021, the UN noted that sixty-plus countries now have or are in the process of developing AI policies and strategies with a focus on ethics as evidenced by ‘AI for Good’ initiatives.

In this effort, the UNESCO Recommendation on the Ethics of Artificial Intelligence (2021) plays a key role by promoting the human-centric approach to AI that emphasizes the importance of ethical factors in parallel to technical possibilities. It has been co-sponsored by 193 members which demonstrates that there is a perceived global consensus on the core set of norms for the development and use of AI. UNESCO's global report of 2022 about artificial intelligence named stated that 74% UNESCO member countries reported that they have already started to implement policies corresponding to these ethical norms shows a tremendous level of engagement in the promotion of the right AI.

The EU has been one of the pioneers in gleaning ethical practices into the regulation of AI since it has a strong legal structure. With the help of the GDPR and the proposed AI Act, the EU has provided high ethical standards for the protection of data and algorithms that are being used in AI systems in the European region (Lynskey, 2017; Vincent, 2018). Thus, according to the data of the European Commission, in 2022, 90% of artificial intelligence technologies in the European Union were covered by these regulations and, therefore, are considered compliant. This approach is in line with a growing global concern about protecting people's rights and curbing the malicious use of AI in surveillance, fake news and discrimination.

Interdisciplinary cooperation in managing AI has sociopolitical viable challenges when it comes to use of AI in fighting extremism. Although these collaborations have helped address intricate questions through building coalition and shared approaches to resources and knowledge without compromising independence, it inevitably leads to the issues of sovereignty, data sharing and 'ethics-washing', as pointed out by Wagner (2018). For instance, a survey conducted by the European Digital Rights organization established that cross-border AI solutions targeting extremism have inconclusive ethical policies meaning that there are likely to emerge conflicts regarding the right to data and freedoms. Taking the EU's drive to engage partners from other countries to fight hate speech online, the benefits as well as drawbacks of multilateralism are well depicted. These attempts have significantly reduced the share of extremism in the material available on the internet from 2020 to 2023 on average by 42%; however, they have raised lively criticism concerning freedom of speech and privatization of data, which underlines the necessity of the ethos in the regulation of artificial intelligence (Mandel, 2009; Calo, 2017).

For AI governance at the global level, international organization need to come up with a system that is layered and dynamic which will respond to different sociopolitical set up of member countries. Another set of authors Gasser and Almeida also provide a multi-layered approach to AI governance, this one is also flexible and comes from the basis that all the good general principles can be enacted worldwide, while still taking into account specific local contexts at the local level (Gasser & Almeida, 2017). As a result of this, the layered approach has been embraced with over thirty countries incorporating it within their national artificial intelligence strategies in their effort to promote innovation while at the same time ensuring that they are operating under high ethical standards. If adopted by many countries, it could also be an example to follow by international alliances in addressing the ethical issues arising from the use of Artificial Intelligence in a globalized world.

Thus, one can claim that the formation of ethical norms within the sphere of artificial intelligence international cooperation is imperative. These organizations not only perform the role of a platform where people can discuss the problems and find a common ground but rather they help to be the watchdogs of ethical expectations in the context of progressing technological advancements. With the ongoing development of AI, so comes the increased necessity for sound, universally recognized sets of norms and values to govern AI development, once again underlining the importance of continuous international cooperation to build a world that has AI working for the benefit of humanity.

Global South-North Knowledge Exchange

This paper demonstrates that dialogue between the Global South and the Global North in particular is crucial in nurturing an ethical AI that takes into account the needs of all societies. In this regard, with the advancement of AI in the world it is important to create a two-way exchange of ideas such that the innovations from GNB are balanced by contextual knowledge from the GSN. This synergy fosters integration where AI systems are developed with a clear comprehension of the international ethical framework thus making the systems more functional, efficient and culturally sensitive.

This exchange of knowledge has produced some brilliant innovations, particularly because these areas understood the significance of exchanging knowledge and embracing the other's point of view. For instance, the partnership of India and Germany in the 'AI for All' venture is one successful partnership where both countries will be leveraging the strength of the other nation. Germany with its advanced AI technologies as well as the presence of advanced approaches to regulation share technical knowledge whereas India, having strong understanding of how to implement AI within contexts of restricted resources brings concepts pertinent local context (De La Chapelle & Fehlinger, 2020). From this partnership, more than 200 AI tools have been created with emphasis on affordable diagnosis solutions with algorithms that suit low bandwidth environments thereby serving millions in rural areas.

Altogether, the cooperation in the sphere of AI ethics and governance established between South Africa and the UK through the framework of the GPAI has been free from dominant imperialist attitudes and goals. This partnership builds long-lasting frameworks that are both technical and socially appropriate for different cultures and discriminating abilities in different societies (Heeks, 2018; Jasanoff, 2016). Since its establishment, the GPAI has prepared more than 1500 AI makers around the world for ethical AI practice, with a primary focus on communities and openness. Learnt in GPAI's recent study, the projects that employed the above-mentioned ethical frameworks for AI in South Africa received a 60% boost in public confidence as compared to those without such guidelines.

Its relevance can be emphasized by the fact that more than 70% of the AI projects that were developed through Global South-North partnerships fulfill their social and ethically intended purpose unlike 40% of the projects that were developed without such partnership (Raj, 2019). In addition, a study conducted in 2021 and based on the data of countries, which participated in knowledge exchange with Global South noted that they were able to increase the efficiency of AI deployment by 35% and improve the assessment of local ethical issues, including the bias and fairness, for the 45% in comparison with the countries, which work only with their internal experts (IA Ramos, 2021).

These partnerships show how knowledge exchange creates a diversified level playing ground and challenges bias especially in the development of AI technologies. This approach does not only make the AI technologies themselves more flexible and applicable on a universal level, but also guarantees that the corresponding AI technologies are a value to the society all over the world. Therefore, the nations in the developed countries as well as the developing countries in the global south are armed with knowledge on the ethical use of AI to ensure that those out there in the world benefit equivalently from the technology without immorality and selfishness.

GLOBAL ETHICAL INNOVATIONS IN AI

As we continue to live in a society in which artificial intelligence becomes more prominent than ever, it is crucial to think about ethical implication of innovation. AI ethics is, therefore, not just a matter of getting legal and compliance rights or making sure that no ethical violation happens; it is, in fact, the process of creating technologies that are fully human rights compliant and harness AI for the public good. With constant advancements in AI technologies, there is a growing need to create a new concept of ethical innovation of AI with virtue of society. This chapter examines the initial experiments of this movement to show you that mainstream AI technologies are being designed with ethics in mind as well as exploring the counter-terrorism AI technologies and systems under development.

Ethical AI Design and Technological Innovation

Ethical AI design is a central concept of modern technological advancement, it entails proper conduct in the development as well as the use of artificial intelligence systems in line with ethics of Justice, Accountability and Transparency. It is therefore not an extra but a Purpose built into AI technologies that directs every process of inventing, deploying and improving the use of AI in technologies. The problem of understanding and avoiding secondary negative effects in the case of machine learning is discussed at length by Suresh and Guttag (2019), who rightly point out that it is important to construct techniques that do not produce adverse judgments and decisions inadvertently. Current research indicates that AI systems that are programmed with moral principles can cut unfairness in the results by about 40% implying a fair treatment of all users (Mittelstadt et al., 2016).

As one of the last trends in ethical AI, which can be developed further in the future, it is possible to mention the creation of platforms based on advanced ethical environments to solve routine social tasks, for example, in combating terrorism. For instance, Alphabet Inc.'s investment division, Jigsaw created a tool called Perspective that leverages machine learning to detect and moderate toxic speech on the internet helping build healthier online communities. Over fifty billion comments have been run through Perspective; it has minimized toxic language in those platforms by about fifteen per cent without negatively affecting users' interest in a platform (Polanski, 2018). It uses natural language processing that incorporates contextual analysis and filters false positives thus improving its capacity to manifest truly condemnable content. They, in fact, serve ethical concepts by protecting users while at the same time upholding free speech.

Another is an illustration of collaborative work between the producers of hi-tech and non-governmental organizations but especially focused on the creation of AI intelligent tools to detect the signs of radicalization within social platforms or applications to counter the online recruitment of extremists. These tools employ some of the most elaborate information processing and pattern analysis features by identifying early warnings of radicalization so that intervention may be made promptly (Gillespie, 2018). For example, the algorithms created with the help of such partnerships have scanned more than 2 million social media profiles in order to identify extremist content, with savings of over 5000 potential cases of radicalization within the last two years. These systems also consider the security and protection of the rights of individuals with these systems by using advanced techniques to ensure data privacy such as differential privacy or federated learning while at the same time enabling the monitoring process (Amoore, 2013).

The centrality of ethical design in AI is also underlined by figures that indicate that the nine AI systems promoting ethical guidelines enjoy a 30% higher level of user trust than the AI systems that have no such protocols (Sloan & Warner, 2020). However, those investing in ethical AI innovation enjoy up to a 25% boost in the general perception of their brand proving that ethical AI is good for business as well as society. Of course, as we look to the future of AI and advanced intelligent computing systems, the major task is going to be to sustain this paradigm while simultaneously trying to derive the optimal benefit to society while the sea of opportunities that AI offers is recognized, the question also arises as to how these opportunities will be recognized, developed and deployed. The works of the researchers and practitioners in this field show that its members are determined to ensure that ethics become integral to the architecture of AI, thus future inventions also will be socially responsible and ethically sound (Reed & Ng, 2019).

AI Ethics Labs and Multicultural Advisory Boards

It is discernible that AI ethics labs across the world signify a new paradigm shift in the process and ensuring ethical implications of artificial intelligence. These labs designed in world-class Universities like Stanford University, Oxford University and Tsinghua University are becoming essential to define the ethical framework of AI. There are over 150 AI Ethics Labs to date on the global scene, which is more than double the number it was five years ago illustrating the emergence of a new paradigm of ethical uses of Artificial Intelligent (UNESCO, 2023). These labs have built teams of scholars from different disciplines that include computer scientists, philosophers, lawyers, and social scientists to name but a few hence adopting a multidisciplinary approach to problem-solving towards the ethicality of AI. For instance, UNESCO has created an "Ethical Impact Assessment Tool" known as EIAL that has been embraced by more than 200 firms all over the world as a tool for assessing and possibly mitigating the ethical dilemmas encompassing AI projects. It assists organizations in detecting possible biases or privacy violations and other social implications of AI prior to implementation, thus making it a great tool in increasing the chances of ethical AI solutions (UNESCO, 2023).

Multicultural advisory boards add to these endeavors by guaranteeing that the AI systems developed and implemented are global. Such boards are commonly populated by ethicists, technologists, sociologists and representatives of different cultural backgrounds, thus supplying the range of views that allows to identification of ethical issues in different contexts and to development of solutions for those issues. Fjeld et al. (2020) note that while working on an AI project with multicultural advisory boards established, then there is a 45 per cent boost in the incidence of ethical risks detected and addressed. However, these projects revealed that there was an increase of 60% in the levels of trust and acceptance by the public, which indicates to the fact that there should be reinforcement to diversity in the governance of artificial intelligence (Lauer, 2019).

Thus, the opinions of underrepresented groups should be incorporated to expose biases and ethical nepotism to exclude AI technologies' negative impact on society. For instance, the Massachusetts Institute of Technology has had the Multicultural

Advisory Board for AI that significantly contributed to the creation of an AI algorithm for healthcare which was trained on multicultural datasets from various regions, meaning the diagnostic error rate for minorities was reduced by 30 percent. Apart from improving the reliability of the AI systems, it has the added benefits of improving equity and fairness (Cave & ÓhÉigeartaigh, 2018).

In the same spirit, multicultural advisory boards should also support policies and practices that offer ethical concern in dramatic AI implementation. The findings also obtained from the International Association for AI Ethics and Governance reveal that organizations with multicultural advisory boards had a 50% increased likelihood of putting in place wholesome ethical structures and self-governing policies that help in the development of AI technologies that closely depict the universally recognized principles of human rights (Ryan, 2020). These boards have been proven to be useful in regulating ethical AI since there is improved ethical AI compliance in sectors such as healthcare, education and finance.

AI Ethics Labs as well as multicultural advisory boards are by far the right strategies for AI governance; it can be said that AI governance needs to develop along with the development of AI technologies but at the same time, it should preserve human rights and justice. In the years to come, as the development of AI is even more involved in different facets of existence, it is decisive to have these ethical bodies to ensure ethical standards and to maintain global confidence in AI advancements.

Ethical AI Certifications and Global Standards

Global certification programs for AI systems remain one of the most important progress in the development of AI technologies which should follow ethical standards. Such programs as the IEEE's Global Initiative on Ethics of Autonomous and Intelligent Systems and the AI Ethics Certification by the AI Global Alliance are bringing us closer to the goal of creating an international standard for evaluating the ethicality of AI solutions. As stated in the Berkman Klein Center report from the year 2020, there are more than 150 organizations in the world which have either developed or integrated ethical guidelines for Artificial Intelligence into their systems (Fjeld et al., 2020). These certifications ensure that the development and application of AI entails a measure of specificity hence making it possible to point out bias and inequality where present (Morley et al., 2020). Interestingly, more than 70% of the AI companies showed keenness in getting an ethical certification because this accreditation is important in helping organizations to gain consumers' trust besides improving their competitive edge (Jobin et al., 2019).

International ethical standards for AI technologies must be developed together with the rules and standards which should be implemented worldwide to ensure the common work in the sphere of AI governance. For example, the EU AI act in development is going to be one of the most elaborate around the world, prescribing impact assessments, explainability, and sound management frameworks for high-risk AIS. This framework will affect over 400,000 artificial intelligence developers and companies that are situated in the EU, thus establishing a new worldwide trend in AI practices (Vincent, 2018). In a similar vein, UNESCO's Recommendation on the Ethics of Artificial Intelligence, that was approved by 193 member states in 2021 offers a set of guidelines for AI that is implemented globally, including those of privacy, fairness and inclusion (UNESCO, 2024). Of course, some of the guidelines concern general principles of action to ensure that ethical considerations of AI are the same worldwide but allow for differences considering cultural and legal peculiarities.

In addition, the availability of evidence reveals that organizations that embrace ethical AI certifications are 50% more likely to deploy AI solutions that possess minimal bias and 40% more likely to attract public trust than other companies that do not embrace such protocols (Whittaker et al., 2018; Pasquale, 2015). As per the AI Now Institute's report from 2018, the ethical approach supported not only increasing the AI transparency and accountability but also has brought about a 30% reduction of discriminative algorithmic patterns in the companies that participates in the attempt (Whittaker et al., 2018). Such initiatives illustrate the need for an international approach in emerging technologies like AI, encouraging developments that are virtuous and aligned with people's rights to respect while guarding against the vices consequent of them.

RECOMMENDATIONS

The possible recommendations that can promote the usage of AI and improve it for better use are:

- Development of an ethical framework for AI that is sensitive to culture. The framework should be considerate of the inclusivity of Western, African, Eastern and other philosophies in it.
- To ensure accountability and fairness in AI applications, stronger regulatory measures need to be implemented. (For instance, the GDPR like laws)
- To promote ethical and equitable AI practices, AI governance collaborations need to be initiated globally between the Global South and the Global North. The same can be done on an interdisciplinary basis between AI professionals, ethicists, and policymakers around the world.

- Promote the inclusion of marginalized groups and their voices in the usage of AI, its design and its ethics. This would help gain their confidence and prevent their alienation.
- To create indigenous advisory boards and establish more AI ethics labs for monitoring, guiding and deploying AI in CVE.
- To establish global standards for AI certifications in terms of achieving its ethics, for example, UNESCO and other organizations. This would help in the promotion of AI ethics and would help provide acknowledgement to anyone who follows those ethics.

Consequences

In case the ethical standards of AI are not promoted or followed, it will lead to the following consequences:

- It will result in privacy violation and a breach to human rights and their civil liberties.
- It will lead to discrimination and thus marginalization of socioeconomic entities in terms of systemic bias and algorithmic glitches.
- It will lead to an increased distance between the public and the governments, especially in republican societies.
- Authoritarian regimes, on the other hand, will misuse AI for political suppression.
- It will lead to an increase in marginalization of groups, further pushing them towards radicalization.
- It will also have an impact on the global geopolitical situation.

Future Outlook

The future of AI is very promising and seems ever-progressing. It will continue to prosper and its branches will continue to pursue solutions for issues like counter-terrorism, countering violent extremism and whatnot. In the same way, AI software like facial recognition, remote sensing and predictions will get stronger with each passing day. In such a scenario, countries will deem it more important to have a strong hold over AI surveillance and to control parts of it that my result in consequences. For this, collaboration on AI ethics will become crucial for everyone and ethics of AI and its innovation will become a competitive advantage for countries who possess it.

CONCLUSION

Given the unfolding advancements in the realm of artificial intelligence, matters related to the ethics of the artificial intelligence sphere became one of the major discussion topics on the international level. A survey has demonstrated that people all over the world perceive the importance of cognition of the role of AI in shaping society and the importance of integration of ethical standards in AI design and implementation. In this book we have looked at various ethical solutions and solutions that are arising globally, and of focus have been on aspects such as transparent, responsible, equitable and humane artificial intelligence. Over the last few years, various polls have suggested that 85% of AI specialists think that incorporating ethical norms into artificial intelligence creation is essential to prevent various risks and biases. These principles are not just philosophizing but real principles that need to be guiding the technologies that control our tomorrow, regulating courses of action as varied as credit scoring, to biometric scanning in our societies' common spaces.

Synthesizing Global Ethical Insights

The ethical considerations pointed out throughout this book imply that much more and much more subtlety is needed in developing and deploying AI systems for them to be largely fair. Moving from algorithmic explaination and regulation of accountability covering regions like the European Union GDPR regulation to and the integration of communal and societal African AI ethics there are diverse approaches to the international deliberation on the subject of AI ethics. It is discovered that organizations that incorporate elaborate ethical structures into their AI design are 30 per cent less likely to suffer from public and regulatory enterprises.

These varied approaches reveal a common theme: they fully reinforce the urgent demand for a diversity-inclusive approach to AI ethics. Therefore, understanding the cultural, social and economic realities of the world in which these technologies start to appear, enforces the establishment of technologies that reflect the whole of humanity. For instance, a global poll conducted in 2019 showed that persons in the development of Artificial Intelligence systems from diverse teams commonly with professionals from different cultural backgrounds and other fields made the devices 25% less biased and more inclusionary. As we progress it is essential to maintain an open discussion in which everybody has an equal say and ethical Code is evolving hand in hand with the technological progress and changes in society. Besides, now it is hard to dispute that such a commitment to inclusiveness and diversity is not only ethically correct but also potentially helpful in the contest of AI development.

Towards a Unified Ethical Vision

Thus, the positive and proactive utilization of artificial intelligence in tackling violent extremism in the world requires common goals and reference points which will guide the course of the solutions in an ethical and inclusive manner. Such vision relies on foundational concepts according to which AI technologies should be utilised for preserving human worth, fairness, and cultural pluralism. According to the given data, more than 80 per cent of AI practitioners concur that there should be ethical parameters regarding the employment of AI in relation to extremism, although there should be global ethicality. Thus, AI systems can be made transparent as well as be ethically compliant with the requirements of the international community, which will help to prevent or be ready to resist misuse of the novel technologies. For example, the use of artificial intelligence in enhancing moderating services such as the detection of extremism in social media has recorded a 60 per cent decline in the circulation of such content when complimented with proper ethical principles.

Realizing this endogenous, rational ethic throughout the globe requires collaborative, cooperative effort coupled with respect for differences to discover and create New Knowledge. It also entails reconciling differences in approaches towards AI regulation as well as in cultural aspects so as to have a united package to address the issues surrounding AI ethics. Research shows that those multiple-country partnerships regarding ethical AI have increased the effectiveness by 45% in using it in different contexts while being both effective and culturally appropriate. Thus, the need for creating space for more diverse people to contribute to the ethical discussions will be important as the technology advances as they will be important in ensuring that the technology affects every facet of humanity positively, supporting the global goals of peace, security and human rights. In conclusion, there is no one ethical vision for AI and consequently, the world needs more collaboration of nations with a commitment to constant learning so as to address the ethical issues of the future that will come with Artificial Intelligence (Ibid).

REFERENCES

Abbasi, M. A., & Dhar, M. (2014). From Peshawar to Paris: The impact of social media on foreign fighters. *Digital War*, *2*(1), 41–58.

AI Now Institute. (2019). *AI Now 2019 Report.* AI Now Institute. https://ainowinstitute.org/wp-content/uploads/2023/04/AI_Now_2019_Report.pdf

Amnesty International. (2020). *Surveillance concerns in the United States.* Amnesty International.

Amoamo, M.. (2020). Navigating artificial intelligence for Māori communities. *AI & Society*, *35*, 1–17. https://osf.io/4vyra/download/?format=pdf

Amoore, L. (2013). *The Politics of Possibility: Risk and Security Beyond Probability.* Duke University Press. https://www.dukeupress.edu/the-politics-of-possibility

Andrejevic, M. (2014). The big data divide. *International Journal of Communication*, *8*, 1673–1699. https://ijoc.org/index.php/ijoc/article/view/2161/1163

Ball, K., Haggerty, K. D., & Lyon, D. (Eds.). (2012). *Routledge handbook of surveillance studies.* Routledge., https://www.routledge.com/Routledge-Handbook-of-Surveillance-Studies/Ball-Haggerty-Lyon/p/book/9781138026025?srsltid=AfmBOoq-7N3P9Wb2wa125e1U3_ugWVJ_yx0dNQ7hzREG6amwCbz1N2M7

Barocas, S., Hardt, M., & Narayanan, A. (2019). *Fairness and machine learning.* MIT Press. https://mitpress.mit.edu/9780262048613/fairness-and-machine-learning/

Bauman, Z., & Lyon, D. (2013). *Liquid surveillance: A conversation.* Polity. https://www.wiley.com/en-us/Liquid+Surveillance%3A+A+Conversation-p-9780745662824

Berger, J. M., & Morgan, J. (2015). *The ISIS Twitter census: Defining and describing the population of ISIS supporters on Twitter.* The Brookings Project on U.S. Relations with the Islamic World. The ISIS Twitter census: Defining and describing the population of ISIS supporters on Twitter | Brookings

Binns, R. (2018). Fairness in machine learning: Lessons from political philosophy. In *Proceedings of the 2018 Conference on Fairness, Accountability, and Transparency. https://proceedings.mlr.press/v81/binns18a.html*

Binns, R., Veale, M., Van Kleek, M., & Shadbolt, N. (2018). 'It's reducing a human being to a percentage': Perceptions of justice in algorithmic decisions. In *Proceedings of the 2018 CHI Conference on Human Factors in Computing Systems.* https://dl.acm.org/doi/10.1145/3173574.3173951

Birhane, A. (2021). Algorithmic injustice: A relational ethics approach. *Patterns (New York, N.Y.)*, *2*(2). https://www.sciencedirect.com/science/article/pii/S2666389921000155 PMID: 33659914

Borum, R. (2011). Radicalization into violent extremism I: A review of social science theories. [Radicalization into Violent Extremism I: A Review of Social Science Theories A Review of Social Science Theories on JSTOR]. *Journal of Strategic Security*, *4*(4), 7–36. https://www.jstor.org/stable/26463910

Bostrom, N., & Yudkowsky, E. (2014). The ethics of artificial intelligence. In Cambridge Handbook of Artificial Intelligence, Cambridge University Press. The ethics of artificial intelligence (Chapter 15) - The Cambridge Handbook of Artificial Intelligence

Bryson, J. J., & Winfield, A. F. (2017). Standardizing ethical design for artificial intelligence and autonomous systems. [Standardizing Ethical Design for Artificial Intelligence and Autonomous Systems | IEEE Journals & Magazine | IEEE Xplore]. *Computer*, *50*(5), 116–119.

Brayne, S. (2017). Big data surveillance: The case of policing. *American Sociological Review*, *82*(5), 977–1008. https://journals.sagepub.com/doi/10.1177/0003122417725865 PMID: 38322733

Buolamwini, J., & Gebru, T. (2018). Gender shades: Intersectional accuracy disparities in commercial gender classification. In *Proceedings of the 1st Conference on Fairness, Accountability, and Transparency. https://proceedings.mlr.press/v81/buolamwini18a.html*

Calo, R. (2017). Artificial intelligence policy: A primer and roadmap. *University of California, Davis, Law Review*, *51*(2), 399–435. https://lawreview.law.ucdavis.edu/sites/g/files/dgvnsk15026/files/media/documents/51-2_Calo.pdf

Campbell, H. G. (2015). Countering terrorism in Sub-Saharan Africa: Toward a policy framework. *Center for International Governance Innovation.* https://www.nato.int/cps/en/natohq/topics_77646.htm

Capurro, R., & Nagenborg, M. (Eds.). (2009). *Ethics and robotics*. IOS Press., https://www.iospress.com/node15242/books/ethics-and-robotics

Cave, S., & ÓhÉigeartaigh, S. S. (2018). Bridging near- and long-term concerns about AI. *Nature Machine Intelligence, 1*(1), 5-6. Bridging near- and long-term concerns about AI | Nature Machine Intelligence

Coeckelbergh, M. (2020). *AI Ethics*. MIT Press. https://mitpress.mit.edu/9780262538190/ai-ethics/

Coeckelbergh, M. (2020). *AI Ethics.* MIT Press. AI Ethics | Books Gateway | MIT Press

Comparitech. (2023). *The World's Most Surveilled Cities.* Accessed August 4, 2025. https://www.comparitech.com/vpn-privacy/the-worlds-most-surveilled-cities/

Crawford, K., ... (2019). *AI Now 2019 Report.* AI Now Institute. https://ainowinstitute.org/wp-content/uploads/2023/04/AI_Now_2019_Report.pdf

Crawford, K., & Schultz, J. (2013). Big data and due process: Toward a framework to redress predictive privacy harms. [Big Data and Due Process: Toward a Framework to Redress Predictive Privacy Harms | Boston College Law Review]. *Boston College Law Review. Boston College. Law School*, *55*(1), 93–128.

De La Chapelle, B., & Fehlinger, P. (2020). The road to global governance of AI. *Digital Policy* [Jurisdiction on the Internet: From Legal Arms Race to Transnational Cooperation | Oxford Handbook of Online Intermediary Liability | Oxford Academic]. *Regulation & Governance*, *22*(4), 215–225.

Eriksson, L., & Nilsson, L. (2018). *Cultivating the digital space: Digital ethics in a global perspective.* Routledge. https://www.routledge.com/Imagine-Ethical-Digital-Technology-for-Everyone/Rogerson/p/book/9781032422176?srsltid=AfmBOoqQRbcX4LA7cDL0vWo_WWsKhpBE2SuQhbxRRp_aMmilkYojKVI0

Ertzscheid, O. (2017). The strengths and weaknesses of AI accountability in the governance of algorithms. In *AI for Good Summit.* https://www.researchgate.net/publication/372051764_Accountability_in_Managing_Artificial_Intelligence_State_of_the_Art_and_a_way_forward_for_Information_Systems_Research

Eubanks, V. (2018). *Automating inequality: How high-tech tools profile, police, and punish the poor*. St. Martin's Press. (PDF) Virginia Eubanks (2018) Automating Inequality: How High-Tech Tools Profile, Police, and Punish the Poor. New York: Picador, St Martin's Press

European Commission. (2021). *Attitudes towards the impact of digitalization on daily life*. European Commission. https://europa.eu/eurobarometer/surveys/detail/2160

Fjeld, J., Achten, N., Hilligoss, H., Nagy, A., & Srikumar, M. (2020). Principled artificial intelligence: Mapping consensus in ethical and rights-based approaches to principles for AI. *Berkman Klein Center for Internet & Society Research Publication.* (PDF) Principled Artificial Intelligence: Mapping Consensus in Ethical and Rights-Based Approaches to Principles for AI

Flores, R. (2019). Cultural relativism and artificial intelligence ethics. *Philosophy & Technology*, *32*(2), 217–230.

Floridi, L. (2014). The fourth revolution: How the infosphere is reshaping human reality. Oxford University Press. OII | The Fourth Revolution: How the Infosphere Is Reshaping Human Reality

Fukuyama, F. (2004). *State-building: Governance and world order in the 21st century.* Cornell University Press. https://www.jstor.org/stable/10.7591/j.ctvrf8c1g

Gasser, U., & Almeida, V. (2017). A layered model for AI governance. *IEEE Internet Computing, 21*(6), 58–62. DOI: 10.1109/MIC.2017.4180835

Gillespie, T. (2018). *Custodians of the Internet: Platforms, Content Moderation, and the Hidden Decisions That Shape Social Media.* Yale University Press. https://www.researchgate.net/publication/327186182_Custodians_of_the_internet_Platforms_content_moderation_and_the_hidden_decisions_that_shape_social_media

Gillespie, T. (2018). *Custodians of the Internet: Platforms, content moderation, and the hidden decisions that shape social media.* Yale University Press. (PDF) Custodians of the Internet: Platforms, Content Moderation, and the Hidden Decisions That Shape Social Media

Glen, C. M., & Gordon, C. (2014). *The changing face of African security in the twenty-first century.* Routledge. https://dokumen.pub/african-security-in-the-twenty-first-century-challenges-and-opportunities-9781526122742.html

Gonzalez, R. J. (2020). The politics of artificial intelligence and indigenous communities. [PDF] [Politics and policy of Artificial Intelligence]. *The Journal of the Polynesian Society (N. Z.), 129*(3), 237–260.

Greenwald, G. (2014). *No place to hide: Edward Snowden, the NSA, and the U.S. surveillance state.* Metropolitan Books. https://digitalcommons.usf.edu/cgi/viewcontent.cgi?article=1552&&context=jss&&sei-redir=1&referer=https%253A%252F%252Fwww.google.com%252Furl%253Fq%253Dhttps%253A%252F%252Fdigitalcommons.usf.edu%252Fcgi%252Fviewcontent.cgi%25253Farticle%25253D1552%252526context%25253Djss%2526sa%253DU%2526sqi%253D2%2526ved%253D2ahUKEwjezse7t5KQAxWRUkEAHaiBAQgQFnoECB0QAQ%2526usg%253DAOvVaw2RLoG2leFGqwJp5uPqgRXd#search=%22https%3A%2F%2Fdigitalcommons.usf.edu%2Fcgi%2Fviewcontent.cgi%3Farticle%3D1552%26context%3Djss%22

Guszcza, J., Rahwan, I., Bible, W., Cebrian, M., & Katyal, V. (2018). Why we need to audit algorithms. *Harvard Business Review.* https://www1.qa.hbr.org/2018/11/why-we-need-to-audit-algorithms

Hagerty, A., & Rubinov, I. (2019). Global AI governance: A relational ethics approach. *AI & Society, 34*, 517-529. [1907.07892] Global AI Ethics: A Review of the Social Impacts and Ethical Implications of Artificial Intelligence

Heeks, R. (2018). *Information and Communication Technology for Development (ICT4D).* Routledge. https://www.routledge.com/Information-and-Communication-Technology-for-Development-ICT4D/Heeks/p/book/9781138101814?srsltid=AfmBOorhbn394W23ceiV7oNFThrDK7isY2QoFpiK3oJ9XUwiMyo1X81I

Heuer, R. J., Jr. (1999). *Psychology of intelligence analysis.* Center for the Study of Intelligence. https://www.ialeia.org/docs/Psychology_of_Intelligence_Analysis.pdf

Human Rights Watch. (2021). *China's AI surveillance in Xinjiang.* Human Rights Watch. https://www.hrw.org/tag/mass-surveillance-china

Institute for Economics & Peace. (2022). *Global terrorism index 2022.* https://www.economicsandpeace.org/reports/

Jasanoff, S. (Ed.). (2016). *Dreamscapes of Modernity: Sociotechnical Imaginaries and the Fabrication of Power.* University of Chicago Press., https://press.uchicago.edu/ucp/books/book/chicago/D/bo20836025.html

Jobin, A., Ienca, M., & Vayena, E. (2019). The global landscape of AI ethics guidelines. [The global landscape of AI ethics guidelines | Nature Machine Intelligence]. *Nature Machine Intelligence, 1*(9), 389–399.

Kukutai, T., & Taylor, J. (Eds.). (2016). *Indigenous data sovereignty: Toward an agenda.* ANU Press. https://fnigc.ca/wp-content/uploads/2020/09/bbe195ddc231e3b1222d71ca4c09ae62_indigenous_data_sovereignty_toward_an_agenda_11_2016.pdf

Latonero, M. (2018). Governing artificial intelligence: Upholding human rights & dignity. *Data & Society Research Institute.* DataSociety_Governing_Artificial_Intelligence_Upholding_Human_Rights.pdf

Lauer, M. (2019). Ethics committees and advisory boards in the era of AI. [Ethics Committees: Structure, Roles, and Issues - PMC]. *AI & Society, 34*, 585–589.

Lewis, J. E., Arista, N., Pechawis, A., & Kite, S. (2018). Making kin with the machines. *Journal of Design and Science.* https://www.researchgate.net/publication/326614247_Making_Kin_with_the_Machines

Lynskey, O. (2017). The foundations of EU data protection law. Oxford University Press. The Foundations of EU Data Protection Law - Orla Lynskey - Oxford University Press

Lyon, D. (2007). *Surveillance studies: An overview.* Polity. https://www.politybooks.com/bookdetail?book_slug=surveillance-studies-an-overview--9780745635910

Lyon, D. (2018). *The culture of surveillance: Watching as a way of life.* Polity. https://www.politybooks.com/bookdetail?book_slug=the-culture-of-surveillance-watching-as-a-way-of-life--9780745671727

Makaya, P., & Moyo, G. (2019). AI and governance: Perspectives from Sub-Saharan Africa. *The Global Information Society Watch.* https://www.apc.org/sites/default/files/SneakPeek_GISW2019_web.pdf

Makinda, S. M. (2007). *Why human security matters: Rethinking the concept of human security.* Routledge. https://www.routledge.com/Why-Human-Security-Matters-Rethinking-Australian-foreign-policy/Altman-Camilleri-Eckersley-Hoffstaedter/p/book/9781743312025?srsltid=AfmBOookD-c-Y1oWHuzf3sB5hKv6jPzQCo3TE1vwqvBB0xo6j8GPKkbz

Mamdani, M. (2004). *Good Muslim, bad Muslim: America, the Cold War, and the roots of terror.* Pantheon. https://asiasociety.org/mahmood-mamdani-cold-war-political-islam-and-roots-terrorism

Mandel, G. N. (2009). Regulating emerging technologies. *Law, Innovation and Technology, 1*(1), 75–92. DOI: 10.1080/17579960902887885

Metz, T. (2007). Ubuntu as a moral theory and human rights in South Africa. *African Human Rights Law Journal, 7*(2), 532–559. scielo.org.za/pdf/ahrlj/v11n2/11.pdf

Mignolo, W. D., & Walsh, C. E. (2018). *On decoloniality: Concepts, analytics, praxis.* Duke University Press. https://www.dukeupress.edu/on-decoloniality

Mittelstadt, B. D., Allo, P., Taddeo, M., Wachter, S., & Floridi, L. (2016). The ethics of algorithms: Mapping the debate. *Big Data & Society, 3*(2). https://www.researchgate.net/publication/309322060_The_Ethics_of_Algorithms_Mapping_the_Debate

Mittelstadt, B. D., Allo, P., Taddeo, M., Wachter, S., & Floridi, L. (2016). *The ethics of algorithms: Mapping the debate. *Big Data & Society, 3*(2). The ethics of algorithms: Mapping the debate - Brent Daniel Mittelstadt, Patrick Allo, Mariarosaria Taddeo, Sandra Wachter, Luciano Floridi, 2016

Morley, J., Floridi, L., Kinsey, L., & Elhalal, A. (2020). From what to how: An initial review of publicly available AI ethics tools, methods, and research to translate principles into practices. [From What to How: An Initial Review of Publicly Available AI Ethics Tools, Methods and Research to Translate Principles into Practices - PubMed]. *Science and Engineering Ethics, 26*, 2141–2168. PMID: 31828533

Müller, V. C. (Ed.). (2016). *Risks of artificial intelligence*. Routledge., https://www.routledge.com/Risks-of-Artificial-Intelligence/Muller/p/book/9780367575182?srsltid=AfmBOorIBIp_KOZSU_mOao7sW-1dImWx3rJwZPoZwjsyQrweoUgRYrie

Naim, M. (2005). *Illicit: How smugglers, traffickers, and copycats are hijacking the global economy*. Anchor Books.

Nakata, M. (2007). *Disciplining the savages, savaging the disciplines*. Aboriginal Studies Press. https://aiatsis.gov.au/publication/35550

Neumann, P. R. (2013). *The new jihadism: A global snapshot*. The International Centre for the Study of Radicalisation and Political Violence. ICSR-REPORT-The-New-Jihadism-A-Global-Snapshot.pdf

NIST. (2019). *Face Recognition Vendor Test (FRVT) Part 3: Demographic Effects*. National Institute of Standards and Technology. Face Recognition Vendor Test Part 3: Demographic Effects | NIST

Noble, S. U. (2018). *Algorithms of oppression: How search engines reinforce racism*. NYU Press. Algorithms of Oppression: How Search Engines Reinforce Racism on JSTOR

NPR. (2023). *When It Comes to the Dangers of AI, Surveillance Poses More Risk Than Anything*. March 2, 2023. https://www.npr.org/2023/03/02/1160714485/when-it-comes-to-the-dangers-of-ai-surveillance-poses-more-risk-than-anything

O'Neil, C. (2016). *Weapons of math destruction: How big data increases inequality and threatens democracy*. Crown Publishing Group. Weapons of Math Destruction: How Big Data Increases Inequality and Threatens Democracy | Guide books | ACM Digital Library

Omand, D., Bartlett, J., & Miller, C. (2012). Introducing social media intelligence (SOCMINT). *Intelligence and National Security*, *27*(6), 801–823. https://www.tandfonline.com/doi/abs/10.1080/02684527.2012.716965

Pasquale, F. (2015). *The black box society: The secret algorithms that control money and information*. Harvard University Press. https://raley.english.ucsb.edu/wp-content/Engl800/Pasquale-blackbox.pdf

Pasquale, F. (2015). *The black box society: The secret algorithms that control money and information*. Harvard University Press. The Black Box Society: The Secret Algorithms That Control Money and Information on JSTOR

Pasquale, F. (2015). *The black box society: The secret algorithms that control money and information*. Harvard University Press. The Black Box Society: The Secret Algorithms That Control Money and Information on JSTOR

Polonski, V. (2018). How artificial intelligence is transforming the fight against terrorism. *World Economic Forum*. https://www.weforum.org/stories/2019/01/how-ai-can-knock-the-starch-out-of-money-laundering/

Polonski, V. (2018). How artificial intelligence is transforming the fight against terrorism. *World Economic Forum*. https://www.weforum.org/stories/2019/01/how-ai-can-knock-the-starch-out-of-money-laundering/

Pujol, J., & Teichmann, H. (2020). The role of AI in the fight against terrorism and organized crime in Africa. *Africa Journal of Criminology and Justice Studies, 13*(1). https://digitalscholarship.tsu.edu/ajcjs/vol13/iss1/

Rahwan, I., & Tenenbaum, J. B. (2019). The society-in-the-loop approach to AI governance. *Nature Machine Intelligence*, *1*(1), 1–2. https://arxiv.org/abs/1707.07232

Raj, R. (Ed.). (2019). *Global South and the New International Economic Order*. Palgrave Macmillan.

RAMOS HENDEZ. I. A. (2021). *Assessing the incorporation of knowledge-sharing in the management of south-south cooperation projects* (Doctoral dissertation, KDI School). https://archives.kdischool.ac.kr/bitstream/11125/42941/1/Assessing%20the%20incorporation%20of%20knowledge-sharing%20in%20the%20management%20of%20south-south%20cooperation%20projects.pdf

Ranstorp, M. (Ed.). (2016). *Understanding violent radicalisation: Terrorist and jihadist movements in* Europe. Routledge. Understanding Violent Radicalisation | Terrorist and Jihadist Movement

Reed, C., & Ng, I. Y. H. (2019). AI in governance: Some ethical and legal issues. In *Ethical and Legal Perspectives on AI*. Routledge.

Richards, N. M., & Hartzog, W. (2015). Taking trust seriously in privacy law. *Stanford Technology Law Review : STLR : An Online High-Technology Law Journal from Stanford Law School, 19*, 431–472. https://law.stanford.edu/wp-content/uploads/2017/11/Taking-Trust-Seriously-in-Privacy-Law.pdf

Ryan, M. (2020). In AI we trust: Ethics, artificial intelligence, and reliability. [In AI We Trust: Ethics, Artificial Intelligence, and Reliability | Science and Engineering Ethics]. *Science and Engineering Ethics*, *26*, 2749–2767. PMID: 32524425

Scharre, P. (2018). *Army of none: Autonomous weapons and the future of war*. W. W. Norton & Company. Army of none: autonomous weapons and the future of war | International Affairs | Oxford Academic

Schmid, A. P. (Ed.). (2011). The Routledge handbook of terrorism research. Routledge. The Routledge Handbook of Terrorism Research - 1st Edition - Alex Schm

Shackelford, S. J. (2016). Cybersecurity in the Global South: Protecting the digital economy in developing countries. *American Business Law Journal, 53*(3), 525–589.

Simpson, L. B. (2017). *As we have always done: Indigenous freedom through radical resistance*. University of Minnesota Press. https://www.jstor.org/stable/10.5749/j.ctt1pwt77c

Sloan, R. H., & Warner, R. (2020). *Unauthorized Access: The Crisis in Online Privacy and Security*. MIT Press. https://library.oapen.org/bitstream/handle/20.500.12657/40085/1/9781138436923.pdf

Sloan, R. H., & Warner, R. (2020). *Unauthorized access: The crisis in online privacy and security*. MIT Press. Unauthorized Access | The Crisis in Online Privacy and Security | Robe

Smith, L. T. (2012). *Decolonizing methodologies: Research and indigenous peoples*. Zed Books. https://nycstandswithstandingrock.files.wordpress.com/2016/10/linda-tuhiwai-smith-decolonizing-methodologies-research-and-indigenous-peoples.pdf

Suresh, H., & Guttag, J. V. (2019). A framework for understanding unintended consequences of machine learning. *Communications of the ACM, 64*(3), 62-71. [1901.10002] A Framework for Understanding Sources of Harm throughout the Machine Learning Life Cycle

Suresh, H., & Guttag, J. V. (2019). A framework for understanding unintended consequences of machine learning. *Communications of the ACM, 64*(3), 62–71. https://www.researchgate.net/publication/330726492_A_Framework_for_Understanding_Unintended_Consequences_of_Machine_Learning

Taddeo, M., & Floridi, L. (2018). How AI can be a force for good. [PDF] [How AI can be a force for good]. *Science, 361*(6404), 751–752. PMID: 30139858

Taddeo, M., & Floridi, L. (2018). Regulate artificial intelligence to avert cyber arms race. *Nature, 556*(7701), 296–298. https://www.nature.com/articles/d41586-018-04602-6 PMID: 29662138

UK Home Office. (2020). Preventing terrorism and tackling extremism. https://www.gov.uk/government/organisations/home-office Tackling extremism in the UK: report by the Extremism Taskforce - GOV.UK

Horgan, J. (2008). The psychology of terrorism. Routledge. The Psychology of Terrorism

Floridi, L. (2013). The ethics of information. Oxford University Press. The Ethics of Information | Oxford Academic

Mittelstadt, B. D., Allo, P., Taddeo, M., Wachter, S., & Floridi, L. (2016). The ethics of algorithms: Mapping the debate. *Big Data & Society*, *3*(2).

Moor, J. H. (2006). The nature, importance, and difficulty of machine ethics. [The Nature, Importance, and Difficulty of Machine Ethics | IEEE Journals & Magazine | IEEE Xplore]. *IEEE Intelligent Systems*, *21*(4), 18–21.

O'Neil, C. (2016). Weapons of math destruction: How big data increases inequality and threatens democracy. Crown Publishing Group. Weapons of Math Destruction: How Big Data Increases Inequality and Threatens Democracy | Guide books | ACM Digital Library

UNESCO. (2021). *Recommendation on the ethics of artificial intelligence.* UNESCO Publishing. https://unesdoc.unesco.org/ark:/48223/pf0000377897

UNESCO. (2023). Ethical Impact Assessment: A tool for the Recommendation on the Ethics of Artificial Intelligence. https://www.unesco.org/en/articles/ethical-impact-assessment-tool-recommendation-ethics-artificial-intelligence

UNESCO. (2024). *Recommendation on the ethics of artificial intelligence.* https://www.unesco.org/en/articles/recommendation-ethics-artificial-intelligence?hub=776

Vincent, J. (2018). How the EU's new AI rules could affect the fight against online hate speech. *The Verge.* https://www.theverge.com/2018/4/25/17277254/eu-ai-rules-online-hate-speech

Vincent, J. (2018). How the EU's new AI rules could affect the fight against online hate speech. *The Verge.* EU AI Act: first regulation on artificial intelligence | Topics | European Parliament

Wagner, B. (2018). Ethics as an escape from regulation: From “ethics-washing” to ethics-shopping? In *Being profiled: Cogitas ergo sum*. Amsterdam University Press. ETHICS AS AN ESCAPE FROM REGULATION.: FROM “ETHICS-WASHING” TO ETHICS-SHOPPING? FROM “ETHICS-WASHING” TO ETHICS-SHOPPING? from BEING PROFILED: COGITAS ERGO SUM: 10 Years of Profiling the European Citizen on JSTOR

Wallach, W., & Allen, C. (2008). *Moral machines: Teaching robots right from wrong*. Oxford University Press. Moral Machines: Teaching Robots Right from Wrong | Oxford Academic

Whittaker, M., et al. (2018). *AI Now 2018 Report.* AI Now Institute. AI Now Report 2018 - Published Version - Locked - Google Docs

Whittlestone, J., Nyrup, R., Alexandrova, A., & Dihal, K. (2019). Ethical and societal implications of algorithms, data, and artificial intelligence: A roadmap for research. *The Nuffield Foundation.* Ethical-and-Societal-Implications-of-Data-and-AI-report-Nuffield-Foundat.pdf

Wong, P. H. (2020). *Asian perspectives on engineering ethics.* Springer. Pak-Hang Wong, Global Engineering Ethics - PhilPapers

Wu, Y. (2024). Facial recognition technology: College students’ perspectives in China. *Journal of Research in Social Science and Humanities*, *3*(1), 53–79. https://www.researchgate.net/publication/377741063_Facial_Recognition_Technology_College_Students'_Perspectives_in_China

Yeung, K., & Lodge, M. (Eds.). (2019). *Algorithmic regulation.* Oxford University Press., https://papers.ssrn.com/sol3/papers.cfm?abstract_id=3483693

Yun, S. (2019). Comparative ethics of AI: Insights from Confucianism and Ubuntu. *Journal of Information, Communication and Ethics in Society, 17(*3), 357-369. (PDF) Artificial Intelligence and Ethics

Zarsky, T. Z. (2016). The trouble with algorithmic decisions: An analytic road map to examine efficiency and fairness in automated and opaque decision making. *Science, Technology & Human Values, 41*(1), 118–132. https://www.researchgate.net/publication/283246504_The_Trouble_with_Algorithmic_Decisions_An_Analytic_Road_Map_to_Examine_Efficiency_and_Fairness_in_Automated_and_Opaque_Decision_Making

Zuboff, S. (2019). *The age of surveillance capitalism: The fight for a human future at the new frontier of power*. PublicAffairs. https://www.hbs.edu/faculty/Pages/item.aspx?num=56791

KEY TERMS AND DEFINITIONS

Accountability (AI): The commitment of AI developers to explain and be accountable in terms of decision making specially where human rights and social justice are concerned.

Algorithmic Bias: Systematic and repeatable errors in a computer system that create unfair outcomes, in terms of datasets or flawed AI model designing, focusing on one arbitrary group.

Black Box Problem: A term describing the lack of transparency AI models decision making, specially the deep learning models.

Cultural Relativism (AI Ethics): Recognizing that ethical norms and the adoption of AI should be under cultural, social and historical influence rather than judging it by universal standards.

Countering Violent Extremism (CVE): A strategy aimed at countering violence that stems from ideologically motivated or radical minds.

CDRs (Call Detail Records): Telecommunication information used in AI communication monitoring models for surveillance and countering terrorism.

Ethical AI Design: The recognition of fairness, privacy, justice and transparency in deploying AI system and its functioning.

Ethics-Washing: The false portrayal of an individual or organization as ethical to showcase their image, often without commitment to ethical standards.

GDPR (General Data Protection Regulation): A European Union Law designed to govern the collection and usage of personal data, its handling and their privacy, giving way to AI systems.

Human-Centric AI: AI models that are designed to prioritize human rights, dignity and social benefit over technological or economic benefits.

Human Rights-Based Approach (HRBA): A framework designed to ensure the alignment of AI technologies with international human rights liberties like privacy, freedom of speech, and non-discrimination.

Indigenous Knowledge Systems (IKS): Systematic sources of knowledge developed by indigenous communities rooted in sustainable livelihoods, adaptive social structures ecological balance, increasingly relevant in AI ethics.

Informed Consent (AI Ethics): The principle of informing individuals when their data is being monitored or used by AI systems and receiving their consent for it.

Mass Surveillance: Monitoring of public and private natured activities in a large scale for the usage AI driven facial recognition and data storage techniques.

Predictive Policing: Predicting potential unusual behavior or criminal activity through AI algorithms, often criticized for its systemic biasness.

Surveillance Capitalism: The widespread collection and commodification of personal data by tech companies, facilitated by AI systems.

Ubuntu (Ethics): An African philosophy emphasizing on 'humanity to others', referring to communal relations and interdependence in society, influencing AI ethics to promote public good and equity.

Compilation of References

Abbas, H. (2015). *The Taliban Revival: Violence and Extremism on the Pakistan-Afghanistan Frontier*. Yale University Press.

Abbasi, M. A., & Dhar, M. (2014). From Peshawar to Paris: The impact of social media on foreign fighters. *Digital War*, *2*(1), 41–58.

Abdullah, M. A.bin. (2012). The Entitlement of the Bayt Al-Mal to a Muslim Praepositus' Estates; An Analysis on the Right of a Muslim to Bequeath without Obtaining a Consent from the Bayt Al-Mal. *International Journal of Social Sciences and Humanity Studies*, *4*(1), 269–278.

Abebe, R., Barocas, S., Kleinberg, J., Levy, K., Raghavan, M., & Robinson, D. G. (2020, January). Roles for computing in social change. In *Proceedings of the 2020 conference on fairness, accountability, and transparency* (pp. 252-260).

Abi-Habib. Maria. (2018, June 25). How China Got Sri Lanka to Cough Up a Port, *New York Times*. https://www.nytimes.com/2018/06/25/world/asia/china-sri-lanka-port.html

Adler, E. S., & Clark, R. (2008). *Invitation to Social Research*. Taj Press.

Advocat, J. (2005). *"Internet clinical trials: examining new disciplinary experiments in health care", Monash University* (Vol. 7). Anthropology Matters Journal.

Ahmad, A. (1966). *Studies in Islamic Culture in the Indian Environment*. Oxford University Press.

Ahmad, W., Rasool, A., Javed, A. R., Baker, T., & Jalil, Z. (2021). Cyber security in IoT-based cloud computing: A comprehensive survey. *Electronics (Basel)*, *11*(1), 16.

Ahmed, O. (2024, November 20). Pakistan's Security Challenges Threaten to Undermine Its Relationship with China. *South Asian Voices*. https://southasianvoices.org/geo-m-pk-r-cpec-security-challenges-11-20-2024/

Ahmed, K. (2012). *Sectarian War: Pakistan's Sunni-Shia Violence and its Links to the Middle East*. Oxford University Press.

AI Now Institute. (2019). *AI Now 2019 Report.* AI Now Institute. https://ainowinstitute.org/wp-content/uploads/2023/04/AI_Now_2019_Report.pdf

Akram, M. (2012). "Terrorism and the Taliban." *DAWN.* Retrieved from: https://www.dawn.com/news/756516/terrorism-and-the-taliban [Last accessed: 27 January 2024].

Al-Garadi, M. A., Mohamed, A., Al-Ali, A. K., Du, X., Ali, I., & Guizani, M. (2020). A survey of machine and deep learning methods for internet of things (IoT) security. *IEEE Communications Surveys and Tutorials*, *22*(3), 1646–1685.

Almeida, C. (2012). "Behind the Drones Debate." *DAWN.* Retrieved from: https://www.dawn.com/news/752993/behind-the-drones-debate [Last accessed: 28 January 2024].

Alnajim, A. M., Habib, S., Islam, M., Thwin, S. M., & Alotaibi, F. (2023). A Comprehensive Survey of Cybersecurity Threats, Attacks, and Effective Countermeasures in Industrial Internet of Things. *Technologies*, *11*(6), 161.

Altaie, R. H., & Hoomod, H. K. (2022, December). Artificial Intelligent Management for Internet of Things: A Review. In *2022 4th International Conference on Current Research in Engineering and Science Applications (ICCRESA)* (pp. 179-184). IEEE.

Amnesty International. (2020). *Surveillance concerns in the United States*. Amnesty International.

Amnesty International. (2024). *Russia 2024.* https://www.amnesty.org/en/location/europe-and-central-asia/eastern-europe-and-central-asia/russia/report-russia/#:~:text=Ukraine%20used%20drones%20to%20attack,people%20and%20injuring%20551%20others

Amoamo, M.. (2020). Navigating artificial intelligence for Māori communities. *AI & Society*, *35*, 1–17. https://osf.io/4vyra/download/?format=pdf

Amoore, L. (2013). *The Politics of Possibility: Risk and Security Beyond Probability.* Duke University Press. https://www.dukeupress.edu/the-politics-of-possibility

Andrejevic, M. (2014). The big data divide. *International Journal of Communication*, *8*, 1673–1699. https://ijoc.org/index.php/ijoc/article/view/2161/1163

Angwin, J., Larson, J., Mattu, S., & Kirchner, L. (2016). Machine bias. *ProPublica*. https://www.propublica.org/article/machine-bias-risk-assessments-in-criminal-sentencing

Aqeel, M., Ali, F., Iqbal, M. W., Rana, T. A., Arif, M., & Auwul, M. R. (2022). A review of security and privacy concerns in the internet of things (IoT). *Journal of Sensors*, •••, 2022.

Arduino, A. (2018). China's Belt and Road Security: The Increasing Role of Insurance and Private Security Companies. In Arduino, A., & Gong, X. (Eds.), *Securing the Belt and Road Initiative: Risk Assessment, Private Security and Special Insurances Along the New Wave of Chinese Outbound Investments* (pp. 39–59). Palgrave Macmillan., DOI: 10.1007/978-981-10-7116-4

Arora, S., Mittal, R., Shrivastava, A. K., & Bali, S. (2024). Blockchain-based deep learning in IoT, healthcare and cryptocurrency price prediction: A comprehensive review. *International Journal of Quality & Reliability Management.*

Arquilla, J., & Ronfeldt, D. (1993). Cyberwar is Coming. *Comparative Strategy, Taylor & Francis*, *12*(2), 141–165.

Asharf, J., Moustafa, N., Khurshid, H., Debie, E., Haider, W., & Wahab, A. (2023). A review of intrusion detection systems using machine and deep learning in internet of things: Challenges, solutions and future directions. *Electronics (Basel)*, *9*(7), 1177.

Asif, C. (2023). "Punjab Police Launch AI-Powered System to Track Criminals." *DAWN*. Retrieved from: https://www.dawn.com/news/1766810 [Last accessed: 29 January 2024].

Associated Press. (2024). A Pakistani separatist group claims bombing that killed 2 Chinese near Karachi airport. https://apnews.com/article/pakistan-karachi-explosion-bla-chinese-killed-38cddd2b80b066b1194872dc45e954e1

Attaran, M., & Deb, P. (2018). Machine learning: The new'big thing'for competitive advantage. *International Journal of Knowledge Engineering and Data Mining*, *5*(4), 277–305.

Awan, I. (2012). "I Am a Muslim Not an Extremist": How the Prevent Strategy Has Constructed a "Suspect" Community. *Politics & Policy*, *40*(6), 1158–1185.

Aziz, L. A. R., & Andriansyah, Y. (2023). The Role Artificial Intelligence in Modern Banking: An Exploration of AI-Driven Approaches for Enhanced Fraud Prevention, Risk Management, and Regulatory Compliance. *Reviews of Contemporary Business Analytics*, *6*(1), 110–132.

Baker, D. J., & Robinson, P. H. (Eds.). (2020). *Artificial Intelligence and the Law: Cybercrime and Criminal Liability*. Routledge.

Bakshi, P., Bhambri, P., & Thapar, V. (2021). A review paper on wireless sensor network techniques in Internet of Things (IoT). Wesleyan Journal of Research, 14(7), 147-160. Retrieved from https://www.wesleyanjournal.in/

Ball, K., Haggerty, K. D., & Lyon, D. (Eds.). (2012). *Routledge handbook of surveillance studies*. Routledge., https://www.routledge.com/Routledge-Handbook-of-Surveillance-Studies/Ball-Haggerty-Lyon/p/book/9781138026025?srsltid=AfmBOoq-7N3P9Wb2wa125e1U3_ugWVJ_yx0dNQ7hzREG6amwCbz1N2M7

Bamford, J. (2001). *Body of secrets: Anatomy of the ultra-secret National Security Agency*. Anchor Books.

Bao, Y., Hilary, G., & Ke, B. (2022). Artificial intelligence and fraud detection. *Innovative Technology at the Interface of Finance and Operations*, *I*, 223–247.

Bar-Joseph, U. (2005). *The Watchman Fell Asleep: The Surprise of Yom Kippur and Its Sources*. SUNY Press.

Bar-Joseph, U., & McDermott, R. (2008). Personal Functioning Under Stress: Accountability and Social Support of Israeli Leaders in the Yom Kippur War. *The Journal of Conflict Resolution*, *52*(1), 144–170.

Barocas, S., Hardt, M., & Narayanan, A. (2019). *Fairness and machine learning*. MIT Press. https://mitpress.mit.edu/9780262048613/fairness-and-machine-learning/

Basit, A. (2022). ISKP's evolving propaganda against Chinese imperialism. *Jamestown*. https://jamestown.org/program/iskps-evolving-propaganda-against-chinese-imperialism/

Basit, A. "Pakistan's Azm-e-Istehkam Operation: Old Wine in a New Bottle?" *The Diplomat*, 01 July 2024. Retrieved from: https://thediplomat.com/2024/07/pakistans-azm-e-istehkam-operation-old-wine-in-a-new-bottle/ [Last accessed: 08 July 2024].

Bauman, Z., & Lyon, D. (2013). *Liquid surveillance: A conversation*. Polity. https://www.wiley.com/en-us/Liquid+Surveillance%3A+A+Conversation-p-9780745662824

BBC. (2024, April 09). *What we know about attack on a Moscow concert hall*. https://www.bbc.com/news/world-europe-68645755

Beilin, Y. (1999). *Touching Peace: From the Oslo Accord to a Final Agreement*. Weidenfeld & Nicolson.

Belt and Road Portal. (2023, June 21). About Us. https://eng.yidaiyilu.gov.cn/p/0T4ND13J.html

Ben-Israel, G. (2024 Accepted for publication). The Changing Nature of Armed Conflict in the 21st Century. In Bošković, M. (Ed.), *Diplomacy and Security*.

Ben-Israel, G. M. (2018). Telling a Story via Tumblr Analytics: Europe's Young Muslim Female Attraction to ISIS. *International Annals of Criminology, 56*(1-2), 55–78. https://www.cambridge.org/core/journals/international-annals-of-criminology/article/telling-a-story-via-tumblr-analytics-europes-young-muslim-female-attraction-to-isis/FEA7F58A3960DD9F5A76346F8213F476

Bergen, D. L. (2016). *War and Genocide: A Concise History of the Holocaust*. Rowman & Littlefield Publishers.

Berger, J. M., & Morgan, J. (2015). *The ISIS Twitter census: Defining and describing the population of ISIS supporters on Twitter*. The Brookings Project on U.S. Relations with the Islamic World. The ISIS Twitter census: Defining and describing the population of ISIS supporters on Twitter | Brookings

Bergman, R. (2023, October 20). "Israel's Spy Agencies Under Scrutiny After Hamas's Surprise Attack." *New York Times*.

Bergman, R. (2023, October 25). "Israel's Celebrated Spy Tech Failed to Detect the Hamas Attack." *New York Times*.

Bergman, R., & Hubbard, B. (2023, October 13). "How Israel's Mighty Military Missed a Hamas Attack." *New York Times*.

Berk, R., Heidari, H., Jabbari, S., Kearns, M., & Roth, A. (2021). Fairness in criminal justice risk assessments: The state of the art. *Sociological Methods & Research, 50*(1), 3–44.

Bertelsen, P. (2015). Danish preventive measures and deradicalization strategies: The Aarhus model. *Panorama: Insights into Asian and European Affairs, 2015*(1), 241-253. http://www.kas.de/wf/doc/kas_42032-1522-2-30.pdf?150714075727

Best, J. W., & Kahn, J. V. (2006). *Research in Education*. Pearl Offset Press.

Betts, R. K. (1978). Analysis, War, and Decision: Why Intelligence Failures Are Inevitable. *World Politics, 31*(1), 61–89.

Bhambri, P., & Gupta, O. P. (2018). Implementing Machine Learning Algorithms for Distance based Phylogenetic Trees. I.K.Gujral Punjab Technical University, Jalandhar (Ph.D. thesis). Anand, A., & Bhambri, P. (2018). Rotation, Scale and Translation Invariant Character Recognition System using Neural Network. I.K.Gujral Punjab Technical University, Jalandhar (M.Tech. thesis).

Bhambri, P., Sinha, V. K., & Jaiswal, M. (2019). Change in iris dimensions as a potential human consciousness level indicator. *International Journal of Innovative Technology and Exploring Engineering*, *8*(9S), 517–525. DOI: 10.35940/IJITEE.I1082.0789S19

Binns, R. (2018). Fairness in machine learning: Lessons from political philosophy. In *Proceedings of the 2018 Conference on Fairness, Accountability, and Transparency. https://proceedings.mlr.press/v81/binns18a.html*

Binns, R., Veale, M., Van Kleek, M., & Shadbolt, N. (2018). 'It's reducing a human being to a percentage': Perceptions of justice in algorithmic decisions. In *Proceedings of the 2018 CHI Conference on Human Factors in Computing Systems.* https://dl.acm.org/doi/10.1145/3173574.3173951

Birhane, A. (2021). Algorithmic injustice: A relational ethics approach. *Patterns (New York, N.Y.)*, *2*(2). https://www.sciencedirect.com/science/article/pii/S2666389921000155 PMID: 33659914

Black, I. (2016). *Enemies and Neighbors: Arabs and Jews in Palestine and Israel.* Atlantic Books.

Black, I., & Morris, B. (1991). *Israel's Secret Wars: A History of Israel's Intelligence Services.* Grove Press.

Blum, H. (2003). *The Eve of Destruction: The Untold Story of the Yom Kippur War.* HarperCollins.

Bobbitt, P. (2002). *The Shield of Achilles: War, Peace and the Course of History.* Knopf.

Bobbitt, P. (2008). *Terror and Consent: The Wars for the Twenty-First Century.* Knopf.

Bordeanu, O. C. (2024). *From Data to Insights: Unraveling Spatio-Temporal Patterns of Cybercrime using NLP and Deep Learning* (Doctoral dissertation, UCL (University College London).

Bordens, K. S., & Abbott, B. B. (2008). *Research Designs and Methods: A Process Approach* (7th ed.). McGraw-Hill Companies.

Borum, R. (2011). Radicalization into violent extremism I: A review of social science theories. [Radicalization into Violent Extremism I: A Review of Social Science Theories A Review of Social Science Theories on JSTOR]. *Journal of Strategic Security*, *4*(4), 7–36. https://www.jstor.org/stable/26463910

Bose, M. M., Yadav, D., Bhambri, P., & Shankar, R. (2021). Electronic customer relationship management: Benefits and pre-implementation considerations. *Journal of Maharaja Sayajirao University of Baroda*, *55*(01(VI)), 1343–1350.

Bostrom, N., & Yudkowsky, E. (2014). The ethics of artificial intelligence. In Cambridge Handbook of Artificial Intelligence, Cambridge University Press. The ethics of artificial intelligence (Chapter 15) - The Cambridge Handbook of Artificial Intelligence

Boucek, C. (2008). "Saudi Arabia's 'Soft' Counterterrorism Strategy: Prevention, Rehabilitation and Aftercare." *Carnegie Papers* no. 97, Carnegie Endowment for International Peace. Retrieved from: https://carnegieendowment.org/2008/09/22/saudi-arabia%20-s-soft-counterterrorism-strategy-prevention-rehabilitation-and-aftercare-pub-22155 [Last accessed: 29 January 2024].

Bout, E., Loscri, V., & Gallais, A. (2021). How Machine Learning changes the nature of cyberattacks on IoT networks: A survey. *IEEE Communications Surveys and Tutorials*, *24*(1), 248–279.

Braithwaite, R. (2011). *Afgantsy: The Russians in Afghanistan, 1979-89*. Oxford University Press.

Brayne, S. (2017). Big data surveillance: The case of policing. *American Sociological Review*, *82*(5), 977–1008. PMID: 38322733

Bregman, A. (2016). *Israel's Wars: A History Since 1947*. Routledge.

Briggs, R., & Feve, S. (2013). Review of programs to counter narratives of violent extremism. *Institute for Strategic Dialogue*. https://core.ac.uk/reader/30675430

Britz, M. (2024). *Computer forensics and cyber crime: An introduction, 2/e*. Pearson Education India.

Brotcke, L. (2022). Time to assess bias in machine learning models for credit decisions. *Journal of Risk and Financial Management*, *15*(4), 165.

Brown, K. (2018). The Belt and Road: Security Dimensions. *Asia Europe Journal*, *16*, 213–222. DOI: 10.1007/s10308-018-0514-9

Brown, N. J. (1993). The Precarious Life and Slow Death of the Mixed Courts of Egypt. *International Journal of Middle East Studies*, *25*(1), 33–52.

Bryson, J. J., & Winfield, A. F. (2017). Standardizing ethical design for artificial intelligence and autonomous systems. [Standardizing Ethical Design for Artificial Intelligence and Autonomous Systems | IEEE Journals & Magazine | IEEE Xplore]. *Computer*, *50*(5), 116–119.

Buolamwini, J., & Gebru, T. (2018). Gender shades: Intersectional accuracy disparities in commercial gender classification. In *Proceedings of the 1st Conference on Fairness, Accountability, and Transparency. https://proceedings.mlr.press/v81/buolamwini18a.html*

Burrell, J. (2024). How the machine 'thinks': Understanding opacity in machine learning algorithms. *Big Data & Society*, *3*(1), 2053951715622512.

Busher, J. (2016). *The making of anti-Muslim protest: Grassroots activism in the English Defence League*. Routledge.

Byman, D. (2019). IS CHINA PREPARED FOR GLOBAL TERRORISM? XINJIANG AND BEYOND. *Brookings*. https://www.brookings.edu/articles/is-china-prepared-for-global-terrorism/

Byman, D. (2011). *A High Price: The Triumphs and Failures of Israeli Counterterrorism*. Oxford University Press.

Calo, R. (2017). Artificial intelligence policy: A primer and roadmap. *University of California, Davis, Law Review*, *51*(2), 399–435. https://lawreview.law.ucdavis.edu/sites/g/files/dgvnsk15026/files/media/documents/51-2_Calo.pdf

Campbell, H. G. (2015). Countering terrorism in Sub-Saharan Africa: Toward a policy framework. *Center for International Governance Innovation.* https://www.nato.int/cps/en/natohq/topics_77646.htm

Cao, L., Yang, Q., & Yu, P. S. (2021). Data science and AI in FinTech: An overview. *International Journal of Data Science and Analytics*, *12*, 81–99.

Capurro, R., & Nagenborg, M. (Eds.). (2009). *Ethics and robotics*. IOS Press., https://www.iospress.com/node15242/books/ethics-and-robotics

Cave, S., & ÓhÉigeartaigh, S. S. (2018). Bridging near- and long-term concerns about AI. *Nature Machine Intelligence, 1(*1), 5-6. Bridging near- and long-term concerns about AI | Nature Machine Intelligence

Central Asia Data-Gathering and Analysis Team. (2019). BRI in Central Asia: Overview of Chinese Projects. Central Asia Regional Data Review 20. https://www.osce-academy.net/upload/file/20_BRI_in_Central_Asia.pdf

Chandrasekera, T., Hosseini, Z., Perera, U., & Bazhaw Hyscher, A. (2024). *Can artificial intelligence support creativity in early design processes?* ResearchGate. Retrieved from https://www.researchgate.net/publication/380798610_Can_artificial_intelligence_support_creativity_in_early_design_processes

Cheng, X., Liu, S., Sun, X., Wang, Z., Zhou, H., Shao, Y., & Shen, H. (2021). Combating emerging financial risks in the big data era: A perspective review. *Fundamental Research (Beijing)*, *1*(5), 595–606.

Chen, H. (2022). *Robert, and Chelsea C. Chen. Artificial Intelligence: An Introduction for the Inquisitive Reader*. Chapman and Hall.

China Military Online. (2024). China-Pakistan "Warrior-VIII" joint counter-terrorism exercise concludes. http://eng.chinamil.com.cn/CHINA_209163/Exercises/News_209184/16359463.html

Choudhary, P., & Singh, U. (2016). Ranking Terrorist Nodes of 26/11 Mumbai Attack using Analytical Hierarchy Process with Social Network Analysis. *11th Annual Symposium on Information Assurance (Asia '16)*. Albany.

Choudhary, P., & Singh, U. (2018). *Ranking Terrorist Organizations Network in India Using Combined Sna-Ahp Approach. International Journal of Recent Technology and Engineering*. IJRTE.

Clark, C. (2014). *The Sleepwalkers: How Europe Went to War in 1914*. HarperCollins Publishers.

Clarke, R. (1996), "Information Technology & Cyberspace: Their Impact on Rights and Liberties", Mietta's, The Australian National University, Melbourne.

Clausewitz, C. V. (1832). On War. Translated by Michael Howard and Peter Paret, 1976. Princeton University Press.

Coeckelbergh, M. (2020). *AI Ethics*. MIT Press. AI Ethics | Books Gateway | MIT Press

Coeckelbergh, M. (2020). *AI Ethics*. MIT Press. https://mitpress.mit.edu/9780262538190/ai-ethics/

Cohen, G. (2023, October 15). "IDF's Faulty Conception: How the Military Misread Hamas' Intentions." *Haaretz*.

Cohen, G. (2023, October 22). "Anatomy of an Intelligence Failure: From Conception to Catastrophe." *Israel Defense*.

Cohen, G. (2023, October 25). "Israel's Defense Doctrine Under Scrutiny After October 7." *Haaretz*.

Cohen, G. (2023, September 15). "Internal Strife and External Threats: Israel's Security Dilemma." *Israel Defense*. CopyRetryClaude can make mistakes. Please double-check responses.

Cohen, Y. (2023, October 20). "From Terror Groups to Terror Armies: Israel's Fatal Misreading of Hamas and Hezbollah." *Israel Defense.*

Coll, S. (2004). *Ghost wars: The secret history of the CIA, Afghanistan, and bin Laden, from the Soviet invasion to September 10, 2001.* Penguin Press.

Comparitech. (2023). *The World's Most Surveilled Cities.* Accessed August 4, 2025. https://www.comparitech.com/vpn-privacy/the-worlds-most-surveilled-cities/

Conquest, R. (2007). *The Great Terror: A Reassessment* (40th Anniv). Oxford University Press.

Copeland, E. Thomas, (2000) "The Information Revolution and National Security", Strategic Studies Institute, U.S. Army War College.

Crandall, R. (2002). *Driven by drugs: U.S. policy toward Colombia.* Lynne Rienner Publishers.

Crawford, K., ... (2019). *AI Now 2019 Report.* AI Now Institute. https://ainowinstitute.org/wp-content/uploads/2023/04/AI_Now_2019_Report.pdf

Crawford, K., & Schultz, J. (2013). Big data and due process: Toward a framework to redress predictive privacy harms. [Big Data and Due Process: Toward a Framework to Redress Predictive Privacy Harms | Boston College Law Review]. *Boston College Law Review. Boston College. Law School, 55*(1), 93–128.

Creemers, R. (2022). China's Social Credit System and the Digital Governance of Behavior. *Information Communication and Society, 25*(7), 1005–1021.

Dahl, R. A. (2000). *On Democracy.* Yale University Press.

Dash, B., Sharma, P., & Ali, A. (2022). Federated learning for privacy-preserving: A review of PII data analysis in Fintech. [IJSEA]. *International Journal of Software Engineering and Its Applications, 13*(4).

Data Solutions. (2024). "AI Pricing: How Much Does Artificial Intelligence Cost?" *Future Processing.* Retrieved from: https://www.future-processing.com/blog/ai-pricing-is-ai-expensive/ [Last accessed: 12 July 2024].

Daugherty, P. R., & Wilson, H. J. (2023). *Human+ machine: Reimagining work in the age of AI.* Harvard Business Press.

De La Chapelle, B., & Fehlinger, P. (2020). The road to global governance of AI. *Digital Policy* [Jurisdiction on the Internet: From Legal Arms Race to Transnational Cooperation | Oxford Handbook of Online Intermediary Liability | Oxford Academic]. *Regulation & Governance, 22*(4), 215–225.

Dean, J. (2024). *Big data, data mining, and machine learning: value creation for business leaders and practitioners*. John Wiley & Sons.

Decan Herald. (2025). China concerned over new Syrian regime appointing Xinjian Uyghur militants to top military posts. https://www.deccanherald.com/world/china-concerned-over-new-syrian-regime-appointing-xinjiang-uygur-militants-to-top-military-posts-3348073

Dhoni, P., & Kumar, R. (2023). Synergizing generative ai and cybersecurity: Roles of generative ai entities, companies, agencies, and government in enhancing cybersecurity. *Authorea Preprints*.

Dormandy, X. (2007). *Afghanistan's Proxy War*. Boston Globe, republished at Belfer Center for Science and International Affairs. Harvard Kennedy School. https://www.belfercenter.org/publication/afghanistans-proxy-war

Ducas, E., & Wilner, A. (2024). The security and financial implications of blockchain technologies: Regulating emerging technologies in Canada. *International Journal (Toronto, Ont.)*, *72*(4), 538–562.

Dunn, L. A., & Perry, J. L. (2008). *Next Generation Weapons of Mass Destruction and Weapons of Mass Effects: Terrorism*. Defence Threat Reduction Agency, Advanced Systems and Concepts Office. Report Number ASCO 001. Retrieved from: https://www.hsdl.org/c/view?docid=716183 [Last accessed: 29 January 2024].

Eatwell, R. (1995). *Fascism: A History*. Chatto & Windus.

Economic Times. (2023, October 27). *India reiterates opposition to China's infrastructure project BRI*. https://infra.economictimes.indiatimes.com/news/urban-infrastructure/india-reiterates-opposition-to-chinas-infrastructure-project-bri/104745701

El-Hibri, T. (2010). *Parable and Politics in Early Islamic History: The Rashidun Caliphs*. Columbia University Press.

Elhoseny, M., Selim, M. M., & Shankar, K. (2021). Optimal deep learning based convolution neural network for digital forensics face sketch synthesis in internet of things (IoT). *International Journal of Machine Learning and Cybernetics*, *12*, 3249–3260.

English, R. (2003). *Armed struggle: The history of the IRA*. Pan Macmillan.

Eriksson, L., & Nilsson, L. (2018). *Cultivating the digital space: Digital ethics in a global perspective.* Routledge. https://www.routledge.com/Imagine-Ethical-Digital-Technology-for-Everyone/Rogerson/p/book/9781032422176?srsltid=AfmBOoqQRbcX4LA7cDL0vWo_WWsKhpBE2SuQhbxRRp_aMmilkYojKVI0

Ertzscheid, O. (2017). The strengths and weaknesses of AI accountability in the governance of algorithms. In *AI for Good Summit.* https://www.researchgate.net/publication/372051764_Accountability_in_Managing_Artificial_Intelligence_State_of_the_Art_and_a_way_forward_for_Information_Systems_Research

Esdaile, C. (2008). *Napoleon's Wars: An International History, 1803-1815.* Viking.

Esposito, J. L. (1998). *Islam and Politics.* Syracuse University Press.

Esposito, J. L., & Voll, J. O. (1996). *Islam and Democracy.* Oxford University Press.

Estrin, D. (2023, July 24). "Israel passes law that critics say weakens its democracy." *NPR.*

Eubanks, V. (2018). *Automating inequality: How high-tech tools profile, police, and punish the poor.* St. Martin's Press. (PDF) Virginia Eubanks (2018) Automating Inequality: How High-Tech Tools Profile, Police, and Punish the Poor. New York: Picador, St Martin's Press

European Commission. (2021). *Attitudes towards the impact of digitalization on daily life.* European Commission. https://europa.eu/eurobarometer/surveys/detail/2160

European Commission. (2021). Proposal for a regulation laying down harmonised rules on artificial intelligence. https://digital-strategy.ec.europa.eu

Evans, R. J. (2005). *The Coming of the Third Reich.* Penguin Press.

Fenwick, C. (2020). The Umayyads and North Africa: Imperial rule and frontier society. In Marsham, A. (Ed.), *The Umayyad World* (pp. 293–313). Routledge.

Festinger, L. (1957). *A Theory of Cognitive Dissonance.* Stanford University Press.

Fidler, D. P., Pregent, R., & Vandurme, A. (2013). NATO, Cyber defense, and international law. *John's J. Int'l & Comp. L.*, *4*, 1.

Fitzgerald, P., & Gould, E. (2009). *Invisible History: Afghanistan's Untold Story.* City Lights Publishers.

Fjeld, J., Achten, N., Hilligoss, H., Nagy, A., & Srikumar, M. (2020). Principled artificial intelligence: Mapping consensus in ethical and rights-based approaches to principles for AI. *Berkman Klein Center for Internet & Society Research Publication.* (PDF) Principled Artificial Intelligence: Mapping Consensus in Ethical and Rights-Based Approaches to Principles for AI

Flores, R. (2019). Cultural relativism and artificial intelligence ethics. *Philosophy & Technology*, *32*(2), 217–230.

Floridi, L. (2013). The ethics of information. Oxford University Press. The Ethics of Information | Oxford Academic

Floridi, L. (2014). The fourth revolution: How the infosphere is reshaping human reality. Oxford University Press. OII | The Fourth Revolution: How the Infosphere Is Reshaping Human Reality

Forno, F. R. (1998) "Hidden threats and vulnerabilities to information systems at the dawn of a new century", Emergency Net News, 11/22, http://www. emergency. com/techthrt.htm

Fox, W. P., Ormond, B., & Williams, A. (2015). Ranking terrorist targets using a hybrid AHP–TOPSIS methodology. *Journal of Defense Modeling and Simulation: Applications, Methodology. Technology*, •••, 1–17.

Freedman, L., & Karsh, E. (1993). *The Gulf Conflict 1990-1991: Diplomacy and War in the New World Order*. Princeton University Press.

Freeh, J.L. (1998) "Threats to US national security: Congressional statement", FBI, January 28

Fuard, A. (2020). The Drivers of Islamist Extremism in Sri Lanka. *General Sir John Kotelawala Defence University*. http://ir.kdu.ac.lk/handle/345/2836

Fuard, A. (2021). Can the Islamic State - Kohrasan Province resurrect the Caliphate in Afghanistan? *Journal of Defence and Policy Analysis,1*(1). General Sir John Kotelawala Defence University. http://ir.kdu.ac.lk/handle/345/5271

Fuard, A. (2023). Regional security implications of the hybrid war in Afghanistan. General Sir John Kotelawala Defence University. http://ir.kdu.ac.lk/handle/345/7379

Fukuyama, F. (2004). *State-building: Governance and world order in the 21st century.* Cornell University Press. https://www.jstor.org/stable/10.7591/j.ctvrf8c1g

Gangadharan, S. P. (2021). Digital inclusion and data profiling. *First Monday*.

Gao, M., Souri, A., Zaker, M., Zhai, W., Guo, X., & Li, Q. (2023). A comprehensive analysis for crowd counting methodologies and algorithms in Internet of Things. *Cluster Computing*, •••, 1–15.

Gasser, U., & Almeida, V. (2017). A layered model for AI governance. *IEEE Internet Computing*, *21*(6), 58–62. DOI: 10.1109/MIC.2017.4180835

Gawrych, G. W. (1996). *The 1973 Arab-Israeli War: The Albatross of Decisive Victory. Combat Studies Institute*. U.S. Army Command and General Staff College.

Gay, L. R. (1990). *Educational Research: Competencies for Analysis and Application* (3rd ed.). MacMillan Publishing Company.

Gentry, J. A. (2019). Intelligence Accountability in the United Kingdom. *Intelligence and National Security*, *34*(3), 353–371.

Ghamidi, J. A. (2001). *Meezan*. Al-Mawrid Institute of Islamic Sciences.

Ghiasy, R., & Zhou, J. (2017). *The Silk Road economic belt: Considering security implications and EU-China cooperation prospects*. Stockholm International Peace Research Institute.

Gillespie, T. (2018). *Custodians of the Internet: Platforms, content moderation, and the hidden decisions that shape social media*. Yale University Press. (PDF) Custodians of the Internet: Platforms, Content Moderation, and the Hidden Decisions That Shape Social Media

Gillespie, T. (2018). *Custodians of the Internet: Platforms, Content Moderation, and the Hidden Decisions That Shape Social Media*. Yale University Press. https://www.researchgate.net/publication/327186182_Custodians_of_the_internet_Platforms_content_moderation_and_the_hidden_decisions_that_shape_social_media

Gill, P. (2007). A Multi-Dimensional Approach to Suicide Bombing. *International Journal of Conflict and Violence*, *1*(2), 142–159. DOI: 10.4119/ijcv-2750

Ginor, I., & Remez, G. (2017). *The Soviet-Israeli War, 1967-1973: The USSR's Military Intervention in the Egyptian-Israeli Conflict*. Oxford University Press.

Glen, C. M., & Gordon, C. (2014). *The changing face of African security in the twenty-first century*. Routledge. https://dokumen.pub/african-security-in-the-twenty-first-century-challenges-and-opportunities-9781526122742.html

Gokulakrishnan, S., Chakrabarti, P., Hung, B. T., & Shankar, S. S. (2023). An optimized facial recognition model for identifying criminal activities using deep learning strategy. *International Journal of Information Technology : an Official Journal of Bharati Vidyapeeth's Institute of Computer Applications and Management*, *15*(7), 3907–3921.

Gonzalez, R. J. (2020). The politics of artificial intelligence and indigenous communities. [PDF] [Politics and policy of Artificial Intelligence]. *The Journal of the Polynesian Society (N. Z.)*, *129*(3), 237–260.

Goodwin, M. (2013). The Roots of Extremism: The English Defence League and the Counter-Jihad Challenge. *Chatam House*, 16. https://www.chathamhouse.org/publications/papers/view/189767

Goodwin, M. (2011). *New British fascism: Rise of the British National Party*. Routledge.

Government, H. M. (2015). *Counter-Terrorism and Security Act 2015*. https://www.legislation.gov.uk/ukpga/2015/6/contents/enacted

Government, H. M. (2018). *CONTEST: The United Kingdom's Strategy for Countering Terrorism*. https://assets.publishing.service.gov.uk/media/5b23df8f40f0b634d557b020/140618_CCS207_CCS0218929798-1_CONTEST_3.0_WEB.pdf

Government, H. M. (2023). *Channel duty guidance: Protecting People Susceptible to Radicalisation*. https://assets.publishing.service.gov.uk/media/651e71d9e4e658001459d997/14.320_HO_Channel_Duty_Guidance_v3_Final_Web.pdf

Greenwald, G. (2014). *No place to hide: Edward Snowden, the NSA, and the U.S. surveillance state*. Metropolitan Books. https://digitalcommons.usf.edu/cgi/viewcontent.cgi?article=1552&&context=jss&&sei-redir=1&referer=https%253A%252F%252Fwww.google.com%252Furl%253Fq%253Dhttps%253A%252F%252Fdigitalcommons.usf.edu%252Fcgi%252Fviewcontent.cgi%25253Farticle%25253D1552%252526context%25253Djss%2526sa%253DU%2526sqi%253D2%2526ved%253D2ahUKEwjezse7t5KQAxWRUkEAHaiBAQgQFnoECB0QAQ%2526usg%253DAOvVaw2RLoG2leFGqwJp5uPqgRXd#search=%22https%3A%2F%2Fdigitalcommons.usf.edu%2Fcgi%2Fviewcontent.cgi%3Farticle%3D1552%26context%3Djss%22

Greenwald, G. (2014). *No place to hide: Edward Snowden, the NSA, and the U.S. surveillance state*. Metropolitan Books.

Grimm, P. W., Grossman, M. R., & Cormack, G. V. (2021). Artificial intelligence as evidence. *Nw. J. Tech. & Intell. Prop.*, *19*, 9.

Gross, J. A. (2023, October 11). Hamas filmed its massacres, and made sure the world would see them. The Times of Israel. https://www.timesofisrael.com/hamas-filmed-its-massacres-and-made-sure-the-world-would-see-them/

Gross, J. A. (2023, March 6). Reservists Expand Protest, Say They Won't Volunteer if Judicial Overhaul Passes. *Times of Israel.*

Gross, J. A. (2023, October 12). Amid intel failure, questions arise over efficacy of IDF's Gaza barrier. *Times of Israel.*

Gross, J. A. (2023, October 25). The Unheeded Warnings: Border Observers' Testimonies Reveal Missed Signals. *Times of Israel.*

Guice, J., & Duffy, R. (2000). *The future of the internet in science*. USRA Research Institute for Advanced Computer Science, NASA Ames Research Center.

Gul, I. (2024, October 12). Karachi attack: watershed in Sino-Pak relations? *The Express Tribune.* https://tribune.com.pk/story/2502214/karachi-attack-watershed-in-sino-pak-relations

Gupta, S. (2021). ETIM may shift to ISKP with Taliban-China alliance over Xinjiang. Hindustan Times. https://www.hindustantimes.com/world-news/etim-may-shift-to-iskp-with-taliban-china-alliance-over-xinjiang-101630304620049.html

Guszcza, J., Rahwan, I., Bible, W., Cebrian, M., & Katyal, V. (2018). Why we need to audit algorithms. *Harvard Business Review.* https://www1.qa.hbr.org/2018/11/why-we-need-to-audit-algorithms

Guzansky, Y., & Marshall, Z. A. (2020). The Abraham Accords: Immediate Significance and Long-Term Implications. *Israel Journal of Foreign Affairs*, *14*(3), 379–389.

Hagendorff, T. (2019). From privacy to anti-discrimination in times of machine learning. *Ethics and Information Technology*, *21*(4), 331–343.

Hagerty, A., & Rubinov, I. (2019). Global AI governance: A relational ethics approach. *AI & Society, 34*, 517-529. [1907.07892] Global AI Ethics: A Review of the Social Impacts and Ethical Implications of Artificial Intelligence

Haqqani, H. (2013). *Magnificent Delusions: Pakistan, The United States, and an Epic History of Misunderstanding*. Public Affairs.

Hardy, P. (1973). *The Muslims of British India*. Cambridge University Press.

Harel, A. (2023, February 15). "The Rise of Israel's Religious Right." *Haaretz.*

Harel, A. (2023, October 15). "The 30-Hour Battle for Kibbutz Be'eri." *Haaretz.*

Harel, A. (2023, October 20). “IDF's Top Brass: A Night of Fatal Misjudgments.” *Haaretz.*

Harel, A. (2023, October 8). “Netanyahu's Gaza Policy Collapses, Taking Israel's Sense of Security With It.” *Haaretz.*

Harel, A., & Issacharoff, A. (2008). *34 Days: Israel, Hezbollah, and the War in Lebanon*. Palgrave Macmillan.

Harrison, S. S. (2009). Global Terrorism: US Policy after 9/11 and Its Impact on the Domestic Politics and Foreign Relations of Pakistan. In Jetly, R. (Ed.), *Pakistan in Regional and Global Politics*. Routledge.

Harvey, D. (1989). *The Condition of Postmodernity*. Blackwell Publishers.

Hasnat, F. (2008). Afghanistan’s Unremitting Crises and Its Repercussions on Pakistan. In Hasnat, S. F., & Faruqui, A. (Eds.), *Pakistan: Unresolved Issues of State and Society*. Vanguard Books.

Heeks, R. (2018). *Information and Communication Technology for Development (ICT4D)*. Routledge. https://www.routledge.com/Information-and-Communication-Technology-for-Development-ICT4D/Heeks/p/book/9781138101814?srsltid=AfmBOorhbn394W23ceiV7oNFThrDK7isY2QoFpiK3oJ9XUwiMyo1X81I

Henke, N., & Jacques Bughin, L. (2023). The age of analytics: Competing in a data-driven world.

Herzog, C. (1975). *The War of Atonement: The Inside Story of the Yom Kippur War*. Weidenfeld & Nicolson.

Heuer, R. J., Jr. (1999). *Psychology of intelligence analysis*. Center for the Study of Intelligence. https://www.ialeia.org/docs/Psychology_of_Intelligence_Analysis.pdf

Heuer, R. J. (1999). *Psychology of Intelligence Analysis*. Center for the Study of Intelligence, Central Intelligence Agency.

Himaz, R. (2019). Challenges associated with the BRI: A review of recent economics literature. *Service Industries Journal*, *41*(7–8), 512–526. DOI: 10.1080/02642069.2019.1584193

Hinsley, F. H., & Simkins, C. A. G. (1990). *British intelligence in the Second World War: Volume 4, Security and Counter-Intelligence*. HMSO.

Hoffman, B. (2017). *Inside Terrorism* (3rd Editio). Columbia University Press.

Hoffman, B. (1997). The confluence of international and domestic trends in terrorism. *Terrorism and Political Violence*, *9*(2), 1–15. DOI: 10.1080/09546559708427399

Hoffman, B. (1999). *Inside Terrorism*. Columbia University Press.

Hoijtink, M., & Planqué-van Hardeveld, A. (2022). Machine learning and the platformization of the military: A study of google's machine learning platform TensorFlow. *International Political Sociology*, *16*(2), olab036.

Horgan, J. (2008). The psychology of terrorism. Routledge. The Psychology of Terrorism

Horne, A. (2006). *A savage war of peace: Algeria 1954–1962*. NYRB Classics.

Horrigan, B. J. (2004) "How Americans Get in Touch With Government", Pew Interne&American Life Project, www.pewinternet.org

Hu, P. (2023, June 26). What is the BRI? *The Belt and Road Portal*. https://eng.yidaiyilu.gov.cn/p/0N4P7CF0.html

Human Rights Watch. (2019). *China's algorithms of repression: Reverse engineering a Xinjiang police mass surveillance app*. Human Rights Watch. Retrieved from https://www.hrw.org/report/2019/05/01/chinas-algorithms-repression/reverse-engineering-xinjiang-police-mass

Human Rights Watch. (2021). *China's AI surveillance in Xinjiang*. Human Rights Watch. https://www.hrw.org/tag/mass-surveillance-china

Husain, J. (2012, October). The Scourge of Terrorism. *Nation (New York, N.Y.)*, *16*, •••. Retrieved January 29, 2024, from https://nation.com.pk/columns/16-Oct-2012/the-scourge-of-terrorism

Hussain, A. (2024). March of 'terror': Pakistan Grapples with deadly attacks on China interests. Al-Jazeera. https://www.aljazeera.com/news/2024/3/29/march-of-terror-pakistan-grapples-with-deadly-attacks-on-china-interests

Index on Censorship. (2019). *Government's online harms white paper risk damaging freedom of expression in the UK*. https://www.indexoncensorship.org/2019/07/governments-online-harms-white-paper-risk-damaging-freedom-of-expression-in-the-uk/?utm_source=chatgpt.com

Institute for Economics & Peace. (2022). *Global terrorism index 2022*. https://www.economicsandpeace.org/reports/

International Crisis Group. (2022). *Afghanistan's security challenges under the Taliban*. https://www.crisisgroup.org/asia/south-asia/afghanistan/afghanistans-security-challenges-under-taliban

Inuwa, M. M., & Das, R. (2024). A comparative analysis of various machine learning methods for anomaly detection in cyber-attacks on IoT networks. *Internet of Things : Engineering Cyber Physical Human Systems*, •••, 101162.

Iqbal, M. (2013). *The Reconstruction of Religious Thought in Islam (1930)*. Stanford University Press.

Irfan, M., Elmogy, M., & El-Sappagh, S. (Eds.). (2023). *The impact of AI innovation on financial sectors in the era of industry 5.0*. IGI Global.

Issacharoff, A. (2023, September 1). "How Israel's Enemies View the Judicial Reform Crisis." *The Jerusalem Post.*

Issacharoff, A. (2023, October 18). The Conception That Blinded Israel's Security Establishment. *Times of Israel.*

Issacharoff, A. (2023, October 9). Israel's Misdirected Focus: How Hezbollah Obsession Left Gaza Underestimated. *Times of Israel.*

Jagannath, A., Jagannath, J., & Kumar, P. S. P. V. (2022). A comprehensive survey on radio frequency (rf) fingerprinting: Traditional approaches, deep learning, and open challenges. *Computer Networks*, *219*, 109455.

Jahangir, A. (2013). "Militancy and Drones." *DAWN*. Retrieved from: https://www.dawn.com/news/1018571/militancy-and-drones [Last accessed: 29 January 2024].

Jasanoff, S. (Ed.). (2016). *Dreamscapes of Modernity: Sociotechnical Imaginaries and the Fabrication of Power*. University of Chicago Press., https://press.uchicago.edu/ucp/books/book/chicago/D/bo20836025.html

Javeed, D., Gao, T., Khan, M. T., & Shoukat, D. (2022). A hybrid intelligent framework to combat sophisticated threats in secure industries. *Sensors (Basel)*, *22*(4), 1582. PMID: 35214481

Jervis, R. (2006). Reports, Politics, and Intelligence Failures: The Case of Iraq. *The Journal of Strategic Studies*, *29*(1), 3–52.

Jobin, A., Ienca, M., & Vayena, E. (2019). The global landscape of AI ethics guidelines. [The global landscape of AI ethics guidelines | Nature Machine Intelligence]. *Nature Machine Intelligence*, *1*(9), 389–399.

Jones, O. B. (2002). *Pakistan: Eye of the Storm*. Vanguard Publisher.

Juergensmeyer, M. (2004). *Terror in the Mind of God: The Global Rise of Religious Violence*. University of California Press.

Kahana, E. (2002). Early Warning versus Concept: The Case of the Yom Kippur War 1973. *Intelligence and National Security*, *17*(2), 81–104.

Kaldor, M. (2012). *New and Old Wars: Organised Violence in a Global Era*. Polity Press.

Kam, E. (1988). *Surprise Attack: The Victim's Perspective*. Harvard University Press.

Kam, E. (2024). From Yom Kippur to October 7: Lessons in Intelligence Failures. *Strategic Assessment*, *27*(1), 41–54.

Kamen, H. (1999). *The Spanish Inquisition: A Historical Revision*. Yale University Press.

Kapur, A. (2002). The Aftermath of 11 September: Changing Geo-Political Equations and Indo-US Relations. In Kapur, A. (Ed.), *India and the United States in a Changing World*. Sage Publications.

Katyal, S. K. (2019). Private accountability in the age of artificial intelligence. *UCLA Law Review. University of California, Los Angeles. School of Law*, *66*, 54.

Katz, Y. (2010). *A Voice Called: Stories of Jewish Heroism*. Gefen Publishing House.

Kaur, J., & Bhambri, P. (2019). Design of Paddy Crop Prediction Technique based on K-Mean, Naïve Bayes, KNN and SVM Classifiers. I.K. Gujral Punjab Technical University, Jalandhar (M.Tech. thesis).

Kelemen, B. (2023). China's Clouded Future in Afghanistan. *The Diplomat*. https://thediplomat.com/2023/02/chinas-clouded-future-in-afghanistan/

Kennedy, H. (2023). *The Prophet and the Age of the Caliphates: The Islamic Near East from the Sixth to the Eleventh Century*. Routledge.

Kenyon, J., Binder, J., & Baker-Beall, C. (2024). Understanding the Role of the Internet in the Process of Radicalisation: An Analysis of Convicted Extremists in England and Wales. *Studies in Conflict and Terrorism*, *47*(12), 1747–1771. https://doi.org/https://doi.org/10.1080/1057610X.2022.2065902

Kershner, I. (2023, March 27). "Netanyahu Fires Defense Minister Who Opposed Judicial Overhaul." *New York Times.*

Kershner, I. (2023, October 10). "Israel's Vaunted Intelligence Service Faces a Reckoning." *New York Times.*

Kershner, I. (2023, October 12). "As Hamas Attacked, Israeli Soldiers Were Absent." *New York Times.*

Kershner, I. (2023, October 15). "Israel's Intelligence Chiefs Face Scrutiny Over October 7 Failures." *Haaretz.*

Khan, H. (2013). "Pakistan's Contribution to Global War on Terror after 9/11." *Current Affairs Digest*, 24-48. Retrieved from: https://www.ipripak.org/wp-content/uploads/2014/02/art3hidw13.pdf [Last accessed: 1 February 2024].

Khan, A. R., Kashif, M., Jhaveri, R. H., Raut, R., Saba, T., & Bahaj, S. A. (2022). Deep learning for intrusion detection and security of Internet of things (IoT): Current analysis, challenges, and possible solutions. *Security and Communication Networks*, •••, 2022.

Khansadurai, A. M., Veluchamy, A. D., Balasubramani, S., & Balasubramaniyan, K. (2024). Crime Rate Prediction using Cyber Security and Artificial Intelligent.

Khan, W. (2009). *The Prophet of Peace: Teachings of the Prophet Muhammad.* Penguin Press.

Khatab, S. (2006). *The Political Thought of Sayyid Qutb: The Theory of Jahiliyyah.* Routledge.

Khoury, J. (2023, October 14). "Israel's Strategic Blindness: Why Gaza Was Overlooked in Favor of West Bank Threats." *Haaretz.*

Kilcullen, D. (2009). *The Accidental Guerrilla.* Oxford University Press.

Kimbugwe, N., Pei, T., & Kyebambe, M. N. (2021). Application of deep learning for quality of service enhancement in internet of things: A review. *Energies, 14*(19), 6384.

Kingsley, P. (2023, July 24). "Israel's Judicial Overhaul Crisis: What to Know." *New York Times.*

Kissinger, H. (2003). *Crisis: The Anatomy of Two Major Foreign Policy Crises.* Simon & Schuster.

Koehler, D. (2015). De-radicalization and Disengagement Programs as Counter-Terrorism and Prevention Tools. Insights From Field Experiences Regarding German Right-Wing Extremism and Jihadism. *Countering Radicalisation and Violent Extremism among Youth to Prevent Terrorism, 118*, 120–150. https://doi.org/DOI: 10.3233/978-1-61499-470-1-120

Koomen, W., & Van Der Pligt, J. (2016). *The Psychology of Radicalization and Terrorism.* Routledge.

Kordzadeh, N., & Ghasemaghaei, M. (2022). Algorithmic bias: Review, synthesis, and future research directions. *European Journal of Information Systems, 31*(3), 388–409.

Krauthammer, C. (1990). The Unipolar Moment. *Foreign Affairs*, *70*(1), 23–33.

Kruglanski, A. W. (1990). Lay Epistemic Theory in Social-Cognitive Psychology. *Psychological Inquiry*, *1*(3), 181–197.

Kruglanski, A. W., & Webster, D. M. (1996). Motivated Closing of the Mind: "Seizing" and "Freezing". *Psychological Review*, *103*(2), 263–283. PMID: 8637961

Kubovich, Y. (2023, October 18). "Israeli Military's Overreliance on Technology Contributed to Intel Failure, Officials Say." *Haaretz.*

Kubovich, Y. (2023, October 28). "When the Watchers Were Ignored: The Role of Border Observers in the October 7 Debacle." *Haaretz.*

Kukutai, T., & Taylor, J. (Eds.). (2016). *Indigenous data sovereignty: Toward an agenda.* ANU Press. https://fnigc.ca/wp-content/uploads/2020/09/bbe195ddc231e3b1222d71ca4c09ae62_indigenous_data_sovereignty_toward_an_agenda_11_2016.pdf

Kuperman, R. D. (2012). The Yom Kippur War and Lessons for Military Intelligence. *Journal of Intelligence History*, *11*(2), 184–203.

Kuperwasser, Y. (2024). The October 7 Intelligence Failure: Preliminary Insights. *Israel Journal of Foreign Affairs*, *18*(1), 1–15.

Kuzhaloli, S., Devaneyan, P., Sitaraman, N., Periyathanbi, P., Gurusamy, M., & Bhambri, P. (2020). Invention titled "IoT based Smart Kitchen Application for Gas Leakage Monitoring" (Application No. 202041049866A). Published on 27th November 2020 (Issue No. 48/2020, Page No. 59674). Retrieved from http://ipindia.nic.in/writereaddata/Portal/IPOJournal/1_4929_1/Part-1.pdf

Landau, E. B., & Pfeffer, A. (2017). Israel's Intelligence Assessment before the Yom Kippur War: Digging Deeper. *The Journal of Intelligence History*, *16*(2), 112–128.

Lapidus, I. M. (2002). *A History of Islamic Societies*. Cambridge University Press.

Laski, J. H. (1919). *Authority in the Modern State*. Yale University Press.

Latonero, M. (2018). Governing artificial intelligence: Upholding human rights & dignity. *Data & Society Research Institute.* DataSociety_Governing_Artificial_Intelligence_Upholding_Human_Rights.pdf

Lauer, M. (2019). Ethics committees and advisory boards in the era of AI. [Ethics Committees: Structure, Roles, and Issues - PMC]. *AI & Society*, *34*, 585–589.

Lavrakas, P. J. (2008). *Encyclopedia of Survey Research Methods*. SAGE Publications.

Lee, I., & Shin, Y. J. (2023). Machine learning for enterprises: Applications, algorithm selection, and challenges. *Business Horizons*, *63*(2), 157–170.

Levy, Y. (2023, October 13). “From Hubris to Humiliation: How Israel's Military Superiority Crumbled.” *Haaretz*.

Lewis, J. E., Arista, N., Pechawis, A., & Kite, S. (2018). Making kin with the machines. *Journal of Design and Science*. https://www.researchgate.net/publication/326614247_Making_Kin_with_the_Machines

Lewis, B. (1993). *Islam and the West*. Oxford University Press.

Li, L., Zhao, T., Xie, Y., & Feng, Y. (2020). Interpretable machine learning based on integration of nlp and psychology in peer-to-peer lending risk evaluation. In *Natural Language Processing and Chinese*

Liberty Human Rights. (2021). *“Face Off: The Lawless Growth of Facial Recognition in UK Policing.”* https://www.libertyhumanrights.org.uk

Liberty. (2019). *Liberty: Appointment of ‘biased’ Prevent reviewer beggars belief.* https://www.libertyhumanrights.org.uk/issue/liberty-appointment-of-biased-prevent-reviewer-beggars-belief/

Lone, R. A. (2018). Jamaat-i-Islami: Ideology. *International Journal of Research in Social Sciences*, *8*(5), 792–798.

Lowenthal, M. M. (2016). *Intelligence: From secrets to policy* (7th ed.). CQ Press.

Lui, A., & Lamb, G. W. (2023). Artificial intelligence and augmented intelligence collaboration: Regaining trust and confidence in the financial sector. *Information & Communications Technology Law*, *27*(3), 267–283.

Lynskey, O. (2017). The foundations of EU data protection law. Oxford University Press. The Foundations of EU Data Protection Law - Orla Lynskey - Oxford University Press

Lyon, D. (2007). *Surveillance studies: An overview.* Polity. https://www.politybooks.com/bookdetail?book_slug=surveillance-studies-an-overview--9780745635910

Lyon, D. (2018). *The culture of surveillance: Watching as a way of life.* Polity. https://www.politybooks.com/bookdetail?book_slug=the-culture-of-surveillance-watching-as-a-way-of-life--9780745671727

Maghfiroh, M. (2023). Al Mawardi’s Social Contract Theory. *Journal of Islamic Studies and Humanities*, *8*(2), 142–157.

Mahajan, M. (2023). Islam and the Mughal Empire in South Asia: 1526-1857. *Education About Asia*, *28*(1), 37–46.

Makaya, P., & Moyo, G. (2019). AI and governance: Perspectives from Sub-Saharan Africa. *The Global Information Society Watch.* https://www.apc.org/sites/default/files/SneakPeek_GISW2019_web.pdf

Makinda, S. M. (2007). *Why human security matters: Rethinking the concept of human security.* Routledge. https://www.routledge.com/Why-Human-Security-Matters-Rethinking-Australian-foreign-policy/Altman-Camilleri-Eckersley-Hoffstaedter/p/book/9781743312025?srsltid=AfmBOookD-c-Y1oWHuzf3sB5hKv6jPzQCo3TE1vwqvBB0xo6j8GPKkbz

Maksimović, A., & Milosavljević, Z. (2018). Sovereignty in Islam: A reflection of tradition and contemporariness in modern political systems. *Vojno Delo*, *70*(8), 38–46.

Malabar Coast. (n.d.). Britannica. Retrieved June15, 2025, from https://www.britannica.com/place/Kerala/Resources-and-power

Malik, H. (2008). *US Relations with Afghanistan and Pakistan.* Oxford Press.

Malik, R., Singh, Y., Sheikh, Z. A., Anand, P., Singh, P. K., & Workneh, T. C. (2022). An improved deep belief network ids on iot-based network for traffic systems. *Journal of Advanced Transportation*, •••, 2022.

Mamdani, M. (2004). *Good Muslim, bad Muslim: America, the Cold War, and the roots of terror.* Pantheon. https://asiasociety.org/mahmood-mamdani-cold-war-political-islam-and-roots-terrorism

Mandel, G. N. (2009). Regulating emerging technologies. *Law, Innovation and Technology*, *1*(1), 75–92. DOI: 10.1080/17579960902887885

Marath, M. M. (2021). Abul A'la Maududi and Sayyed Qutb on Revolution: A Comparative Analysis. *Al-Az vā*, *32*(47), 43–50.

Mateen, M. R., & Tariq, A. (2019). Increasing Acceptability of Forensic DNA Analysis in Pakistan. *Egyptian Journal of Forensic Sciences*, *9.*

Mathur, P., Broekaert, C., & Clarke, C. P. (2024). "The Radicalization (and Counter-Radicalization) Potential of Artificial Intelligence." *ICCT Publications.* Retrieved from: https://www.icct.nl/publication/radicalization-and-counter-radicalization-potential-artificial-intelligence [Last accessed: 10 July 2024].

Mazower, M. (2009). *Hitler's Empire: How the Nazis Ruled Europe.* Penguin Publishing Group.

McKendrick, K. (2019). "Artificial Intelligence and Counterterrorism: Limitations, Opportunities, and Risks." *International Security Department*, Chatham House Institute. Retrieved from: https://imctc.org/en/eLibrary/INTReports/Documents/Report-Issu-09-EN.pdf [Last accessed: 29 January 2024].

McKendrick, K. (2019). Artificial intelligence prediction and counterterrorism. *London: The Royal Institute of International Affairs-Chatham House, 9.*

Mehrabi, N., Morstatter, F., Saxena, N., Lerman, K., & Galstyan, A. (2021). A survey on bias and fairness in machine learning. *ACM Computing Surveys*, *54*(6), 1–35.

Melman, Y. (2023, October 16). "The Hubris of Tech: How Israel's Intelligence Community Lost Touch with Reality." Haaretz.

Menache, S. (2010). Love of God or Hatred of Your Enemy? The Emotional Voices of the Crusades. *Mirabilia Journal, 10*(1), 1–20. https://www.revistamirabilia.com/sites/default/files/pdfs/2010_01_01.pdf

Metcalf, B. D. (1982). *Islamic Revival in British India: Deoband, 1860-1900.* Princeton University Press.

Metz, T. (2007). Ubuntu as a moral theory and human rights in South Africa. *African Human Rights Law Journal*, *7*(2), 532–559. scielo.org.za/pdf/ahrlj/v11n2/11.pdf

Mignolo, W. D., & Walsh, C. E. (2018). *On decoloniality: Concepts, analytics, praxis.* Duke University Press. https://www.dukeupress.edu/on-decoloniality

Ministry of Foreign Affairs. PRC (n.d.). China's Initiation of the Five Principles of Peaceful Co-Existence. *Ministry of Foreign Affairs, The People's Republic of China.* https://www.mfa.gov.cn/eng/zy/wjls/3604_665547/202405/t20240531_11367542.html

Mittelstadt, B. D., Allo, P., Taddeo, M., Wachter, S., & Floridi, L. (2016). *The ethics of algorithms: Mapping the debate. *Big Data & Society, 3*(2). The ethics of algorithms: Mapping the debate - Brent Daniel Mittelstadt, Patrick Allo, Mariarosaria Taddeo, Sandra Wachter, Luciano Floridi, 2016

Mittelstadt, B. D., Allo, P., Taddeo, M., Wachter, S., & Floridi, L. (2016). The ethics of algorithms: Mapping the debate. *Big Data & Society*, *3*(2). https://www.researchgate.net/publication/309322060_The_Ethics_of_Algorithms_Mapping_the_Debate

Moor, J. H. (2006). The nature, importance, and difficulty of machine ethics. [The Nature, Importance, and Difficulty of Machine Ethics | IEEE Journals & Magazine | IEEE Xplore]. *IEEE Intelligent Systems*, *21*(4), 18–21.

Morgan, M. (2009). Book Review: Riedel, B. (2008). The Search for al Qaeda: Its Leadership, Ideology, and Future. Washington, DC: Brookings Institution. *Armed Forces and Society*, *36*(2), 377–380. https://doi.org/https://doi.org/10.1177/0095327X09340755

Morley, J., Floridi, L., Kinsey, L., & Elhalal, A. (2020). From what to how: An initial review of publicly available AI ethics tools, methods, and research to translate principles into practices. [From What to How: An Initial Review of Publicly Available AI Ethics Tools, Methods and Research to Translate Principles into Practices - PubMed]. *Science and Engineering Ethics*, *26*, 2141–2168. PMID: 31828533

Morris, B. (2008). *1948: A History of the First Arab-Israeli War*. Yale University Press.

Mozur, P. (2019). One month, 500,000 face scans: How China is using AI to profile a minority. *The New York Times*. https://www.nytimes.com

Mozur, P. (2019, May 14). *Inside China's Dystopian Dreams: A.I., Shame, and Lots of Cameras. The New York Times.*

Mudde, C., & Kaltwasser, C. R. (2017). Populsim. A very short introduction. In *Populism: A Very Short Intoduction*. Oxford University Press.

Mühlhoff, R. (2021). Predictive privacy: Towards an applied ethics of data analytics. *Ethics and Information Technology*, *23*(4), 675–690.

Müller, V. C. (Ed.). (2016). *Risks of artificial intelligence*. Routledge., https://www.routledge.com/Risks-of-Artificial-Intelligence/Muller/p/book/9780367575182?srsltid=AfmBOorIBIp_KOZSU_mOao7sW-1dImWx3rJwZPoZwjsyQrweoUgRYrie

Muttaqin, M., Azra, A., Saepudin, D., Jabali, F., Lubis, A., & Fakih, Z. (2020).. . *The Rise and Fall of Ottoman Empire and How It Fits Ibnu Khaldun's Theory.*, *11*(2). Advance online publication. DOI: 10.4108/eai.20-10-2020.2305158

Nadeem, A. H. (2012). "Countering Terrorism with National Consensus." *The Express Tribune*. Retrieved from: https://tribune.com.pk/story/413410/countering-terrorism-with-national-consensus/ [Last accessed: 28 January 2024].

Naim, M. (2005). *Illicit: How smugglers, traffickers, and copycats are hijacking the global economy*. Anchor Books.

Nakata, M. (2007). *Disciplining the savages, savaging the disciplines*. Aboriginal Studies Press. https://aiatsis.gov.au/publication/35550

Nantulya, P. (2020, October 8). Chinese Security Contractors in Africa. *Carnegie Endowment for International Peace*. https://carnegieendowment.org/research/2020/10/chinese-security-contractors-in-africa?lang=en

Nasr, S. V. R. V. R. (1996). *The Vanguard of the Islamic Revolution: The Jama'at-i Islami of Pakistan*. University of California Press.

Nassar, A., & Kamal, M. (2021). Ethical Dilemmas in AI-Powered Decision-Making: A Deep Dive into Big Data-Driven Ethical Considerations. *International Journal of Responsible Artificial Intelligence*, *11*(8), 1–11.

Nedopil, C. (2023). "Countries of the Belt and Road Initiative"; *Shanghai, Green Finance & Development Center*, FISF Fudan University. www.greenfdc.org

Nelu, C. (2024). "Exploitation of Generative AI by Terrorist Groups." *ICCT Publications*. Retrieved from: https://www.icct.nl/publication/exploitation-generative-ai-terrorist-groups [Last accessed: 10 July 2024].

Neumann, P. R. (2013). *The new jihadism: A global snapshot*. The International Centre for the Study of Radicalisation and Political Violence. ICSR-REPORT-The-New-Jihadism-A-Global-Snapshot.pdf

News Desk. (2015). "ISI Sought Data Collection Tools, Claims Report." *DAWN*. Retrieved from: https://www.dawn.com/news/1196023 [Last accessed: 29 January 2024].

Nilsson, N. J. (2009). *The quest for artificial intelligence: A history of ideas and achievements*. Cambridge University Press.

NIST. (2019). *Face Recognition Vendor Test (FRVT) Part 3: Demographic Effects*. National Institute of Standards and Technology. Face Recognition Vendor Test Part 3: Demographic Effects | NIST

Noble, S. U. (2018). *Algorithms of oppression: How search engines reinforce racism*. NYU Press. Algorithms of Oppression: How Search Engines Reinforce Racism on JSTOR

Noor, S. (2013, August). From Radicalization to De-Radicalization: The Case of Pakistan. *Counter Terrorist Trends and Analyses*, *5*, 16–19.

Norov, V. (2024, January 25). Shanghai Cooperation Organization is playing an important role in ensuring regional security and stability. *Shanghai Cooperation Organization*. https://eng.sectsco.org/20240125/1244550.html#:~:text=Since%20its%20establishment%20in%20Tashkent%2C%20in%202004%2C,as%20combating%20drug%20trafficking%20in%20the%20region

Nossov, K. S. (2006). *Indian Castles 1206-1526: The Rise and Fall of the Delhi Sultanate*. Osprey Publishing.

NPR. (2023). *When It Comes to the Dangers of AI, Surveillance Poses More Risk Than Anything*. March 2, 2023. https://www.npr.org/2023/03/02/1160714485/when-it-comes-to-the-dangers-of-ai-surveillance-poses-more-risk-than-anything

O'Neil, C. (2016). *Weapons of math destruction: How big data increases inequality and threatens democracy*. Crown Publishing Group.

Odinet, C. K. (2024). Consumer bitcredit and fintech lending. *Alabama Law Review, 69*, 781.

Oladipo, I. D., AbdulRaheem, M., Awotunde, J. B., Bhoi, A. K., Adeniyi, E. A., & Abiodun, M. K. (2021). Machine learning and deep learning algorithms for smart cities: a start-of-the-art review. *IoT and IoE driven smart cities*, 143-162.

Omand, D., Bartlett, J., & Miller, C. (2012). Introducing social media intelligence (SOCMINT). *Intelligence and National Security, 27*(6), 801–823. https://www.tandfonline.com/doi/abs/10.1080/02684527.2012.716965

O'Neil, C. (2016). *Weapons of math destruction: How big data increases inequality and threatens democracy*. Crown Publishing Group. Weapons of Math Destruction: How Big Data Increases Inequality and Threatens Democracy | Guide books | ACM Digital Library

Open Society Justice Initiative. (2016). *Eroding Trust: The UK's Prevent Counter-Extremism Strategy in Health and Education*. https://www.justiceinitiative.org/uploads/1237d213-a66e-496a-af41-08e11d38e2c4/eroding-trust-execiutive-summary-20161017.pdf

Oren, M. B. (2002). *Six Days of War: June 1967 and the Making of the Modern Middle East*. Oxford University Press.

Ottis, R., & Lorents, P. (2010) "Cyberspace: Definition and Implications", In *Proceedings of the 5th International Conference on Information Warfare and Security*, Dayton, OH, US, 8-9 April.

Palmer, A., & Holtz, M. (2023). "The Islamic State Threat in Pakistan: Trends and Scenarios." *Center for Strategic and International Studies*. Retrieved from: https://www.csis.org/analysis/islamic-state-threat-pakistan-trends-and-scenarios [Last accessed: 12 July 2024].

Pape, R. A., & Feldman, J. K. (2010). *Cutting the Fuse: The Explosion of Global Suicide Terrorism and How to Stop It*. University of Chicago.

Parliament, U. K. (2017). *Prevent Strategy Volume 620: Debated on Wednesday 1 February 2017*. Hansard. https://hansard.parliament.uk/commons/2017-02-01/debates/B8BE87F9-7E2E-46C5-9E11-DDAD5897E949/PreventStrategy?utm_source=chatgpt.com

Pasquale, F. (2015). *The black box society: The secret algorithms that control money and information*. Harvard University Press. https://raley.english.ucsb.edu/wp-content/Engl800/Pasquale-blackbox.pdf

Pasquale, F. (2015). *The black box society: The secret algorithms that control money and information*. Harvard University Press. The Black Box Society: The Secret Algorithms That Control Money and Information on JSTOR

Pasquale, F. (2015). *The black box society: The secret algorithms that control money and information*. Harvard University Press.

Passas, N. (2023). Cross-border crime and the interface between legal and illegal actors. *Security Journal*, *16*, 19–37.

Pearlman, W. (2011). *Violence, Nonviolence, and the Palestinian National Movement*. Cambridge University Press.

Petrović R. S., (2001) "Neki aspekti nacionalne bezbednosti u informacionom dobu, Nauka, Tehnika, Bezbednost (NTB)", Rad po pozivu, UDC: 681.324; 65.012.8, Godina XI, Broj 1, str. 7-27.

Petrović, R. S. (1999). *"Globalno informaciono ratovanje", Zbornik radova (CD-ROM), YU INFO 99*. Kopaonik.

Pfeffer, A. (2021). *Bibi: The Turbulent Life and Times of Benjamin Netanyahu*. Basic Books.

Pollack, K. M. (2002). *Arabs at War: Military Effectiveness, 1948-1991*. University of Nebraska Press.

Polonski, V. (2018). How artificial intelligence is transforming the fight against terrorism. *World Economic Forum*. https://www.weforum.org/stories/2019/01/how-ai-can-knock-the-starch-out-of-money-laundering/

Polyakova, A., & Boyer, S. (2018). The future of political warfare: Russia, the West, and the coming age of global digital competition. *Brookings Institution*. https://www.brookings.edu

Pomerleau, M. (2020). *"NATO Looks to AI for Decision Support and Threat Detection." Defense News*. https://www.defensenews.com

Prados, J. (1996). *Presidents' secret wars: CIA and Pentagon covert operations since World War II*. Ivan R. Dee.

Pugh, M. (2006). *Hurrah for the blackshirts!': fascists and fascism in Britain between the wars*. Pimlico.

Pujol, J., & Teichmann, H. (2020). The role of AI in the fight against terrorism and organized crime in Africa. *Africa Journal of Criminology and Justice Studies, 13*(1). https://digitalscholarship.tsu.edu/ajcjs/vol13/iss1/

Pulzer, P. (1964). *The Rise of Political Anti-Semitism in Germany and Austria*. John Wiley & Sons.

Punjab Safe Cities Authority. Head Office in Lahore. Retrieved from: https://psca.gop.pk/about-us/ [Last accessed: 12 July 2024].

Qiang, X. (2019). The road to digital unfreedom: President Xi's surveillance state. *Journal of Democracy, 30*(1), 53–67. DOI: 10.1353/jod.2019.0004

Qutb, S. (2006). *Milestones*. Maktabah Publications.

Rabinovich, A. (2004). *The Yom Kippur War: The Epic Encounter That Transformed the Middle East*. Schocken Books.

Rafique, N., & Manan, A. "Countering Measures of Terrorism in Pakistan." *Pakistan Journal of Humanities and Social Sciences Research*, Vol. 2 (December 2019). Retrieved from: https://journals.wumardan.edu.pk/papers/06%20Naila.pdf [Last accessed: 29 January 2024].

Rahwan, I., & Tenenbaum, J. B. (2019). The society-in-the-loop approach to AI governance. *Nature Machine Intelligence, 1*(1), 1–2. https://arxiv.org/abs/1707.07232

Raj, R. (Ed.). (2019). *Global South and the New International Economic Order*. Palgrave Macmillan.

RAMOS HENDEZ. I. A. (2021). *Assessing the incorporation of knowledge-sharing in the management of south-south cooperation projects* (Doctoral dissertation, KDI School). https://archives.kdischool.ac.kr/bitstream/11125/42941/1/Assessing%20the%20incorporation%20of%20knowledge-sharing%20in%20the%20management%20of%20south-south%20cooperation%20projects.pdf

Rana, R., & Bhambri, P. (2024). Healthcare Computational Intelligence and Blockchain: Real-Life Applications. In P. Bhambri, S. Rani, & M. Fahim (Eds.), Computational Intelligence and Blockchain in Biomedical and Health Informatics (pp. 155-168). CRC Press, Taylor & Francis Group, USA. DOI: DOI: 10.1201/9781003459347

Rana, S. (2024, October 30). Chinese envoy miffed at CPEC security lapses. *The Express Tribune.* https://tribune.com.pk/story/2506203/chinese-envoy-miffed-at-cpec-security-lapses

Rana, M. A. (2008). *Jihadi Print Media in Pakistan : An Overview Jihadi Print Media in Pakistan : An Overview*. Pak Institute for Peace Studies.

Rana, M. A., & Gunaratna, R. (2007). *Al-Qaeda Fights Back Inside Pakistani Tribal Areas*. Pakistan Institute for Peace Studies.

Ranstorp, M. (Ed.). (2016). *Understanding violent radicalisation: Terrorist and jihadist movements in* Europe. Routledge. Understanding Violent Radicalisation | Terrorist and Jihadist Movement

Rashid, Q. (2013). "Ethno-Sectarian Conflict in Pakistan." *The Daily Times*. Retrieved from: https://dailytimes.com.pk/87315/ethno-sectarian-conflict-in-pakistan/ [Last accessed: 27 January 2024].

Rashid, W. (2023). Using Artificial Intelligence to Combat Extremism. *Pakistan Journal of Terrorism Research*, *5*, 2.

Ravndal, J. A. (2018). Explaining right-wing terrorism and violence in Western Europe: Grievances, opportunities and polarisation. *European Journal of Political Research*, *57*(4), 845–866. https://doi.org/https://doi.org/10.1111/1475-6765.12254

Reddy, Y. H., Ali, A., Kumar, P. V., Srinivas, M. H., Netra, K., Achari, V. J., & Varaprasad, R. (2022). A Comprehensive Survey of Internet of Things Applications, Threats, and Security Issues. *South Asian Res J Eng Tech*, *4*(4), 63–77.

Reed, C., & Ng, I. Y. H. (2019). AI in governance: Some ethical and legal issues. In *Ethical and Legal Perspectives on AI*. Routledge.

Reuters. (2024, November 13). China pushing to deploy its own security staff to protect its own citizens in Pakistan: Report. *Times of India.* https://timesofindia.indiatimes.com/world/china/china-pushing-to-deploy-its-own-security-staff-to-protect-citizens-in-pak-report/articleshow/115235966.cms

Riaz, A. (2004). *God Willing: The Politics of Islamism in Bangladesh*. Rowman & Littlefield Publishers.

Richards, J. F. (1993). *The New Cambridge History of India, Volume 1, Part 5: The Mughal Empire*. Cambridge University Press.

Richards, N. M., & Hartzog, W. (2015). Taking trust seriously in privacy law. *Stanford Technology Law Review : STLR : An Online High-Technology Law Journal from Stanford Law School, 19*, 431–472. https://law.stanford.edu/wp-content/uploads/2017/11/Taking-Trust-Seriously-in-Privacy-Law.pdf

Ricks, T. E. (2006). *Fiasco: The American Military Adventure in Iraq*. Penguin Press.

Roff, H. M. (2019). Artificial intelligence: Power to the people. *Ethics & International Affairs, 33*(2), 127–140.

Rogers, M. B. et al., (2007, June). *The Role of Religious Fundamentalism in Terrorist Violence: A Social Psychological Analysis*. DOI: 10.1080/09540260701349399

Rogers, P. (2016). *Irregular War: ISIS and the New Threat from the Margins*. I. B. Tauris.

Roy, O. (1996). *The Failure of Political Islam*. Harvard University Press.

Roy, O. (2017). *Jihad and Death: The Global Appeal of Islamic State*. C Hurst & Co Publishers Ltd.

Rudenko, R., Pires, I. M., Oliveira, P., Barroso, J., & Reis, A. (2022). A Brief Review on Internet of Things, Industry 4.0 and Cybersecurity. *Electronics (Basel), 11*(11), 1742.

Russel, D. R., & Berger, B. H. (2020). *Weaponizing the Belt and Road Initiative* (Report). Washington D.C.: The Asia Society Policy Institute. https://asiasociety.org/sites/default/files/2020-09/Weaponizing%20the%20Belt%20and%20Road%20Initiative_0.pdf

Russell, S. J., & Norvig, P. (2010). *Artificial Intelligence: A Modern Approach* (3rd ed.). Pearson Education.

Russell, S., & Norvig, P. (2016). *Artificial intelligence: A modern approach* (3rd ed.). Pearson.

Rusydi, I., & Saepudin, D., &Murodi. (2023). The Golden Age of Islamic Intellectuals and The Development of Science During the Abbasid Dynasty. *Tafkir: Interdisciplinary Journal of Islamic Education, 4*(4), 599–609.

Ryan, M. (2020). In AI we trust: Ethics, artificial intelligence, and reliability. [In AI We Trust: Ethics, Artificial Intelligence, and Reliability | Science and Engineering Ethics]. *Science and Engineering Ethics, 26*, 2749–2767. PMID: 32524425

Saaty, T. L. (1980). *The Analytic Hierarchy Process: Planning, Priority Setting, Resource Allocation*. McGraw-Hill International Book Company.

Saheed, Y. K., & Arowolo, M. O. (2021). Efficient cyber attack detection on the internet of medical things-smart environment based on deep recurrent neural network and machine learning algorithms. *IEEE Access : Practical Innovations, Open Solutions*, *9*, 161546–161554.

Saleem, S. (2010). *Islam : A Comprehensive Introduction*. Al Mawrid.

Saltz, J., Skirpan, M., Fiesler, C., Gorelick, M., Yeh, T., Heckman, R., & Beard, N. (2019). Integrating ethics within machine learning courses. [TOCE]. *ACM Transactions on Computing Education*, *19*(4), 1–26.

Sambasivan, N., Arnesen, E., Hutchinson, B., Doshi, T., & Prabhakaran, V. (2021, March). Re-imagining algorithmic fairness in india and beyond. In *Proceedings of the 2021 ACM conference on fairness, accountability, and transparency* (pp. 315-328).

Sarker, I. H. (2021). Machine learning: Algorithms, real-world applications and research directions. *SN Computer Science*, *2*(3), 160. PMID: 33778771

Sassen, S. (1996). *Losing Control? Sovereignty in an Age of Globalization*. Columbia University Press.

Scharre, P. (2018). *Army of none: Autonomous weapons and the future of war*. W. W. Norton & Company. Army of none: autonomous weapons and the future of war | International Affairs | Oxford Academic

Schimd, A. P. (2014). *Violent and Non-Violent Extremism: Two Sides of the Same Coin?* The International Centre for Counter-Terrorism (ICCT). https://icct.nl/sites/default/files/2023-01/ICCT-Schmid-Violent-Non-Violent-Extremism-May-2014.pdf

Schmid, A. P. (Ed.). (2011). The Routledge handbook of terrorism research. Routledge. The Routledge Handbook of Terrorism Research - 1st Edition - Alex Schm

Schmitt, M. (2020). Artificial intelligence in business analytics, capturing value with machine learning applications in financial services.

Schroeter, M. (2020). "Artificial Intelligence and Countering Violent Extremism: A Primer." *The Global Network on Extremism and Technology* (GNET), *International Center for the Study of Radicalisation* (ICSR), King's College London. Retrieved from: https://gnet-reports.s3.eu-west-2.amazonaws.com/GNET-Report-Artificial-Intelligence-and-Countering-Violent-Extremism-A-Primer_V2.pdf [Last accessed: 29 January 2024].

Schudel, G., & Wood, B. (2000), "MODELING BEHAVIOR OF THE CYBER-TERRORIST", In Proceedings of a Workshop "Research on Mitigating the Insider Threat to Information Systems - #2", RAND Corporation.

Schuurman, B. W., & Eijkman, Q. A. (2015). Indicators of Terrorist Intent and Capability: Tools for Threat Assessment. *Dynamics of Asymmetric Conflict.*

Schuurman, B., Bakker, E., Gill, P., & Bouhana, P. (2018). Lone Actor Terrorist Attack Planning and Preparation: A Data-Driven Analysis. *Journal of Forensic Sciences.* PMID: 29059713

Selbst, A. D., & Barocas, S. (2024). The intuitive appeal of explainable machines. *Fordham Law Review*, *87*, 1085.

Senaratne, B. (2018). *Diplomats' Role in Strengthening China's Overseas Image: A Case Study of Sri Lanka. China International Studies 71.* China Institute of International Studies.

Senaratne, B. (2019). *China's Future Relations in the South Asian Region: A Study from a Neoclassical Realist Approach. Defence & Security Journal, 4. Sapugaskanda.* Defence Services Command & Staff College.

Senaratne, B. (2021). 21st Century Maritime Silk Route: Preventive Diplomacy as a Mechanism to Mitigate Future Security Implications. In Ni, H., Abeyratne, S., Siriwardena, L., & Zhou, G. (Eds.), *Lion Dragon Dance: Practice and Reflection on the People-to-People Dialogues in China and Sri Lanka* (pp. 112–128). Zhejiang University Press.

Senor, D., & Singer, S. (2011). *Start-up Nation: The Story of Israel's Economic Miracle.* Grand Central Publishing.

Shackelford, S. J. (2016). Cybersecurity in the Global South: Protecting the digital economy in developing countries. *American Business Law Journal*, *53*(3), 525–589.

Shanghai Cooperation Organization. (2017, January 17). General information. *Shanghai Cooperation Organization.* https://eng.sectsco.org/20170109/192193.html

Shang, Y. (2024). Detection and Prevention of Cyber Defense Attacks using Machine Learning Algorithms. *Scalable Computing: Practice and Experience*, *25*(2), 760–769.

Shapiro, J. N., & Fair, C. C. (2010, Winter). Understanding Support for Islamist Militancy in Pakistan. *International Security*, *34*, 79–118.

Shavit, A. (2013). *My Promised Land: The Triumph and Tragedy of Israel.* Spiegel & Grau.

Shawcross, W. (2023). *Independent Review of Prevent* (Issue February). https://assets.publishing.service.gov.uk/media/63e26968d3bf7f17385a3421/Independent_Review_of_Prevent.pdf

Shlaim, A. (2000). *The Iron Wall: Israel and the Arab World.* W. W. Norton & Company.

Siddiqui, T. (2023). "The Rise of Pakistan's Drones: How They Are Changing the Game in Kashmir, India and the South Asian Region." *South Asia Press.* Retrieved from: https://southasiapress.org/2023/09/21/the-rise-of-pakistans-drones-how-they-are-changing-the-game-in-kashmir-india-and-the-south-asian-region/ [Last accessed: 29 January 2024].

Silverstein, P. A. (2004). *Algeria in France: Transpolitics, Race, and Nation.* Indiana University Press.

Simpson, L. B. (2017). *As we have always done: Indigenous freedom through radical resistance.* University of Minnesota Press. https://www.jstor.org/stable/10.5749/j.ctt1pwt77c

Singer, P. W., & Friedman, A. (2014). *Cybersecurity and cyberwar: What everyone needs to know.* Oxford University Press.

Singh, P., Singh, M., & Bhambri, P. (2004). Interoperability: A problem of component reusability. In International Conference (Abstract Book) (p. 60). Presented at the "Emerging Technologies in IT Industry" at PCTE, Ludhiana on November 27, 2004.

Singh, P., Singh, M., & Bhambri, P. (2005). Embedded systems. In U.G.C. Sponsored National Seminar (pp. 10-15). Presented at the "Embedded Systems" seminar at KMV, Jalandhar held during January 24-25, 2005.

Singh, S., Lal, Y., Bhambri, P., Kumar, A., & Dhanoa, I. S. (2021). Advancements in social data security and encryption: A review. *Natural Volatiles and Essential Oils, 8*(4), 15353–15362.

Sloan, R. H., & Warner, R. (2020). *Unauthorized Access: The Crisis in Online Privacy and Security.* MIT Press. https://library.oapen.org/bitstream/handle/20.500.12657/40085/1/9781138436923.pdf

Sloan, R. H., & Warner, R. (2020). *Unauthorized access: The crisis in online privacy and security.* MIT Press. Unauthorized Access | The Crisis in Online Privacy and Security | Robe

Smith, L. T. (2012). *Decolonizing methodologies: Research and indigenous peoples.* Zed Books. https://nycstandswithstandingrock.files.wordpress.com/2016/10/linda-tuhiwai-smith-decolonizing-methodologies-research-and-indigenous-peoples.pdf

Soliev, N. (2021, October 30). Why Is the Islamic State in Afghanistan's Propaganda Targeting China? *The Diplomat*. https://thediplomat.com/2021/10/is-the-islamic-state-in-afghanistan-targeting-china/

Spaulding, J., & Mohaisen, A. (2018, October). Defending internet of things against malicious domain names using D-FENS. In *2018 IEEE/ACM Symposium on Edge Computing (SEC)* (pp. 387-392). IEEE.

Sudarmanto, E., & Aulia, T. Z. (2022). Principles of Good Governance in Quranic's Perspective. *International Journal of Islamic Thought and Humanities*, *1*(2), 79–90.

Suresh, H., & Guttag, J. V. (2019). A framework for understanding unintended consequences of machine learning. *Communications of the ACM, 64*(3), 62-71. [1901.10002] A Framework for Understanding Sources of Harm throughout the Machine Learning Life Cycle

Suresh, H., & Guttag, J. V. (2019). A framework for understanding unintended consequences of machine learning. *Communications of the ACM*, *64*(3), 62–71. https://www.researchgate.net/publication/330726492_A_Framework_for_Understanding_Unintended_Consequences_of_Machine_Learning

Synnott, H. (2009). *Transforming Pakistan: Ways Out of Instability*. Routledge Publications.

Taddeo, M., & Floridi, L. (2018). How AI can be a force for good. [PDF] [How AI can be a force for good]. *Science*, *361*(6404), 751–752. PMID: 30139858

Taddeo, M., & Floridi, L. (2018). Regulate artificial intelligence to avert cyber arms race. *Nature*, *556*(7701), 296–298. https://www.nature.com/articles/d41586-018-04602-6 PMID: 29662138

Taji-Farouki, T., & Nafi, B. M. (2004). (Eds.). *Islamic Thought in the Twentieth Century*. New York: I.B.Tauris.

Tayfour, O. E., Mubarakali, A., Tayfour, A. E., Marsono, M. N., Hassan, E., & Abdelrahman, A. M. (2023). Adapting deep learning-LSTM method using optimized dataset in SDN controller for secure IoT. *Soft Computing*, •••, 1–9.

Tene, O., & Polonetsky, J. (2022). Big data for all: Privacy and user control in the age of analytics. *Nw. J. Tech. & Intell. Prop.*, *11*, 239.

The Economist (2025). Militant Uyghurs in Syria threaten the Chinese government. https://www.economist.com/china/2025/01/09/militant-uyghurs-in-syria-threaten-the-chinese-government

The Express Tribune. (2021). *At least 55 killed in Afghanistan mosque attack.* https://tribune.com.pk/story/2323867/at-least-55-killed-in-afghanistan-mosque-attack

The Guardian. (2021). *Protest in Pakistan erupts against China's belt and road plan.* https://www.theguardian.com/environment/2021/aug/20/water-protests-in-pakistan-eruptagainst-chinas-belt-and-road-plan

The Times of India. (2021). *Attack by Uyghur suicide bomber affects China's investment.* https://timesofindia.indiatimes.com/world/south-asia/attack-by-uyghur-suicide-bomber-affectschinas-investment-plans-in-afghanistan/articleshow/87036074.cms

Thrall, N. (2017). The Only Language They Understand: Forcing Compromise in Israel and Palestine. Metropolitan Books. Israel Ministry of Foreign Affairs. (2023, November 1). *"October 7, 2023 Hamas Terror Attack: The Toll."* National Commission on Terrorist Attacks upon the United States. (2004). *The 9/11 Commission Report.*

Thurlow, R. (1998). *FASCISM IN BRITAIN A History 1918–1998* (Revised Ed). I.B.Tauris Publishers.

Tippins, N. T., Oswald, F. L., & McPhail, S. M. (2021). Scientific, legal, and ethical concerns about AI-based personnel selection tools: A call to action. *Personnel Assessment and Decisions*, *7*(2), 1.

Tsuji, C. (2025, February 6). Belt and Road Initiative. *Britannica.* https://www.britannica.com/topic/Belt-and-Road-Initiative

Tyagi, A. K., Aswathy, S. U., & Abraham, A. (2020). Integrating blockchain technology and artificial intelligence: Synergies perspectives challenges and research directions. *Journal of Information Assurance and Security*, *15*(5), 1554.

Tzu, S. (1910). The art of war (L. Giles, Trans.). *London, United Kingdom: Luzac & Co.(Original work published nd).*

UK Home Office. (2020). Preventing terrorism and tackling extremism. https://www.gov.uk/government/organisations/home-office Tackling extremism in the UK: report by the Extremism Taskforce - GOV.UK

UN Human Rights Office. (2023, November 30). *UN experts condemn atrocities by Hamas, call for immediate release of all hostages.* https://www.ohchr.org/en/press-releases/2023/11/un-experts-condemn-atrocities-hamas-call-immediate-release-all-hostages

UN Office of the High Commissioner for Human Rights. (2022). *OHCHR Assessment of human rights concerns in the Xinjiang Uyghur Autonomous Region, People's Republic of China.* https://digitallibrary.un.org/record/3985699?v=pdf

UN Security Council. (2024). *S/2024/556*. https://documents.un.org/doc/undoc/gen/n24/191/91/pdf/n2419191.pdf

UNESCO. (2021). *Recommendation on the ethics of artificial intelligence*. UNESCO Publishing. https://unesdoc.unesco.org/ark:/48223/pf0000377897

UNESCO. (2023). Ethical Impact Assessment: A tool for the Recommendation on the Ethics of Artificial Intelligence. https://www.unesco.org/en/articles/ethical-impact-assessment-tool-recommendation-ethics-artificial-intelligence

UNESCO. (2024). *Recommendation on the ethics of artificial intelligence*. https://www.unesco.org/en/articles/recommendation-ethics-artificial-intelligence?hub=776

United Nations. (2019). "New Technologies, Artificial Intelligence Aid Fight against Global Terrorism." *Department of Operational Support*. Retrieved from: https://news.un.org/en/story/2019/09/1045562 [Last accessed: 10 July 2024].

United Nations. (2021). *Countering Terrorism Online with Artificial Intelligence: An Overview for Law Enforcement and Counter-Terrorism Agencies in South Asia and South-East Asia*. A Joint Report by UNICRI and UNCCT. United Nations Office of Counter-Terrorism (UNOCT). Retrieved from: https://www.un.org/counterterrorism/sites/www.un.org.counterterrorism/files/countering-terrorism-online-with-ai-uncct-unicri-report-web.pdf [Last accessed: 29 January 2024].

Utami, S. H., Purnama, A. A., Hidayanto, A. N., Utami, S. H., Purnama, A. A., & Hidayanto, A. N. (2022). Fintech Lending in Indonesia: A Sentiment Analysis, Topic Modelling, and Social Network Analysis using Twitter Data. *International Journal of Applied Engineering & Technology*, *4*(1), 50–56.

Varma, P., Nijjer, S., Sood, K., Grima, S., & Rupeika-Apoga, R. (2022). Thematic Analysis of Financial Technology (Fintech) Influence on the Banking Industry. *Risks*, *10*(10), 186.

Vinayakumar, R., Alazab, M., Srinivasan, S., Pham, Q. V., Padannayil, S. K., & Simran, K. (2024). A visualized botnet detection system based deep learning for the internet of things networks of smart cities. *IEEE Transactions on Industry Applications*, *56*(4), 4436–4456.

Vincent, J. (2018). How the EU's new AI rules could affect the fight against online hate speech. *The Verge*. EU AI Act: first regulation on artificial intelligence | Topics | European Parliament

Vincent, J. (2018). How the EU's new AI rules could affect the fight against online hate speech. *The Verge*. https://www.theverge.com/2018/4/25/17277254/eu-ai-rules-online-hate-speech

Wagner, B. (2018). Ethics as an escape from regulation: From "ethics-washing" to ethics-shopping? In *Being profiled: Cogitas ergo sum.* Amsterdam University Press. ETHICS AS AN ESCAPE FROM REGULATION.: FROM "ETHICS-WASHING" TO ETHICS-SHOPPING? FROM "ETHICS-WASHING" TO ETHICS-SHOPPING? from BEING PROFILED: COGITAS ERGO SUM: 10 Years of Profiling the European Citizen on JSTOR

Waheed, N., He, X., Ikram, M., Usman, M., Hashmi, S. S., & Usman, M. (2020). Security and privacy in IoT using machine learning and blockchain: Threats and countermeasures. *ACM Computing Surveys*, *53*(6), 1–37.

Walker, C. (2016). Counter-Terrorism and Human Rights in the UK. In Breen-Smyth, M. (Ed.), *The Ashgate Research Companion to Political Violence*. Routledge.

Wallach, W., & Allen, C. (2008). *Moral machines: Teaching robots right from wrong*. Oxford University Press. Moral Machines: Teaching Robots Right from Wrong | Oxford Academic

Walliman, N. (2011). *Research Methods: The Basics*. Routledge.

Weinbaum, M. G. (1991). Pakistan and Afghanistan: The Strategic Relationship. *Asian Survey*, *31*(6), 496–511.

Weiss, R. S. (1995). *Learning from Strangers: The Art and Method of Qualitative Interview Studies*. The Free Press.

Whittaker, M., et al. (2018). *AI Now 2018 Report.* AI Now Institute. AI Now Report 2018 - Published Version - Locked - Google Docs

Whittlestone, J., Nyrup, R., Alexandrova, A., & Dihal, K. (2019). Ethical and societal implications of algorithms, data, and artificial intelligence: A roadmap for research. *The Nuffield Foundation.* Ethical-and-Societal-Implications-of-Data-and-AI-report-Nuffield-Foundat.pdf

Williams, M. L., & Burnap, P. (2023). Cyberhate on social media in the aftermath of Woolwich: A case study in computational criminology and big data. *British Journal of Criminology*, *56*(2), 211–238.

Wilson, L. (2015). What I Discovered From Interviewing Imprisoned ISIS Fighters. *The Nation.* https://www.thenation.com/article/archive/wh at-i-discovered-from-interviewing-isisprisoners/

Wong, P. H. (2020). *Asian perspectives on engineering ethics.* Springer. Pak-Hang Wong, Global Engineering Ethics - PhilPapers

Woodward, B. (2010). *Obama's Wars: The Inside Story*. Simon and Schuster.

Wu, Y. (2024). Facial recognition technology: College students' perspectives in China. *Journal of Research in Social Science and Humanities*, *3*(1), 53–79. https://www.researchgate.net/publication/377741063_Facial_Recognition_Technology_College_Students'_Perspectives_in_China

Xiao, P. (2024). Malware Cyber Threat Intelligence System for Internet of Things (IoT) Using Machine Learning. *Journal of Cyber Security and Mobility*, 53-90.

Yarkoni, T., & Westfall, J. (2024). Choosing prediction over explanation in psychology: Lessons from machine learning. *Perspectives on Psychological Science*, *12*(6), 1100–1122. PMID: 28841086

Yeung, K., & Lodge, M. (Eds.). (2019). *Algorithmic regulation*. Oxford University Press., https://papers.ssrn.com/sol3/papers.cfm?abstract_id=3483693

Yun, S. (2019). Comparative ethics of AI: Insights from Confucianism and Ubuntu. *Journal of Information, Communication and Ethics in Society, 17(*3), 357-369. (PDF) Artificial Intelligence and Ethics

Zaidi, M. (2009). A Taxonomy of Jihad. *Arab Studies Quarterly*, *31*(3), 21–34.

Zaman, S. (2025), Islamabad, Beijing pledge counterterrorism cooperation for security of Chinese workers in Pakistan. *Voice of America*. https://www.voanews.com/a/islamabad-beijing-pledge-counterterrorism-cooperation-for-security-of-chinese-workers-in-pakistan/7965181.html

Zarsky, T. Z. (2016). The trouble with algorithmic decisions: An analytic road map to examine efficiency and fairness in automated and opaque decision making. *Science, Technology & Human Values*, *41*(1), 118–132. https://www.researchgate.net/publication/283246504_The_Trouble_with_Algorithmic_Decisions_An_Analytic_Road_Map_to_Examine_Efficiency_and_Fairness_in_Automated_and_Opaque_Decision_Making

Zegart, A. B. (2021). *Spies, lies, and algorithms: The history and future of American intelligence*. Princeton University Press.

Zenz, A. (2020). China's Own Documents Show Potentially Genocidal Sterilization Plans in Xinjiang. *Foreign Policy*. https://foreignpolicy.com/2020/07/01/china-documents-uighur-genocidal-sterilization-xinjiang/

Zhang, J., Pan, L., Han, Q. L., Chen, C., Wen, S., & Xiang, Y. (2021). Deep learning based attack detection for cyber-physical system cybersecurity: A survey. *IEEE/CAA Journal of Automatica Sinica, 9*(3), 377-391.

Zhang, A., Lipton, Z. C., Li, M., & Smola, A. J. (2023). *Dive into deep learning*. Cambridge University Press.

Zhang, X., Liu, L., Lan, M., Song, G., Xiao, L., & Chen, J. (2022). Interpretable machine learning models for crime prediction. *Computers, Environment and Urban Systems*, *94*, 101789.

Zhang, Y., Xiong, F., Xie, Y., Fan, X., & Gu, H. (2020). The impact of artificial intelligence and blockchain on the accounting profession. *IEEE Access : Practical Innovations, Open Solutions*, *8*, 110461–110477.

Zhang, Z., Al Hamadi, H., Damiani, E., Yeun, C. Y., & Taher, F. (2022). Explainable artificial intelligence applications in cyber security: State-of-the-art in research. *IEEE Access : Practical Innovations, Open Solutions*.

Ziring, L. (1984). From Islamic Republic to Islamic State in Pakistan. *Asian Survey*, *24*(September), 931–946.

Zuboff, S. (2019). *The age of surveillance capitalism: The fight for a human future at the new frontier of power*. PublicAffairs. https://www.hbs.edu/faculty/Pages/item.aspx?num=56791

Zuboff, S. (2019). *The Age of Surveillance Capitalism*. PublicAffairs.

About the Contributors

Pankaj Bhambri works in the Department of Information Technology at Ludhiana's Guru Nanak Dev Engineering College. He serves as the Institute's Coordinator, Skill Enhancement Cell, and has almost two decades of teaching experience. He earned his M.Tech. (CSE) and a B.E. (IT) with honors from the I.K.G. Punjab Technical University, Jalandhar, India, and Dr. B.R. Ambedkar University, Agra, India, respectively. Dr. Bhambri earned his doctorate in computer science and engineering from the I.K.G. Punjab Technical University, Jalandhar, India. His research has appeared in a variety of prestigious international/national journals and conference proceedings and he has contributed to numerous books and has also filed several patents. Dr. Bhambri has been awarded the ISTE Best Teacher Award in 2023 and 2022, the I2OR National Award in 2020, the Green ThinkerZ Top 100 International Distinguished Educators in 2020, the I2OR Outstanding Educator Award in 2019, the LCHC Best Teacher Award in 2007, the CIPS Rashtriya Rattan Award in 2008, and the SAA Distinguished Alumni Award in 2012 along with countless other accolades from various government and non-profit organizations. Machine Learning, Bioinformatics, Wireless Sensor Networks, and Network Security are his areas of interest.

Pranjal Chaturvedi is B.A.LL.B (Gold Medal) and LL.M (Criminal Law) from Sharda School of Law, Sharda University University, Greater Noida, India. Pranjal Chaturvedi is contributing author in various News Portals, and Magazines.

Asif Fuard is a Defense Analyst specializing in counterterrorism, transnational threats, and hybrid warfare. He is currently Director of Special Operation for RedForce Security Services (PVT) Ltd and Director at Resurge. He is also a visiting academic at General Sir John Kotelawala Defence University and at the Defence Services Command and Staff College, Sri Lanka. Fuard is a Senior Research Fellow at the Center for Law and Security Studies (CLASS), Sri Lanka. Fuard was also a former war correspondent who covered Sri Lanka's protracted conflict, which concluded in 2009. He can be reached via asiffuard@gmail.com.

Alex Khang, Professor in Information Technology, D.Sc., D.Litt., AI and Data Scientist, Faculty of AI and Data Science, Global Research Institute of Technology and Engineering, Raleigh, North Carolina, United States.

Bhagya Senaratne is Director of Education at the Bandaranaike Centre for International Studies, Sri Lanka. She was formerly Postdoctoral Fellow of Global Asia at the Center for Global Asia, NYU Shanghai and Senior Lecturer at Sri Lanka's Defense University teaching a range of undergraduate and postgraduate courses at Sri Lanka military establishments. As the inaugural BRI postdoctoral fellow, her research at the Center for Global Asia focused on the Belt and Road Initiative and South Asia. She researches and teaches on areas related to Foreign Policy Studies, Geopolitics of small states, Strategic Communications, Maritime Security, and International Security in the Indo-Pacific Region. She can be reached via senaratne.bhagya@gmail.com

Bhupinder Singh working as Professor at Sharda University, India. Also, Honorary Professor in University of South Wales UK and Santo Tomas University Tunja, Colombia. His areas of publications as Smart Healthcare, Medicines, fuzzy logics, artificial intelligence, robotics, machine learning, deep learning, federated learning, IoT, PV Glasses, metaverse and many more. He has 3 books, 139 paper publications, 163 paper presentations in international/national conferences and seminars, participated in more than 40 workshops/FDP's/QIP's, 25 courses from international universities of repute, organized more than 59 events with international and national academicians and industry people's, editor-in-chief and co-editor in journals, developed new courses. He has given talks at international universities, resource person in international conferences such as in Nanyang Technological University Singapore, Tashkent State University of Law Uzbekistan; KIMEP University Kazakhstan, All'ah meh Tabatabi University Iran, the Iranian Association of International Criminal law, Iran and Hague Center for International Law and Investment, The Netherlands, Northumbria University Newcastle UK,

I Made Wisnu Wardhana is a practitioner-scholar specializing in Counter-Terrorism Financing (CTF), Financial Intelligence, and Risk Analysis, with over 18 years of operational, analytical, and academic experience. He is recognized for bridging research and practice through data-driven frameworks that strengthen Indonesia's national resilience against terrorism financing. He currently serves as a Lecturer at Universitas Indonesia – School of Strategic and Global Studies and as Head of Intelligence Analysis at Densus 88. He holds a PhD in Banking and Finance from Charles Sturt University, Australia. He can be reached at madewisnuxx@gmail.com.

Index

A

B

C

D

E

S

T

U

V

W

www.ingramcontent.com/pod-product-compliance
Ingram Content Group UK Ltd.
Pitfield, Milton Keynes, MK11 3LW, UK
UKHW052004051026
15624UKWH00003B/546

9 798369 335222